GRANBLUE FANTASY

グランブルーファンタジー

volume.

04

Original story: Cygames   Art: cocho   Layouts: Makoto Fugetsu

CONTENTS

GRANBLUE FANTASY

volume.

04

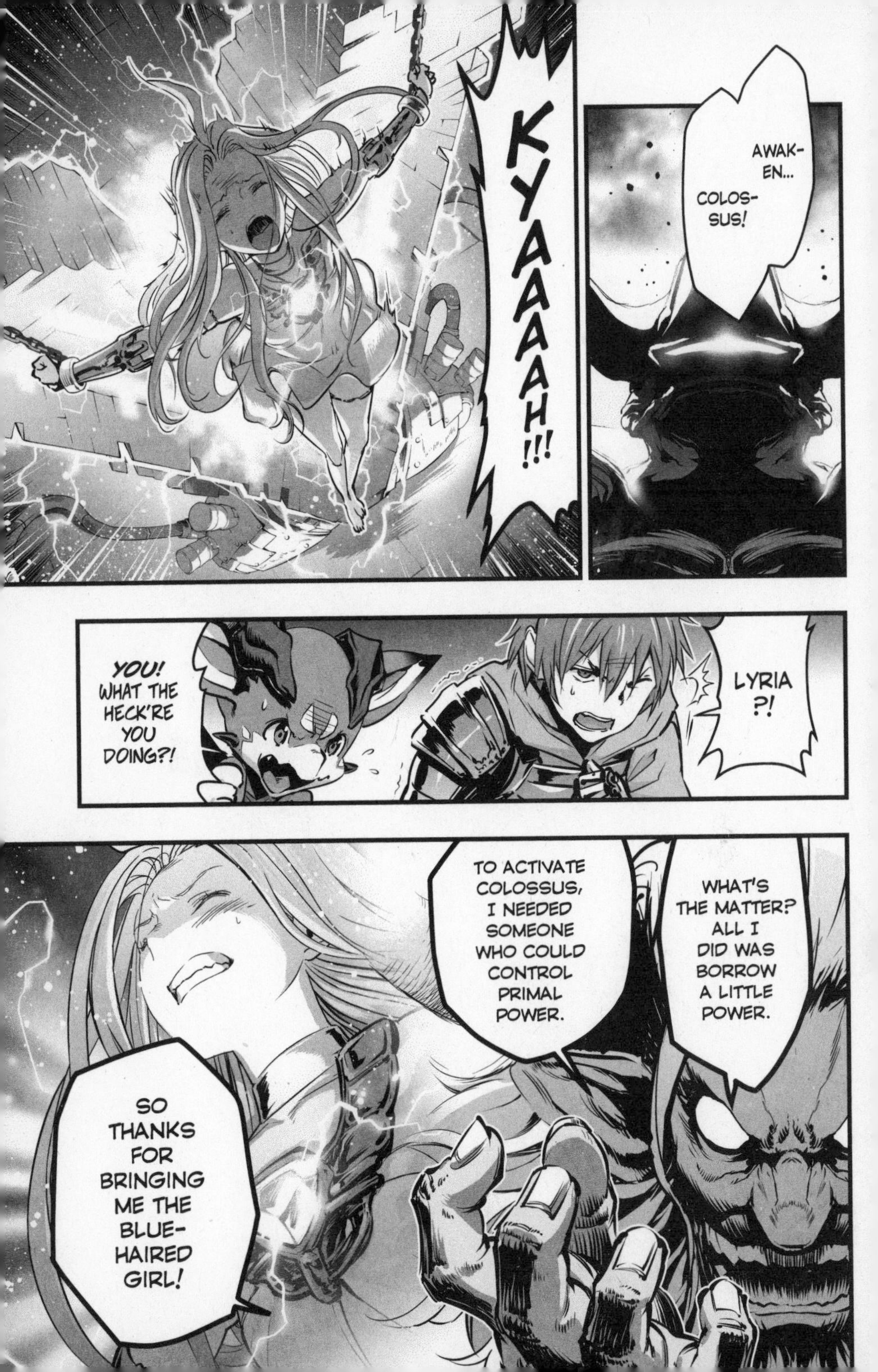
AWAKEN... COLOSSUS!
KYAAAAAH!!!
LYRIA?!
YOU! WHAT THE HECK'RE YOU DOING?!
WHAT'S THE MATTER? ALL I DID WAS BORROW A LITTLE POWER.
TO ACTIVATE COLOSSUS, I NEEDED SOMEONE WHO COULD CONTROL PRIMAL POWER.
SO THANKS FOR BRINGING ME THE BLUE-HAIRED GIRL!

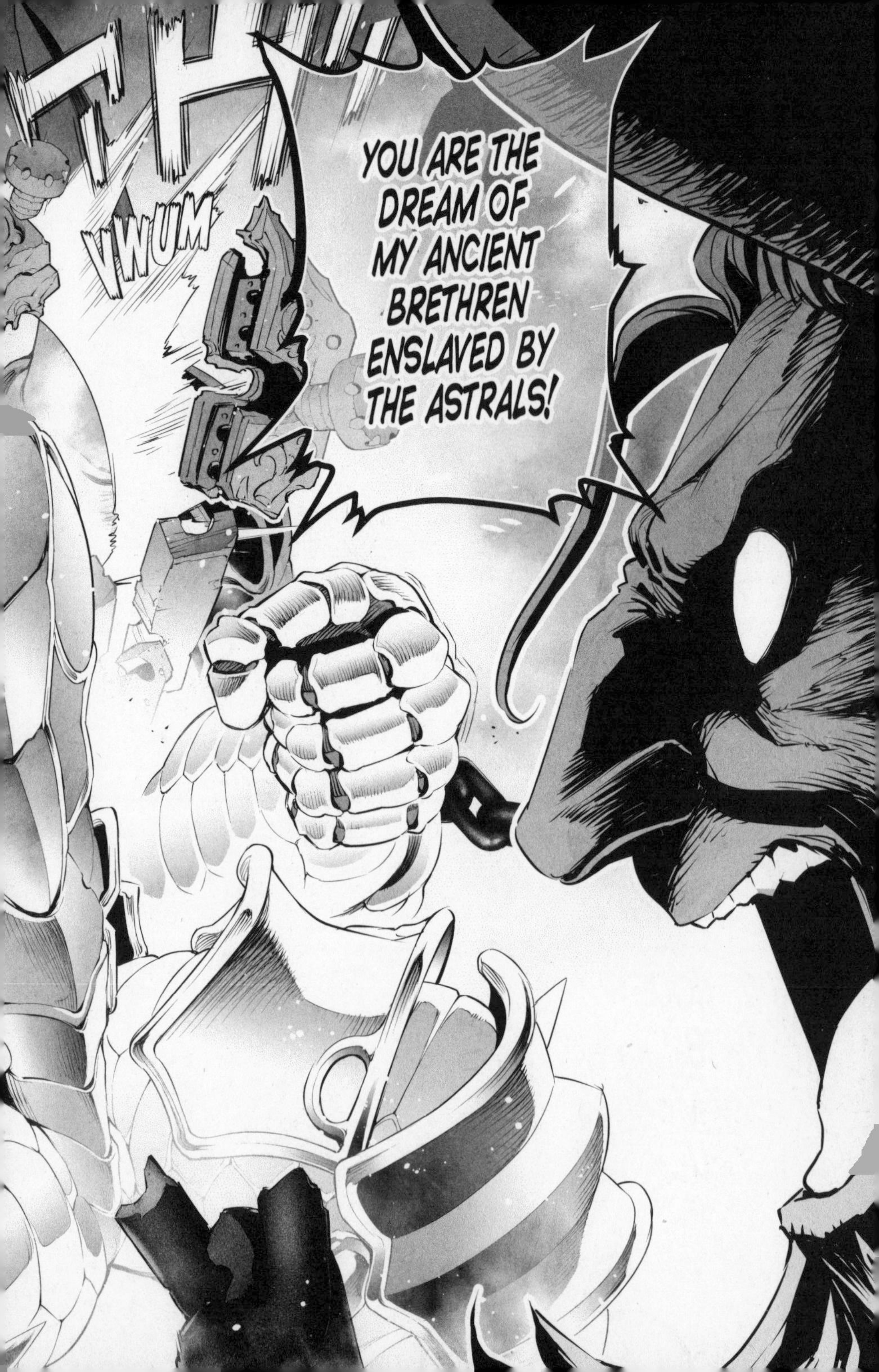
YOU ARE THE DREAM OF MY ANCIENT BRETHREN ENSLAVED BY THE ASTRALS!
VWUM

CHAPTER 20: Colossus

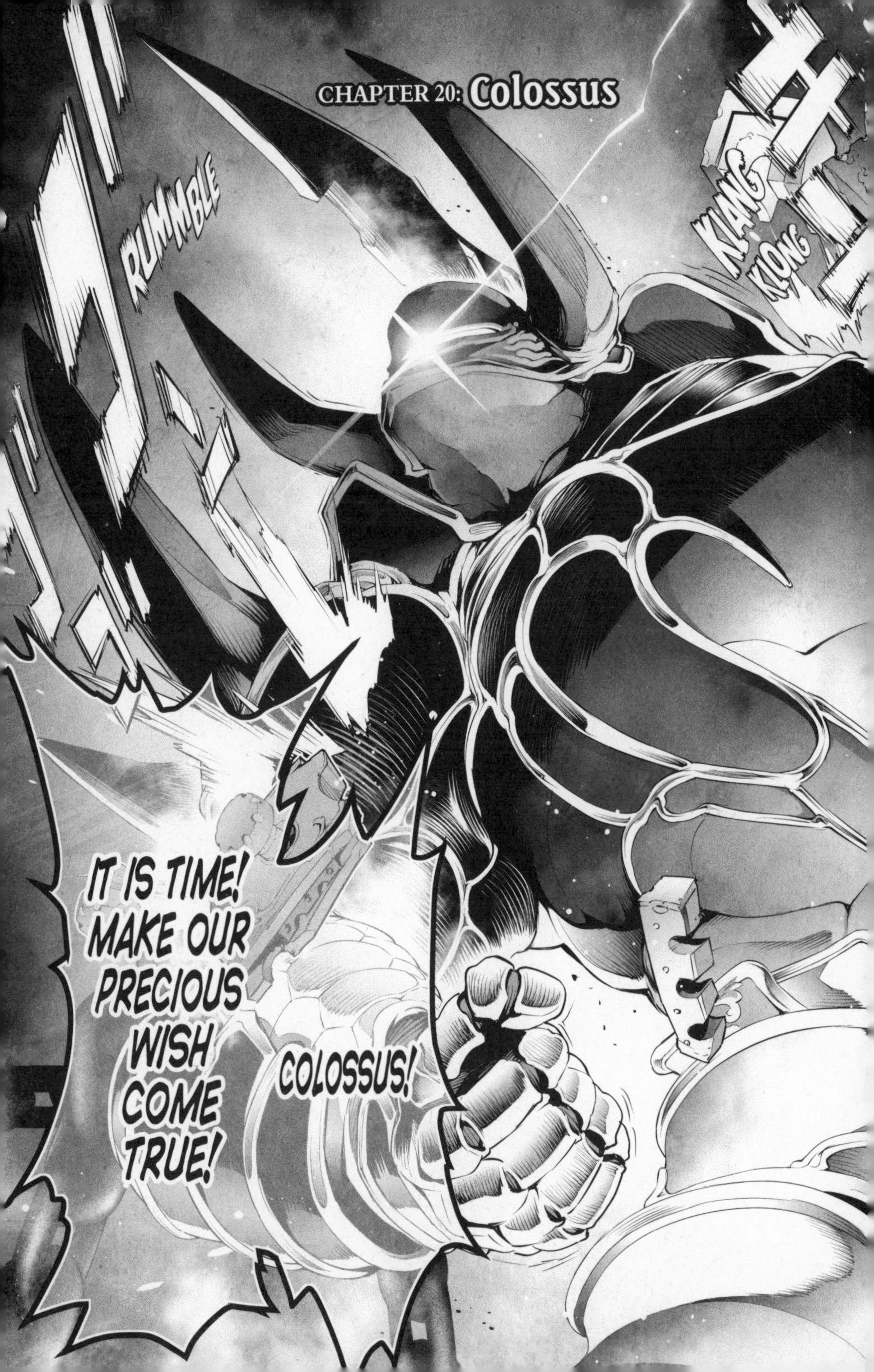
KLANG
KLONG
RUMMBLE
IT IS TIME! MAKE OUR PRECIOUS WISH COME TRUE!
COLOSSUS!

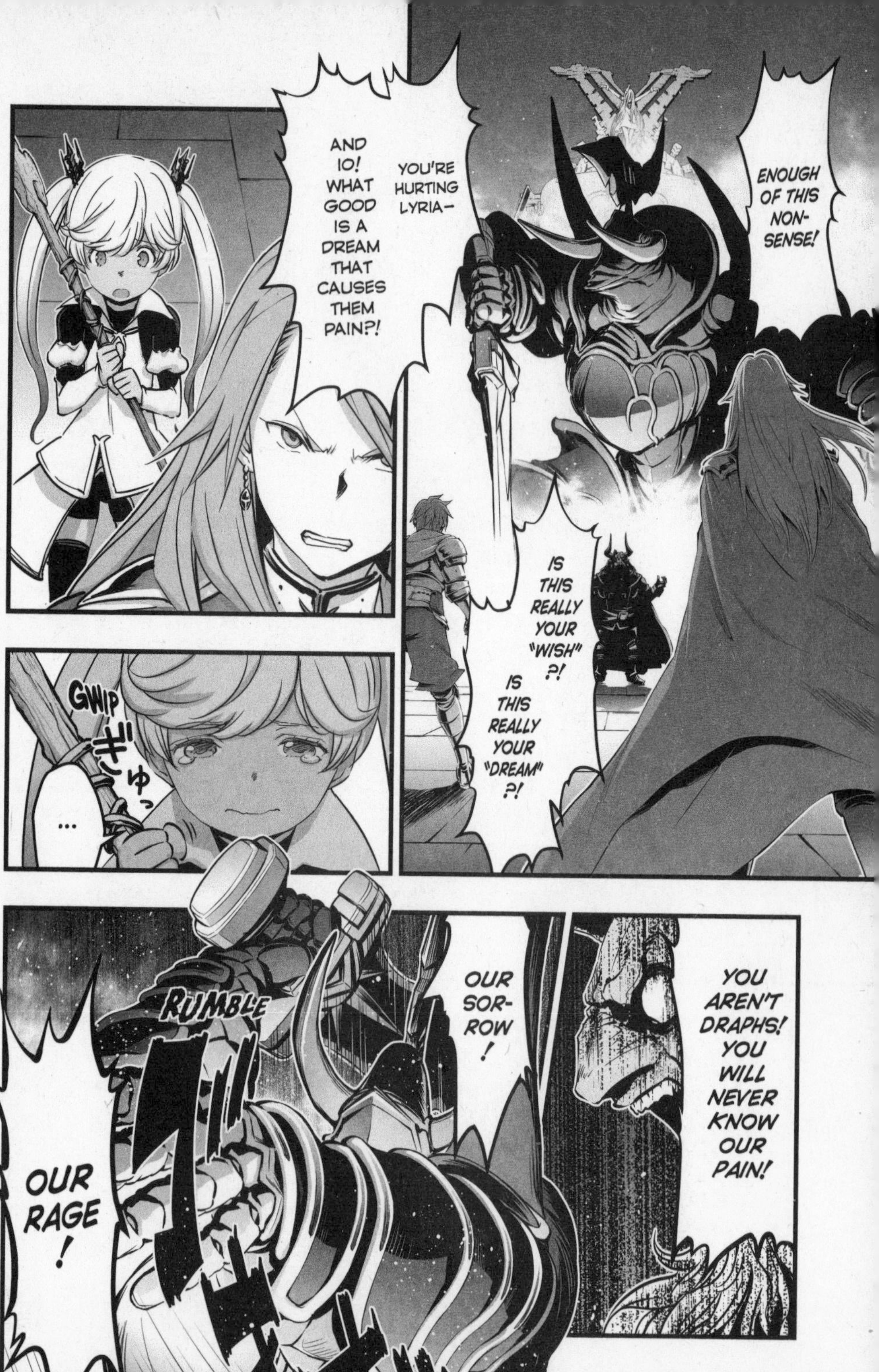
ENOUGH OF THIS NON-SENSE!
YOU'RE HURTING LYRIA—
AND IO! WHAT GOOD IS A DREAM THAT CAUSES THEM PAIN?!
IS THIS REALLY YOUR "WISH"?!
IS THIS REALLY YOUR "DREAM"?!
GWIP
ぎゅっ
...
YOU AREN'T DRAPHS! YOU WILL NEVER KNOW OUR PAIN!
OUR SOR-ROW!
RUMBLE
OUR RAGE!

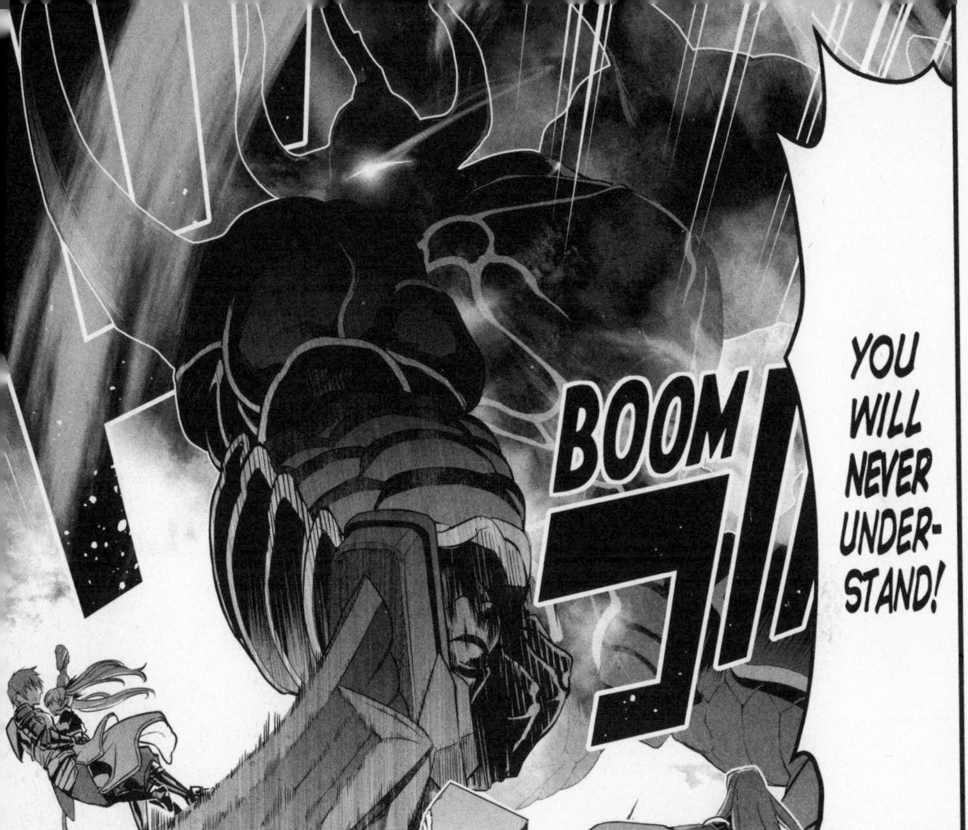
YOU WILL NEVER UNDER-STAND!
BOOM
!!

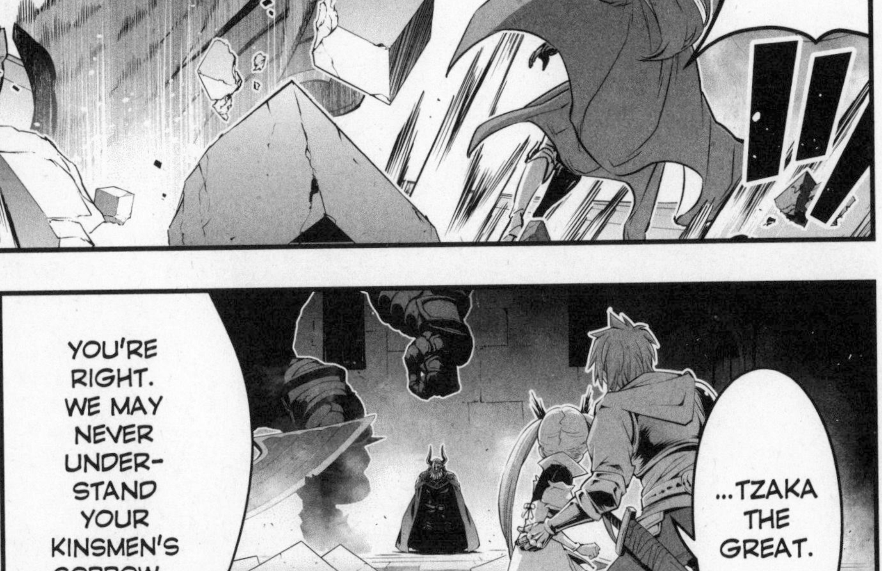
YOU'RE RIGHT. WE MAY NEVER UNDER-STAND YOUR KINSMEN'S SORROW...
...TZAKA THE GREAT.

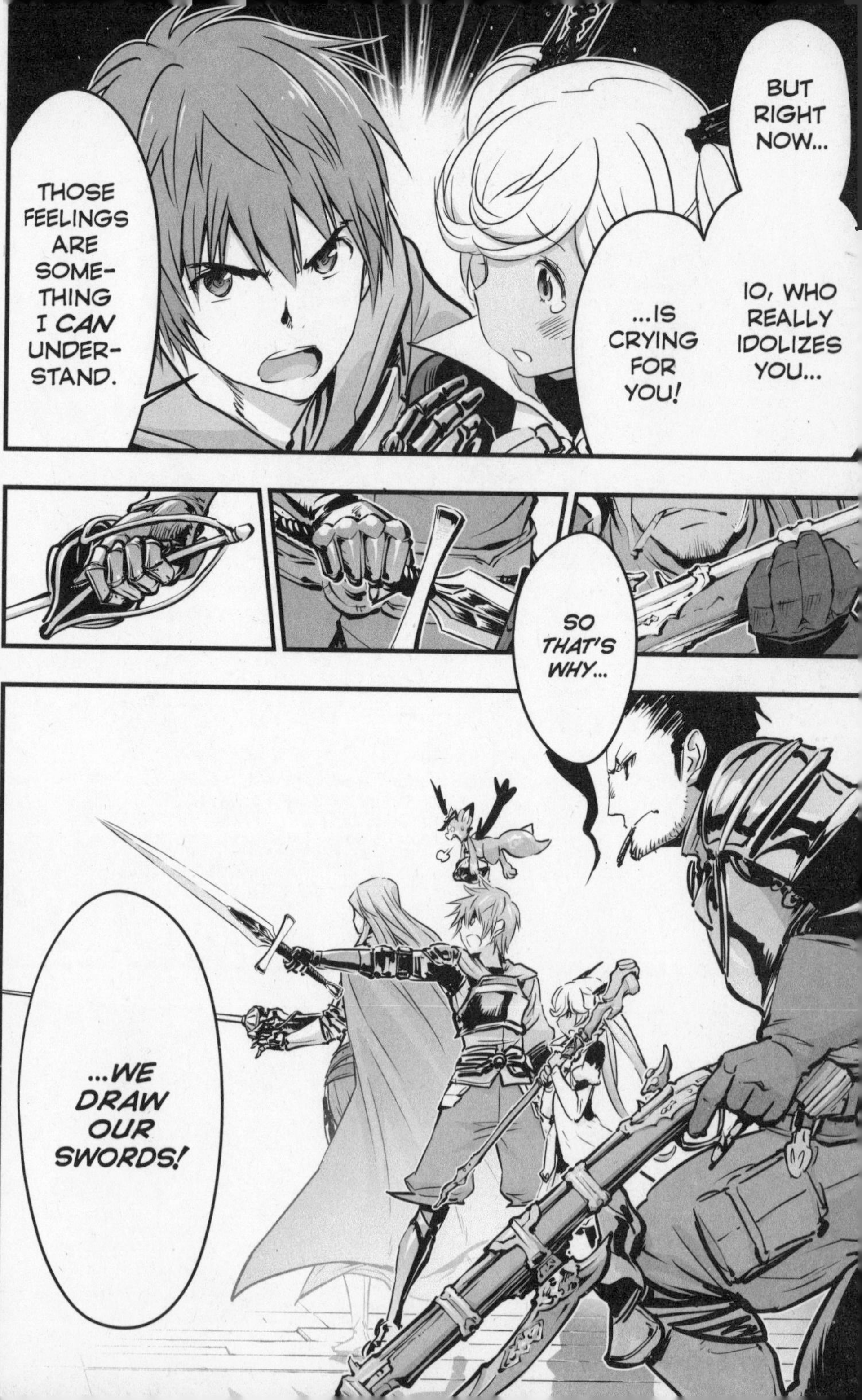
BUT RIGHT NOW...
IO, WHO REALLY IDOLIZES YOU...
...IS CRYING FOR YOU!
THOSE FEELINGS ARE SOME-THING I *CAN* UNDER-STAND.
SO THAT'S WHY...
...WE DRAW OUR SWORDS!

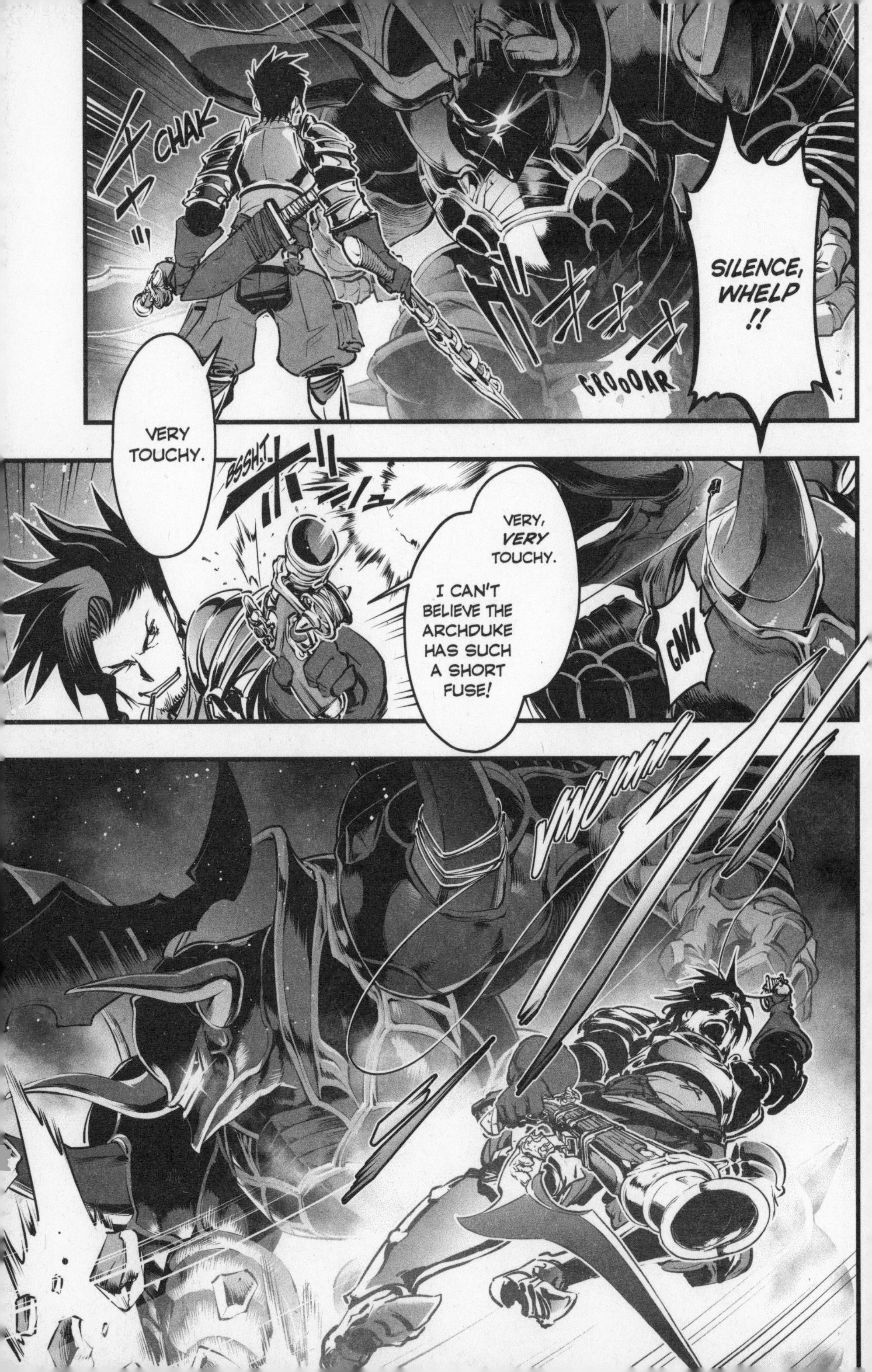
SILENCE, WHELP !!
GROOOAR
CHAK
VERY TOUCHY.
GNK
VERY, *VERY* TOUCHY.
I CAN'T BELIEVE THE ARCHDUKE HAS SUCH A SHORT FUSE!
BSSHT

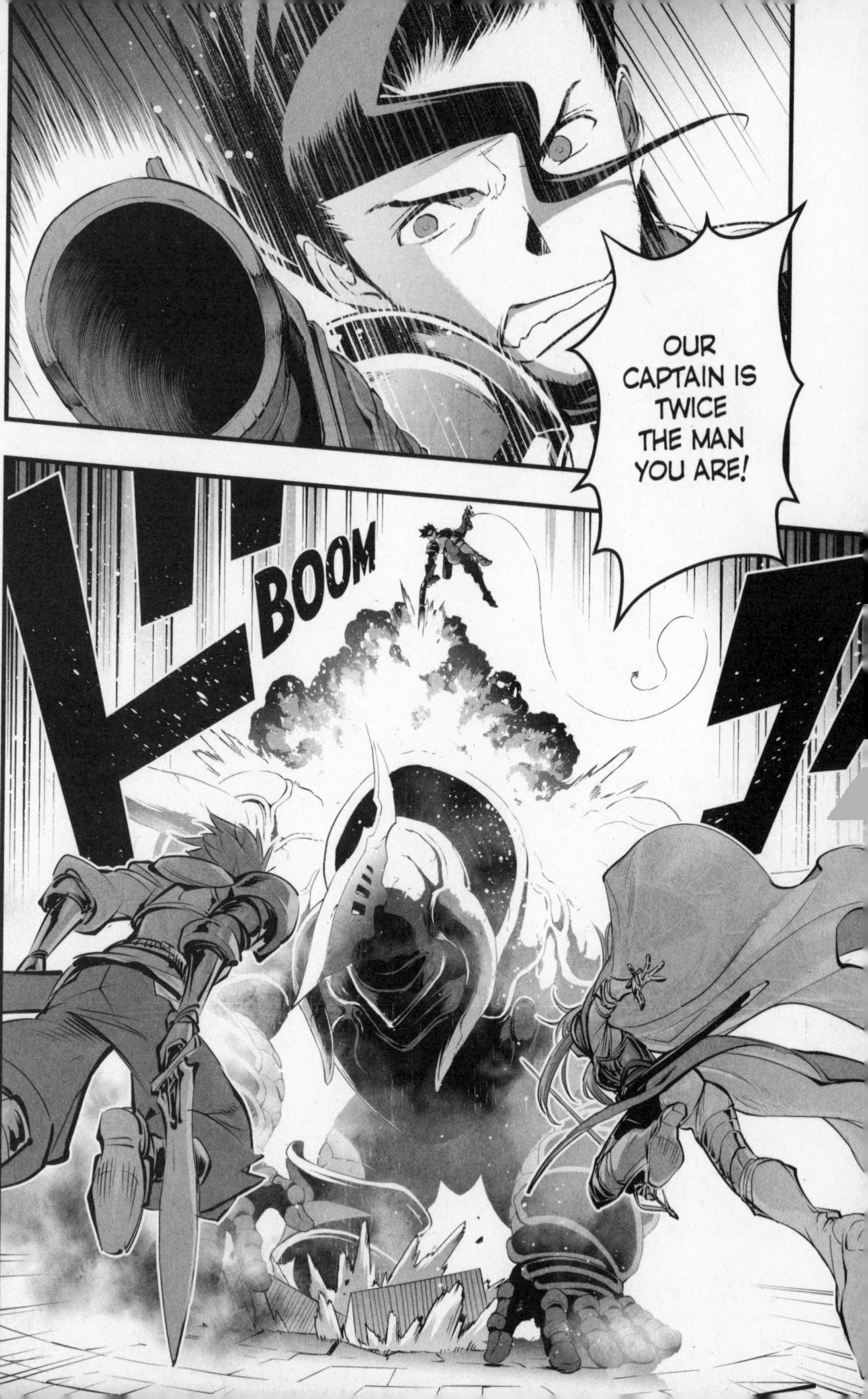
OUR CAPTAIN IS TWICE THE MAN YOU ARE!
BOOM

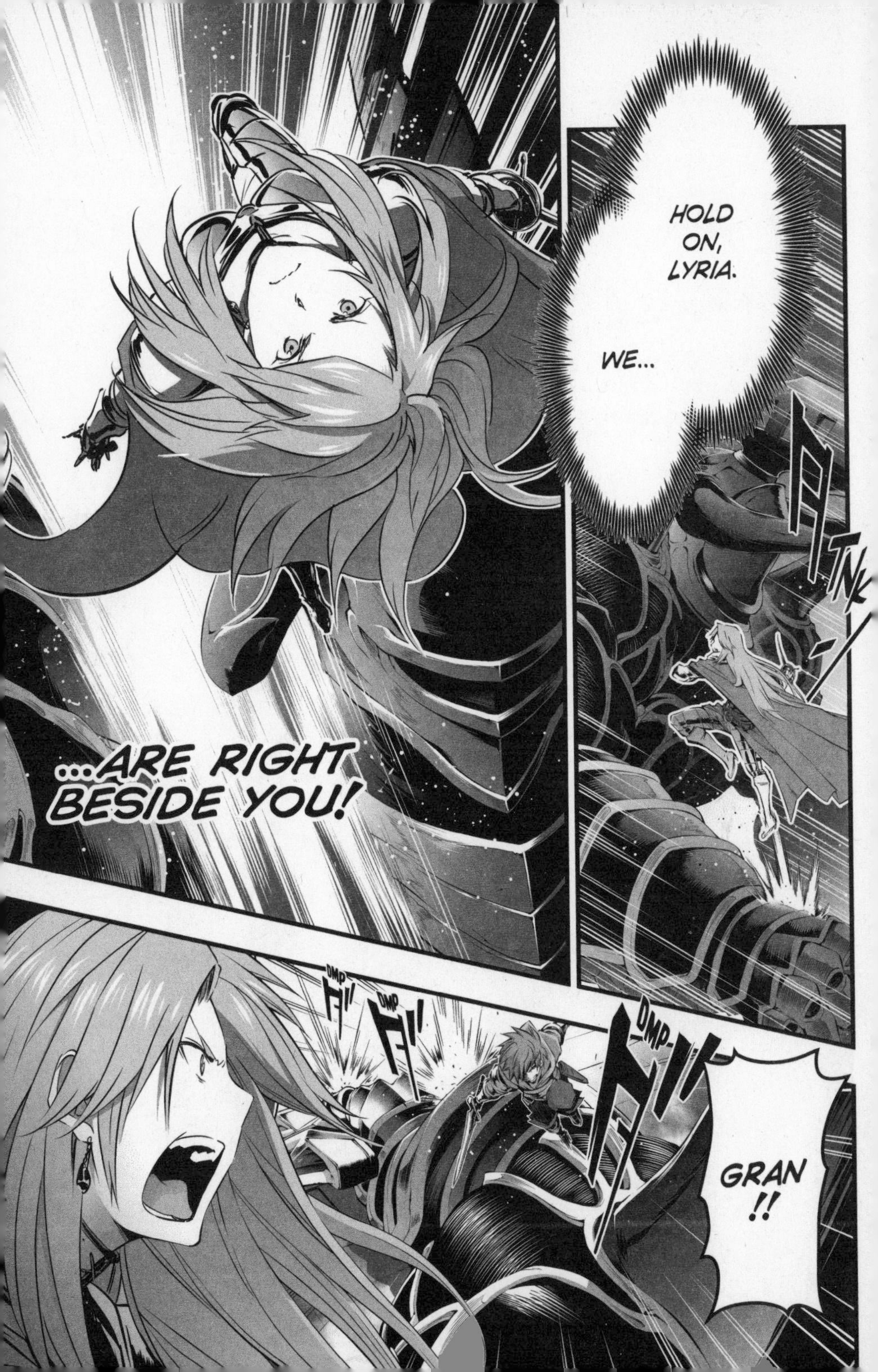
HOLD ON, LYRIA.
WE...
TNK
...ARE RIGHT BESIDE YOU!
DMP-
GRAN !!
DMP
DMP

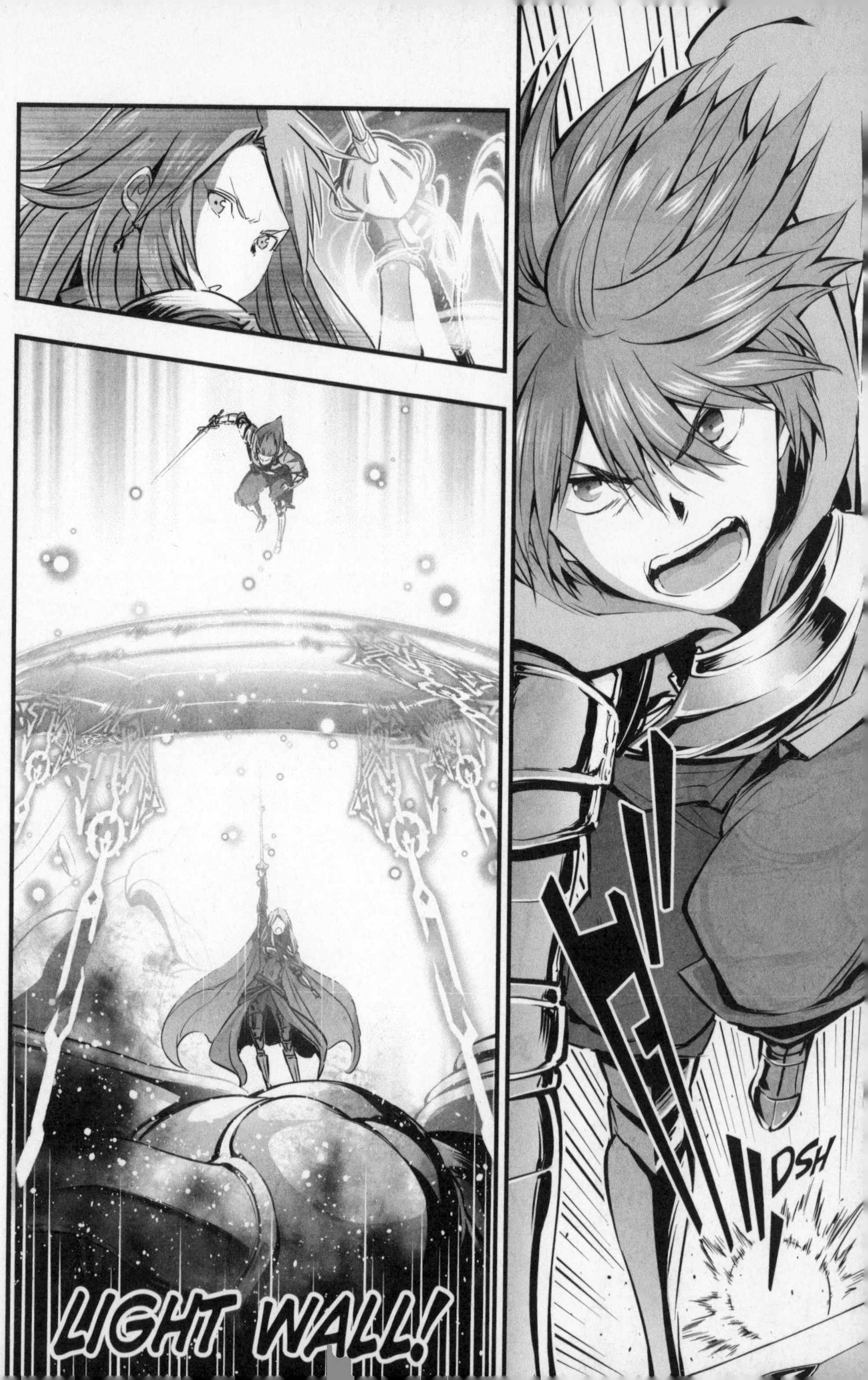
DSH
LIGHT WALL!

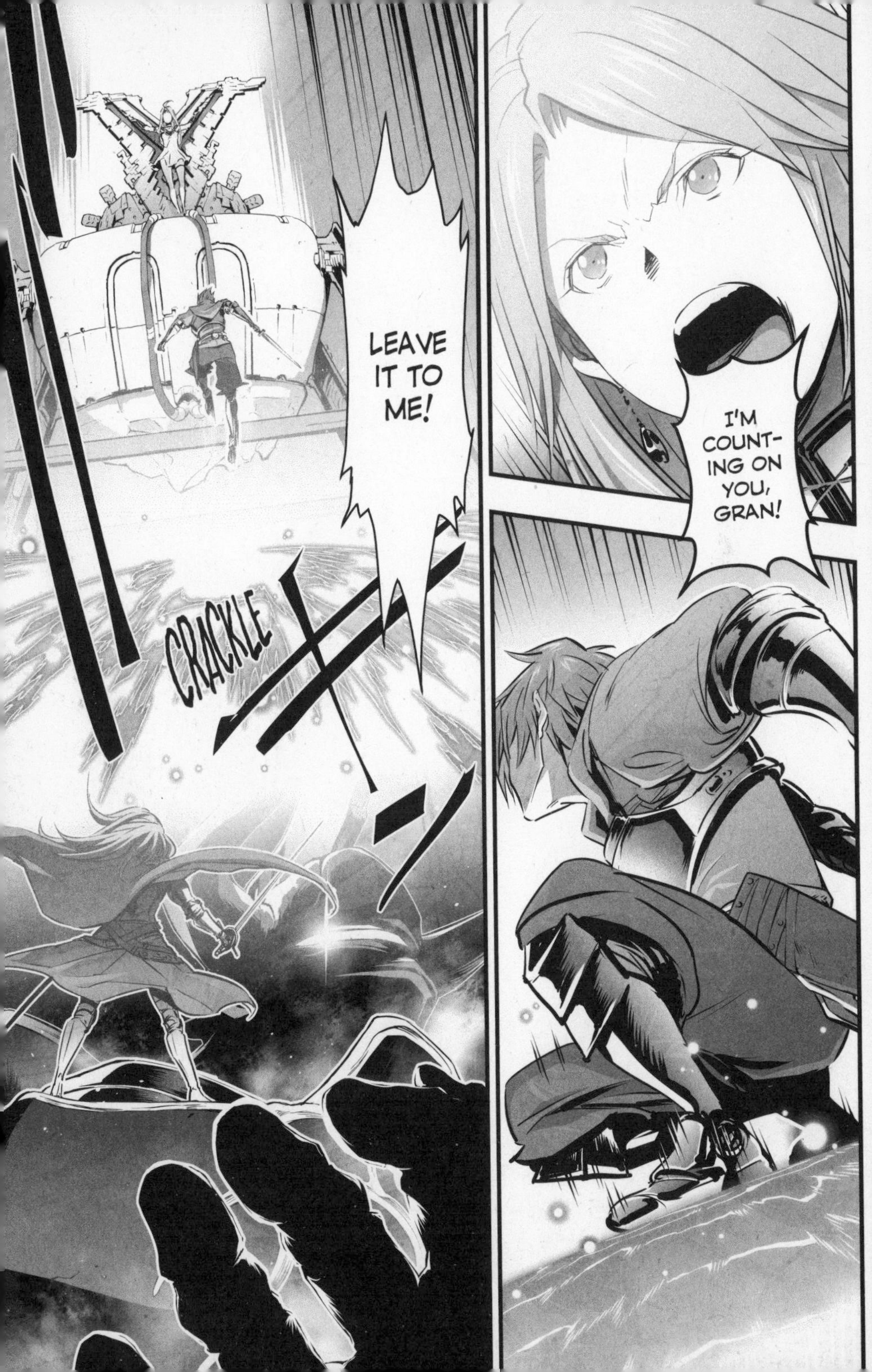
I'M COUNTING ON YOU, GRAN!
LEAVE IT TO ME!
CRACKLE

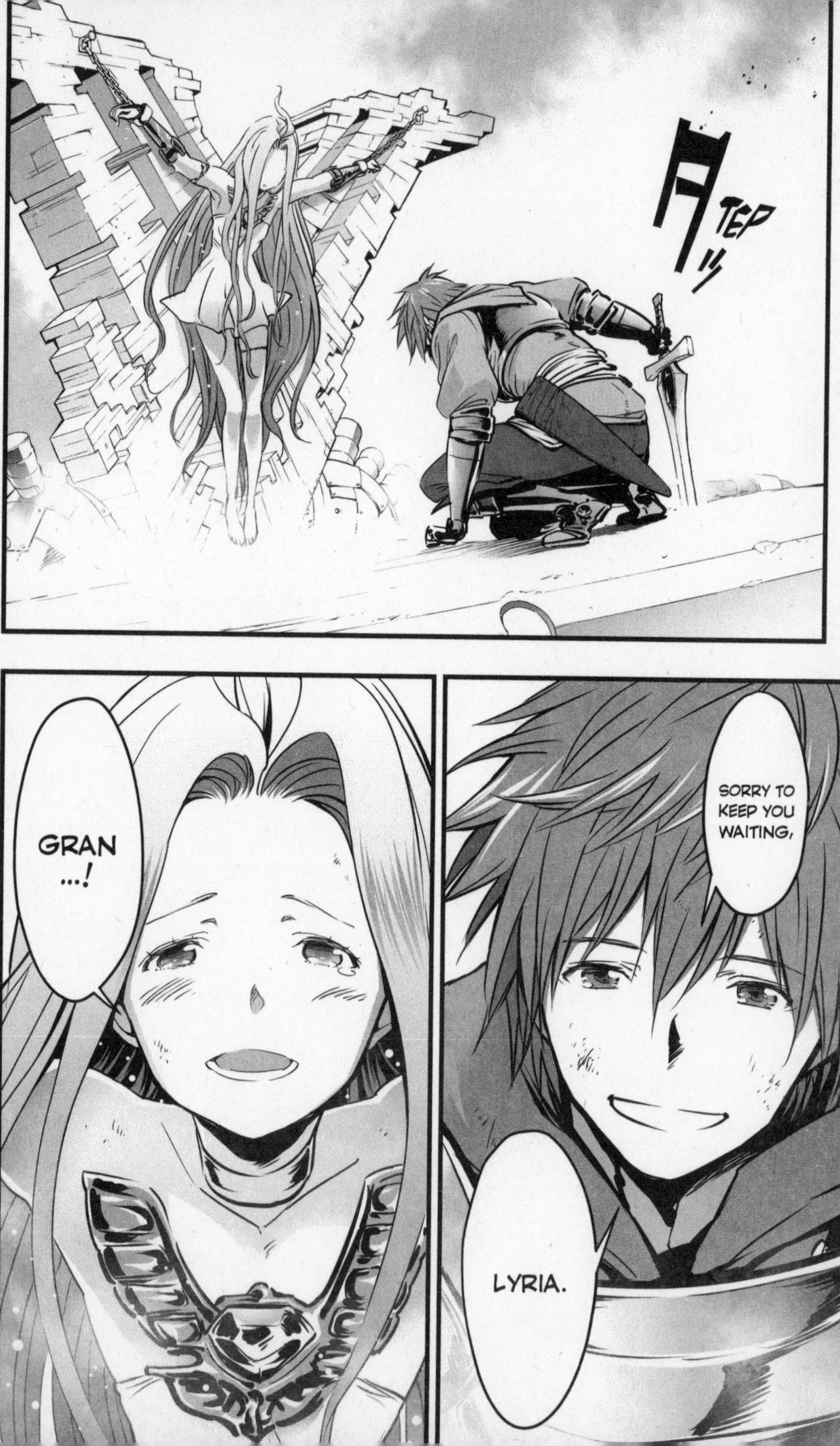
TEP
SORRY TO KEEP YOU WAITING,
LYRIA.
GRAN ...!

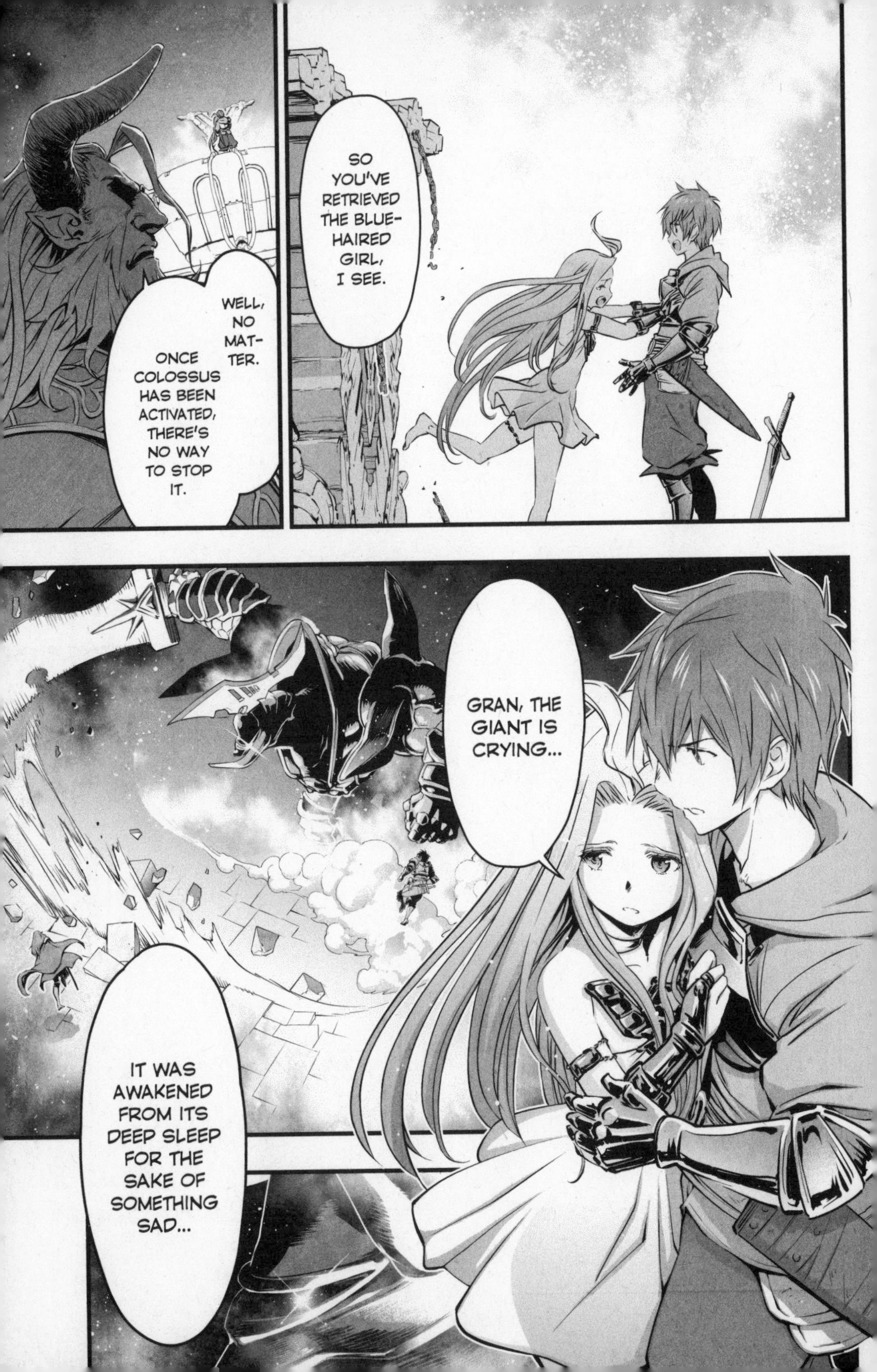
SO YOU'VE RETRIEVED THE BLUE-HAIRED GIRL, I SEE.
WELL, NO MAT-TER.
ONCE COLOSSUS HAS BEEN ACTIVATED, THERE'S NO WAY TO STOP IT.
GRAN, THE GIANT IS CRYING...
IT WAS AWAKENED FROM ITS DEEP SLEEP FOR THE SAKE OF SOMETHING SAD...

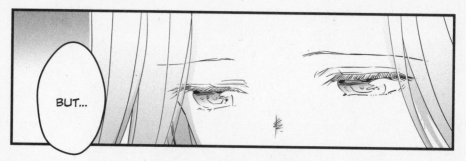

BUT...

THE ARCHDUKE IS CRYING DEEP DOWN, TOO...

SO THAT'S WHY—

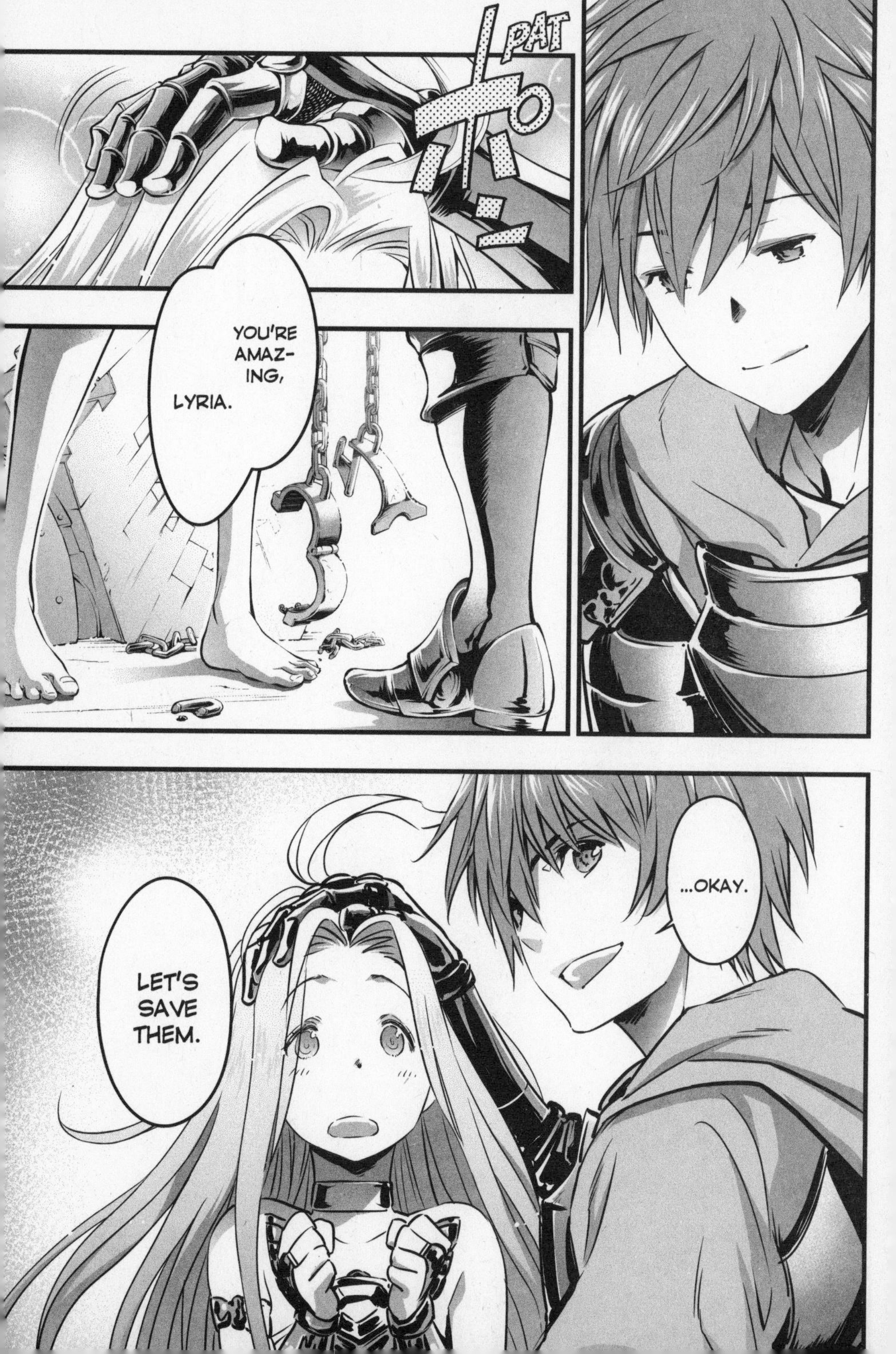
PAT
YOU'RE AMAZ-ING, LYRIA.
...OKAY.
LET'S SAVE THEM.

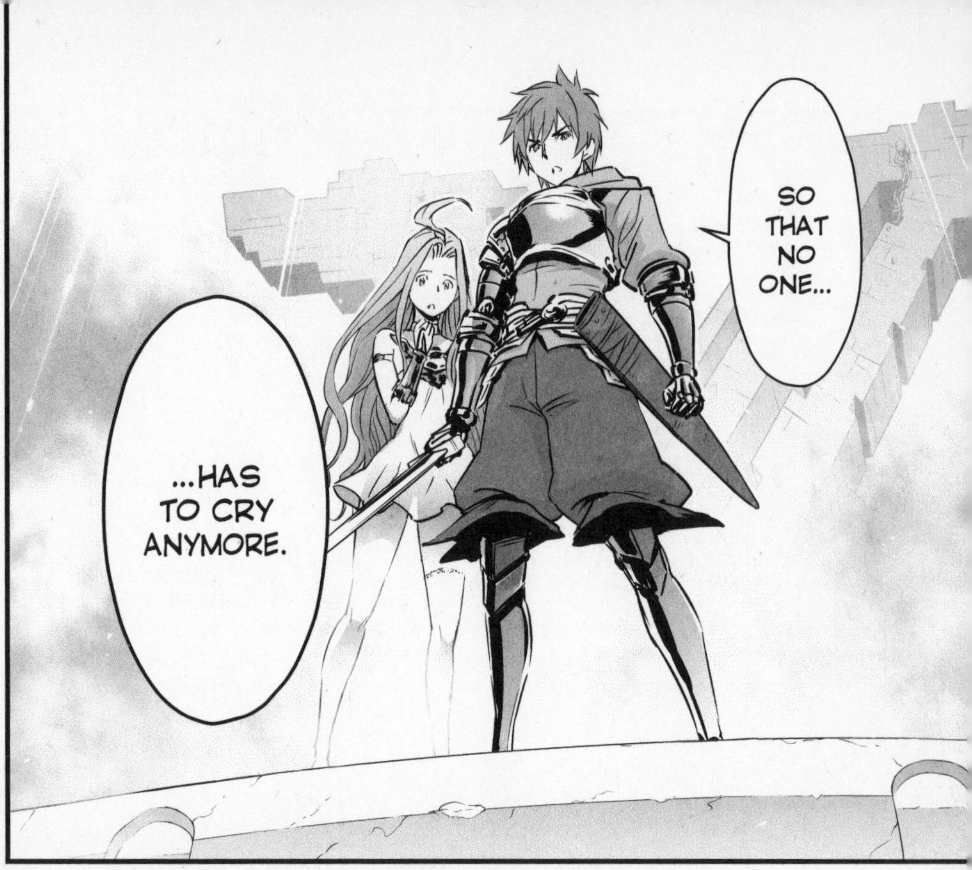
SO THAT NO ONE...
...HAS TO CRY ANYMORE.

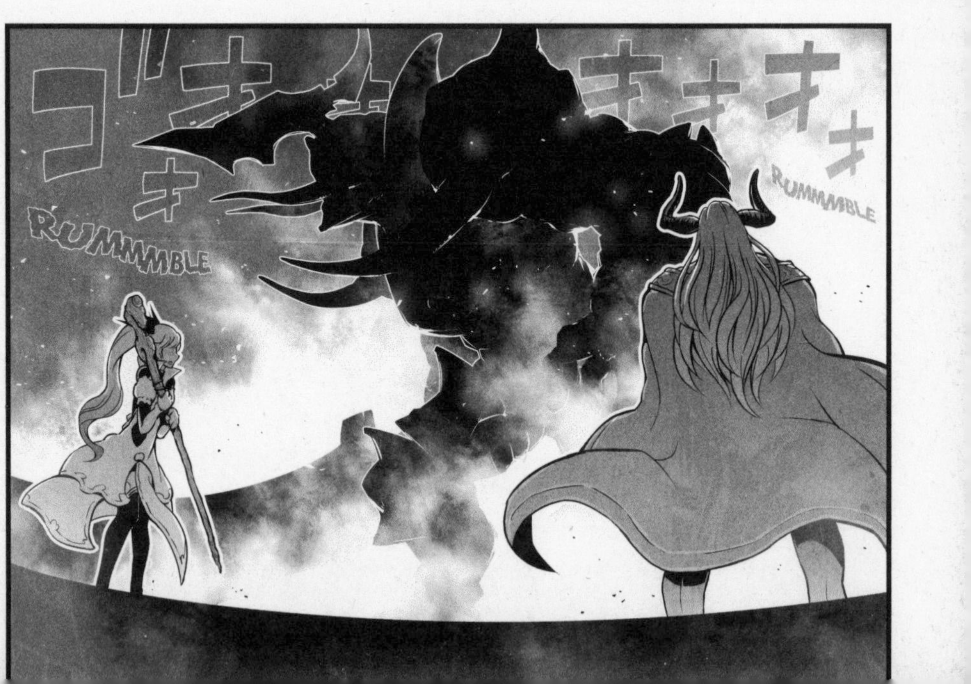
RUMMMBLE
RUMMMMBLE

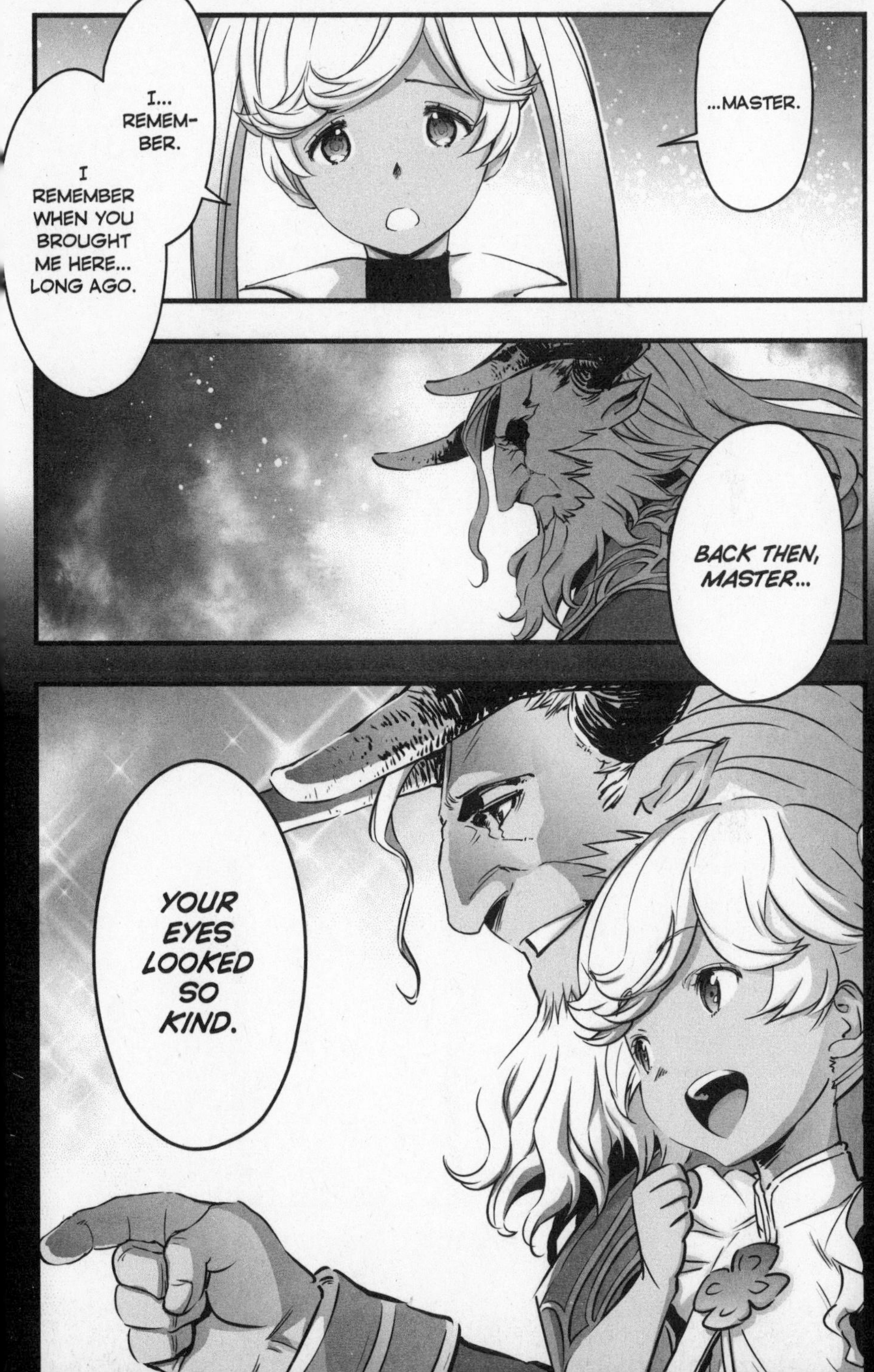
...MASTER.
I... REMEMBER.
I REMEMBER WHEN YOU BROUGHT ME HERE... LONG AGO.
BACK THEN, MASTER...
YOUR EYES LOOKED SO KIND.

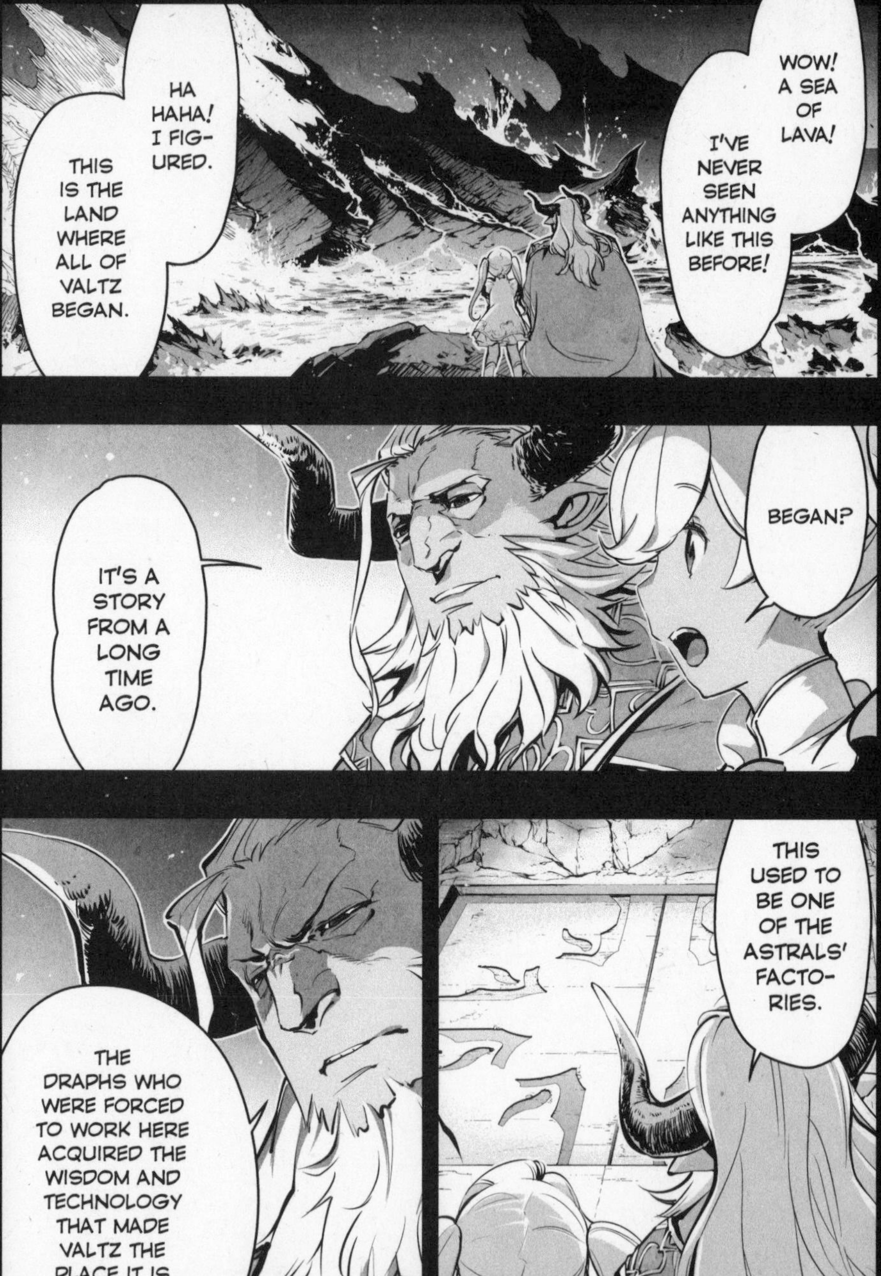
WOW! A SEA OF LAVA!
I'VE NEVER SEEN ANYTHING LIKE THIS BEFORE!
HA HAHA! I FIG-URED.
THIS IS THE LAND WHERE ALL OF VALTZ BEGAN.
BEGAN?
IT'S A STORY FROM A LONG TIME AGO.
THIS USED TO BE ONE OF THE ASTRALS' FACTO-RIES.
THE DRAPHS WHO WERE FORCED TO WORK HERE ACQUIRED THE WISDOM AND TECHNOLOGY THAT MADE VALTZ THE PLACE IT IS TODAY.

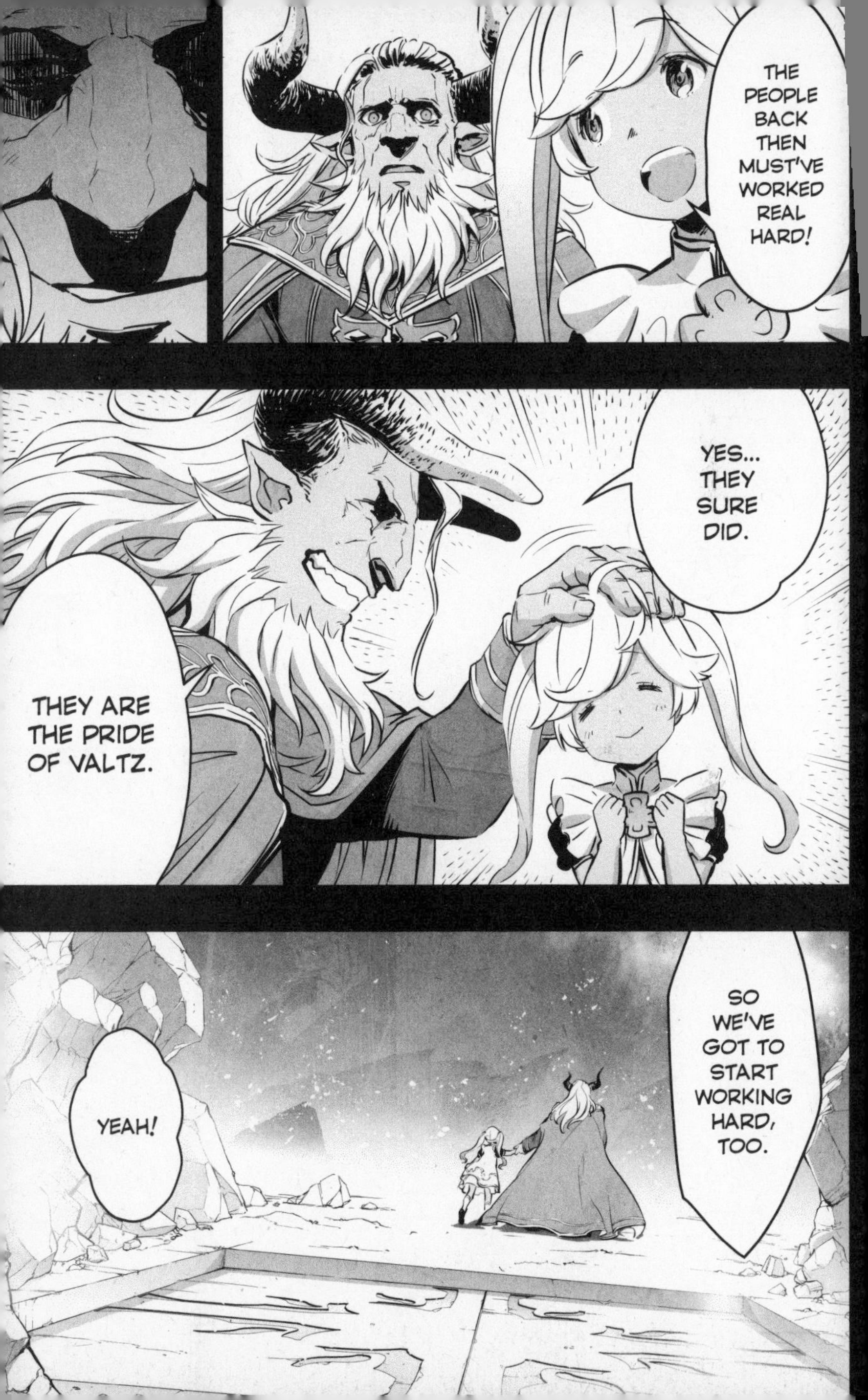
THE PEOPLE BACK THEN MUST'VE WORKED REAL HARD!
YES... THEY SURE DID.
THEY ARE THE PRIDE OF VALTZ.
SO WE'VE GOT TO START WORKING HARD, TOO.
YEAH!

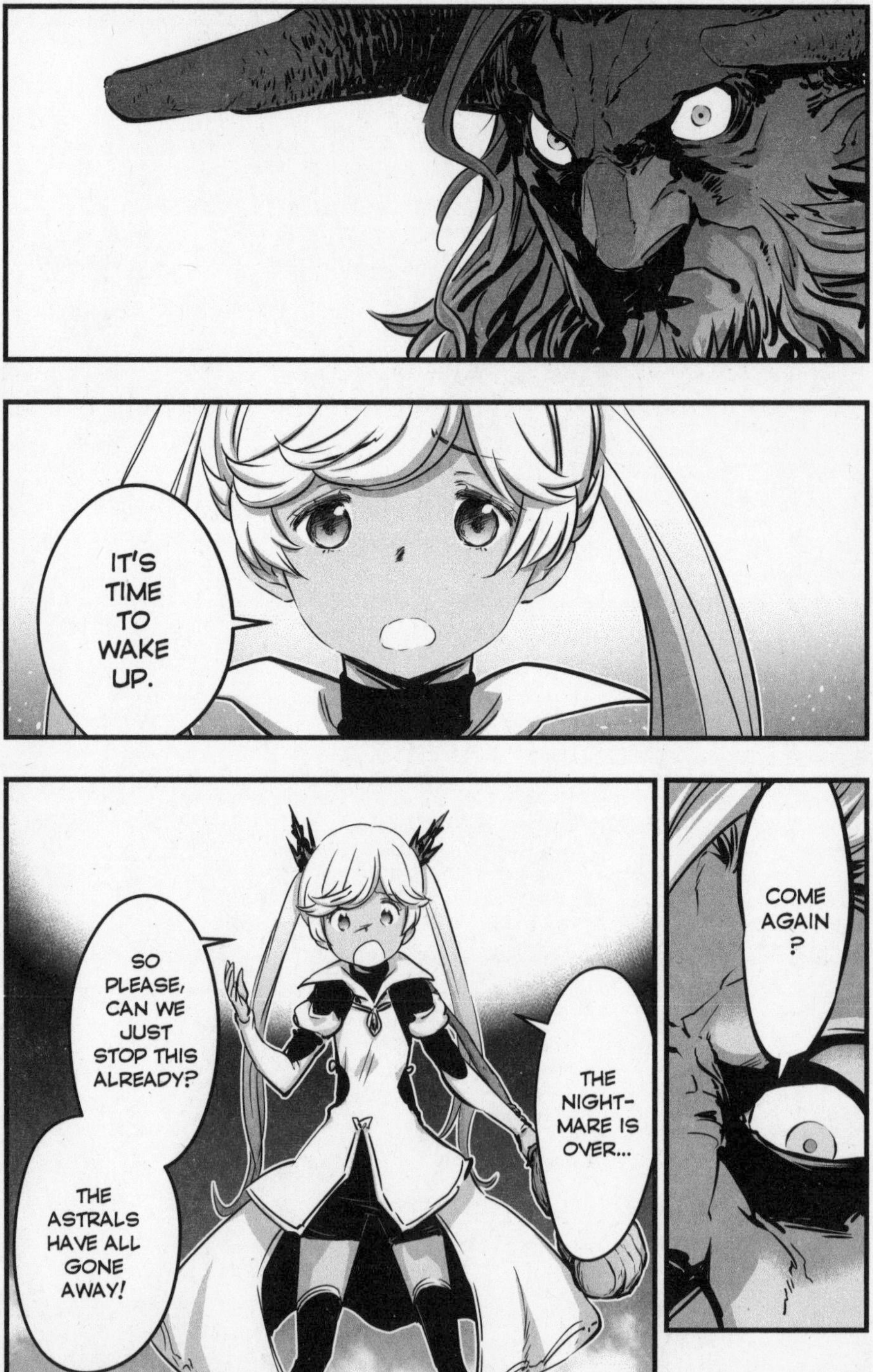
IT'S TIME TO WAKE UP.
COME AGAIN?
THE NIGHTMARE IS OVER...
SO PLEASE, CAN WE JUST STOP THIS ALREADY?
THE ASTRALS HAVE ALL GONE AWAY!

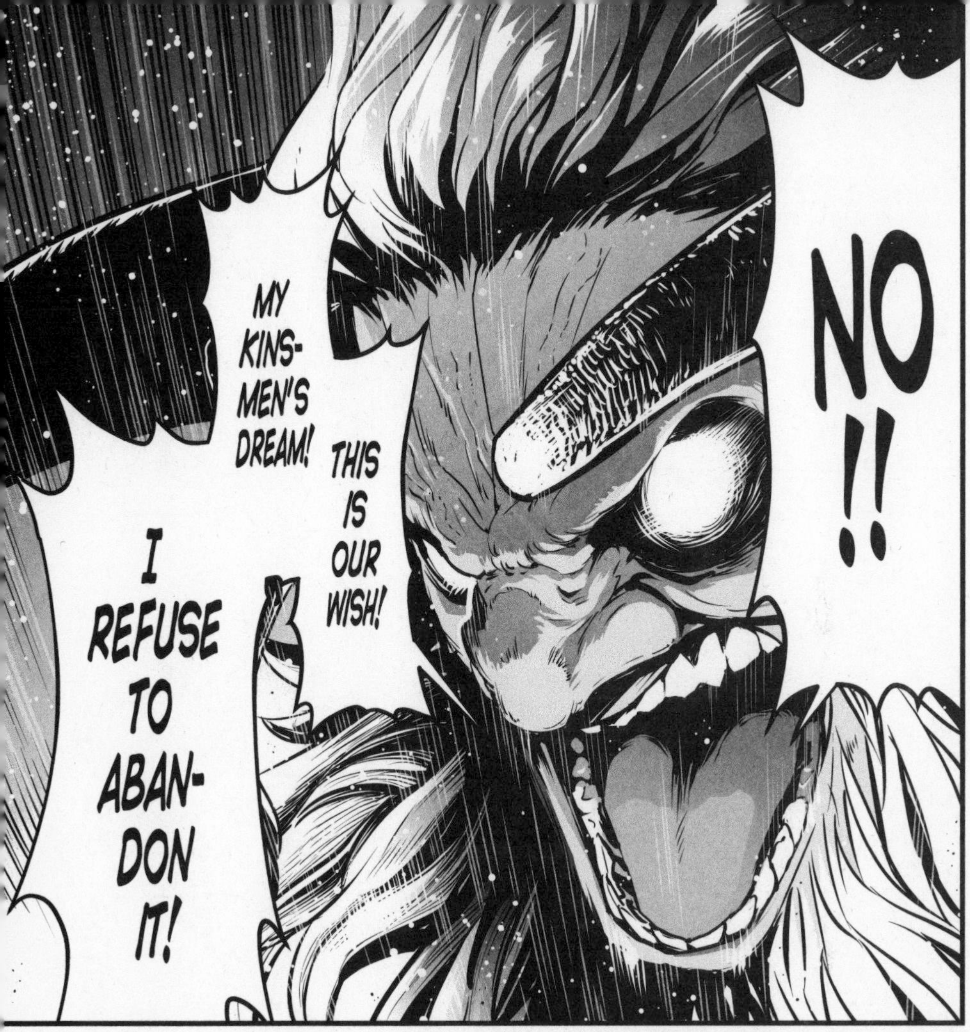
NO!!
THIS IS OUR WISH!
MY KINSMEN'S DREAM!
I REFUSE TO ABANDON IT!

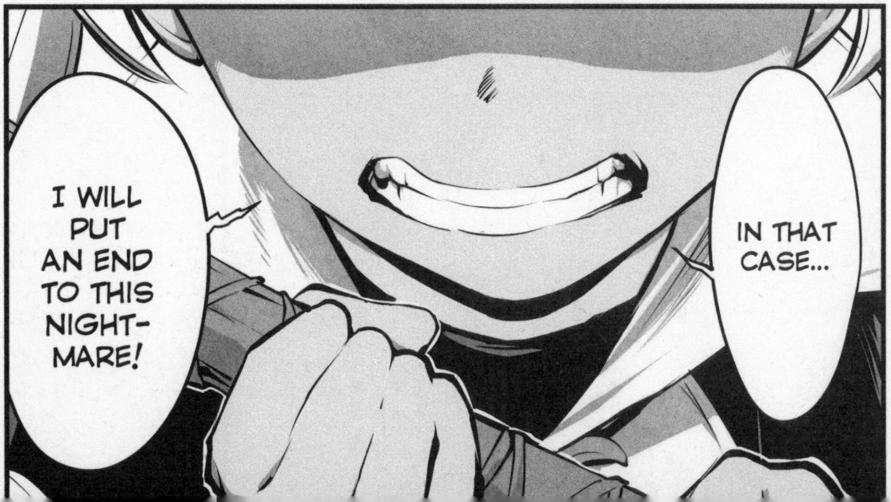
IN THAT CASE...
I WILL PUT AN END TO THIS NIGHTMARE!

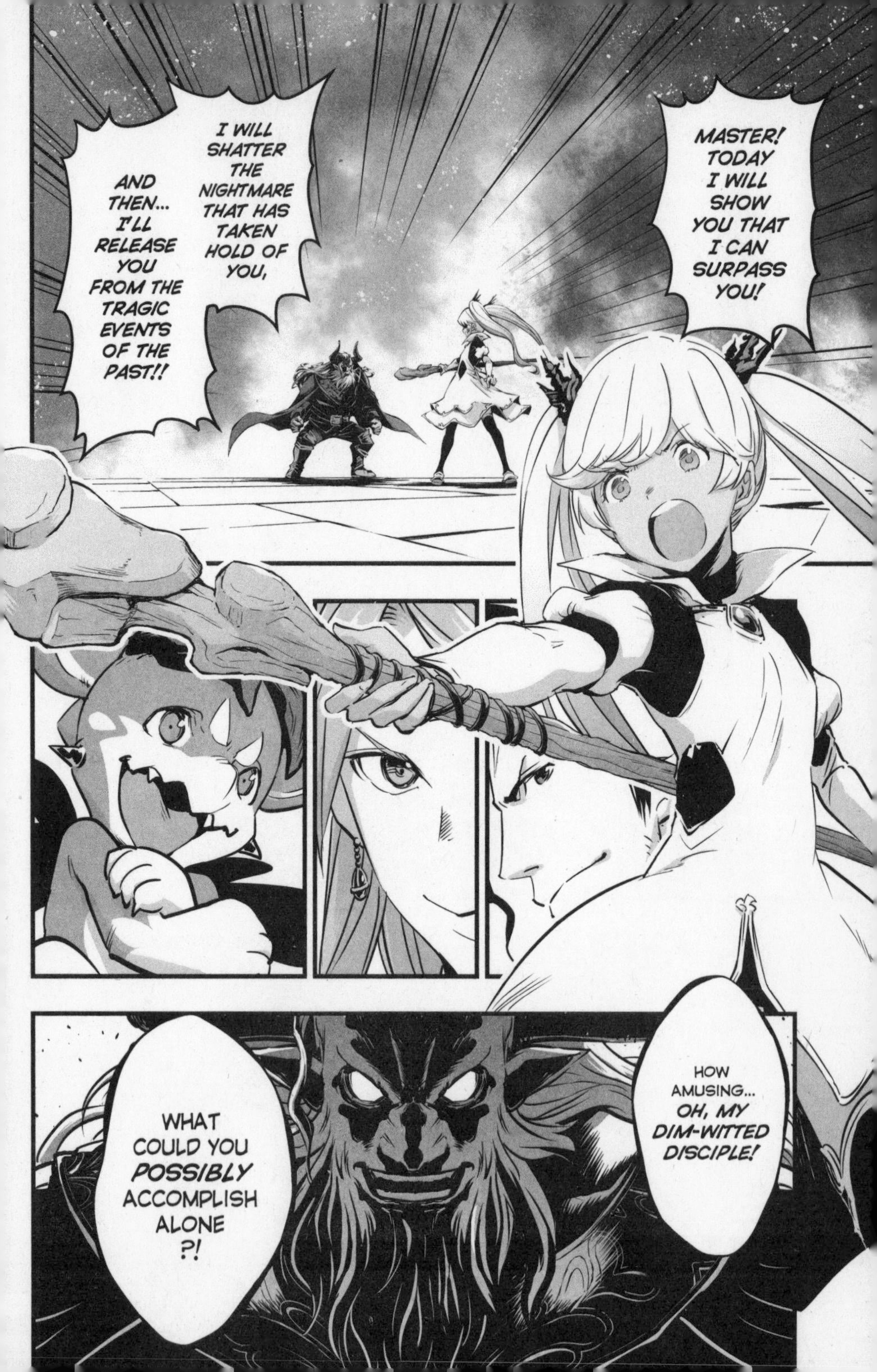
MASTER! TODAY I WILL SHOW YOU THAT I CAN SURPASS YOU!
I WILL SHATTER THE NIGHTMARE THAT HAS TAKEN HOLD OF YOU,
AND THEN... I'LL RELEASE YOU FROM THE TRAGIC EVENTS OF THE PAST!!
HOW AMUSING... OH, MY DIM-WITTED DISCIPLE!
WHAT COULD YOU POSSIBLY ACCOMPLISH ALONE ?!

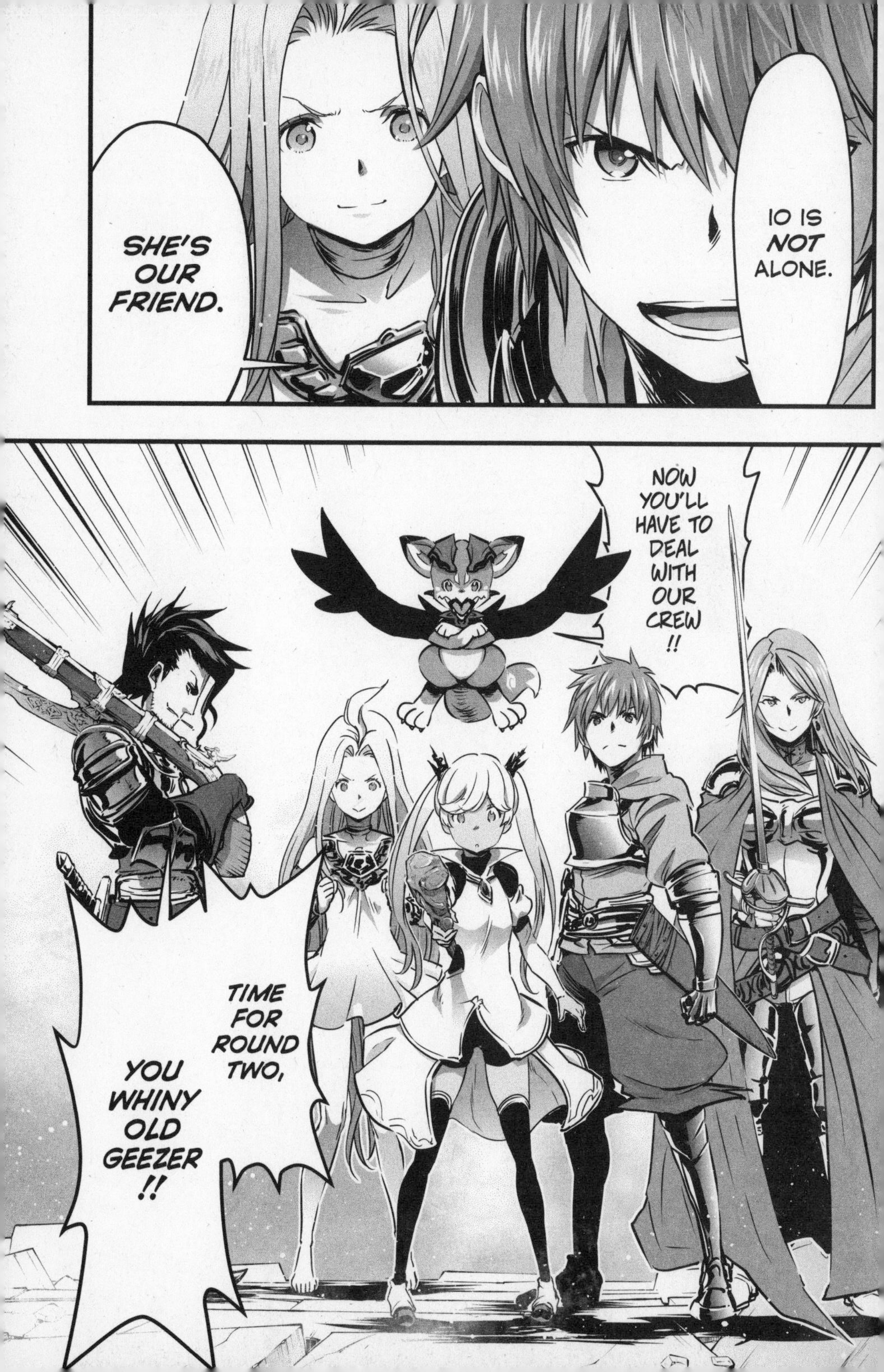
IO IS NOT ALONE.
SHE'S OUR FRIEND.
NOW YOU'LL HAVE TO DEAL WITH OUR CREW!!
TIME FOR ROUND TWO,
YOU WHINY OLD GEEZER!!

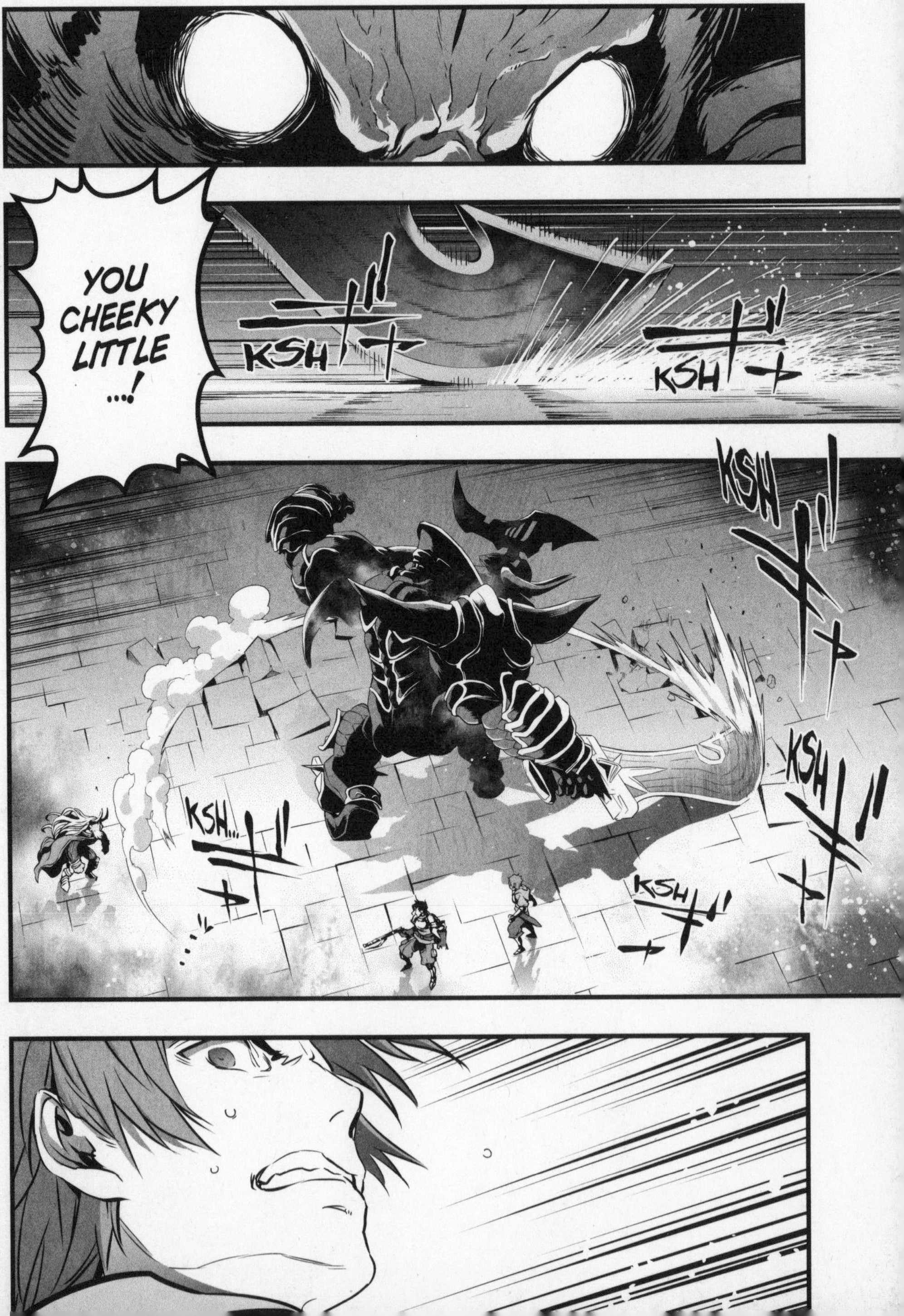
YOU CHEEKY LITTLE ...!
KSH
KSH
KSH
KSH
KSH
KSH...

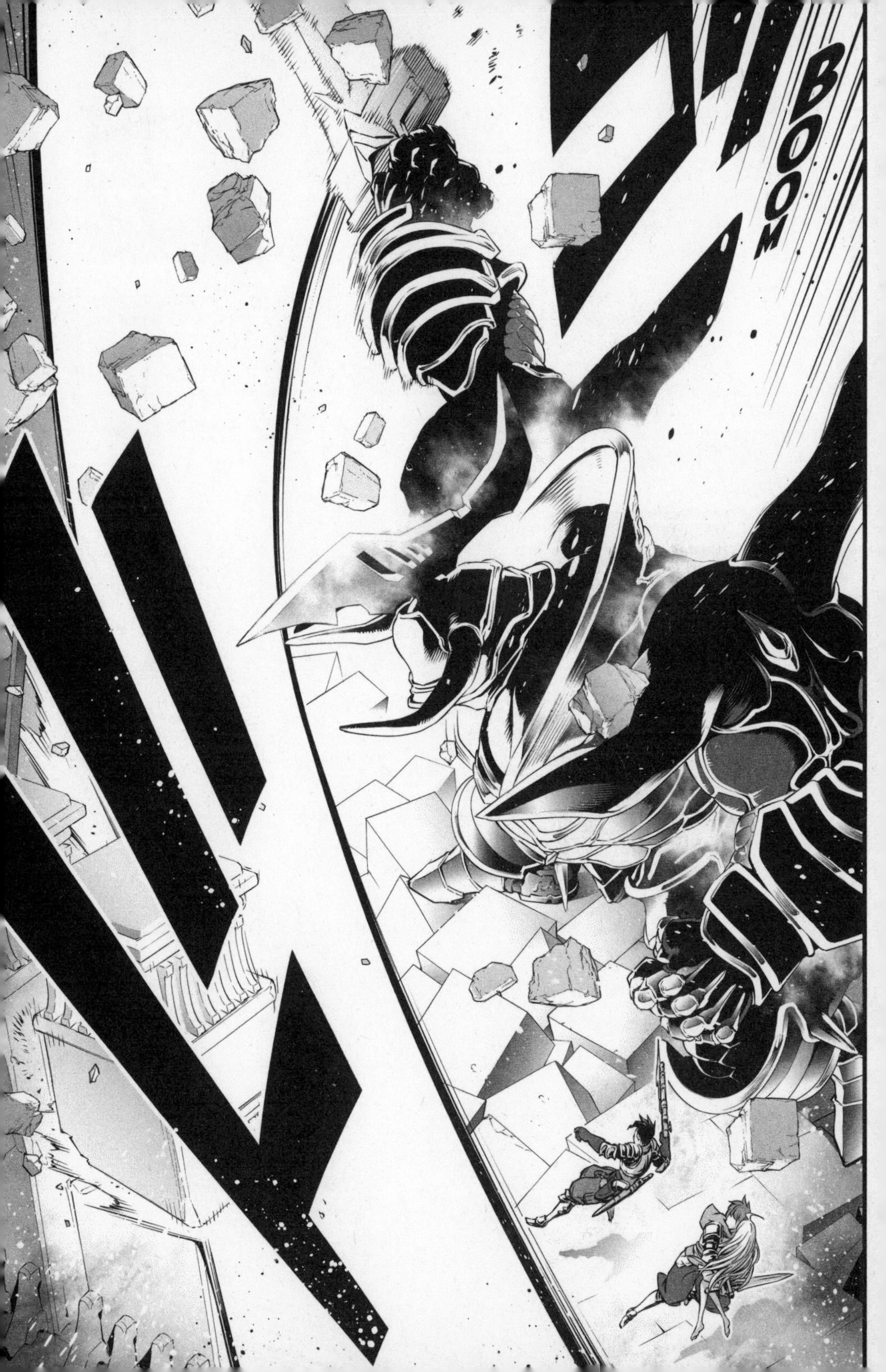
BOOM

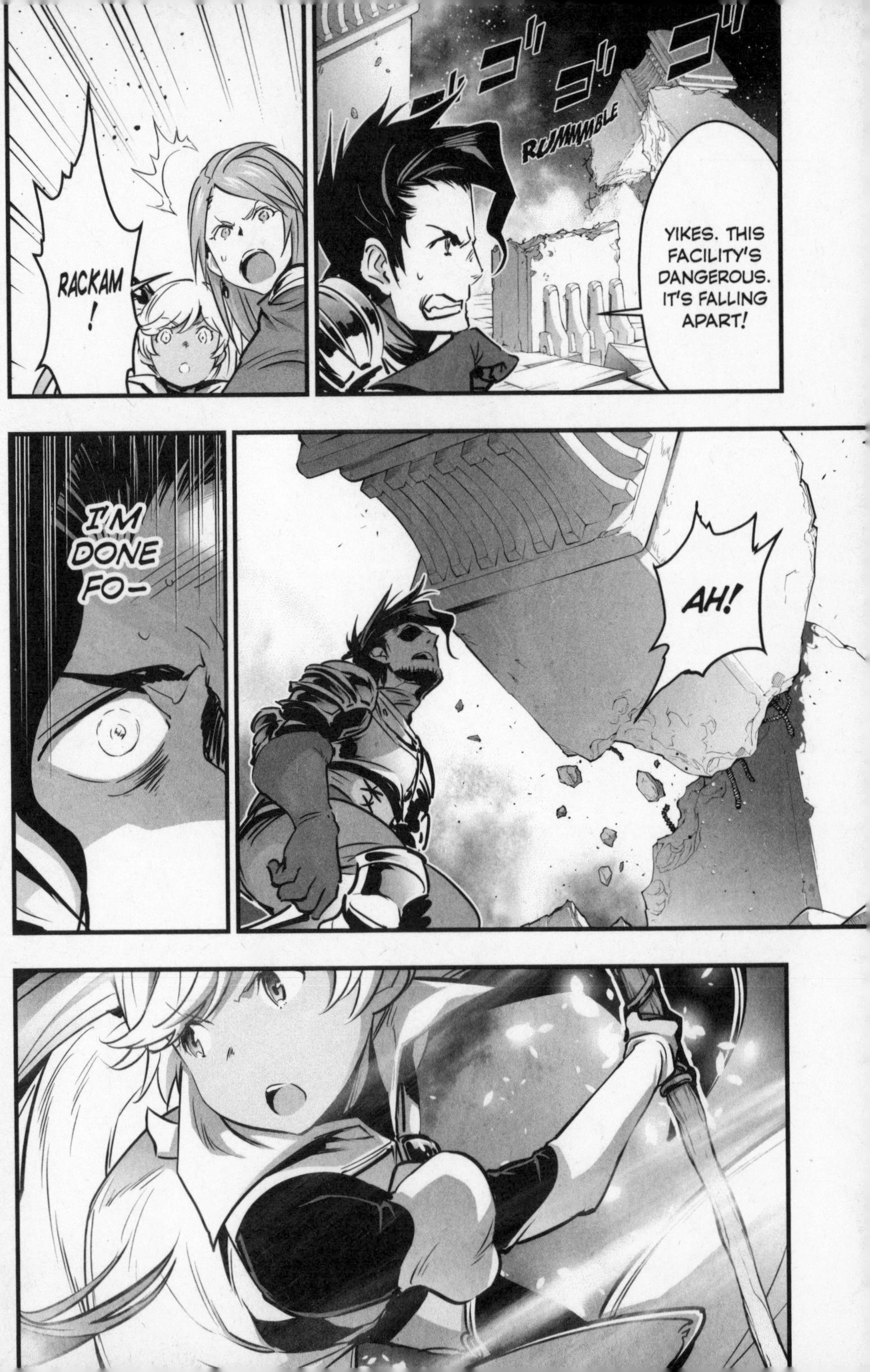
RUMMMBLE
YIKES. THIS FACILITY'S DANGEROUS. IT'S FALLING APART!
RACKAM!
AH!
I'M DONE FO-

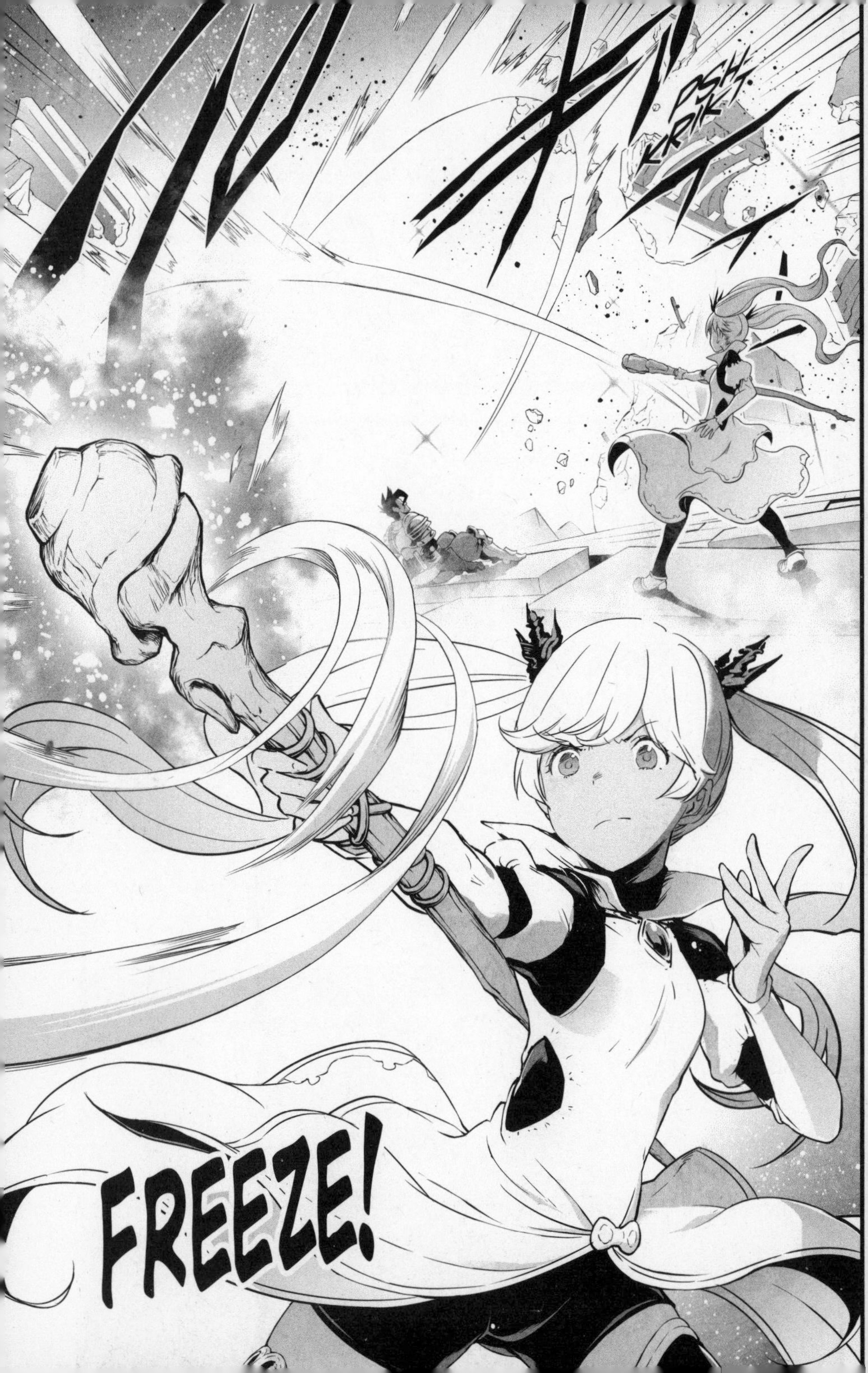
DOSH-KRIK
FREEZE!

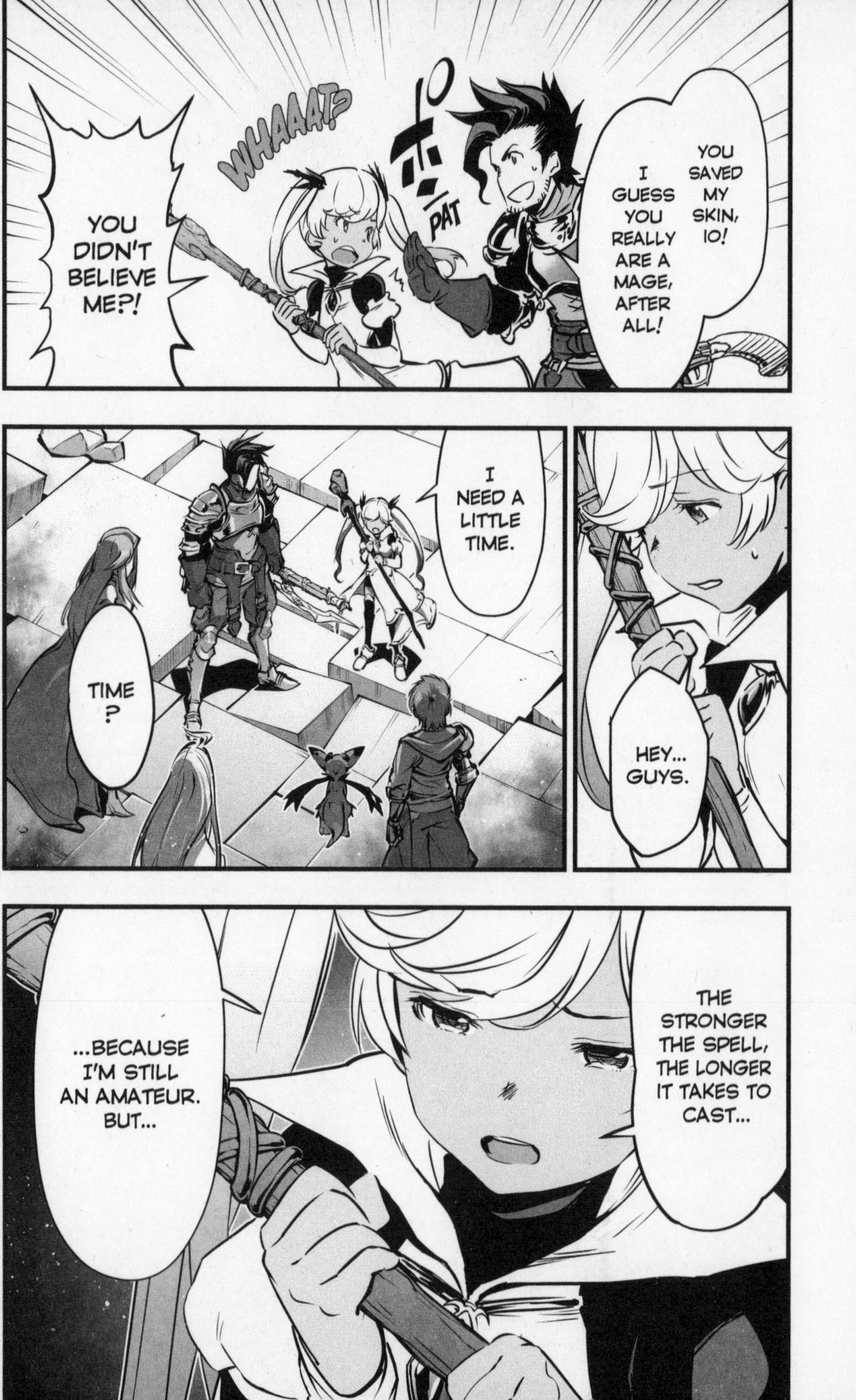
YOU SAVED MY SKIN, IO!
I GUESS YOU REALLY ARE A MAGE, AFTER ALL!
PAT
WHAAAT?!
YOU DIDN'T BELIEVE ME?!
HEY... GUYS.
I NEED A LITTLE TIME.
TIME?
THE STRONGER THE SPELL, THE LONGER IT TAKES TO CAST...
...BECAUSE I'M STILL AN AMATEUR. BUT...

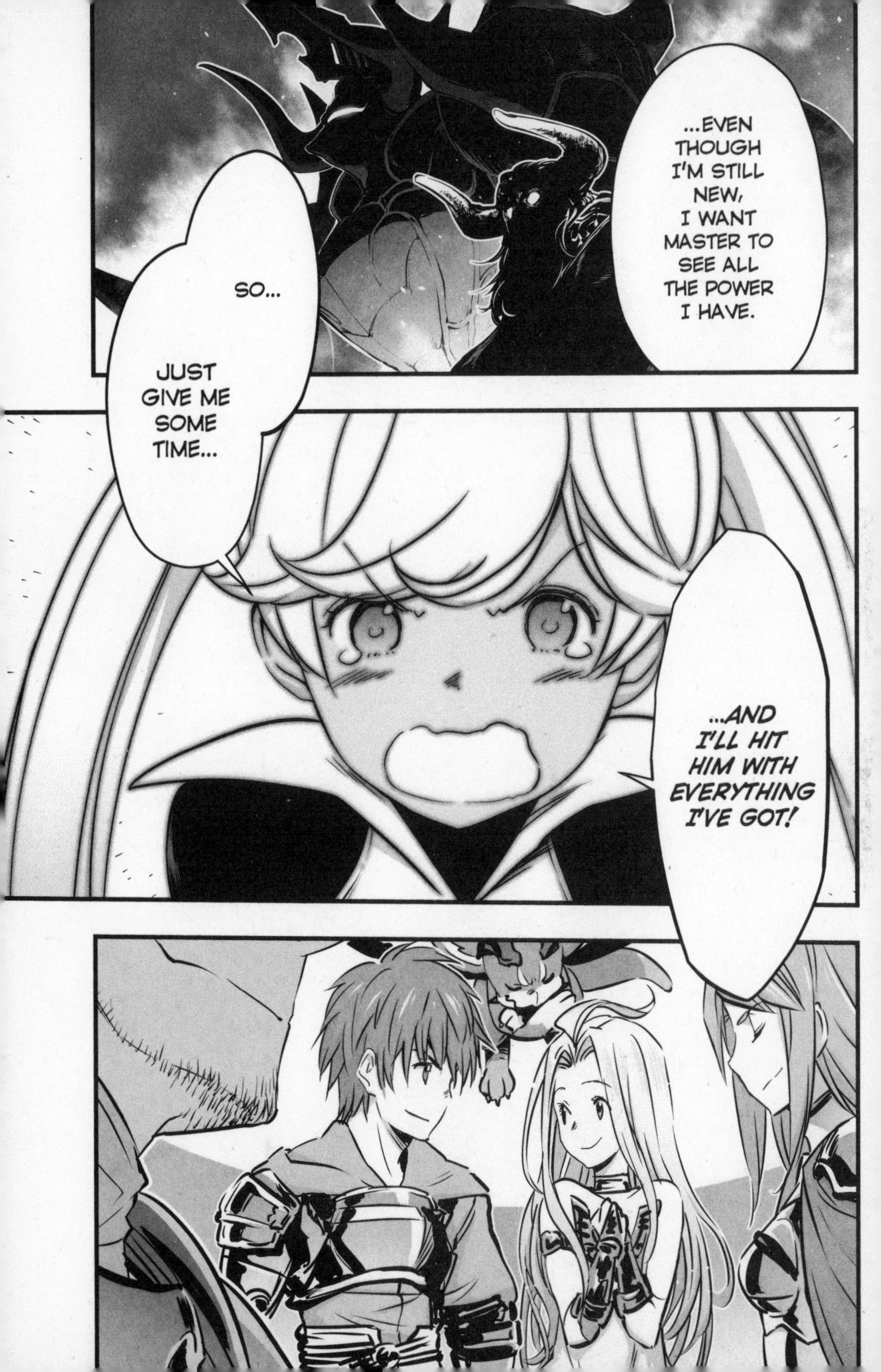
...EVEN THOUGH I'M STILL NEW, I WANT MASTER TO SEE ALL THE POWER I HAVE.
SO...
JUST GIVE ME SOME TIME...
...AND I'LL HIT HIM WITH EVERYTHING I'VE GOT!

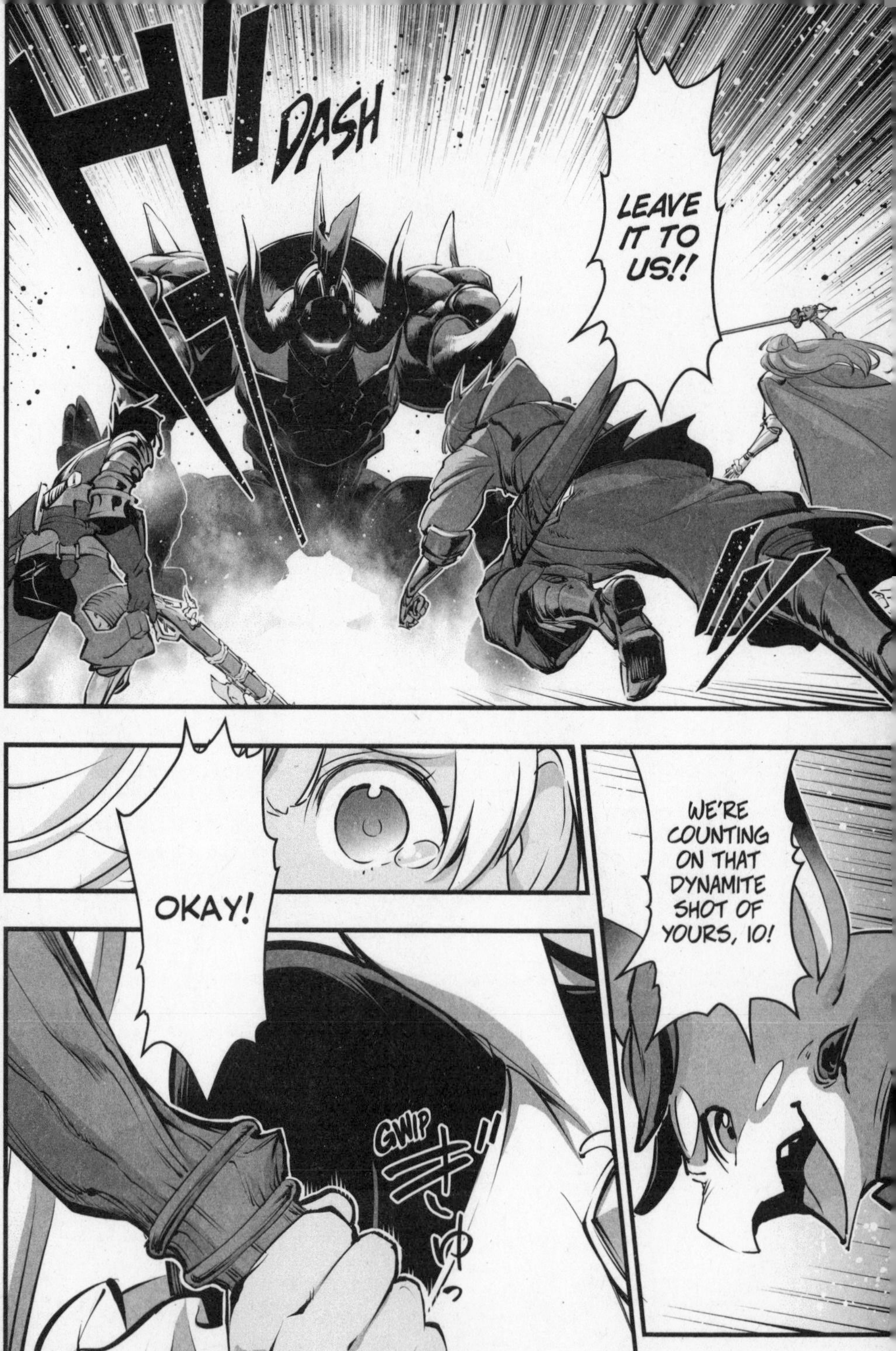
LEAVE IT TO US!!
DASH
WE'RE COUNTING ON THAT DYNAMITE SHOT OF YOURS, IO!
OKAY!
GWIP

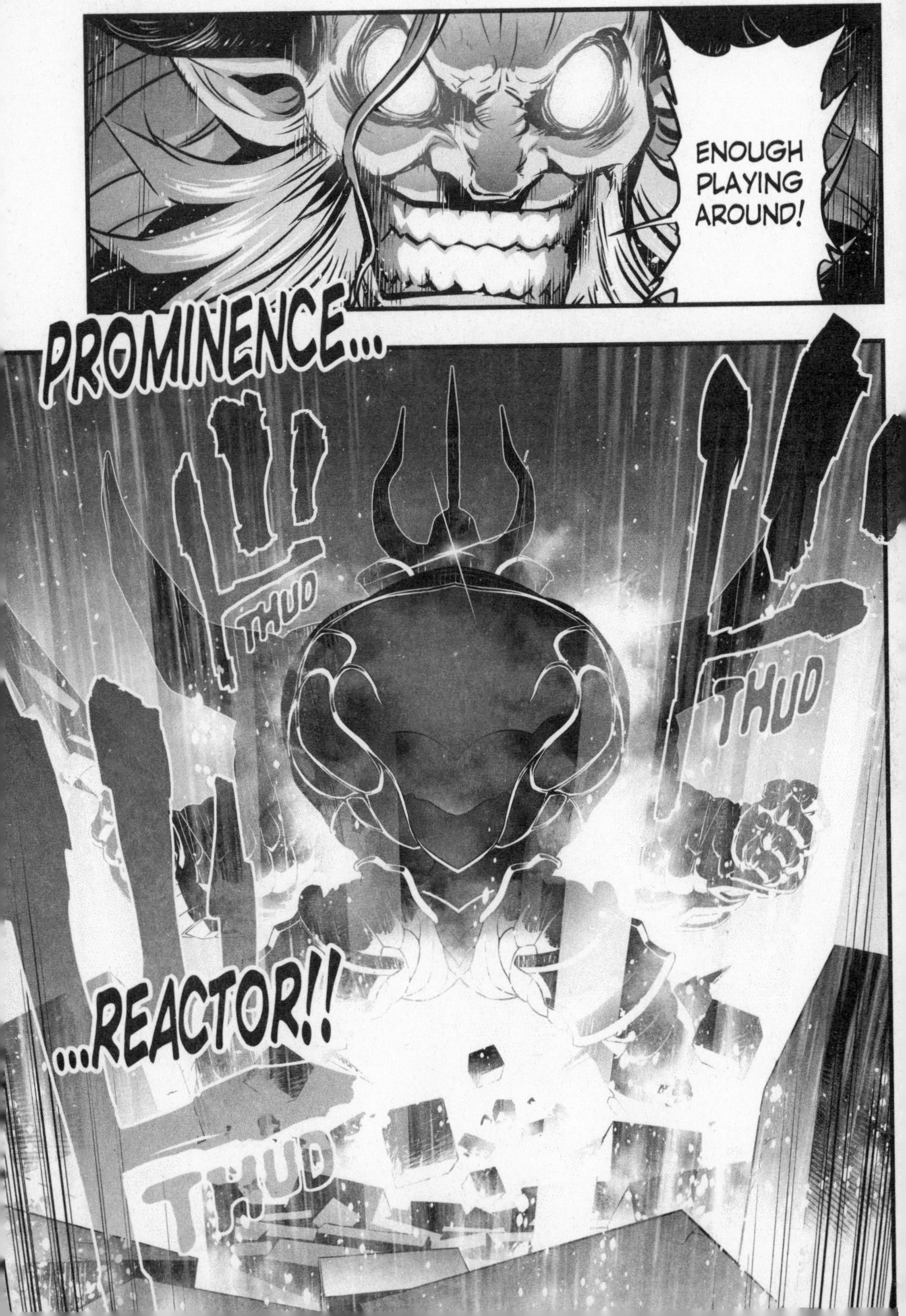
ENOUGH PLAYING AROUND!
PROMINENCE...
THUD
THUD
...REACTOR!!
THUD

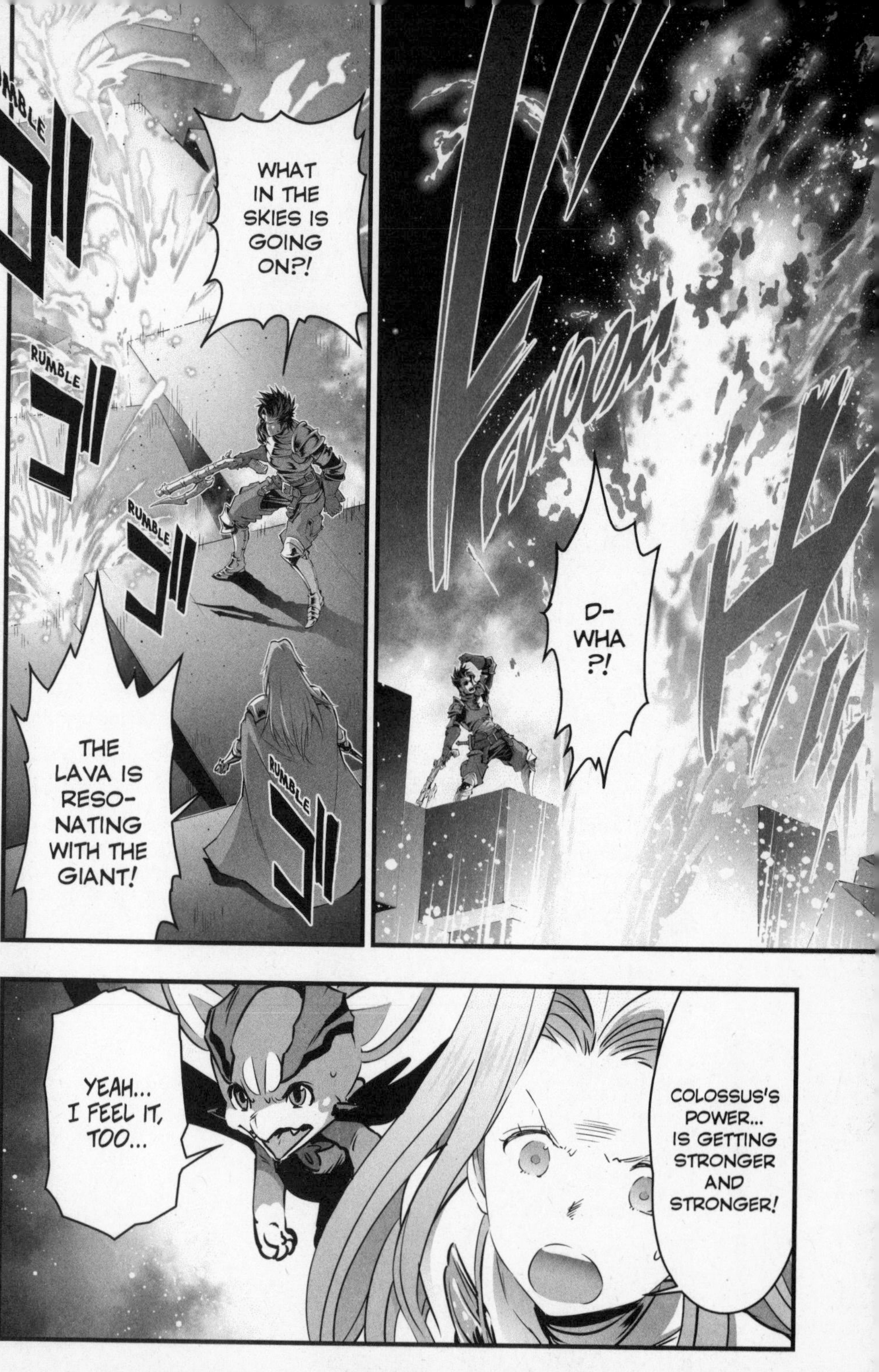
FWOOM
D-WHA?!
WHAT IN THE SKIES IS GOING ON?!
RUMBLE
RUMBLE
RUMBLE
RUMBLE
THE LAVA IS RESO-NATING WITH THE GIANT!
COLOSSUS'S POWER... IS GETTING STRONGER AND STRONGER!
YEAH... I FEEL IT, TOO...

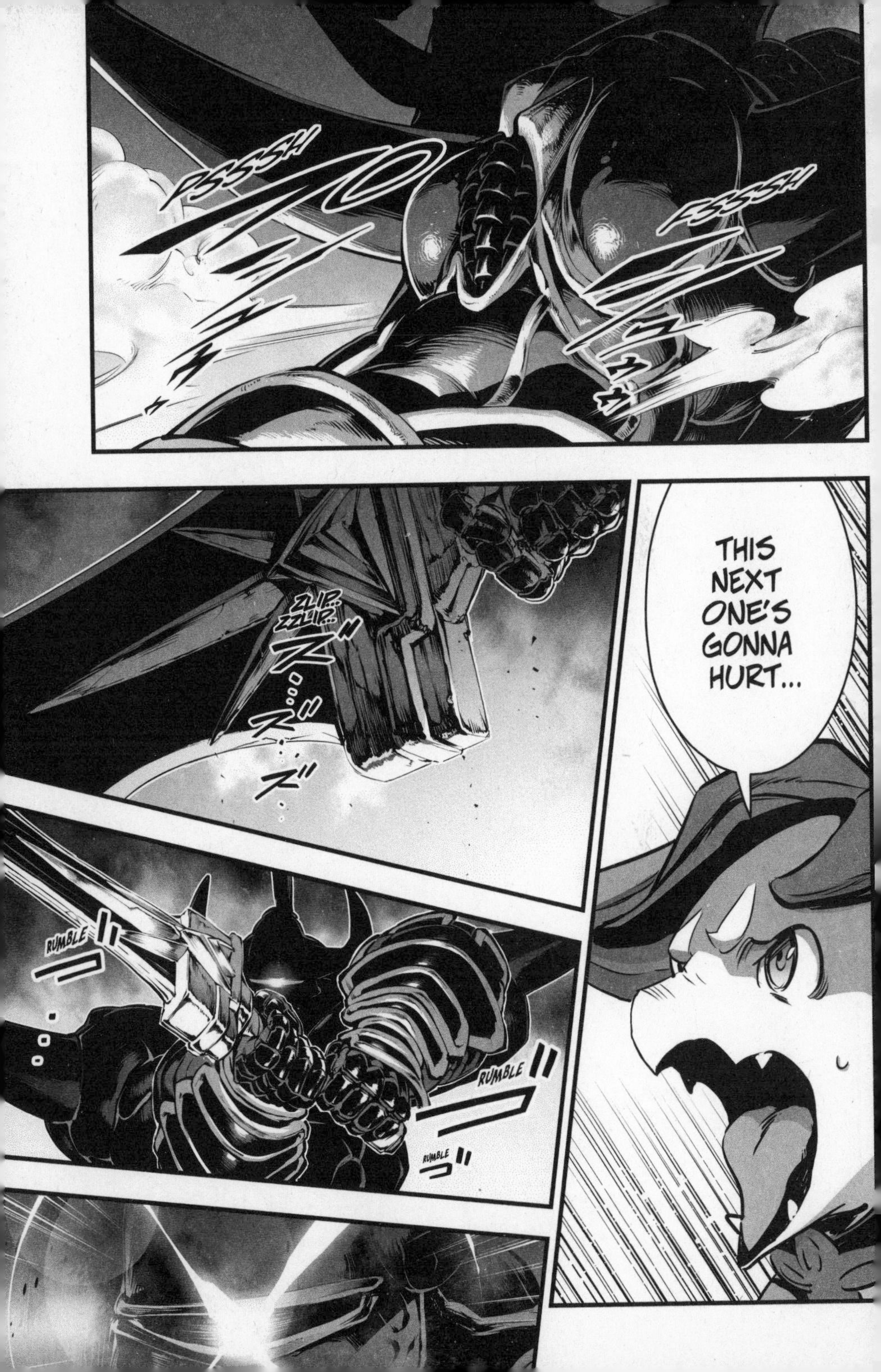
PSSSSH
PSSSSH
THIS NEXT ONE'S GONNA HURT...
ZLIP... ZZLIP...
RUMBLE
RUMBLE
RUMBLE

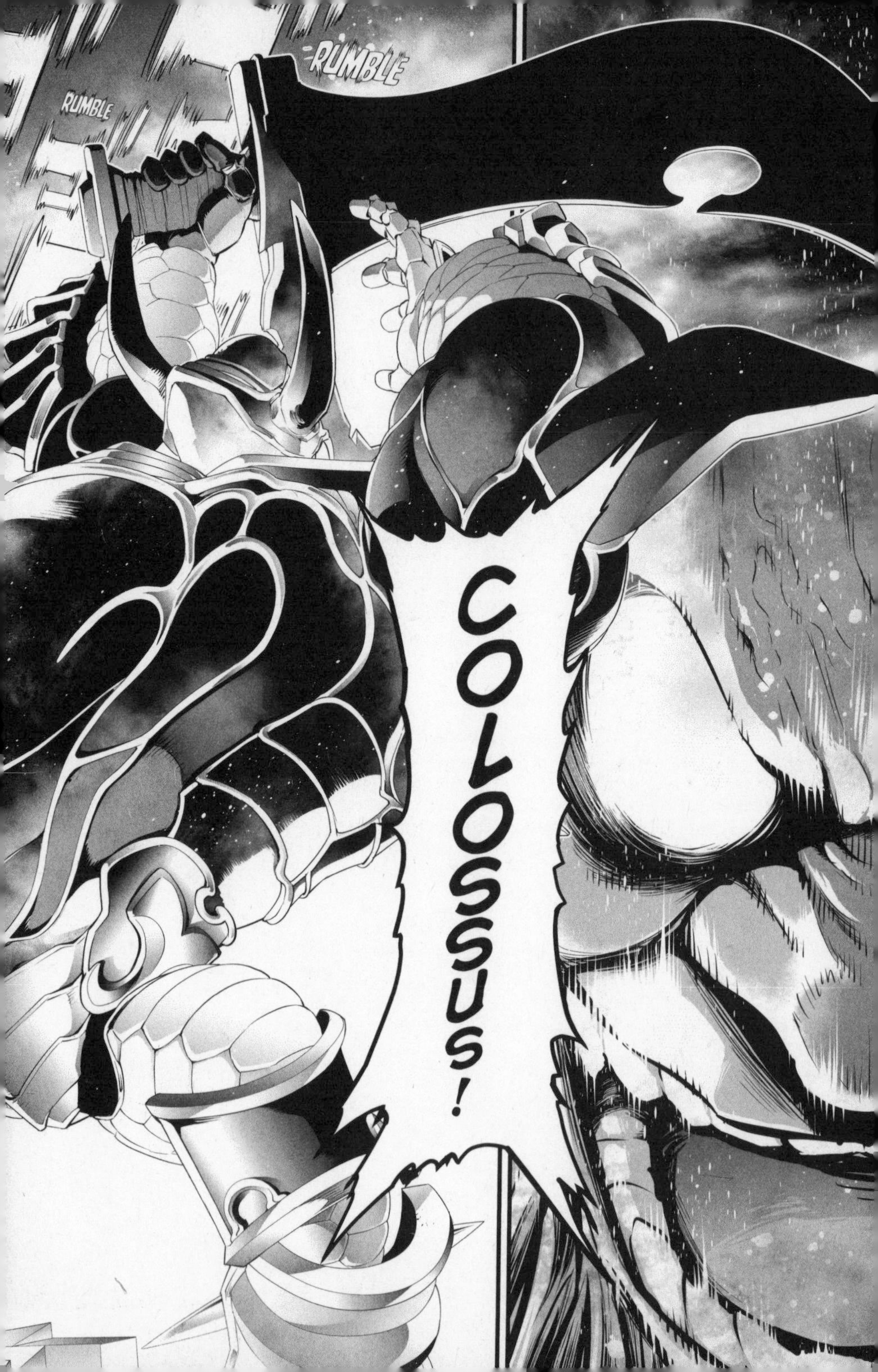
RUMBLE
RUMBLE
COLOSSUS!

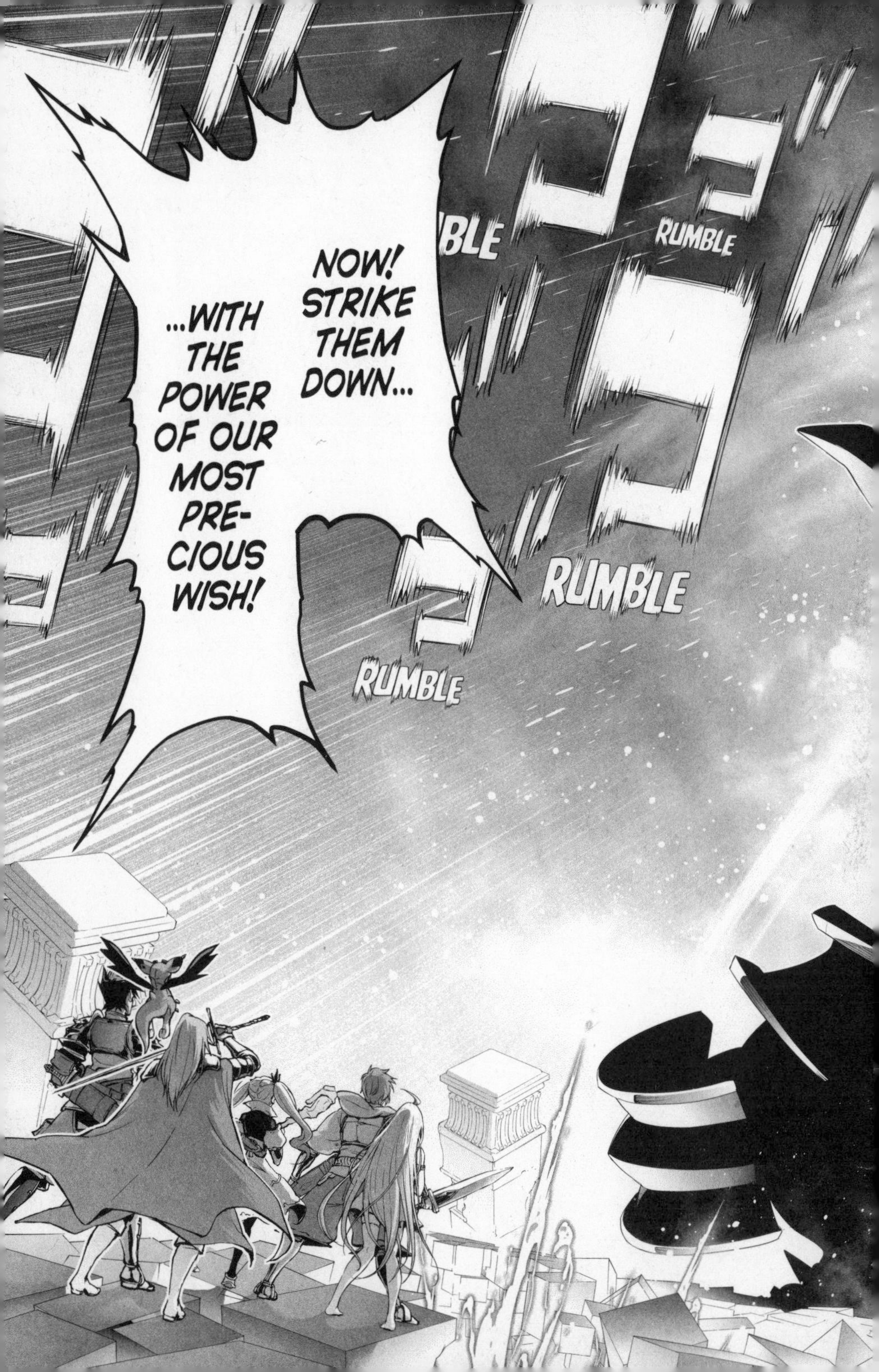
RUMBLE
NOW! STRIKE THEM DOWN... ...WITH THE POWER OF OUR MOST PRE-CIOUS WISH!
RUMBLE
RUMBLE

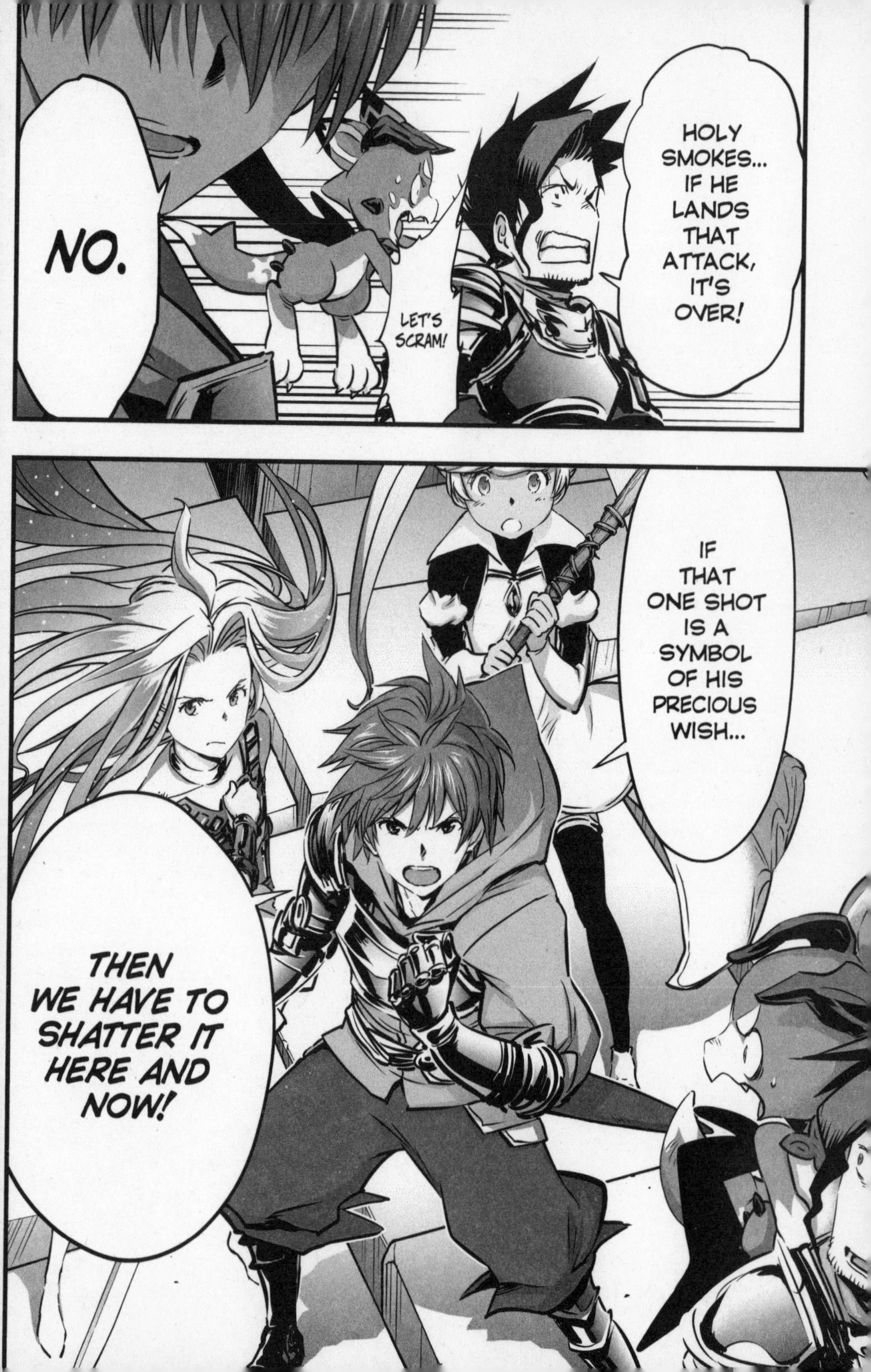
HOLY SMOKES... IF HE LANDS THAT ATTACK, IT'S OVER!
LET'S SCRAM!
NO.
IF THAT ONE SHOT IS A SYMBOL OF HIS PRECIOUS WISH...
THEN WE HAVE TO SHATTER IT HERE AND NOW!

GRANBLUE FANTASY
グランブルーファンタジー

GRANBLUE FANTASY
グランブルーファンタジー

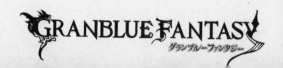

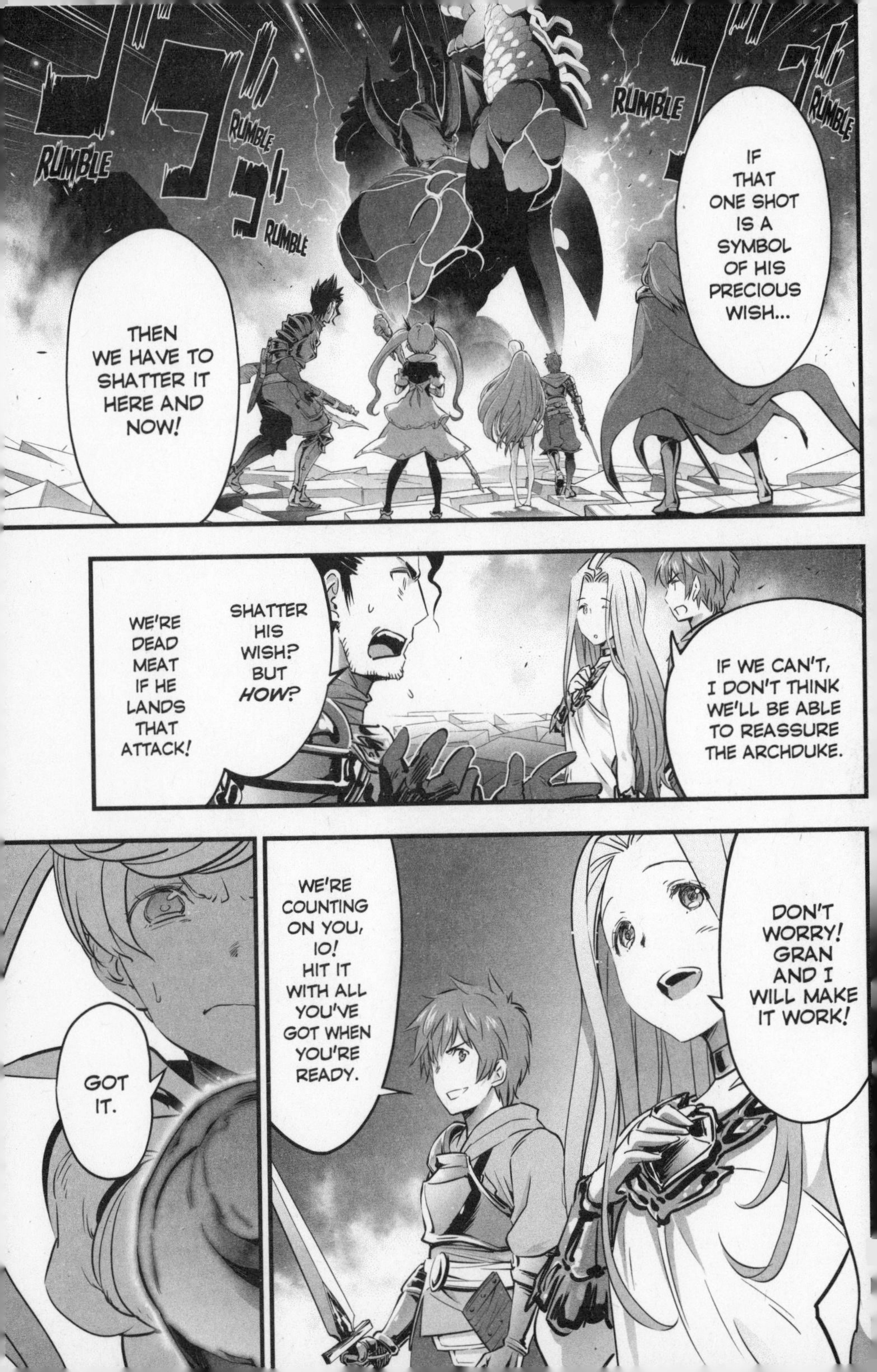
RUMBLE
RUMBLE
IF THAT ONE SHOT IS A SYMBOL OF HIS PRECIOUS WISH...
RUMBLE
RUMBLE
RUMBLE
THEN WE HAVE TO SHATTER IT HERE AND NOW!
IF WE CAN'T, I DON'T THINK WE'LL BE ABLE TO REASSURE THE ARCHDUKE.
SHATTER HIS WISH? BUT *HOW*?
WE'RE DEAD MEAT IF HE LANDS THAT ATTACK!
DON'T WORRY! GRAN AND I WILL MAKE IT WORK!
WE'RE COUNTING ON YOU, IO! HIT IT WITH ALL YOU'VE GOT WHEN YOU'RE READY.
GOT IT.

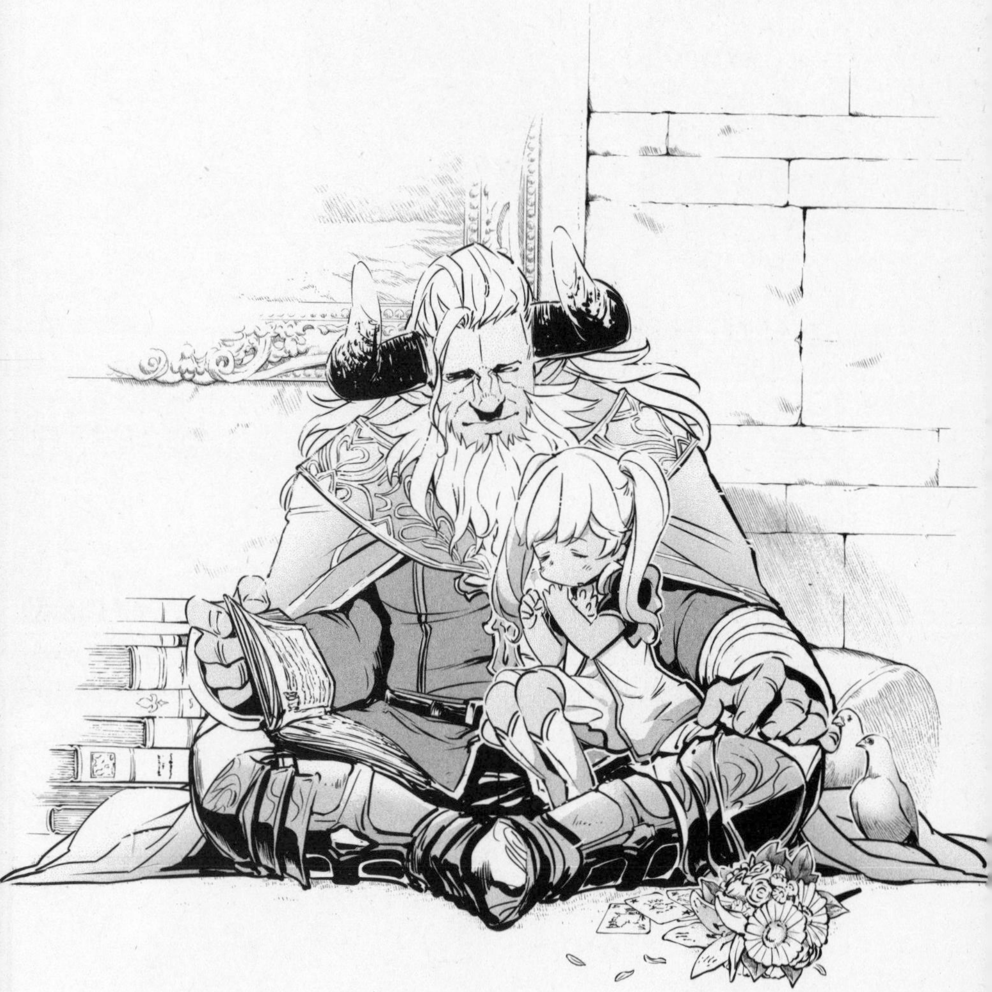

CHAPTER 21: Mage

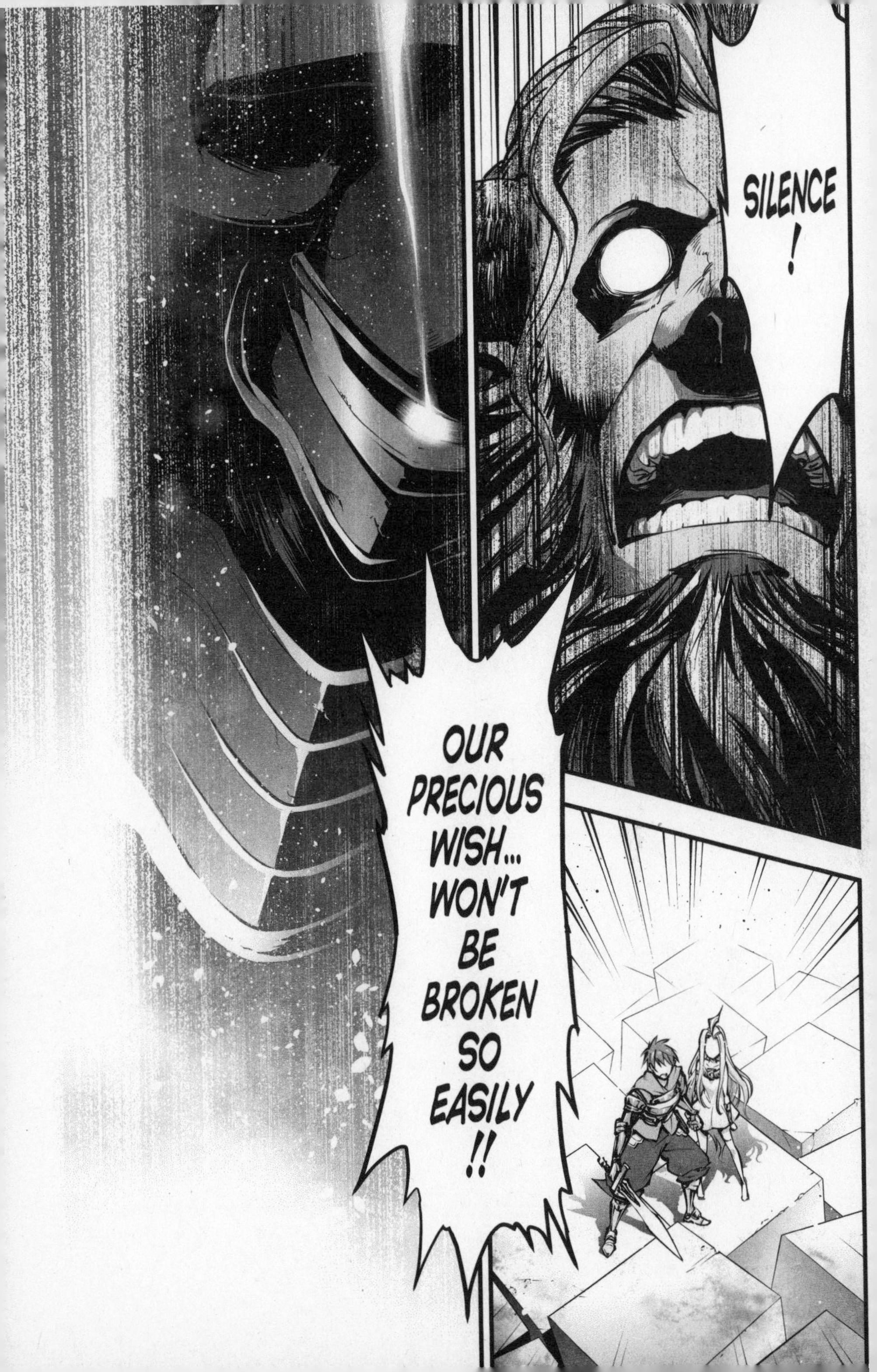
SILENCE !
OUR PRECIOUS WISH... WON'T BE BROKEN SO EASILY !!

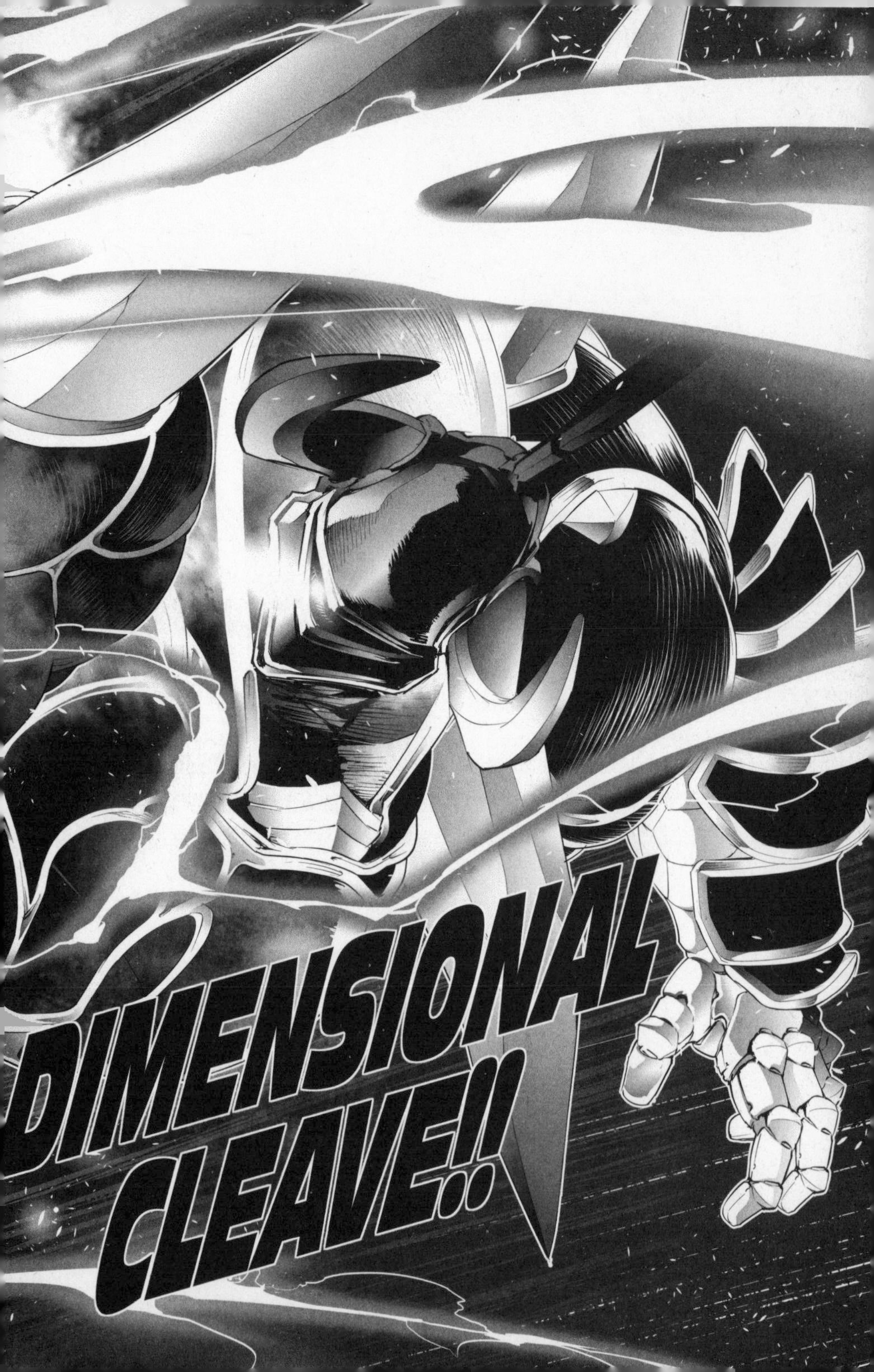
DIMENSIONAL CLEAVE!!

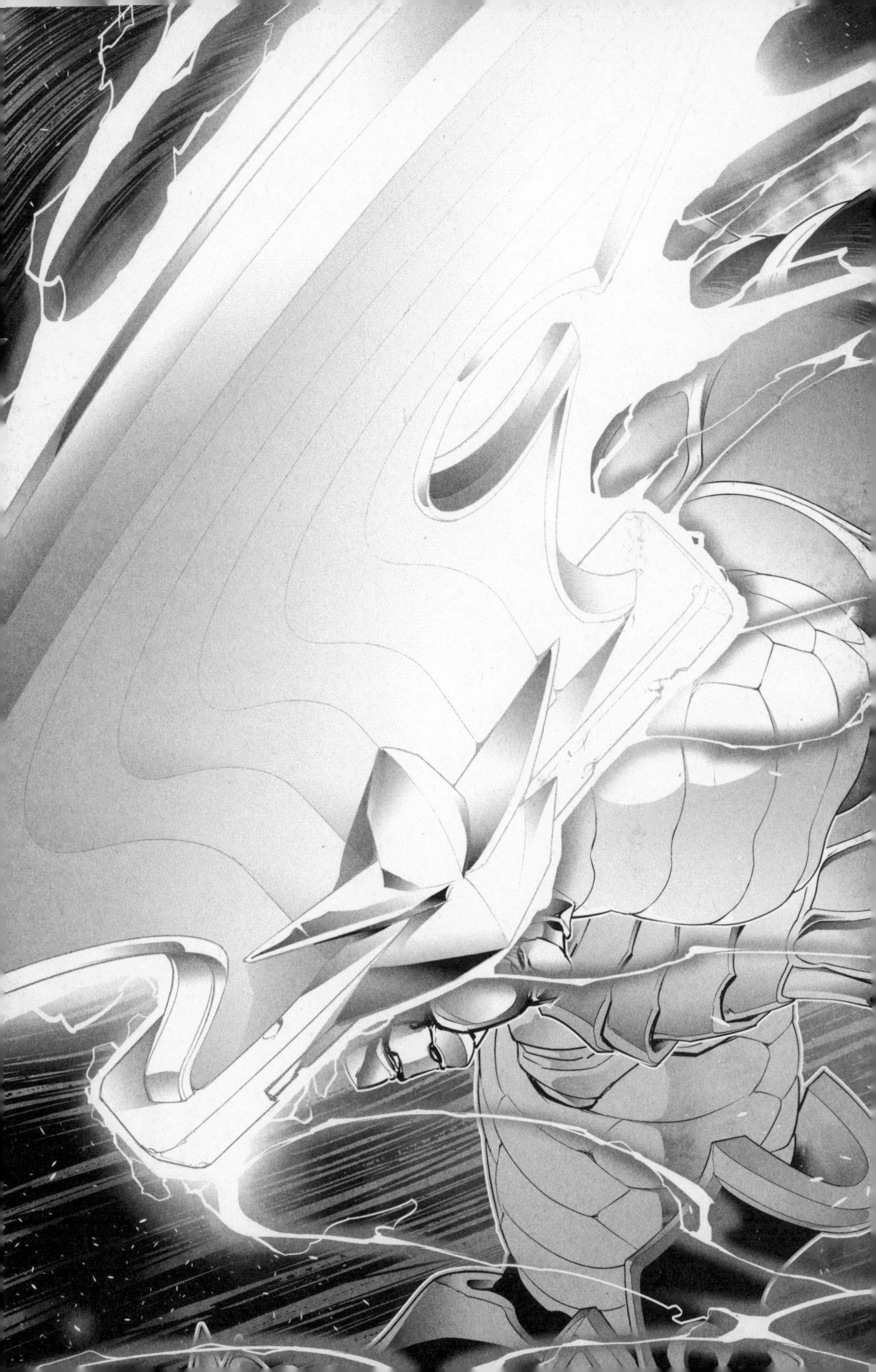

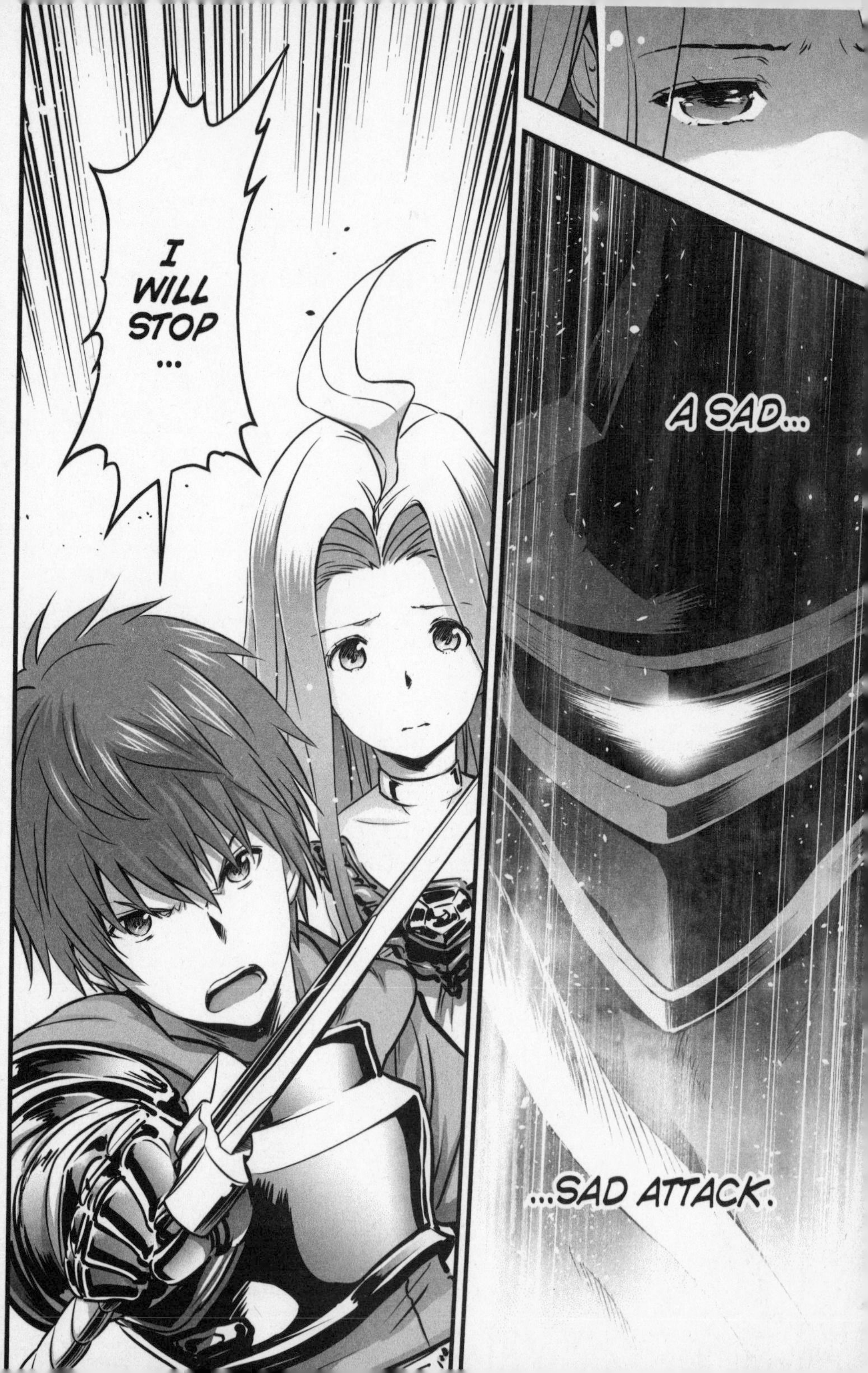
A SAD...
...SAD ATTACK.
I WILL STOP ...

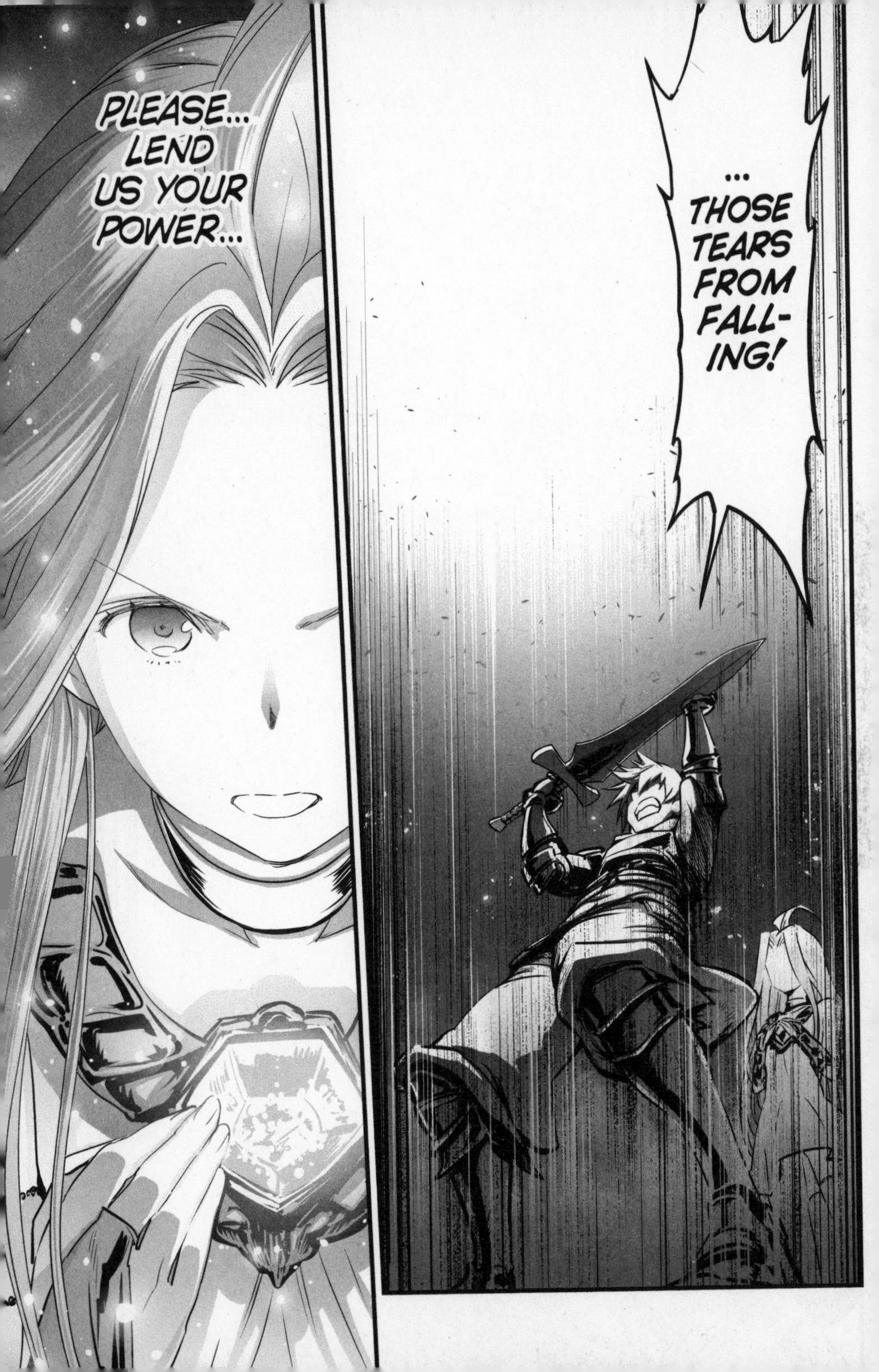
... THOSE TEARS FROM FALL-ING!
PLEASE... LEND US YOUR POWER...

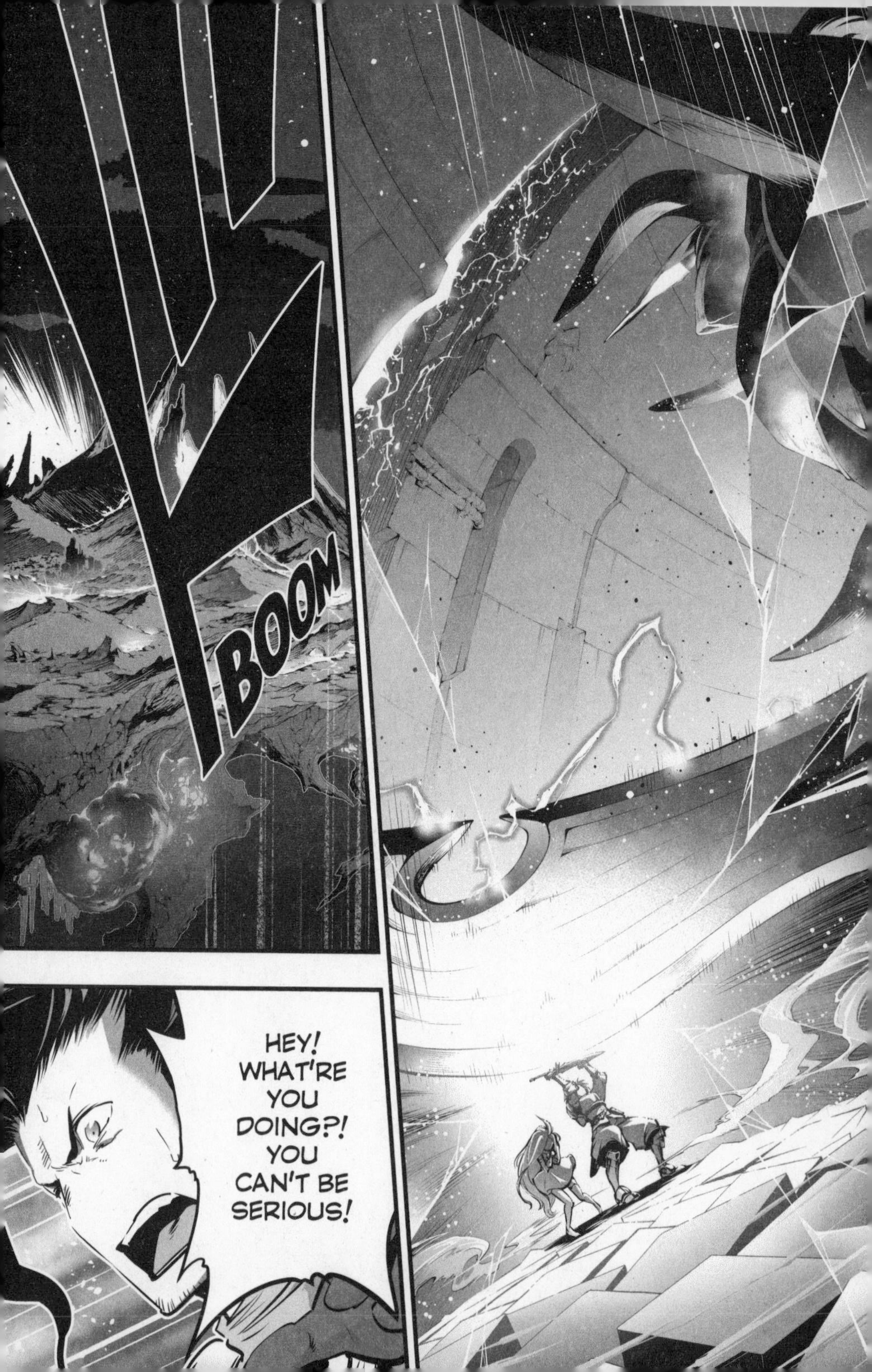
BOOM
HEY! WHAT'RE YOU DOING?! YOU CAN'T BE SERIOUS!

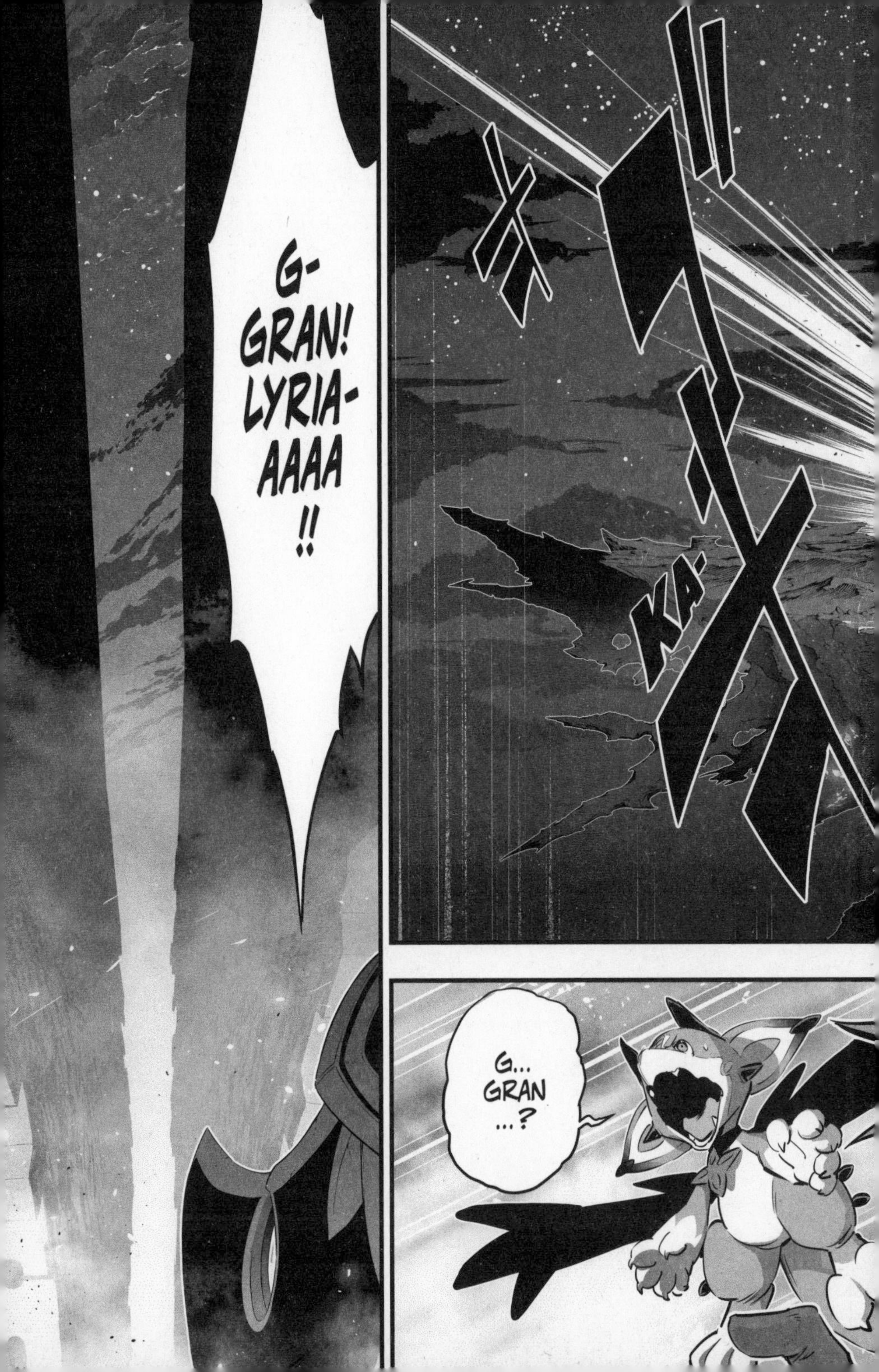
G... GRAN ...?
G- GRAN! LYRIA- AAAA !!

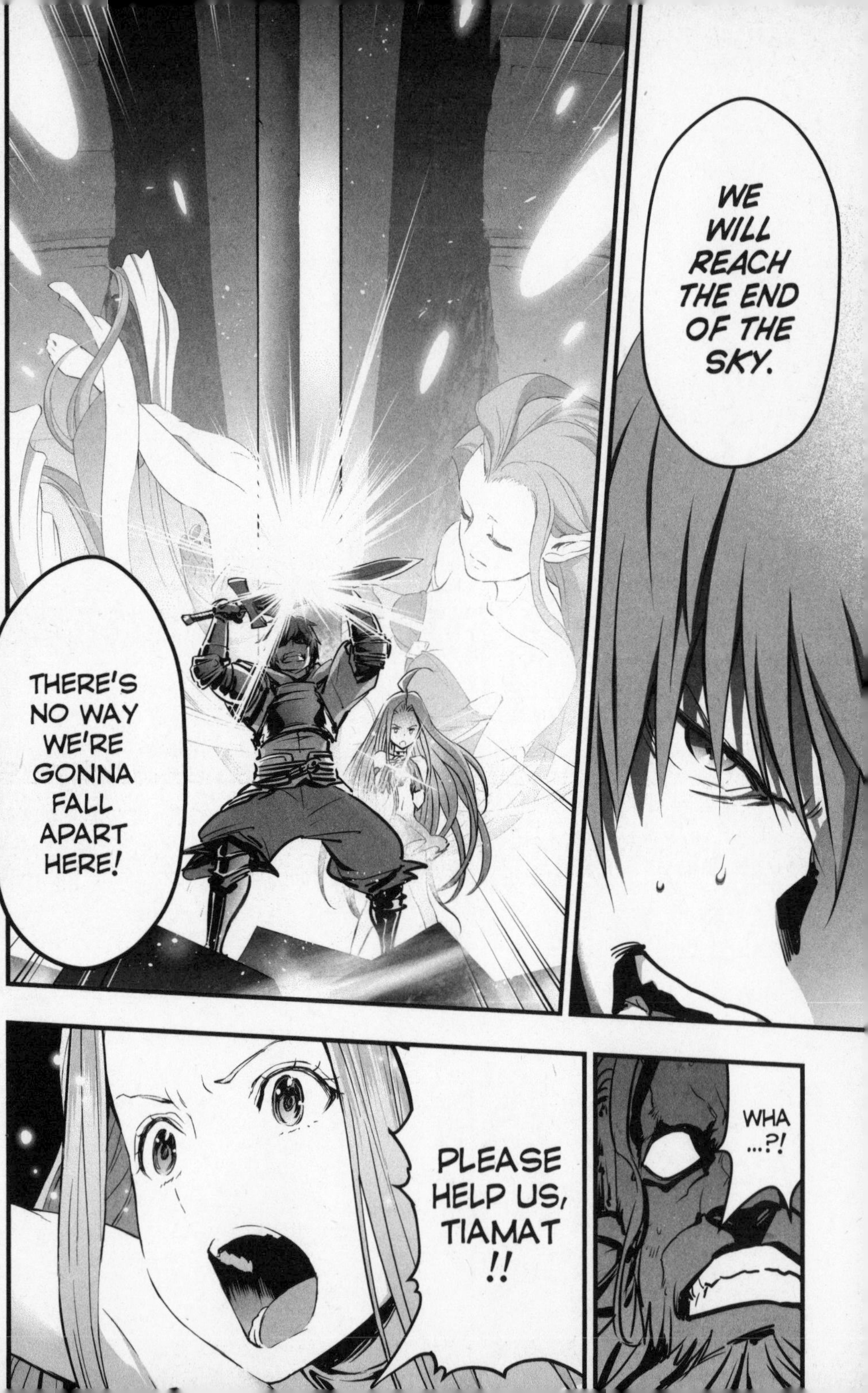
WE WILL REACH THE END OF THE SKY.
THERE'S NO WAY WE'RE GONNA FALL APART HERE!
WHA ...?!
PLEASE HELP US, TIAMAT!!

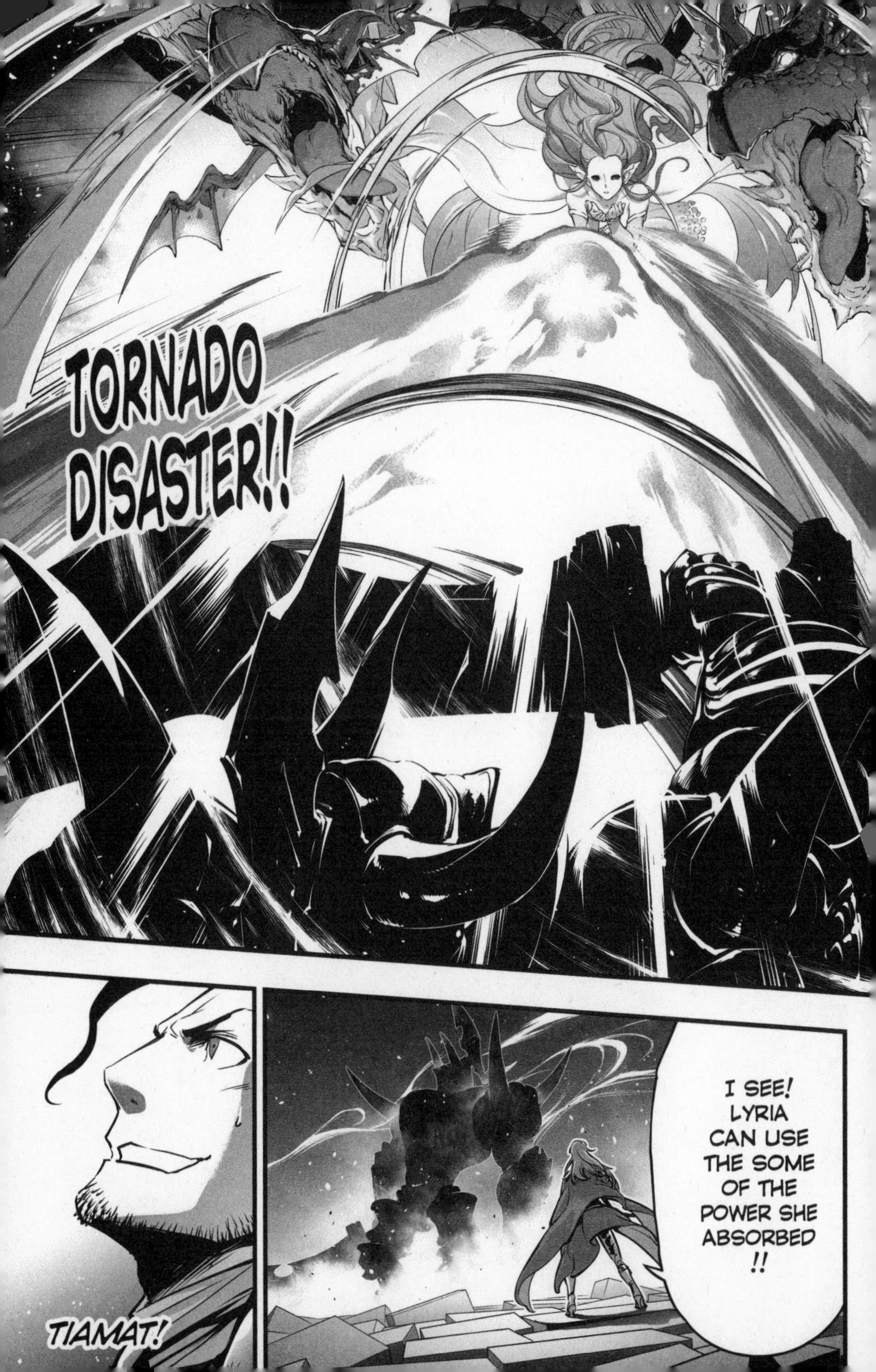
TORNADO DISASTER!!
I SEE! LYRIA CAN USE THE SOME OF THE POWER SHE ABSORBED !!
TIAMAT!

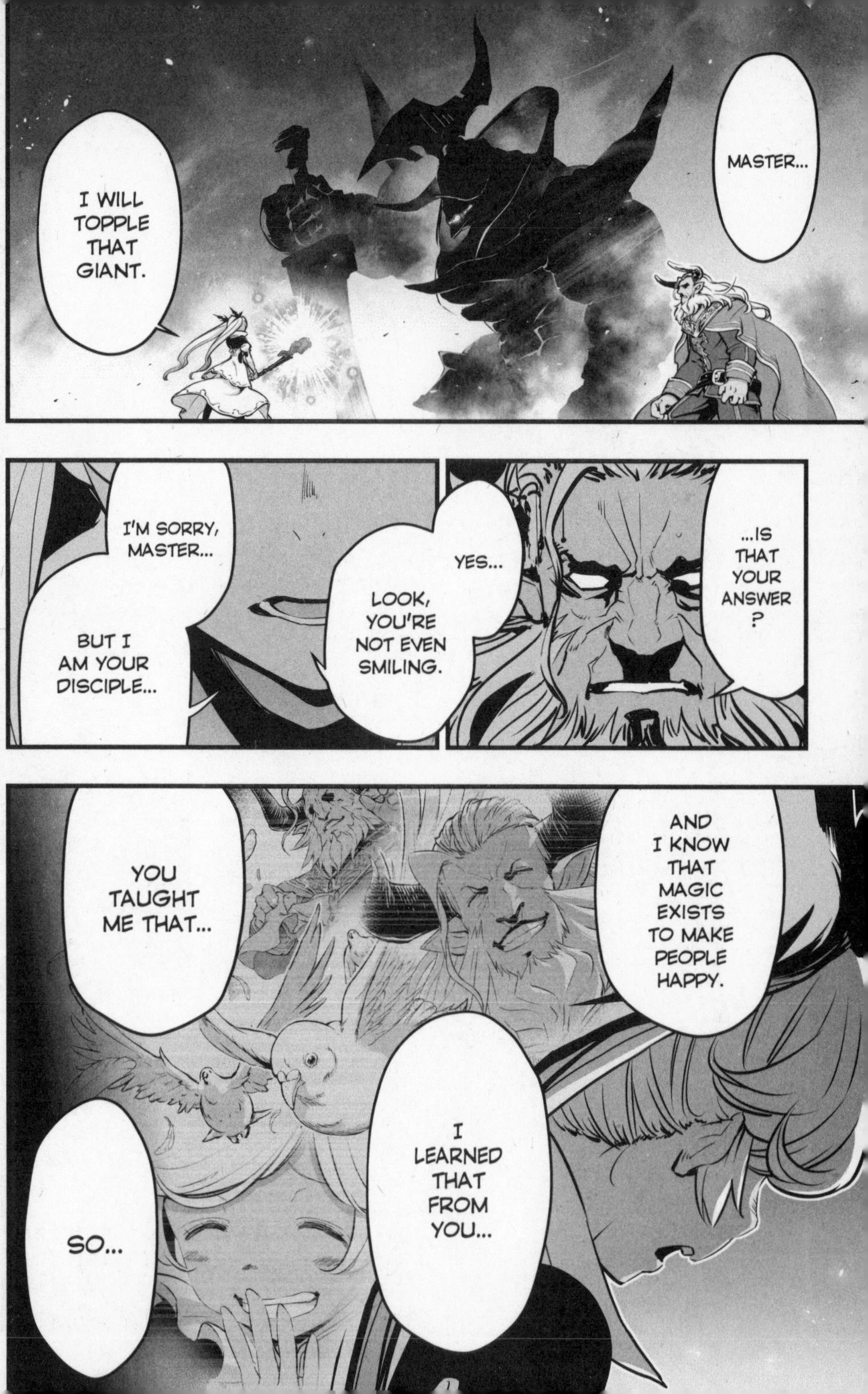
MASTER...
I WILL TOPPLE THAT GIANT.
...IS THAT YOUR ANSWER?
YES... LOOK, YOU'RE NOT EVEN SMILING.
I'M SORRY, MASTER...
BUT I AM YOUR DISCIPLE...
AND I KNOW THAT MAGIC EXISTS TO MAKE PEOPLE HAPPY.
YOU TAUGHT ME THAT...
I LEARNED THAT FROM YOU...
SO...

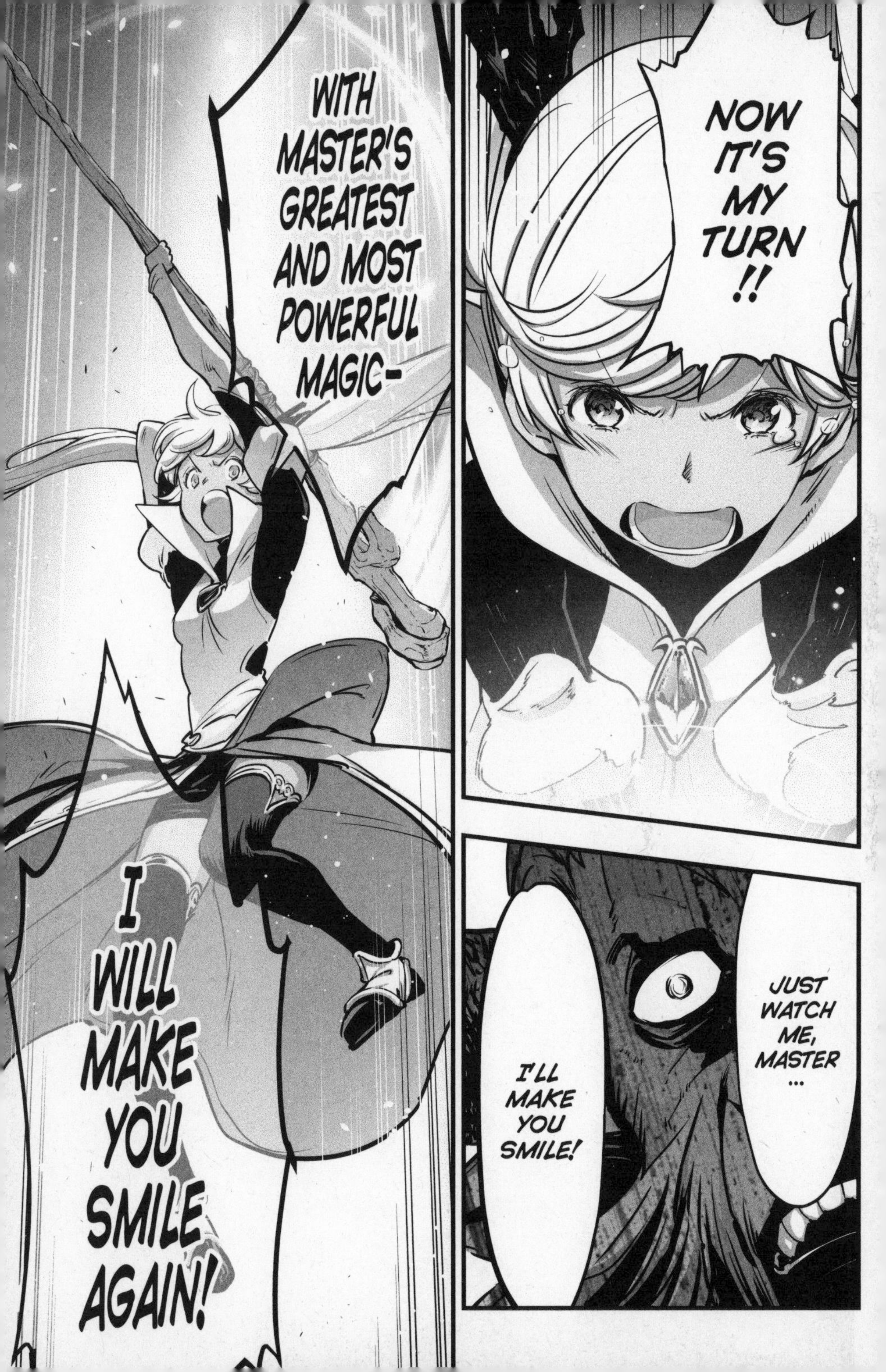
NOW IT'S MY TURN!!
JUST WATCH ME, MASTER...
I'LL MAKE YOU SMILE!
WITH MASTER'S GREATEST AND MOST POWERFUL MAGIC-
I WILL MAKE YOU SMILE AGAIN!

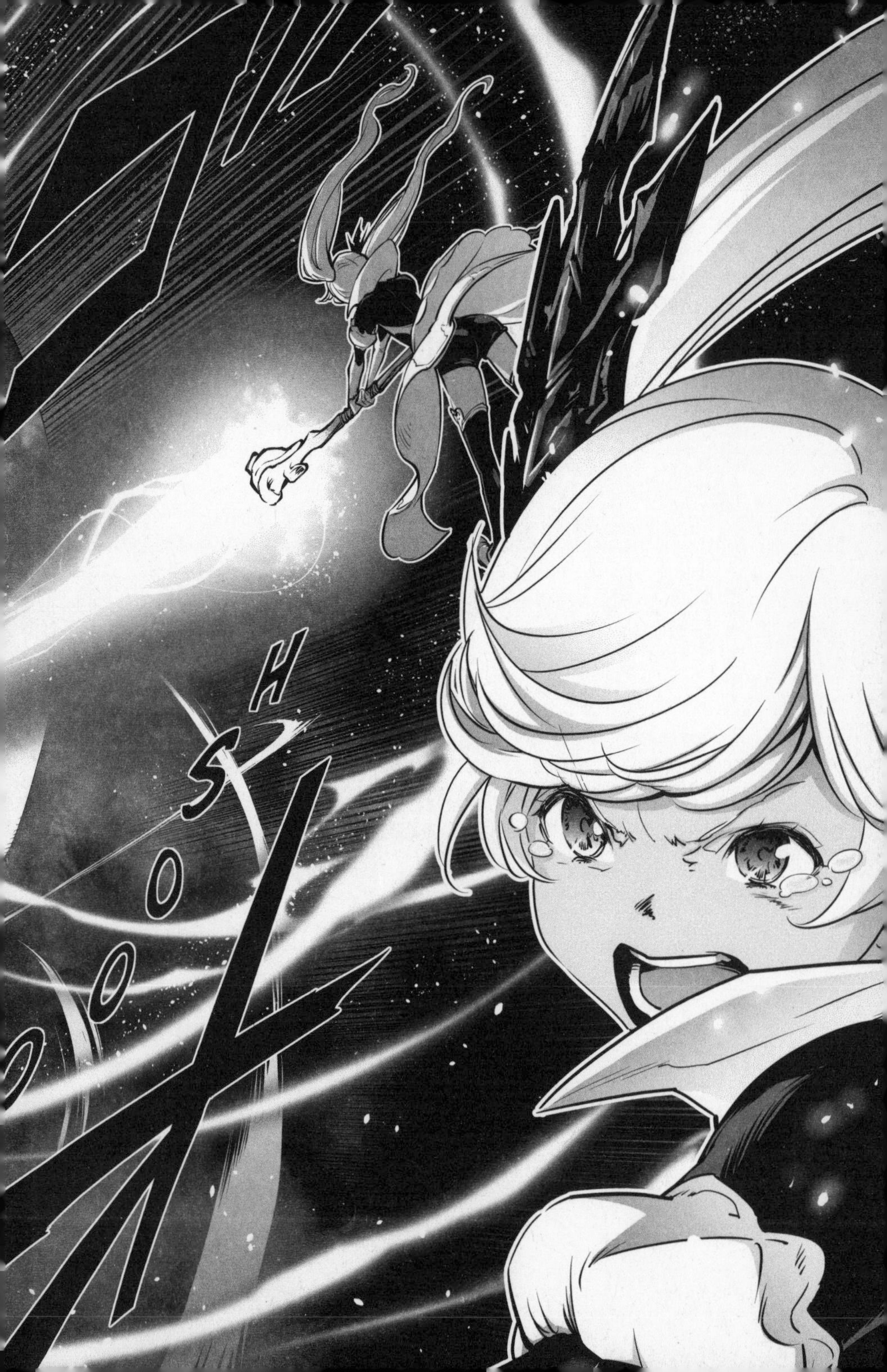
OOOOSH

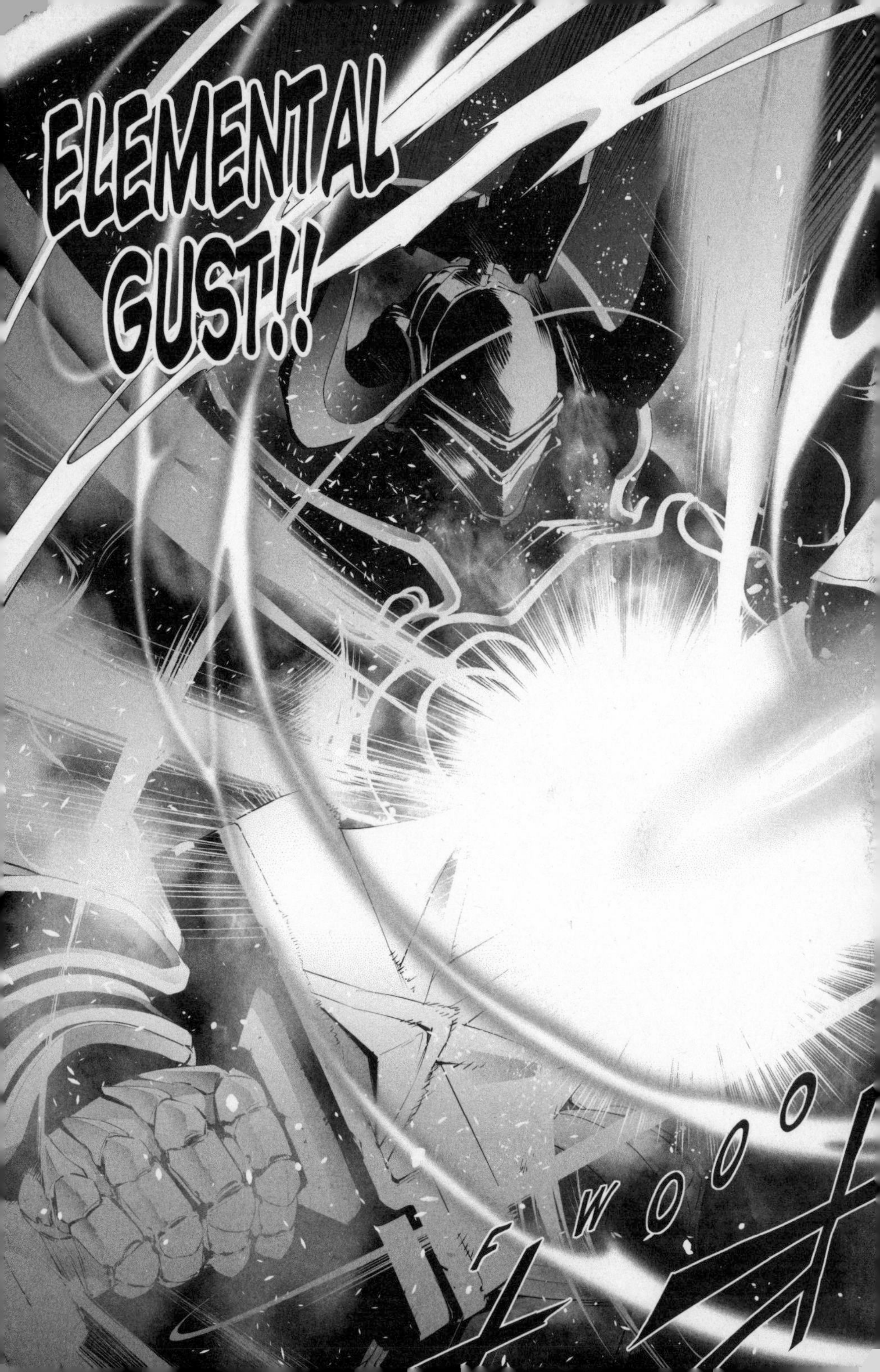
ELEMENTAL GUST!!
FWOOOOOSH

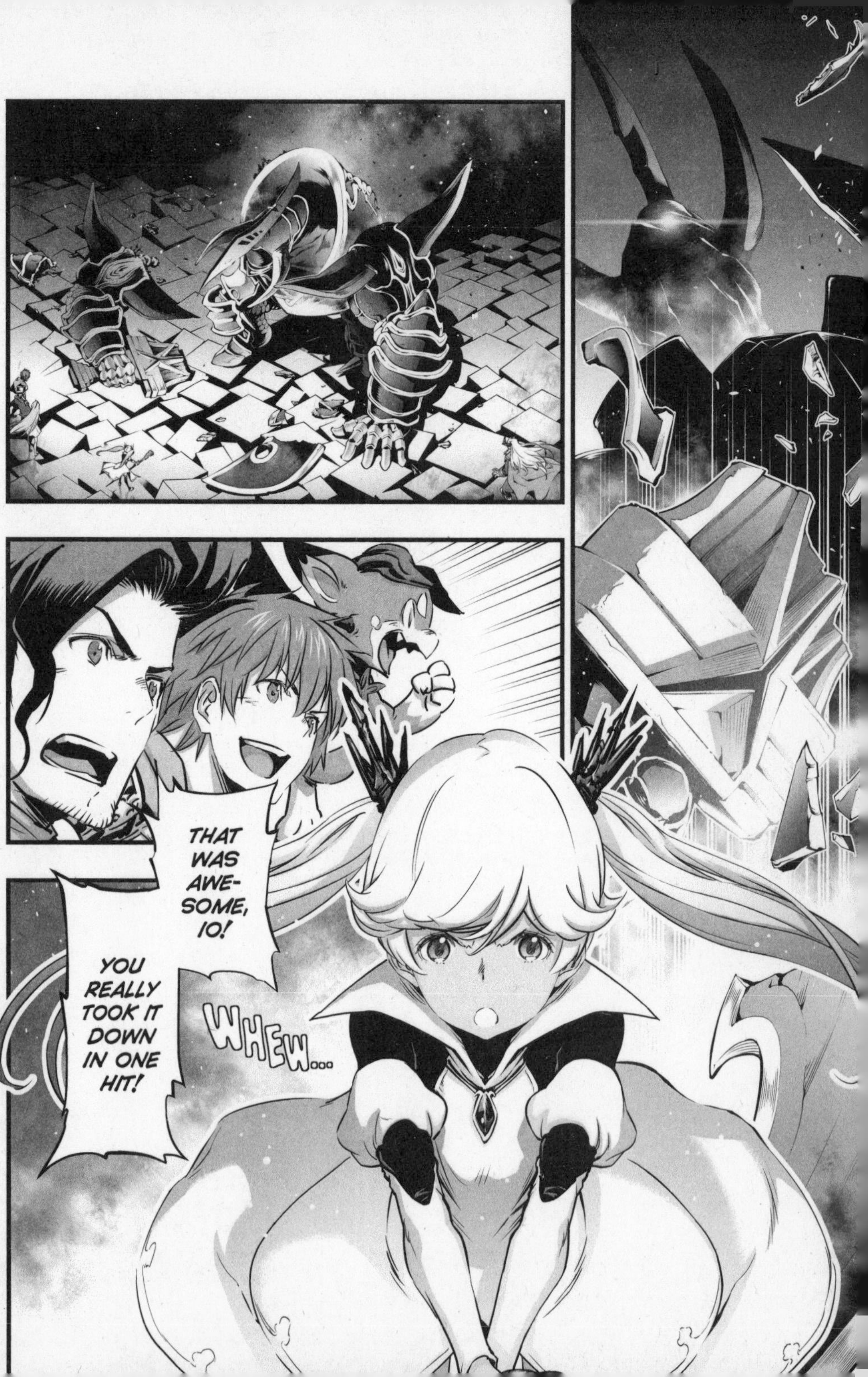
THAT WAS AWE-SOME, IO!
YOU REALLY TOOK IT DOWN IN ONE HIT!
WHEW...

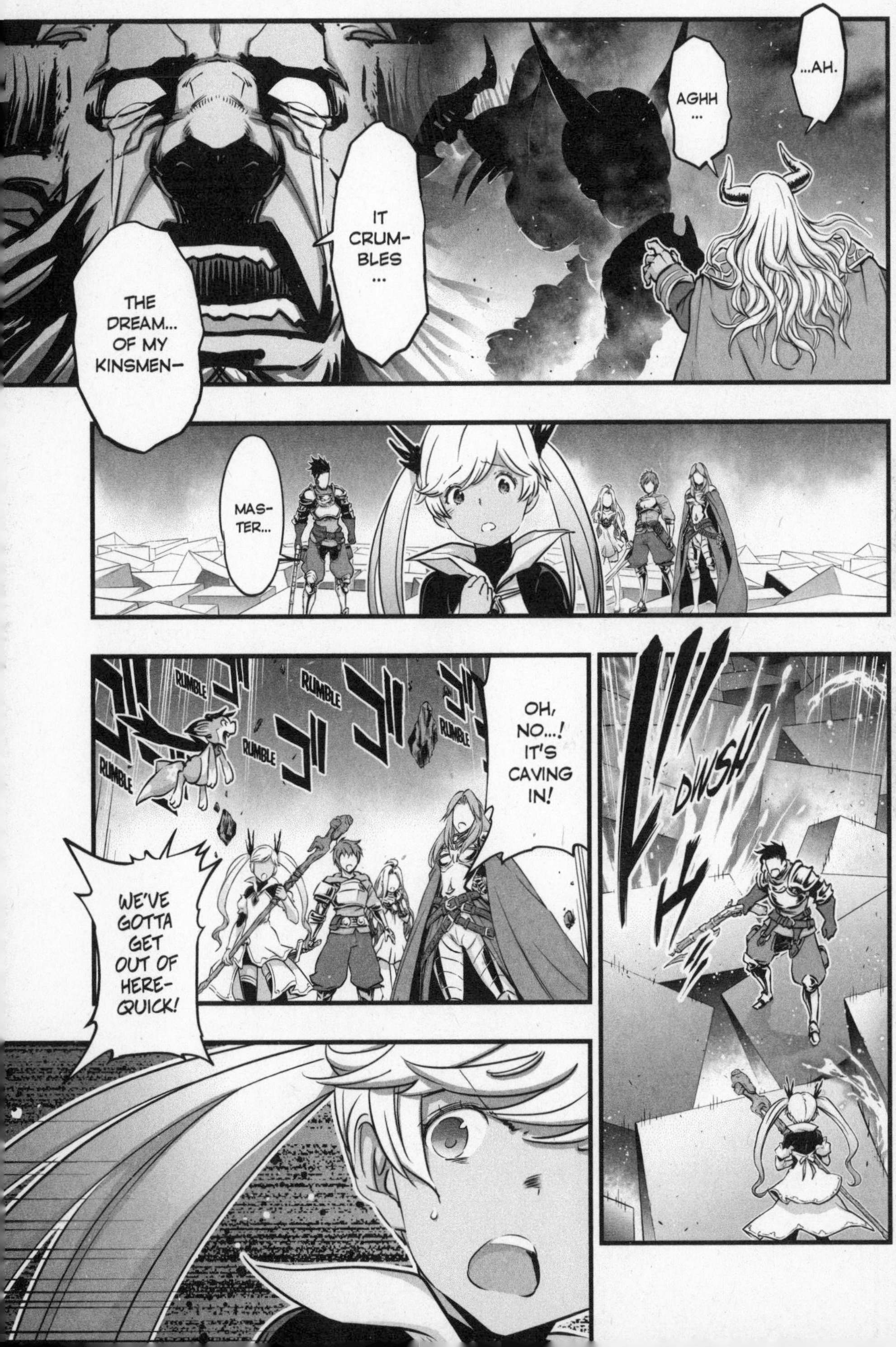
...AH.
AGHH ...
IT CRUMBLES...
THE DREAM... OF MY KINSMEN—
MASTER...
DWSH
RUMBLE
RUMBLE
RUMBLE
RUMBLE
OH, NO...! IT'S CAVING IN!
WE'VE GOTTA GET OUT OF HERE—QUICK!

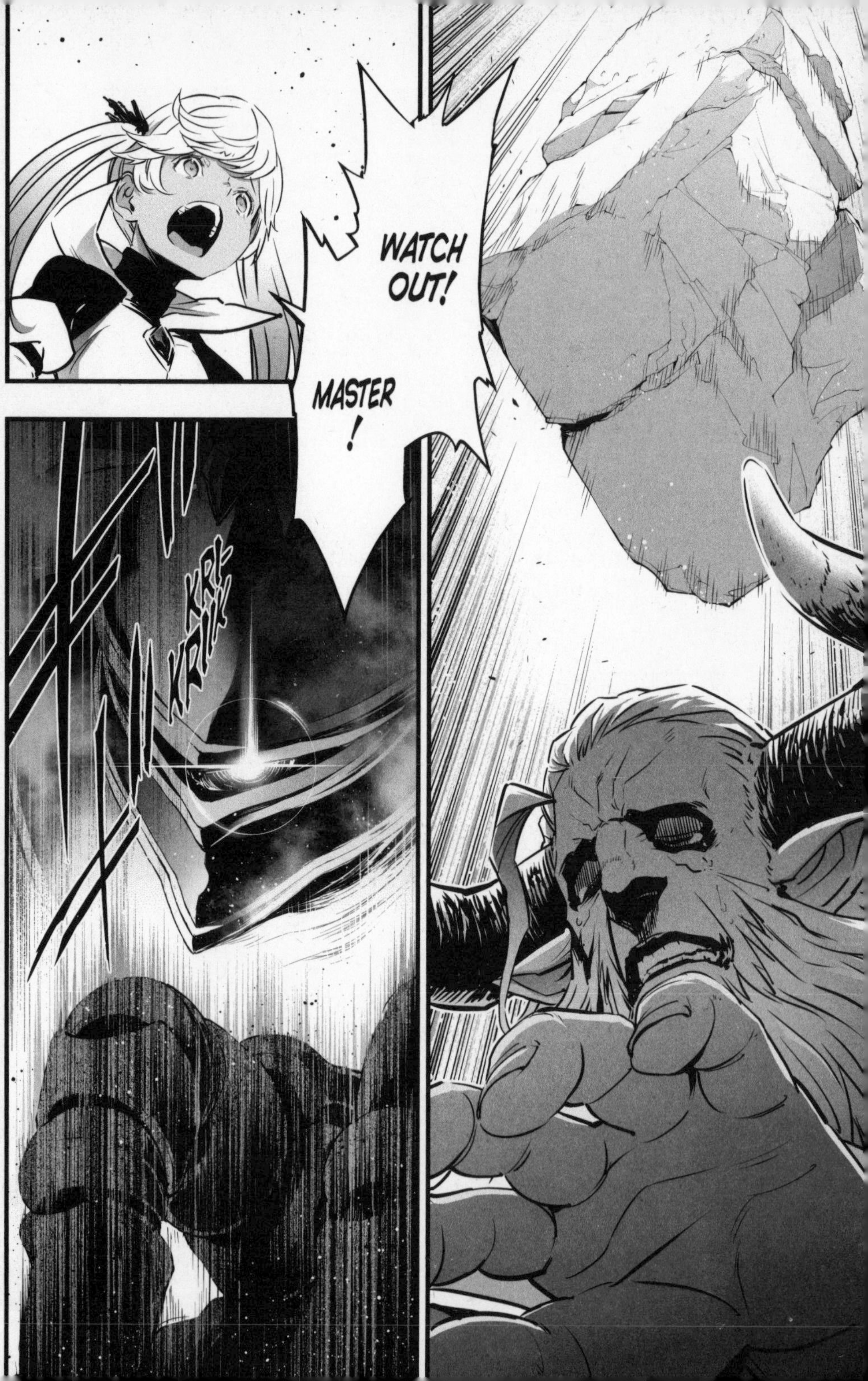
WATCH OUT! MASTER!
KRIK KRIK

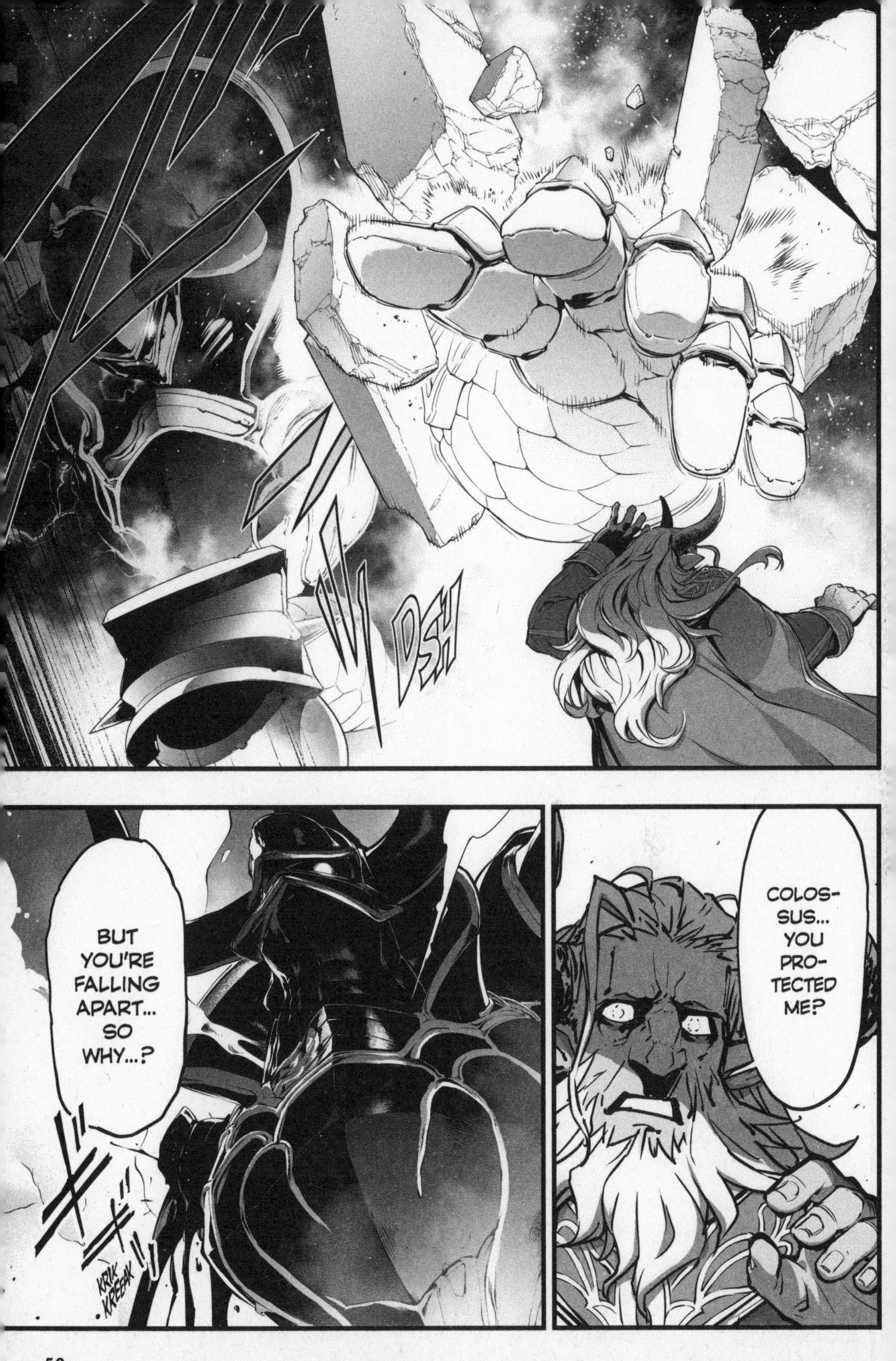
DSH
COLOSSUS... YOU PROTECTED ME?
BUT YOU'RE FALLING APART... SO WHY...?
KRIK KREGAK

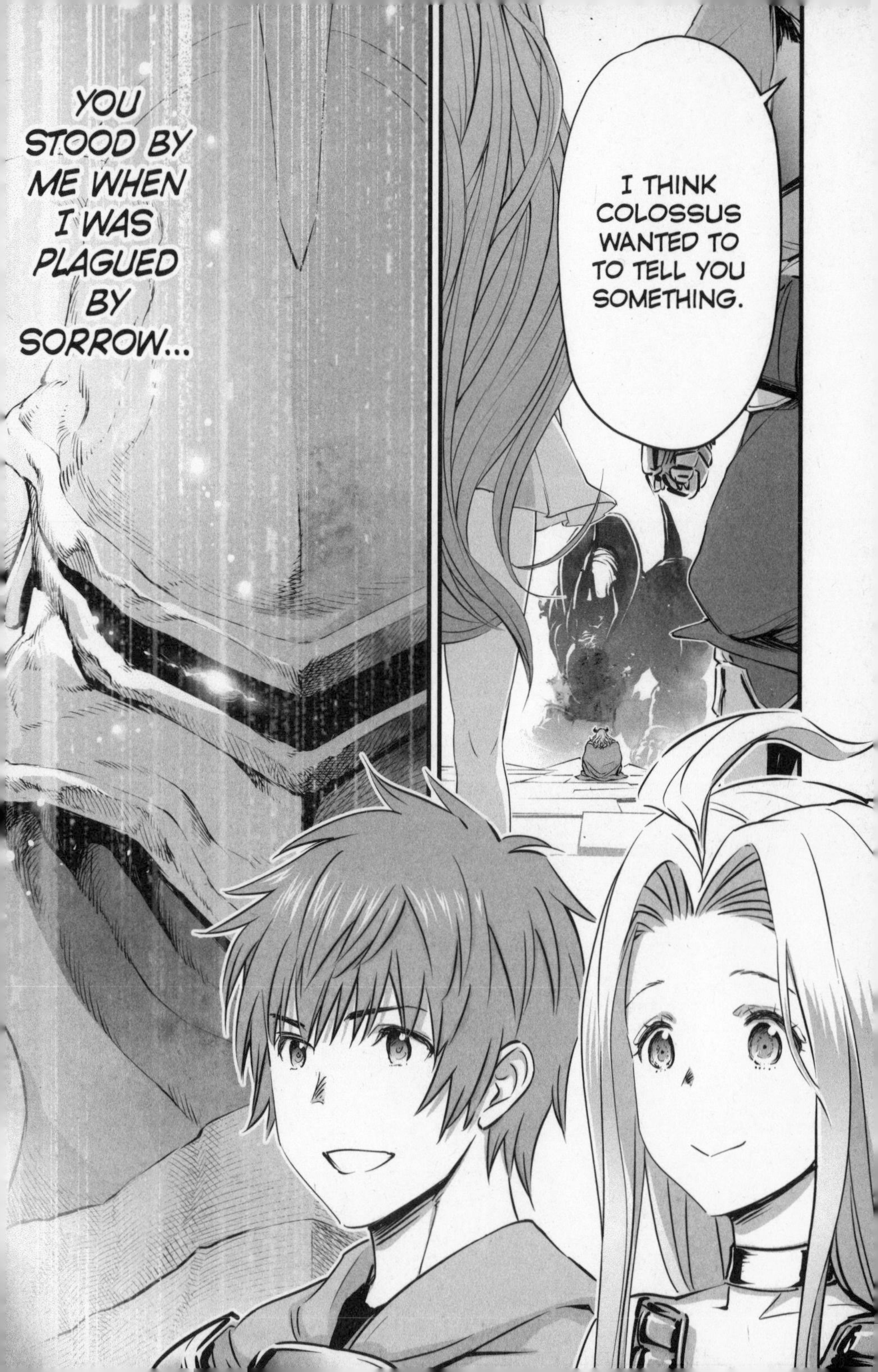
I THINK COLOSSUS WANTED TO TO TELL YOU SOMETHING.
YOU STOOD BY ME WHEN I WAS PLAGUED BY SORROW...

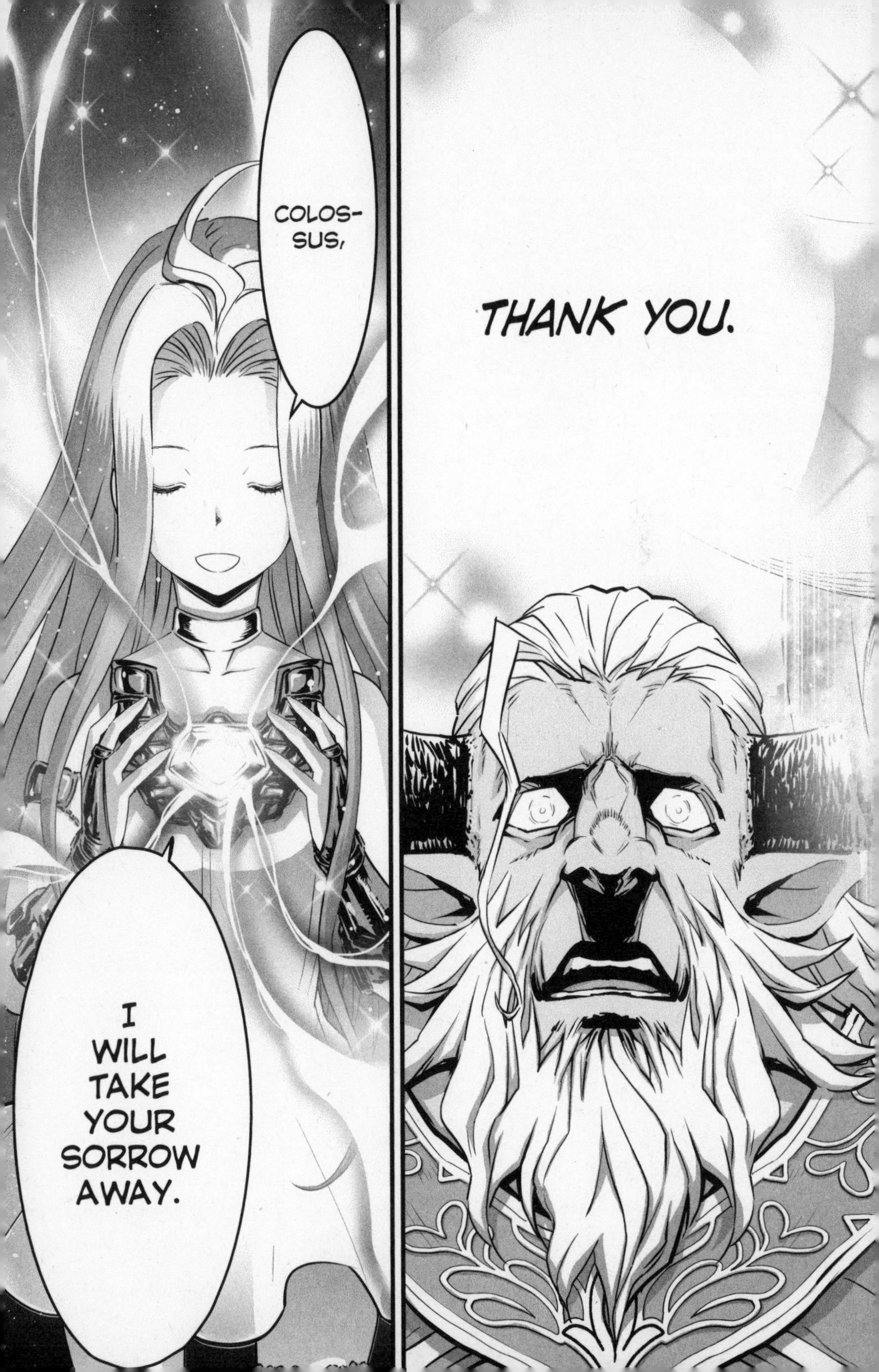
THANK YOU.
COLOS-SUS,
I WILL TAKE YOUR SORROW AWAY.

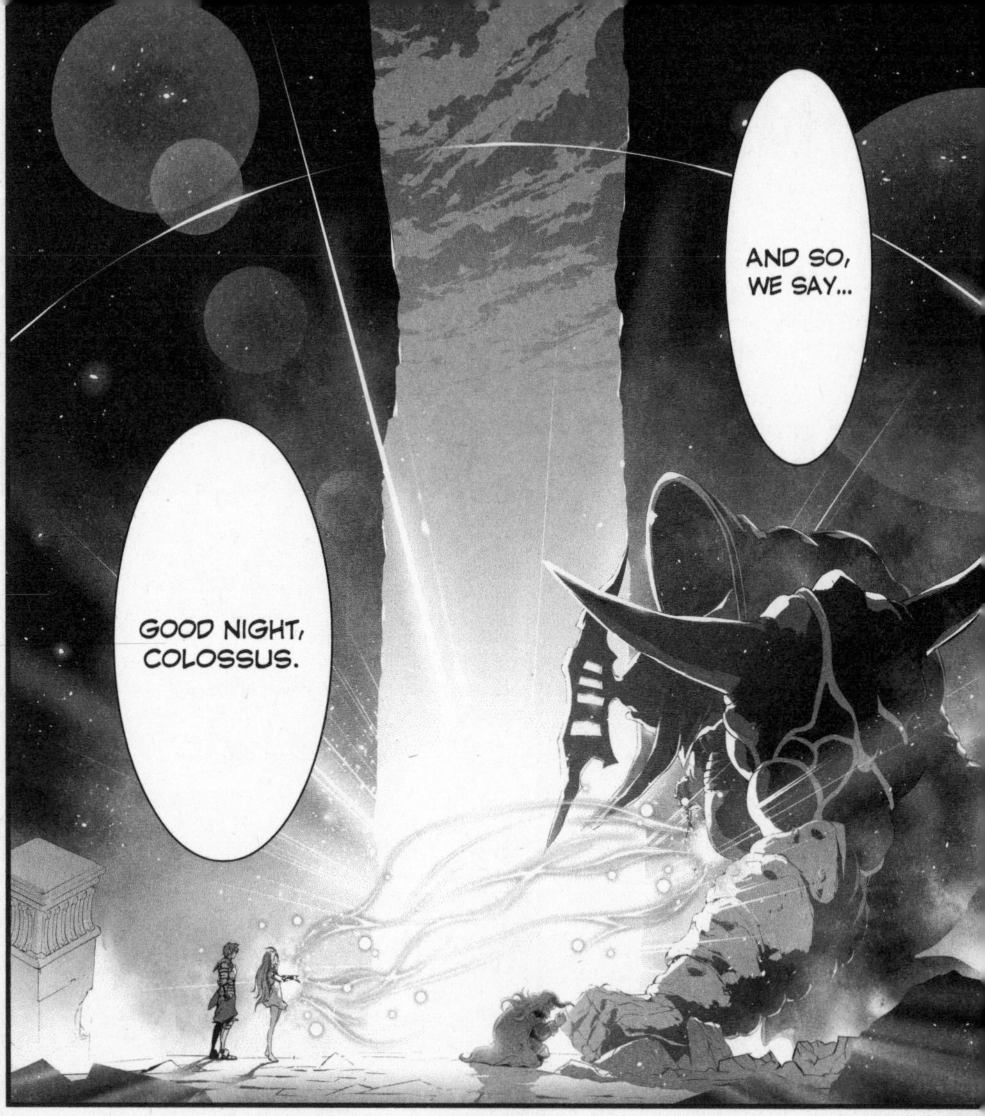
AND SO, WE SAY...
GOOD NIGHT, COLOSSUS.
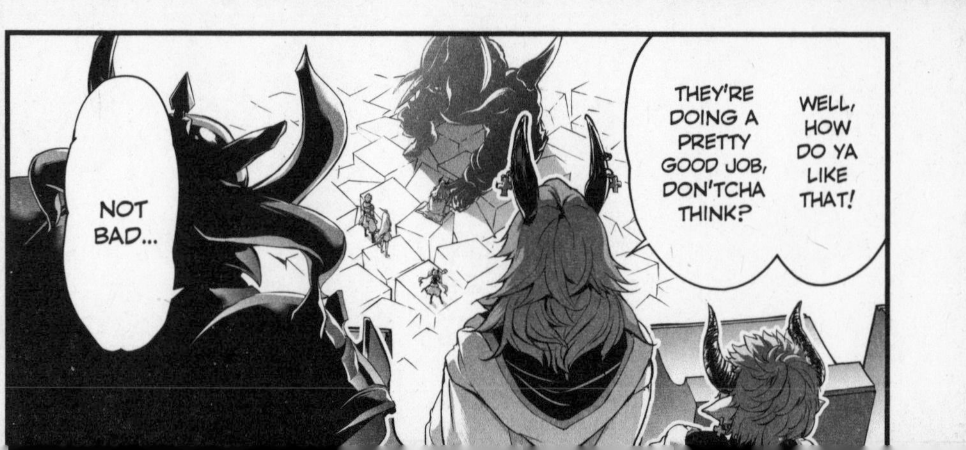
WELL, HOW DO YA LIKE THAT!
THEY'RE DOING A PRETTY GOOD JOB, DON'TCHA THINK?
NOT BAD...

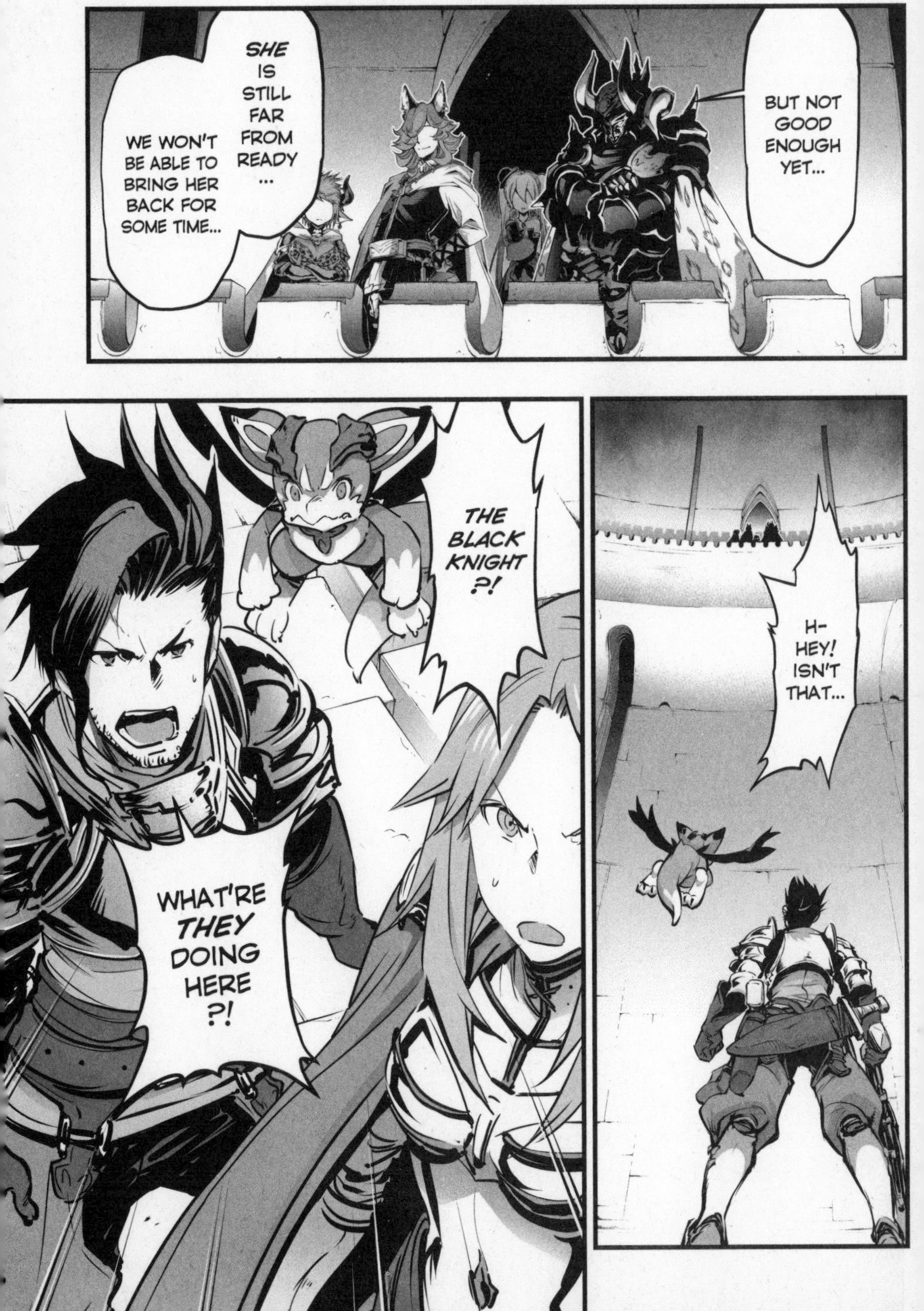
BUT NOT GOOD ENOUGH YET...
SHE IS STILL FAR FROM READY...
WE WON'T BE ABLE TO BRING HER BACK FOR SOME TIME...
H-HEY! ISN'T THAT...
THE BLACK KNIGHT?!
WHAT'RE THEY DOING HERE?!

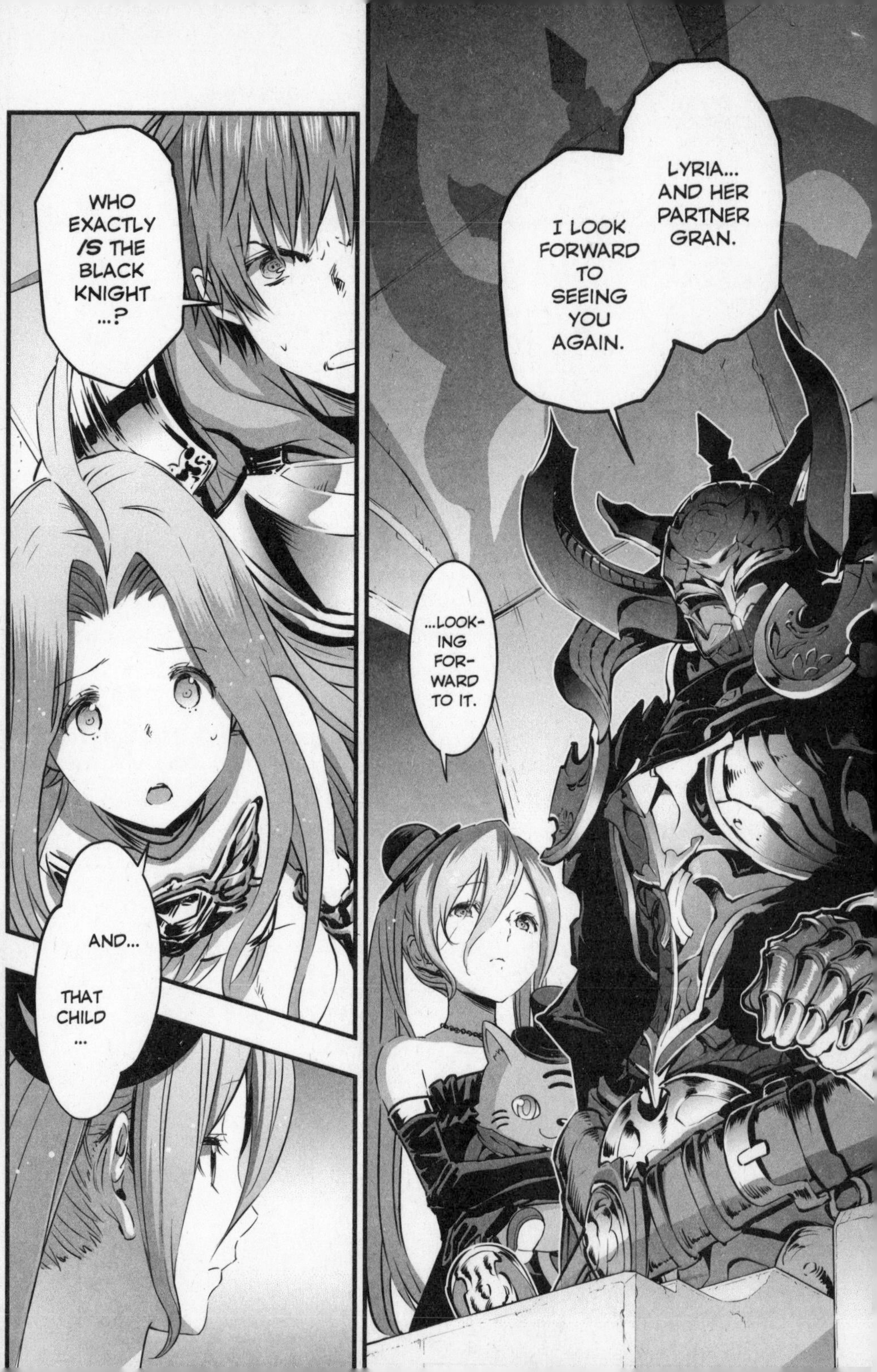
LYRIA... AND HER PARTNER GRAN.
I LOOK FORWARD TO SEEING YOU AGAIN.
...LOOKING FORWARD TO IT.
WHO EXACTLY *IS* THE BLACK KNIGHT ...?
AND...
THAT CHILD ...

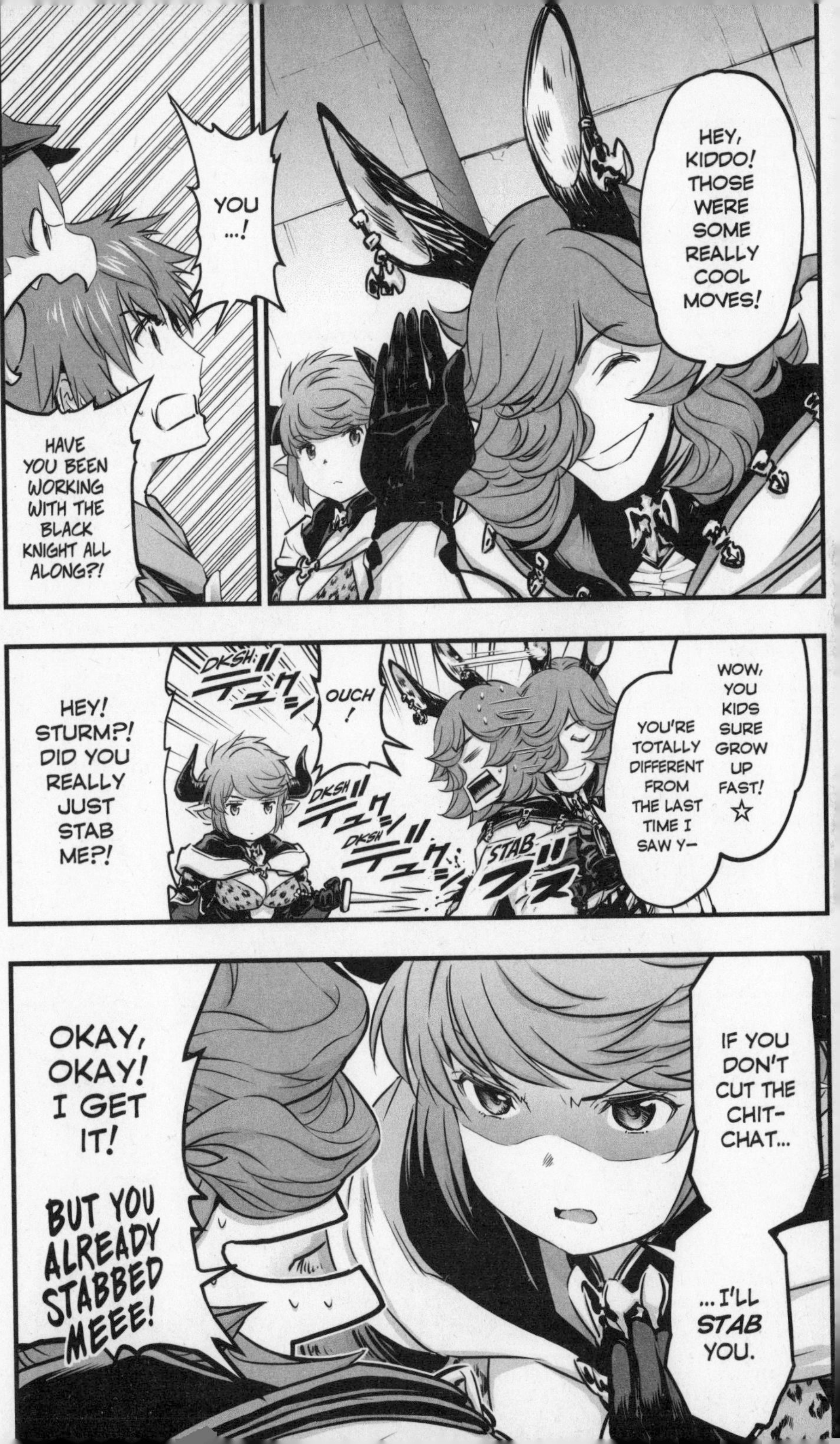
HEY, KIDDO! THOSE WERE SOME REALLY COOL MOVES!
YOU ...!
HAVE YOU BEEN WORKING WITH THE BLACK KNIGHT ALL ALONG?!
WOW, YOU KIDS SURE GROW UP FAST! ☆
YOU'RE TOTALLY DIFFERENT FROM THE LAST TIME I SAW Y—
STAB
DKSH
DKSH
DKSH
OUCH!
HEY! STURM?! DID YOU REALLY JUST STAB ME?!
IF YOU DON'T CUT THE CHIT-CHAT...
...I'LL STAB YOU.
OKAY, OKAY! I GET IT!
BUT YOU ALREADY STABBED MEEE!

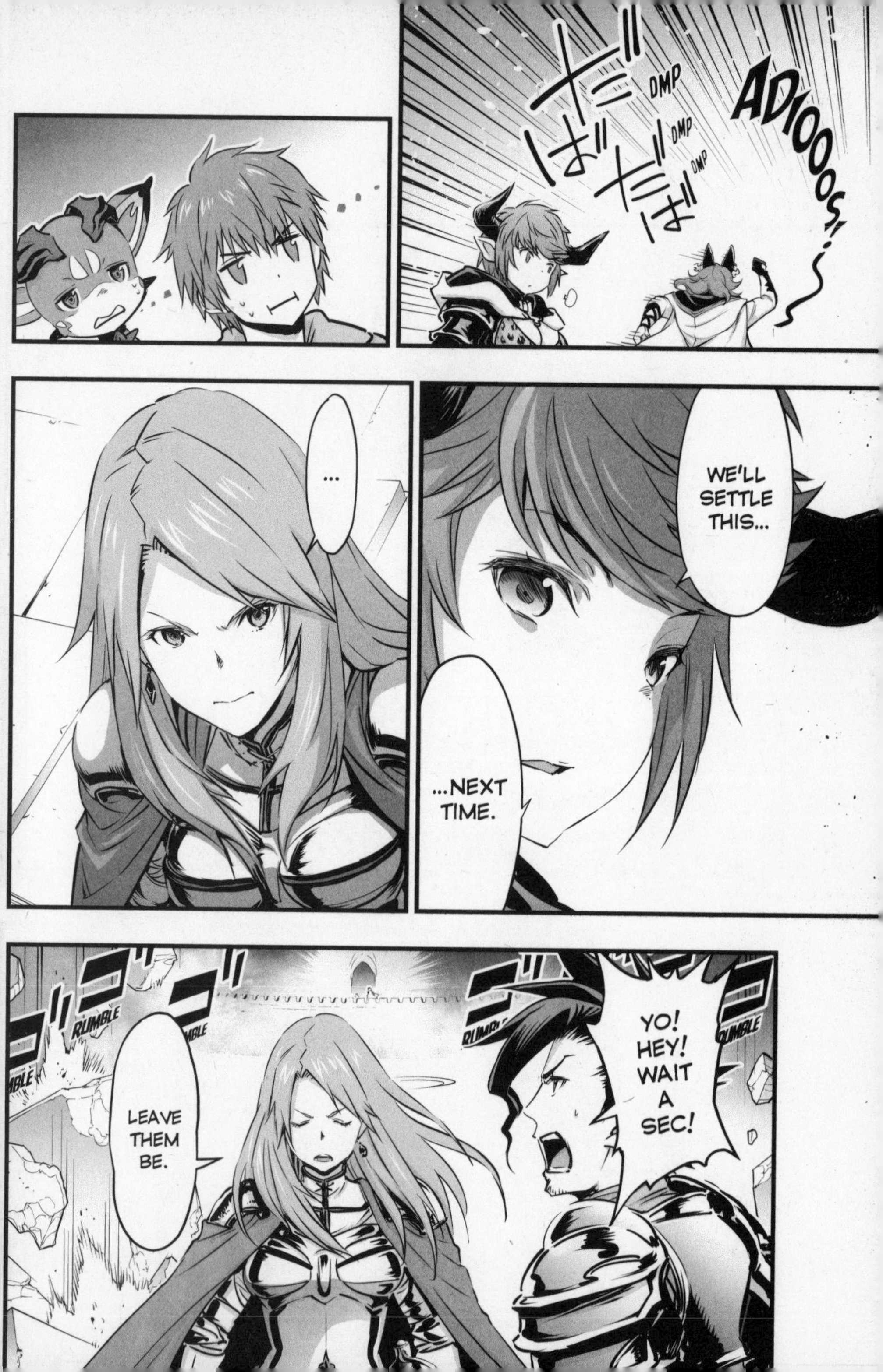
だばだば
DMP
DMP
DMP
ADIOOOS!!
WE'LL SETTLE THIS...
...NEXT TIME.
...
RUMBLE
RUMBLE
YO! HEY! WAIT A SEC!
LEAVE THEM BE.
RUMBLE
RUMBLE
RUMBLE

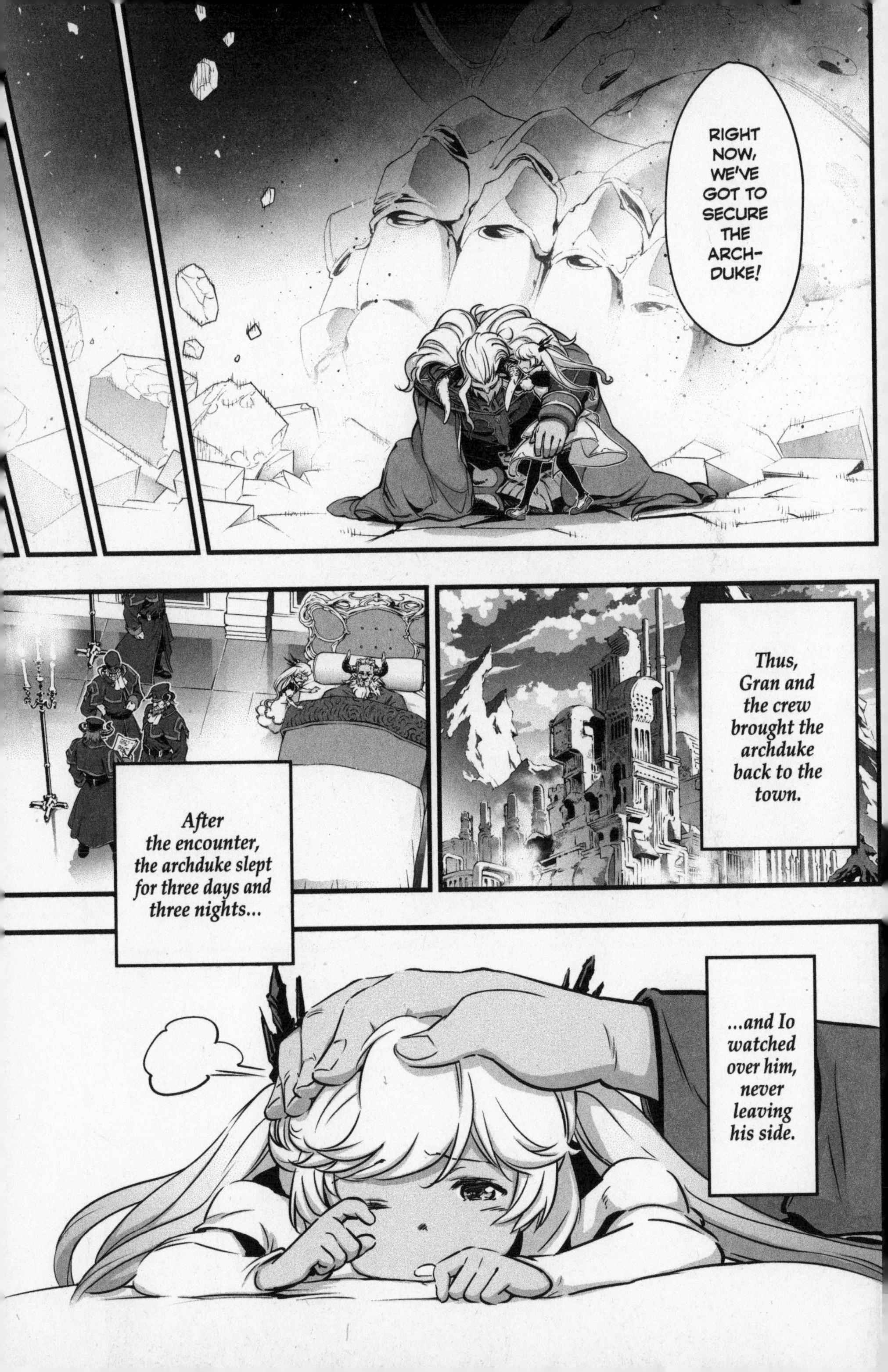
RIGHT NOW, WE'VE GOT TO SECURE THE ARCH-DUKE!
Thus, Gran and the crew brought the archduke back to the town.
After the encounter, the archduke slept for three days and three nights...
...and Io watched over him, never leaving his side.

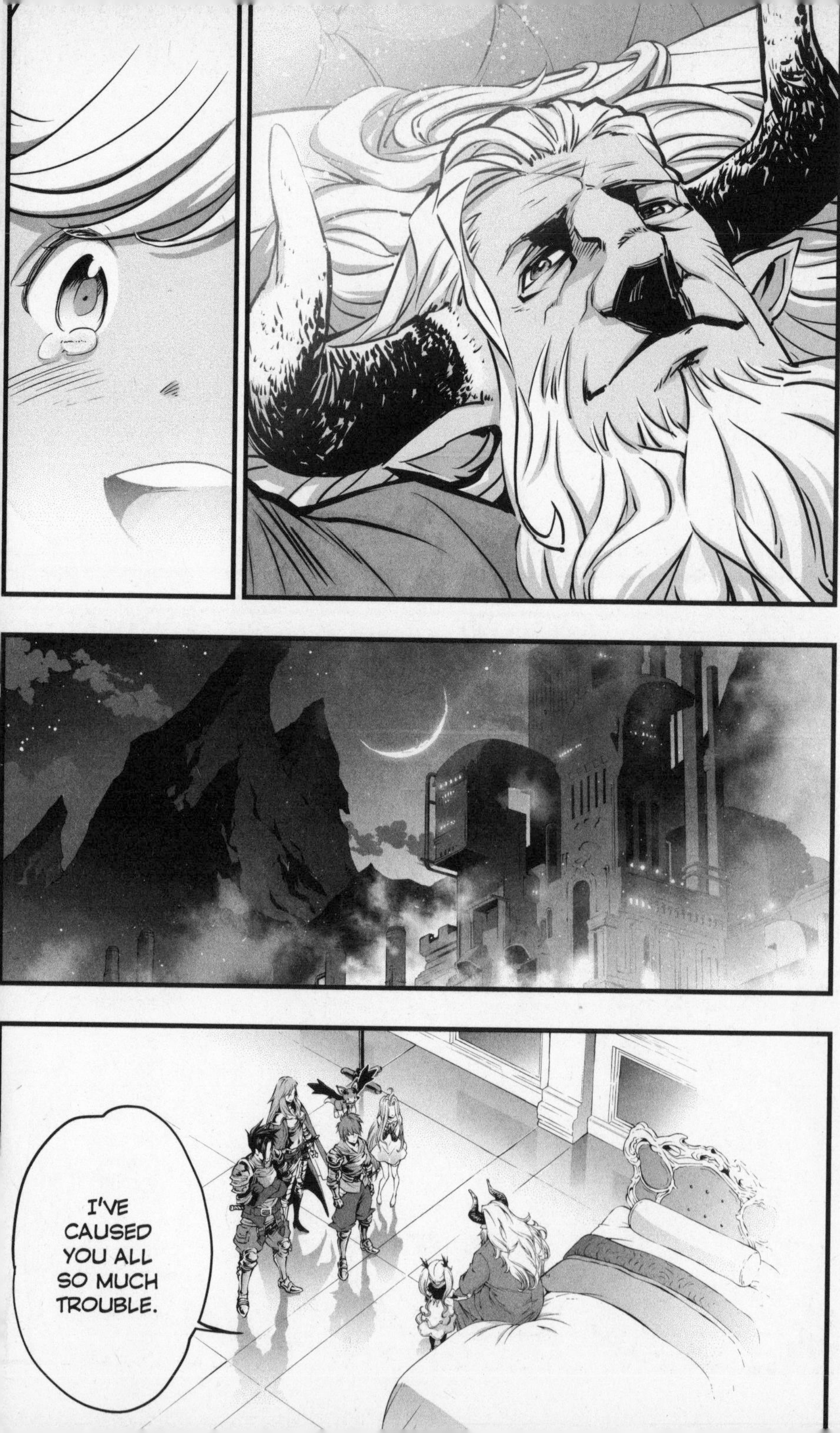
I'VE CAUSED YOU ALL SO MUCH TROUBLE.

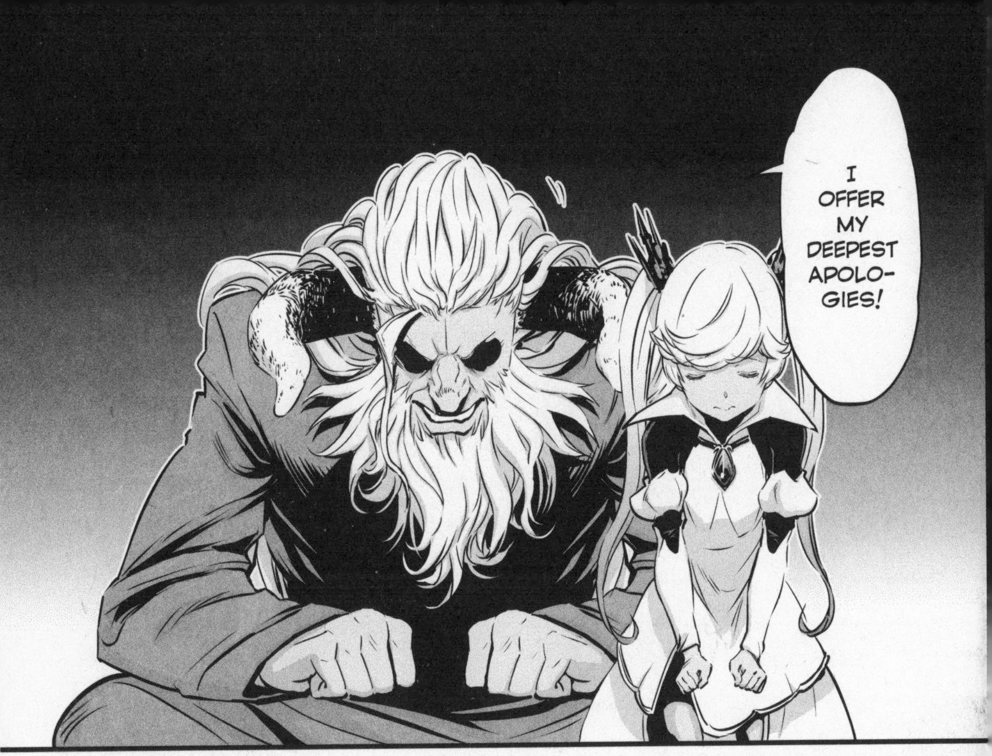
I OFFER MY DEEPEST APOLO-GIES!

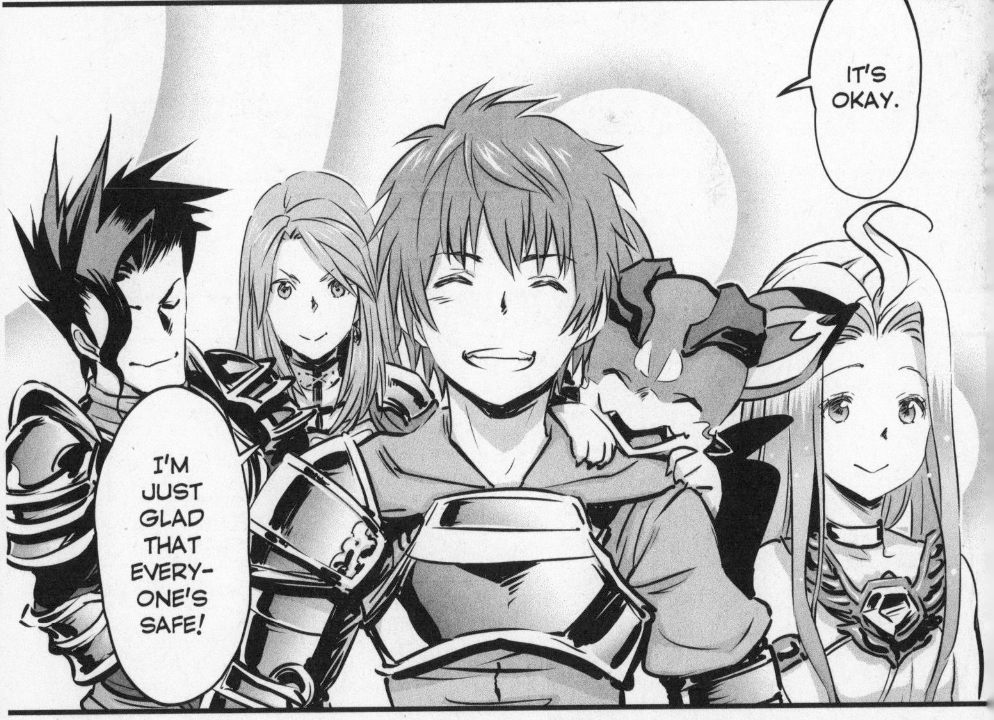
IT'S OKAY.
I'M JUST GLAD THAT EVERY-ONE'S SAFE!

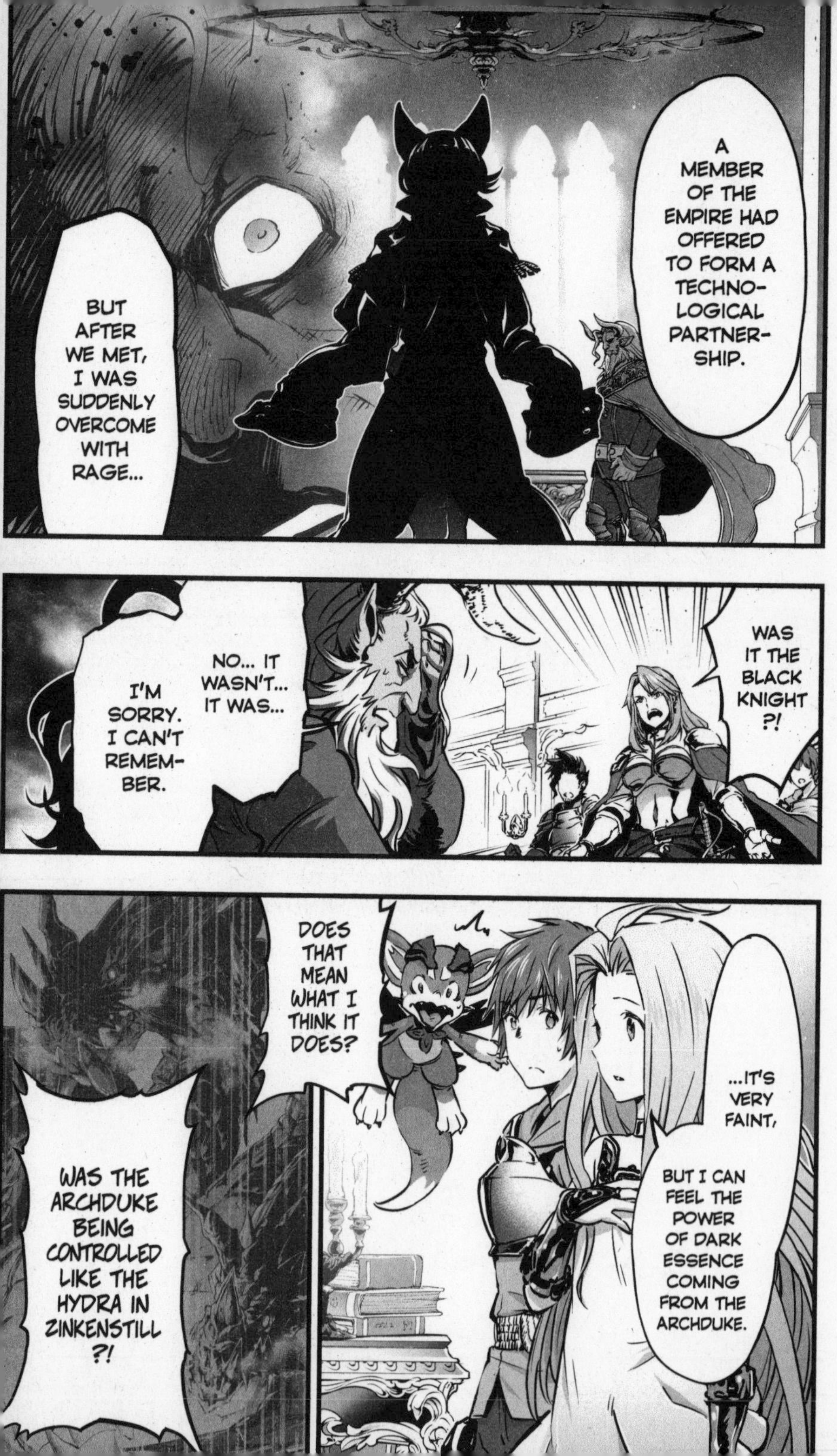
A MEMBER OF THE EMPIRE HAD OFFERED TO FORM A TECHNOLOGICAL PARTNERSHIP.
BUT AFTER WE MET, I WAS SUDDENLY OVERCOME WITH RAGE...
WAS IT THE BLACK KNIGHT?!
NO... IT WASN'T... IT WAS...
I'M SORRY. I CAN'T REMEMBER.
...IT'S VERY FAINT,
BUT I CAN FEEL THE POWER OF DARK ESSENCE COMING FROM THE ARCHDUKE.
DOES THAT MEAN WHAT I THINK IT DOES?
WAS THE ARCHDUKE BEING CONTROLLED LIKE THE HYDRA IN ZINKENSTILL?!

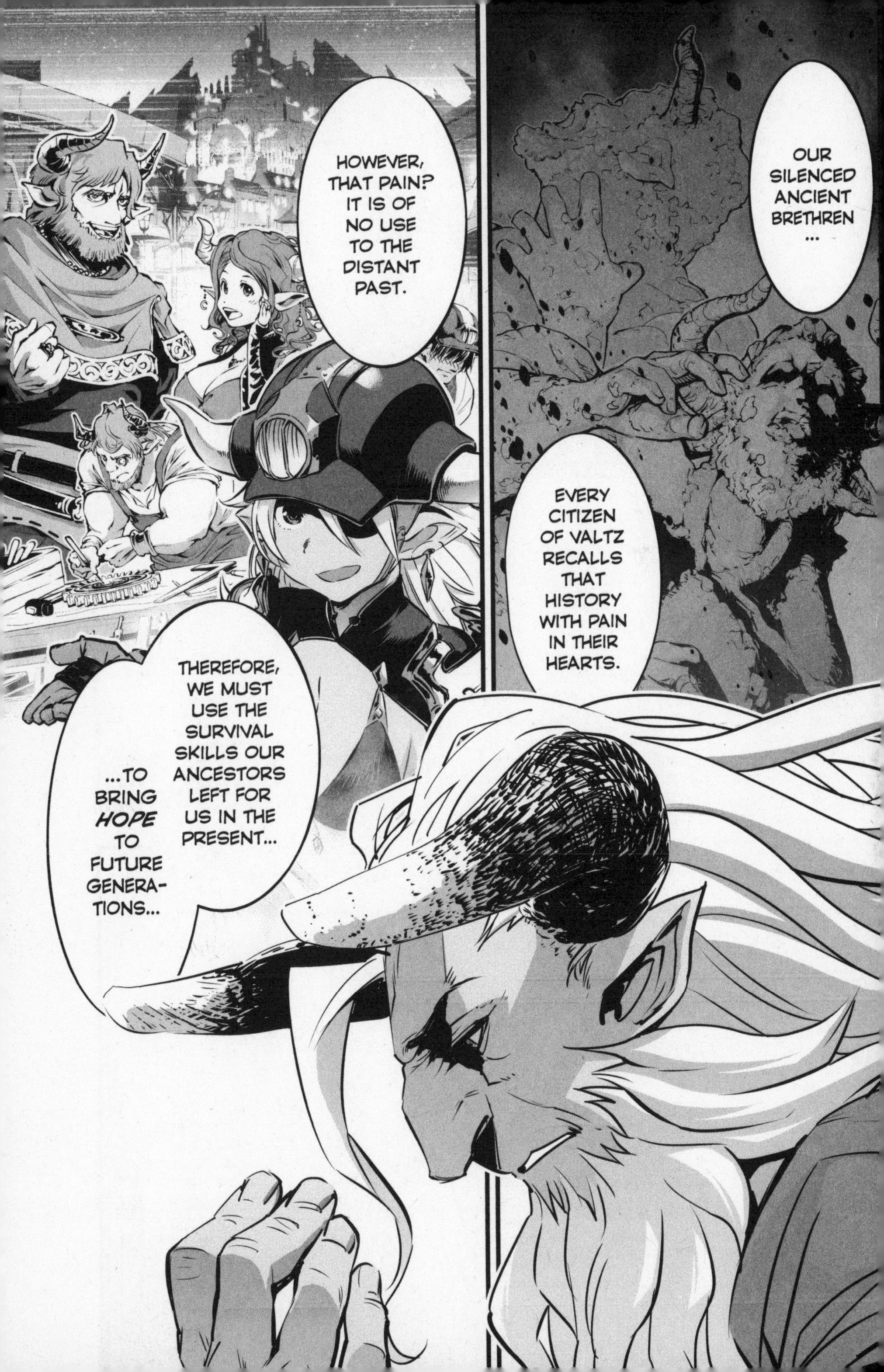
OUR SILENCED ANCIENT BRETHREN ...
EVERY CITIZEN OF VALTZ RECALLS THAT HISTORY WITH PAIN IN THEIR HEARTS.
HOWEVER, THAT PAIN? IT IS OF NO USE TO THE DISTANT PAST.
THEREFORE, WE MUST USE THE SURVIVAL SKILLS OUR ANCESTORS LEFT FOR US IN THE PRESENT...
...TO BRING *HOPE* TO FUTURE GENERATIONS...

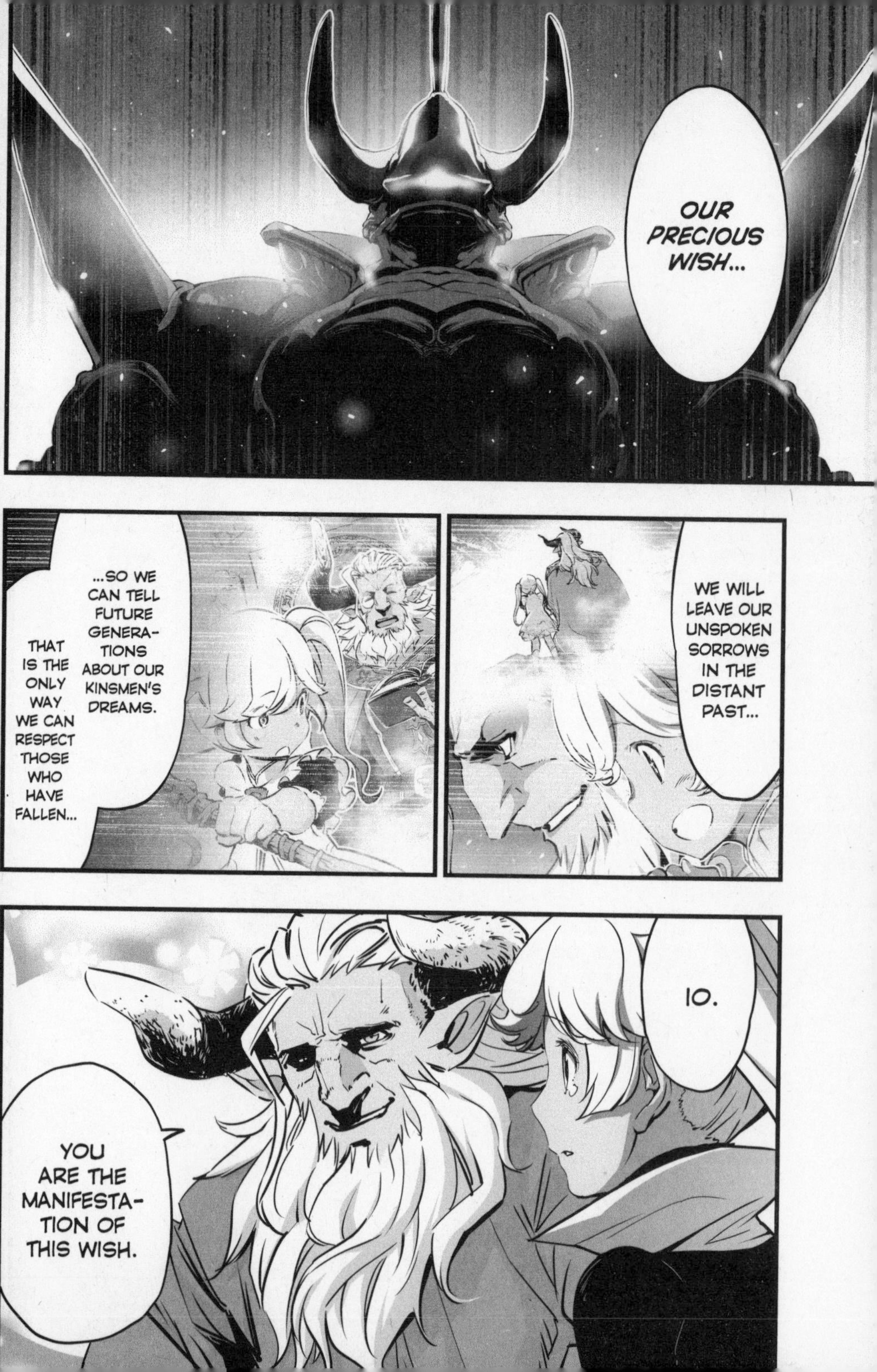
OUR PRECIOUS WISH...
WE WILL LEAVE OUR UNSPOKEN SORROWS IN THE DISTANT PAST...
...SO WE CAN TELL FUTURE GENERA-TIONS ABOUT OUR KINSMEN'S DREAMS.
THAT IS THE ONLY WAY WE CAN RESPECT THOSE WHO HAVE FALLEN...
IO.
YOU ARE THE MANIFESTA-TION OF THIS WISH.

MAS-
TERRR
...

WHAT
ARE
YOU
CRYING
FOR,
IO?

PAT

I
GUESS
YOU'LL
ALWAYS
BE MY
LITTLE
CRYBABY.

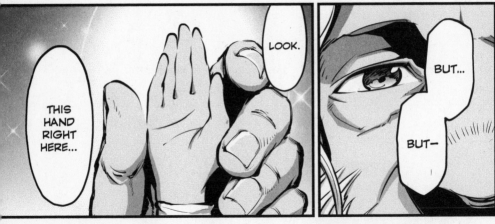

LOOK.

THIS
HAND
RIGHT
HERE...

BUT...

BUT—

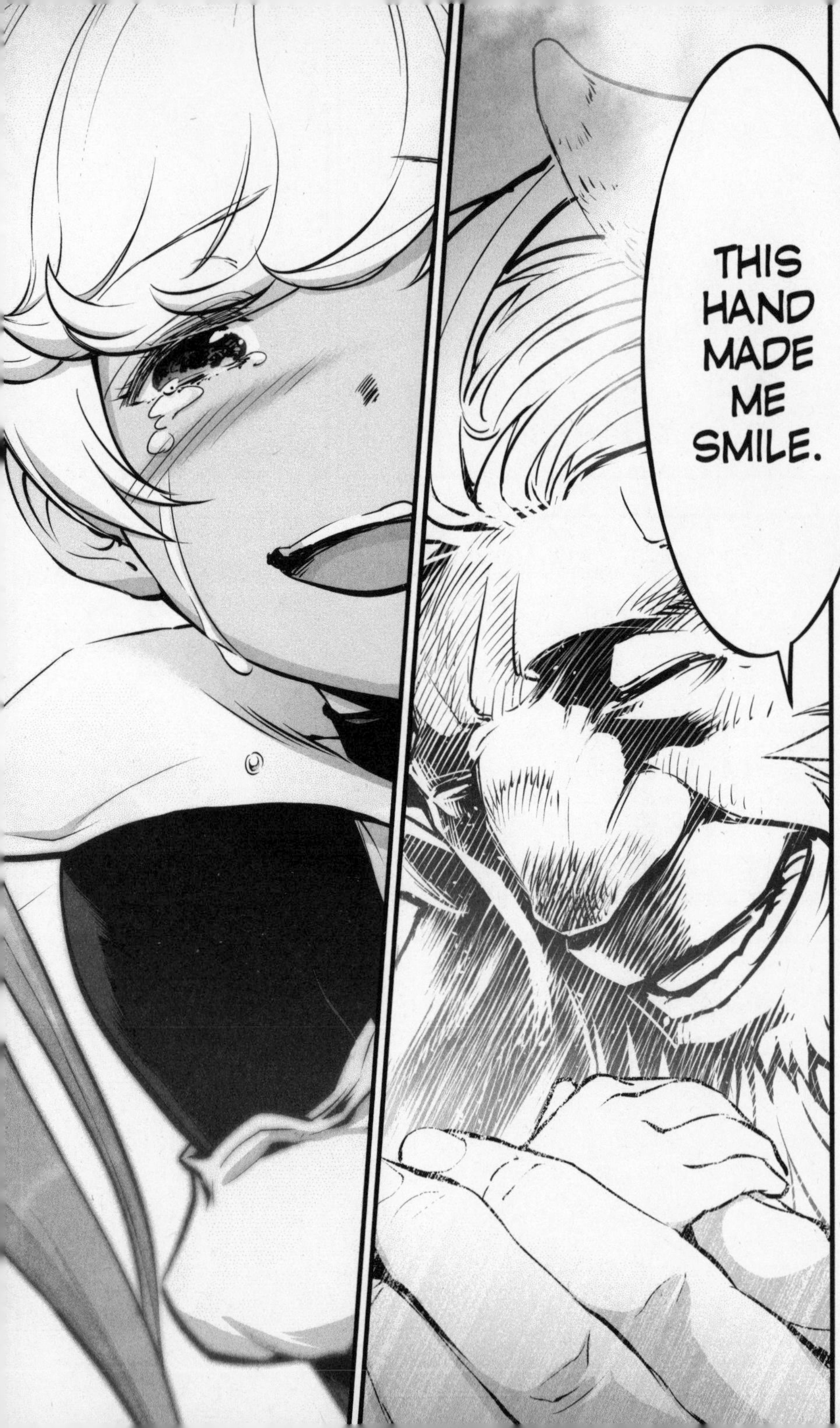
THIS HAND MADE ME SMILE.

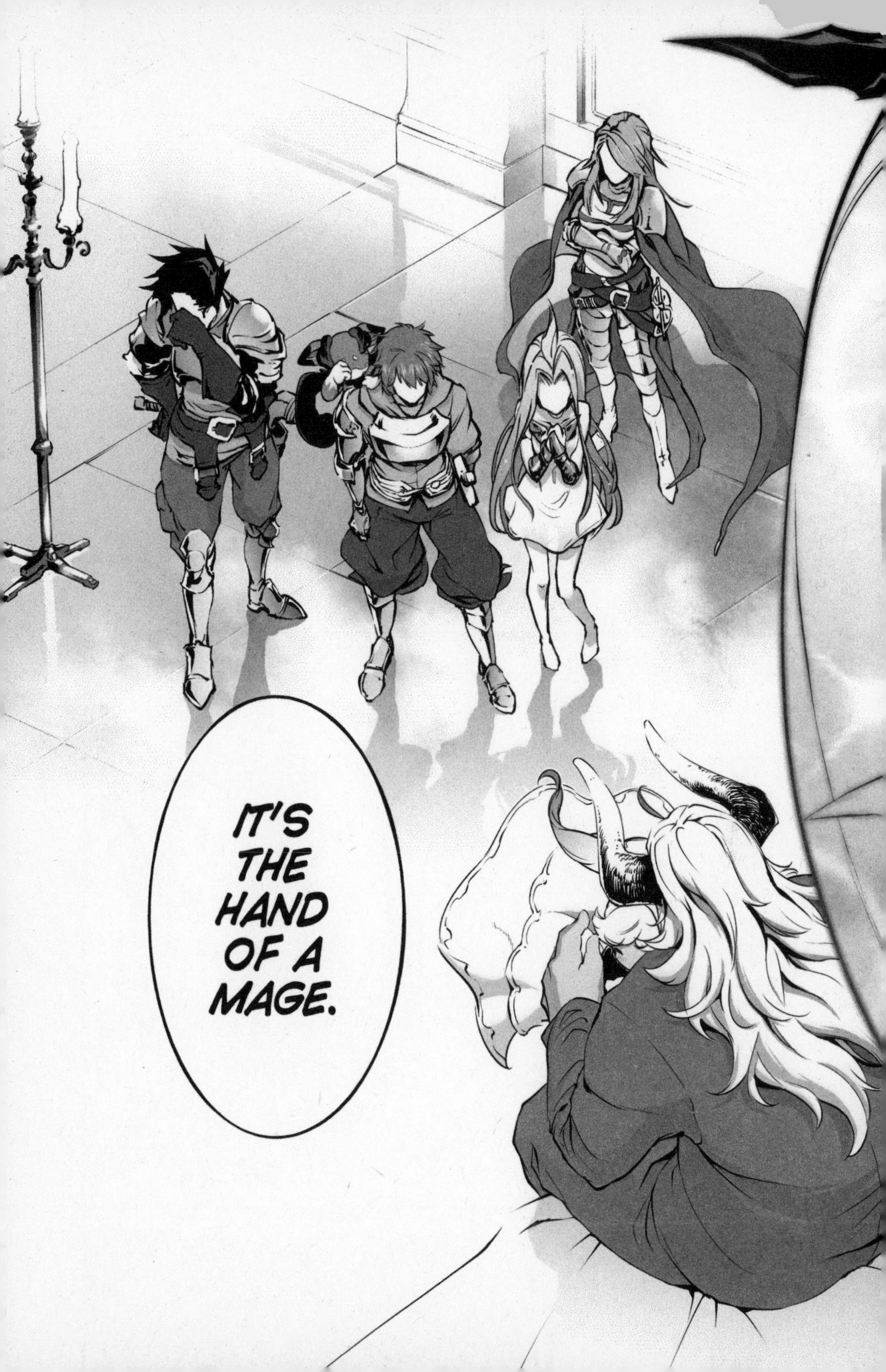
IT'S THE HAND OF A MAGE.

GRANBLUE FANTASY
グランブルーファンタジー

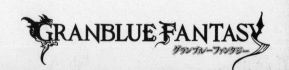

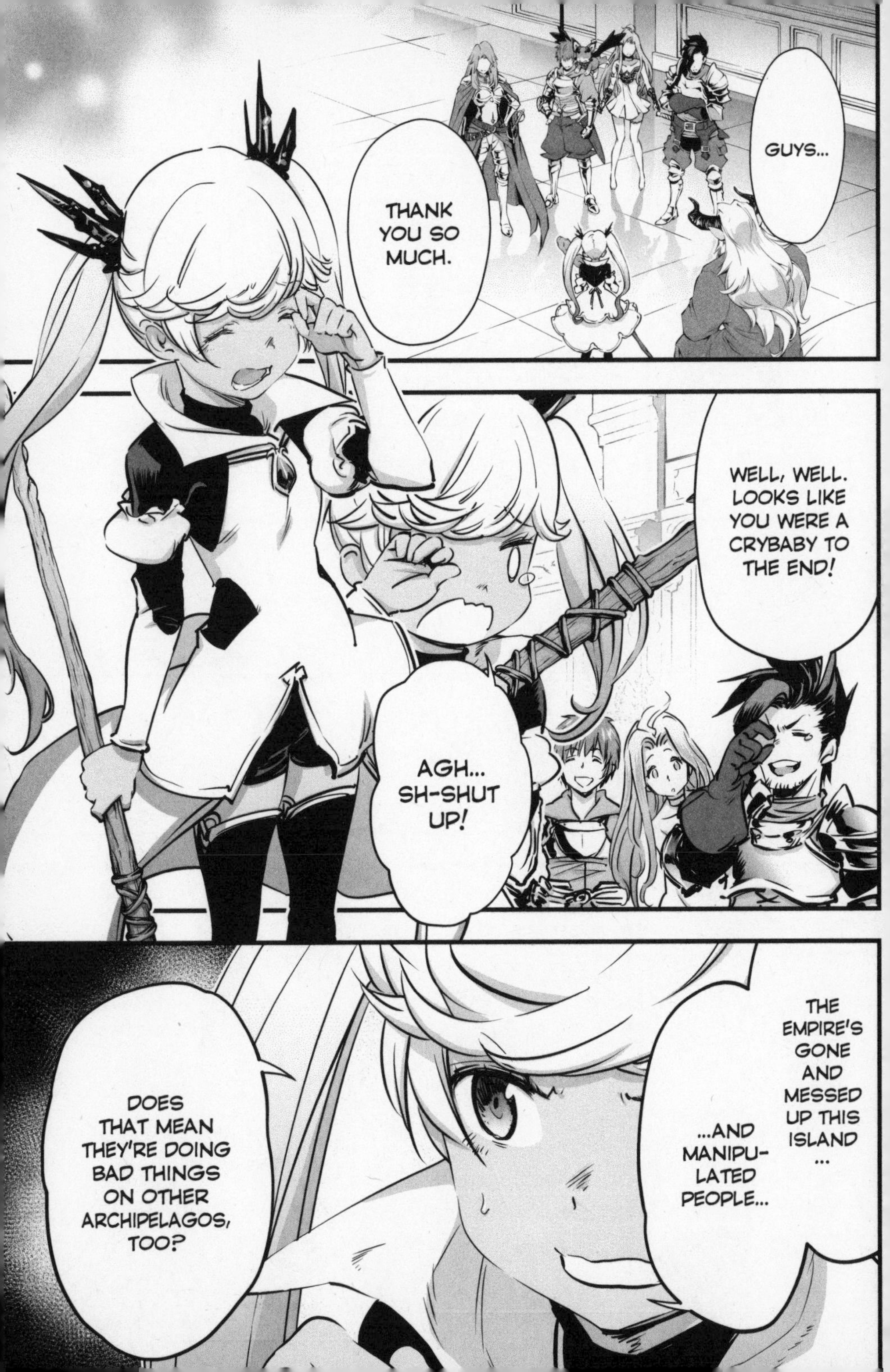
GUYS...
THANK YOU SO MUCH.
WELL, WELL. LOOKS LIKE YOU WERE A CRYBABY TO THE END!
AGH... SH-SHUT UP!
THE EMPIRE'S GONE AND MESSED UP THIS ISLAND...
...AND MANIPU-LATED PEOPLE...
DOES THAT MEAN THEY'RE DOING BAD THINGS ON OTHER ARCHIPELAGOS, TOO?

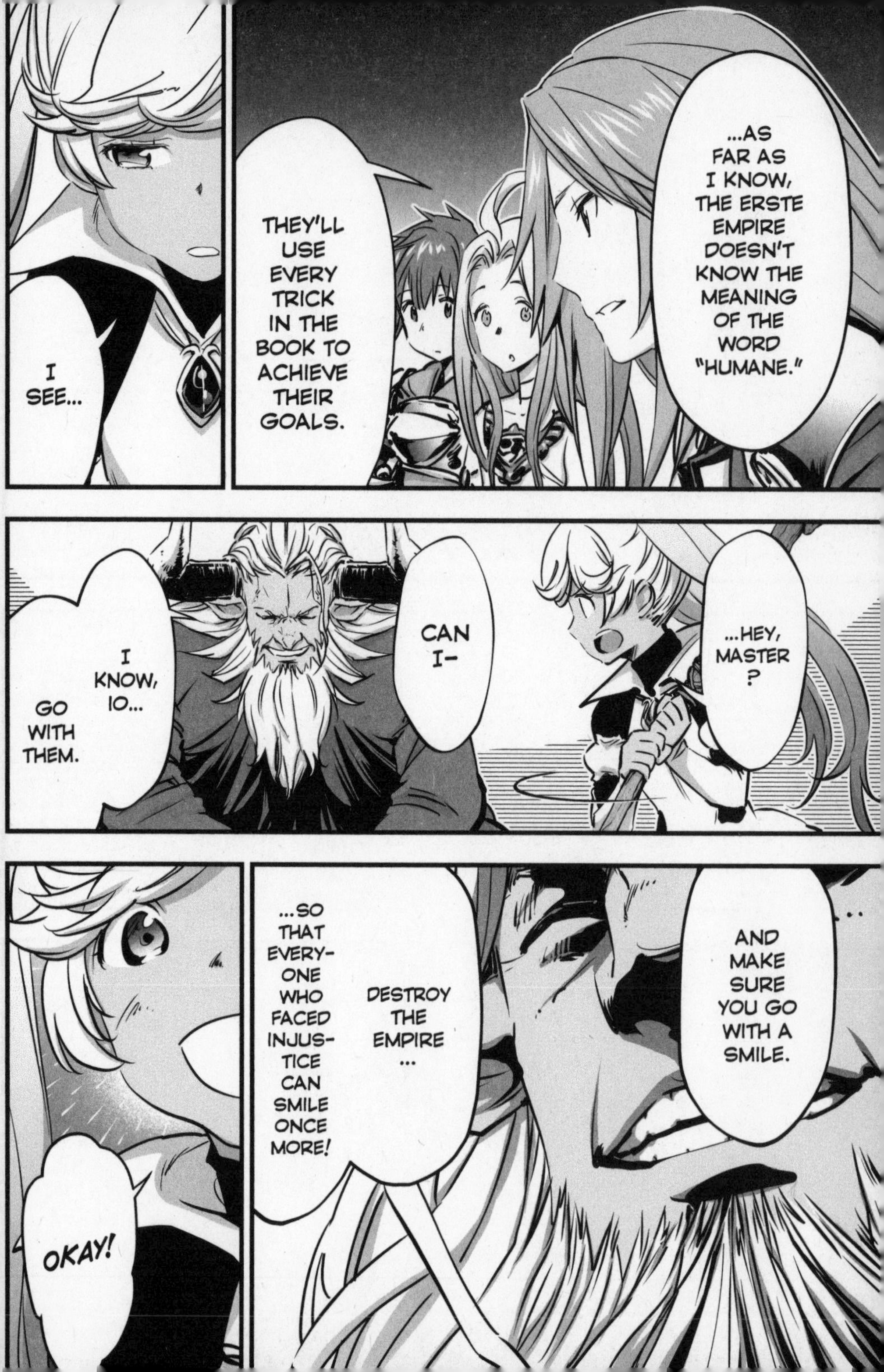
...AS FAR AS I KNOW, THE ERSTE EMPIRE DOESN'T KNOW THE MEANING OF THE WORD "HUMANE."
THEY'LL USE EVERY TRICK IN THE BOOK TO ACHIEVE THEIR GOALS.
I SEE...
...HEY, MASTER?
CAN I-
I KNOW, IO...
GO WITH THEM.
...
AND MAKE SURE YOU GO WITH A SMILE.
DESTROY THE EMPIRE...
...SO THAT EVERY-ONE WHO FACED INJUS-TICE CAN SMILE ONCE MORE!
OKAY!

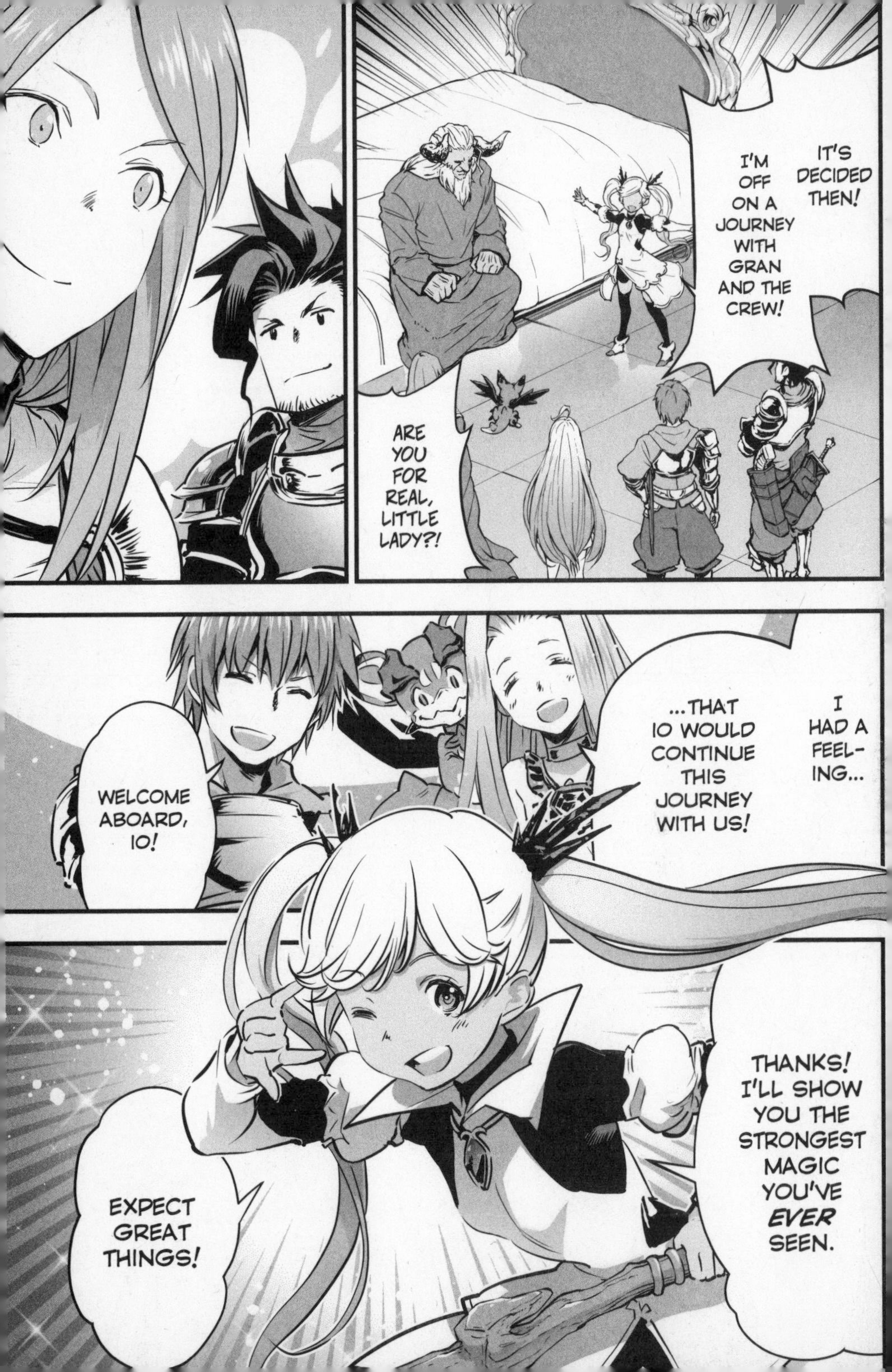
IT'S DECIDED THEN!
I'M OFF ON A JOURNEY WITH GRAN AND THE CREW!
ARE YOU FOR REAL, LITTLE LADY?!
I HAD A FEEL-ING...
...THAT IO WOULD CONTINUE THIS JOURNEY WITH US!
WELCOME ABOARD, IO!
THANKS! I'LL SHOW YOU THE STRONGEST MAGIC YOU'VE *EVER* SEEN.
EXPECT GREAT THINGS!

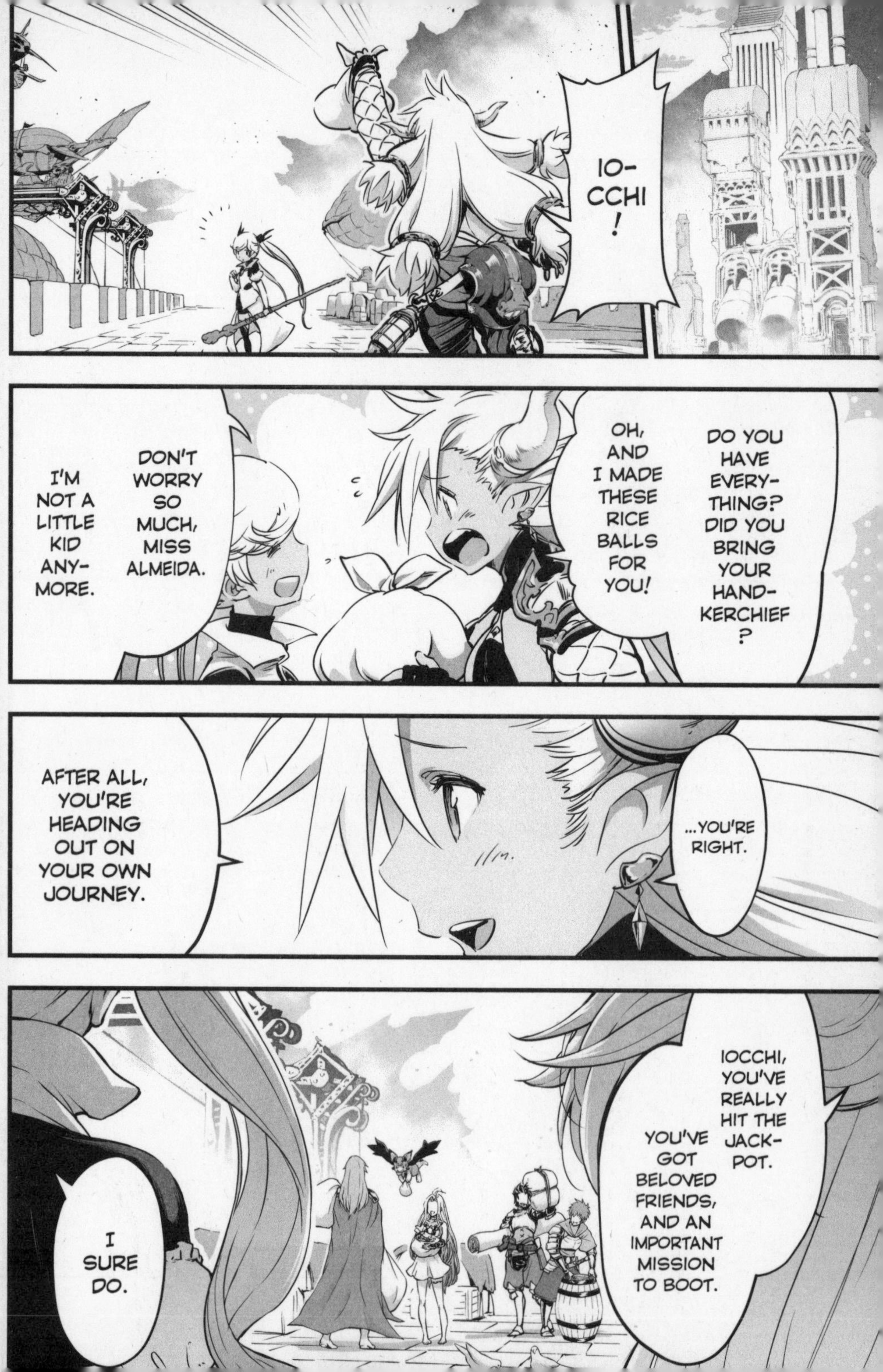
IO-CCHI!
DO YOU HAVE EVERY-THING? DID YOU BRING YOUR HAND-KERCHIEF?
OH, AND I MADE THESE RICE BALLS FOR YOU!
DON'T WORRY SO MUCH, MISS ALMEIDA.
I'M NOT A LITTLE KID ANY-MORE.
...YOU'RE RIGHT.
AFTER ALL, YOU'RE HEADING OUT ON YOUR OWN JOURNEY.
IOCCHI, YOU'VE REALLY HIT THE JACK-POT.
YOU'VE GOT BELOVED FRIENDS, AND AN IMPORTANT MISSION TO BOOT.
I SURE DO.

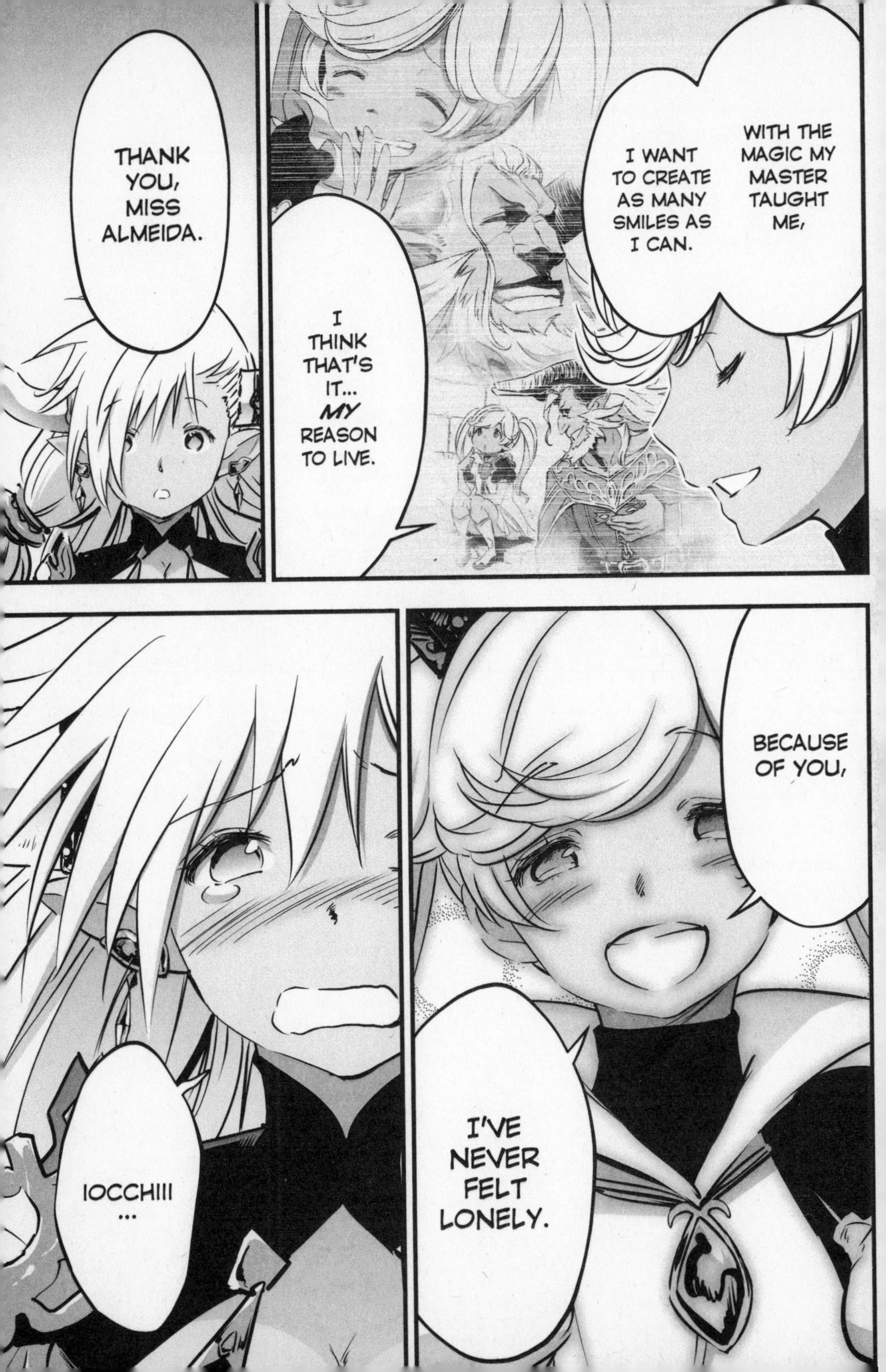
WITH THE MAGIC MY MASTER TAUGHT ME,
I WANT TO CREATE AS MANY SMILES AS I CAN.
I THINK THAT'S IT... MY REASON TO LIVE.
THANK YOU, MISS ALMEIDA.
BECAUSE OF YOU,
I'VE NEVER FELT LONELY.
IOCCHIII ...

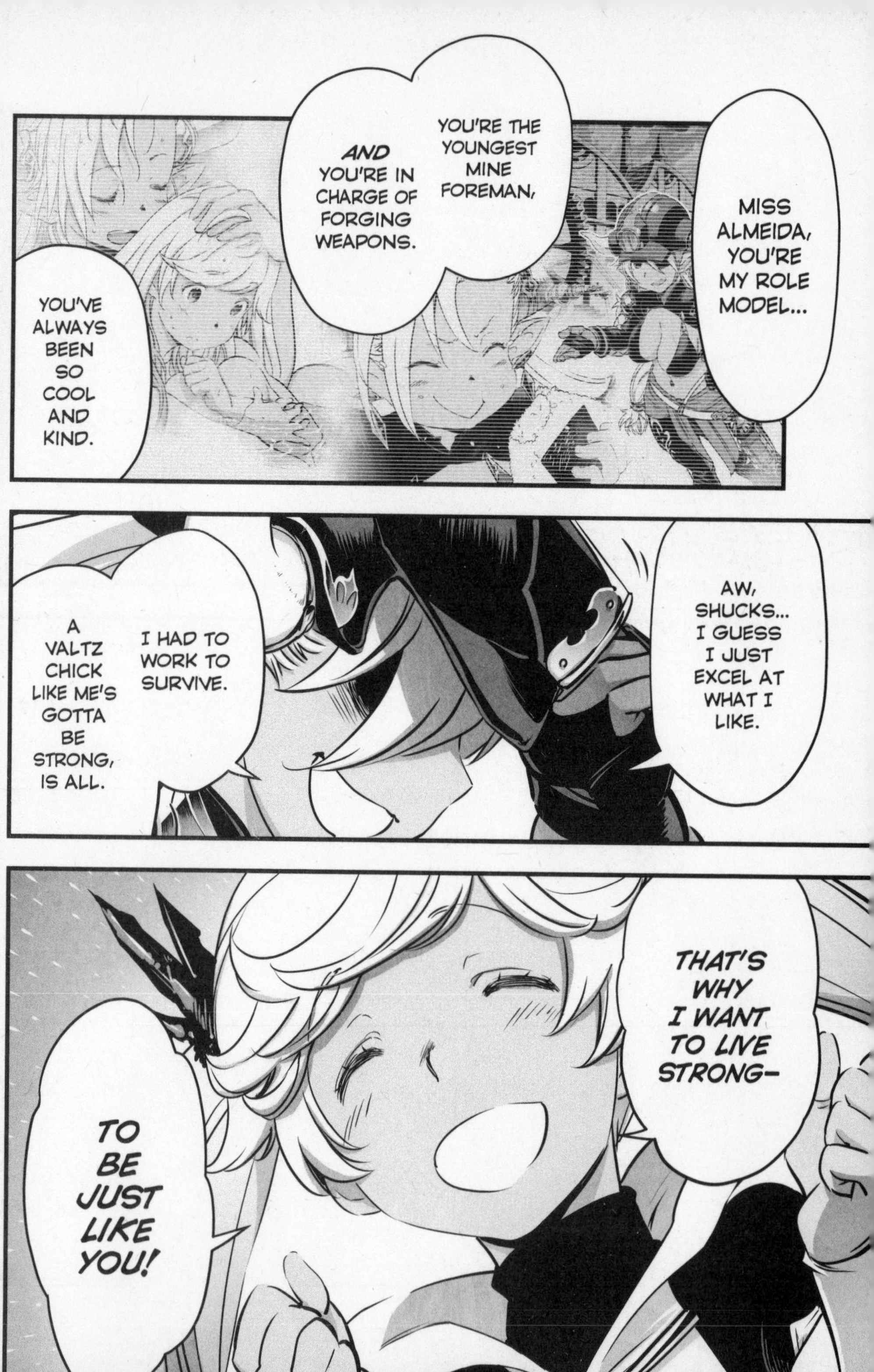
MISS ALMEIDA, YOU'RE MY ROLE MODEL...
YOU'RE THE YOUNGEST MINE FOREMAN,
AND YOU'RE IN CHARGE OF FORGING WEAPONS.
YOU'VE ALWAYS BEEN SO COOL AND KIND.
AW, SHUCKS... I GUESS I JUST EXCEL AT WHAT I LIKE.
I HAD TO WORK TO SURVIVE.
A VALTZ CHICK LIKE ME'S GOTTA BE STRONG, IS ALL.
THAT'S WHY I WANT TO LIVE STRONG–
TO BE JUST LIKE YOU!

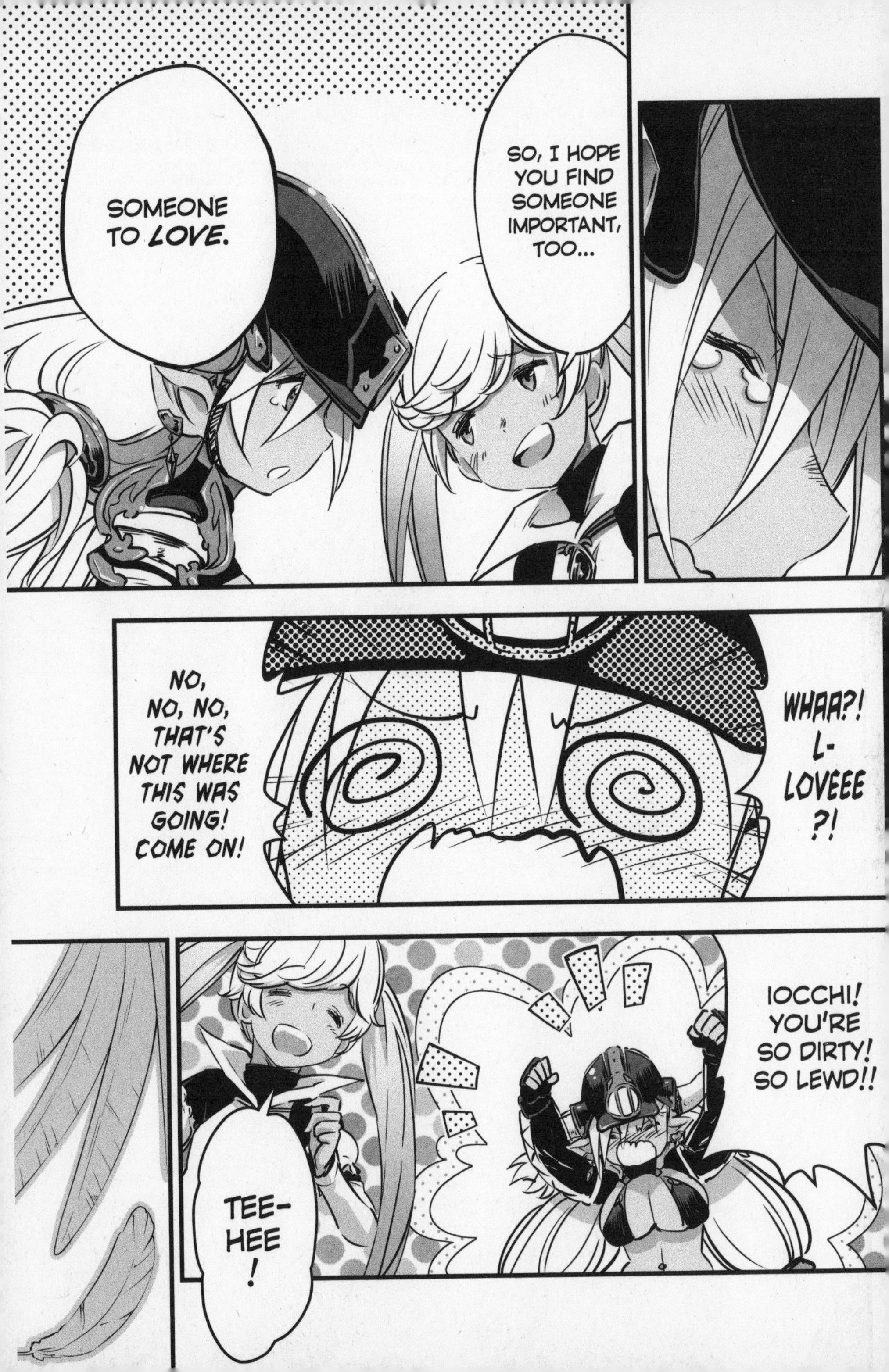
SO, I HOPE YOU FIND SOMEONE IMPORTANT, TOO...
SOMEONE TO *LOVE*.
WHAA?! L-LOVEEE?!
NO, NO, NO, THAT'S NOT WHERE THIS WAS GOING! COME ON!
IOCCHI! YOU'RE SO DIRTY! SO LEWD!!
!!
TEE-HEE!

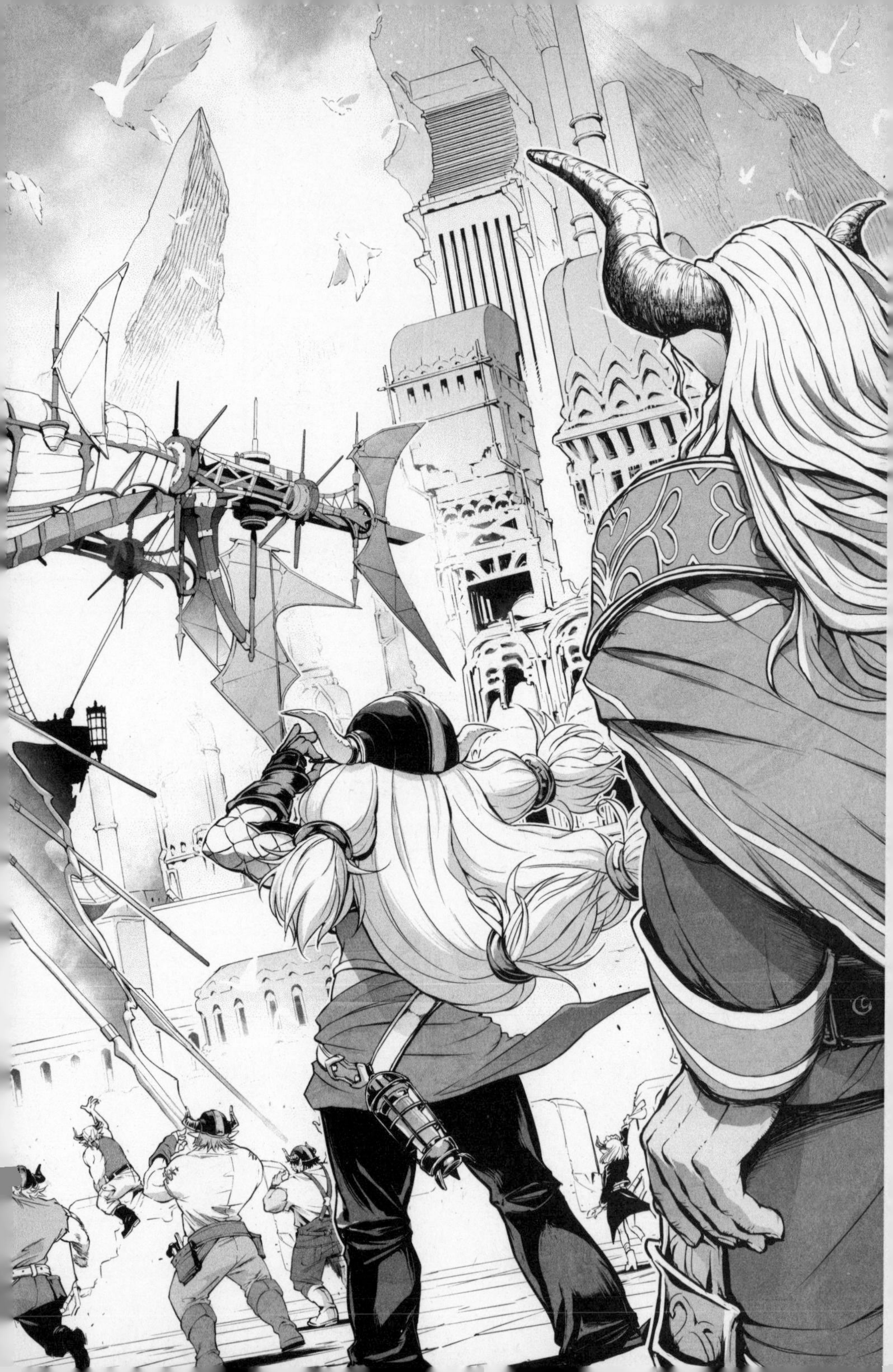

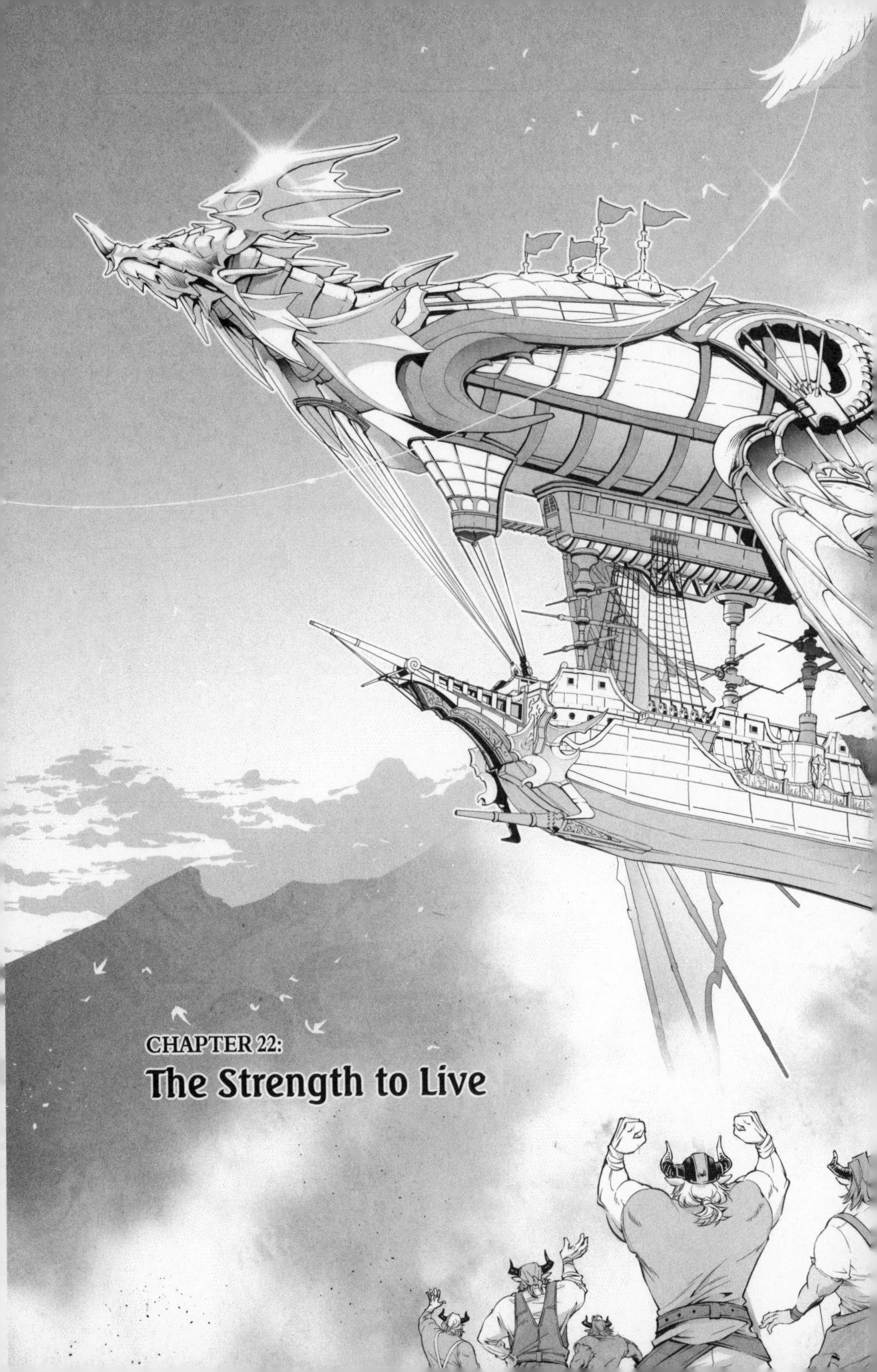

CHAPTER 22:

The Strength to Live

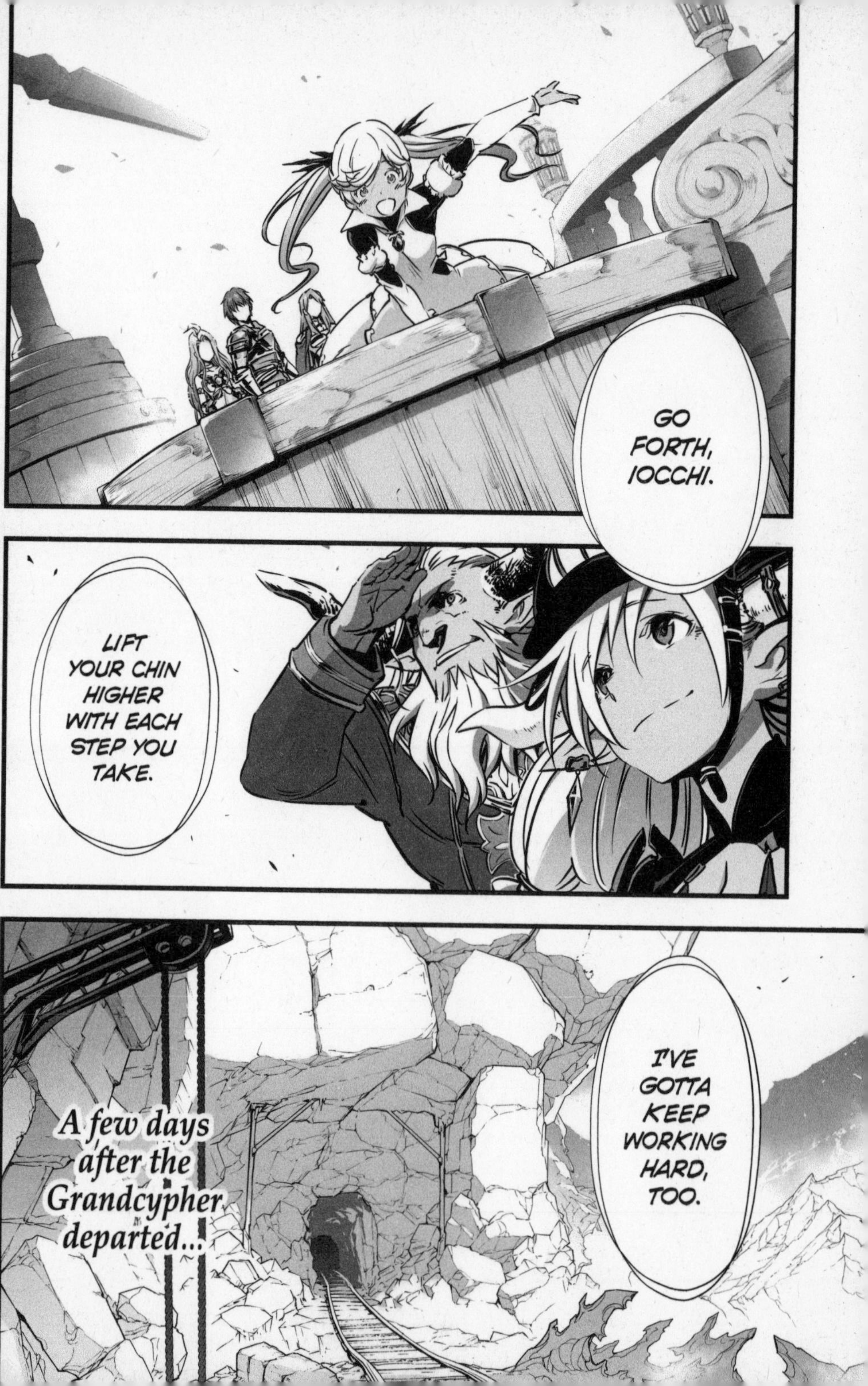
GO FORTH, IOCCHI.
LIFT YOUR CHIN HIGHER WITH EACH STEP YOU TAKE.
I'VE GOTTA KEEP WORKING HARD, TOO.
A few days after the Grandcypher departed...

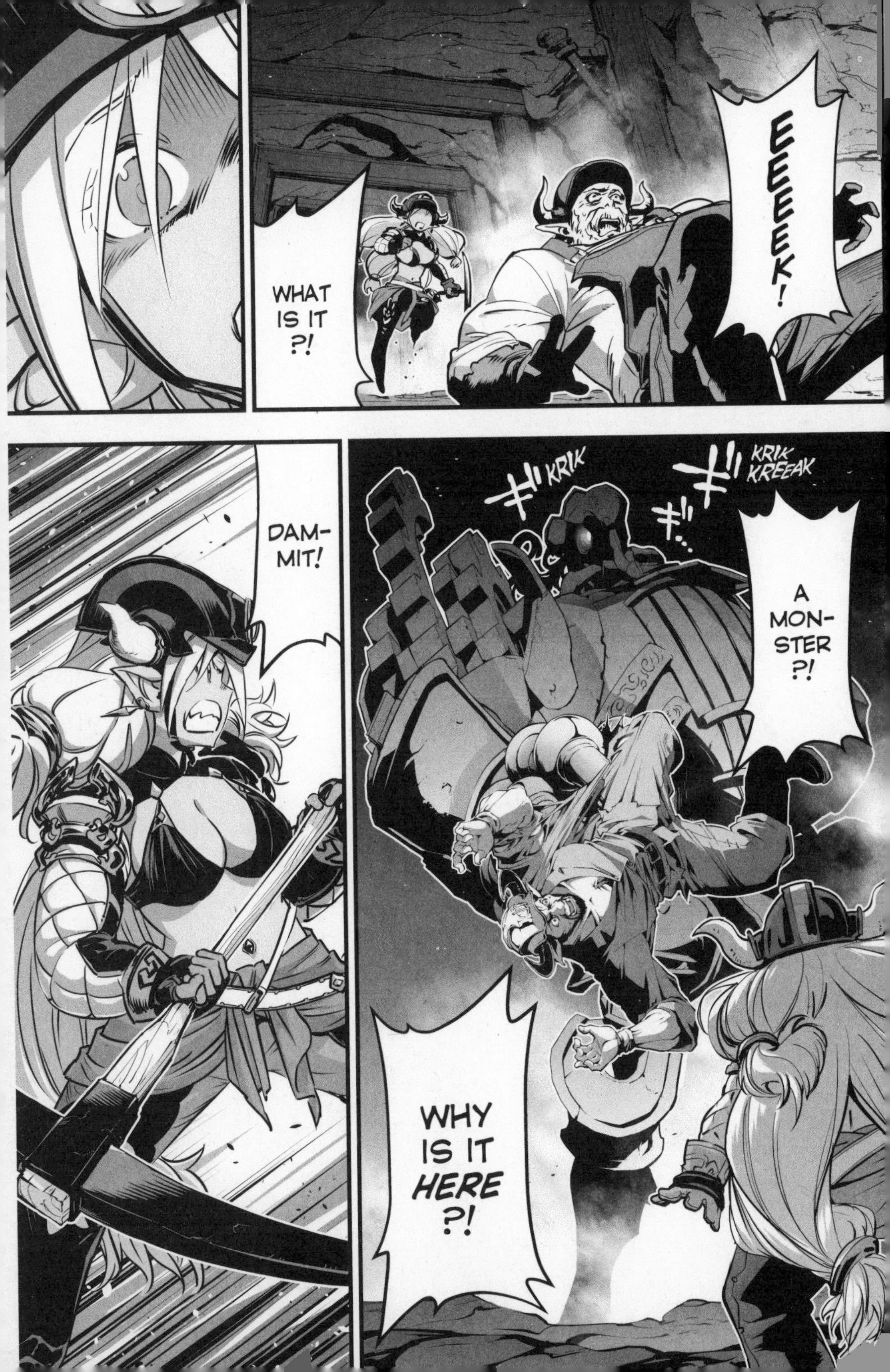
EEEEK!
WHAT IS IT ?!
KRIK KREEAK
KRIK
A MON-STER ?!
WHY IS IT *HERE* ?!
DAM-MIT!

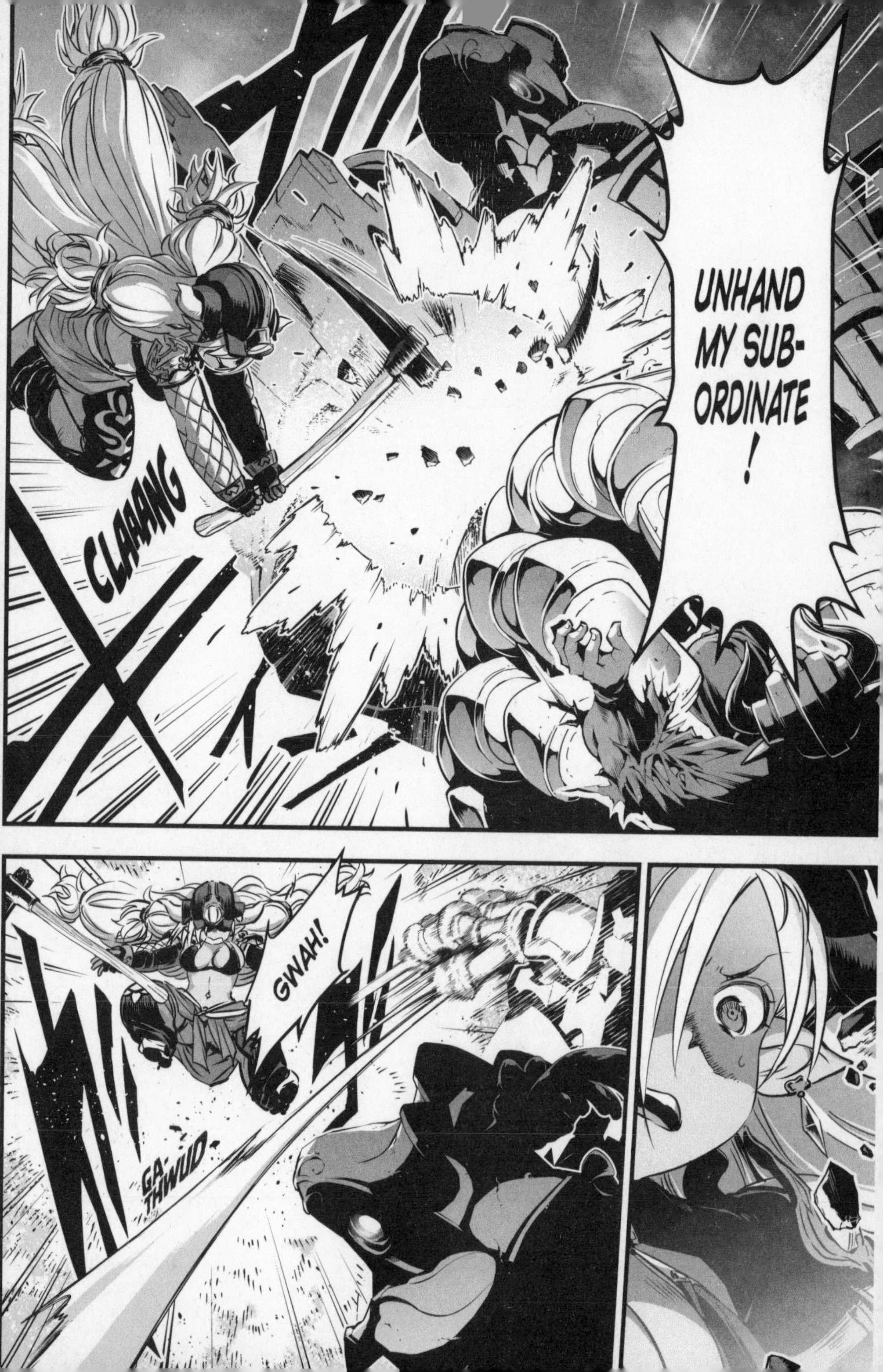
UNHAND MY SUB-ORDINATE!
CLAAANG
GWAH!
GA-THWUD

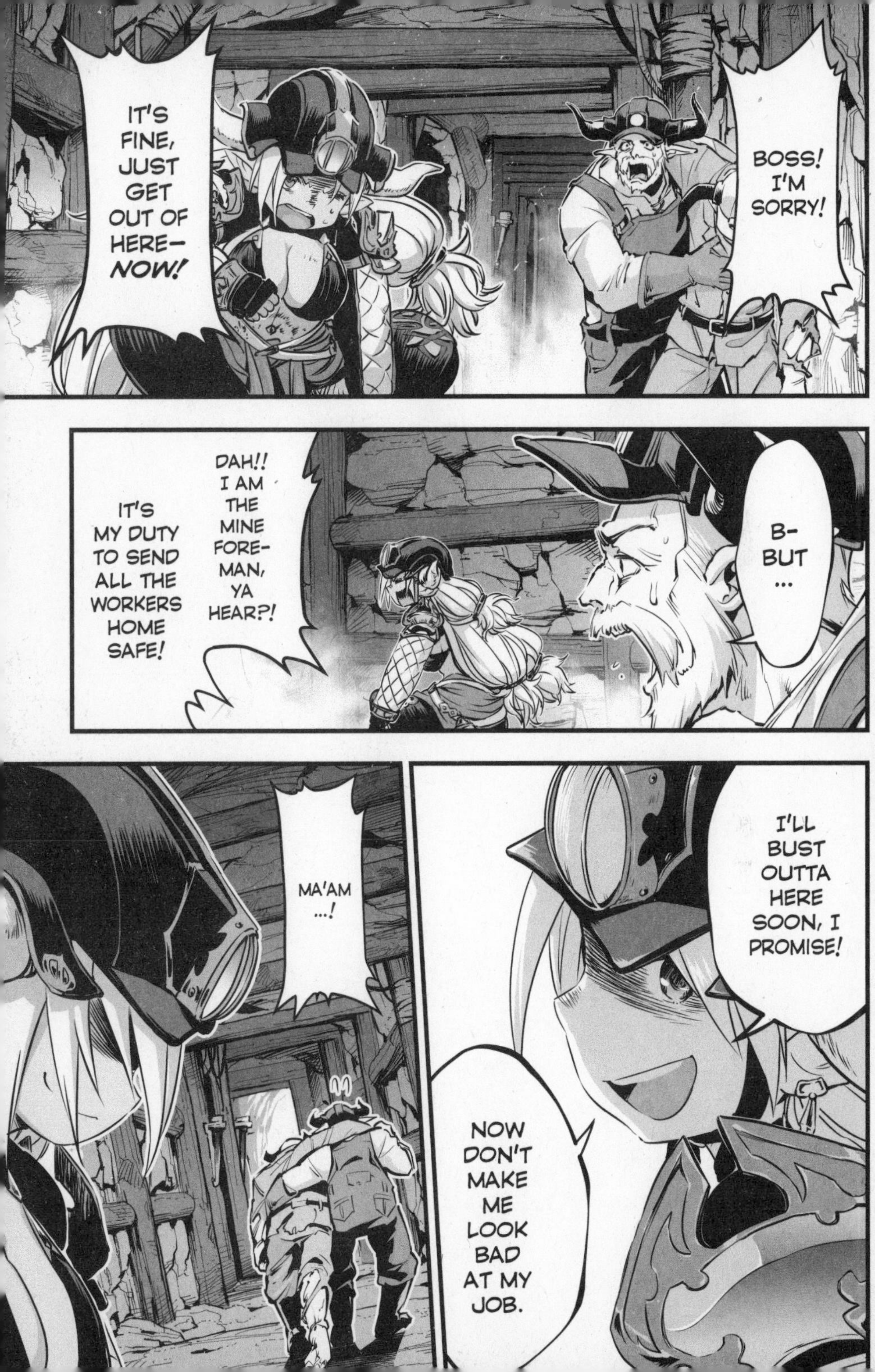
BOSS! I'M SORRY!
IT'S FINE, JUST GET OUT OF HERE— NOW!
B- BUT ...
DAH!! I AM THE MINE FORE- MAN, YA HEAR?!
IT'S MY DUTY TO SEND ALL THE WORKERS HOME SAFE!
I'LL BUST OUTTA HERE SOON, I PROMISE!
NOW DON'T MAKE ME LOOK BAD AT MY JOB.
MA'AM ...!

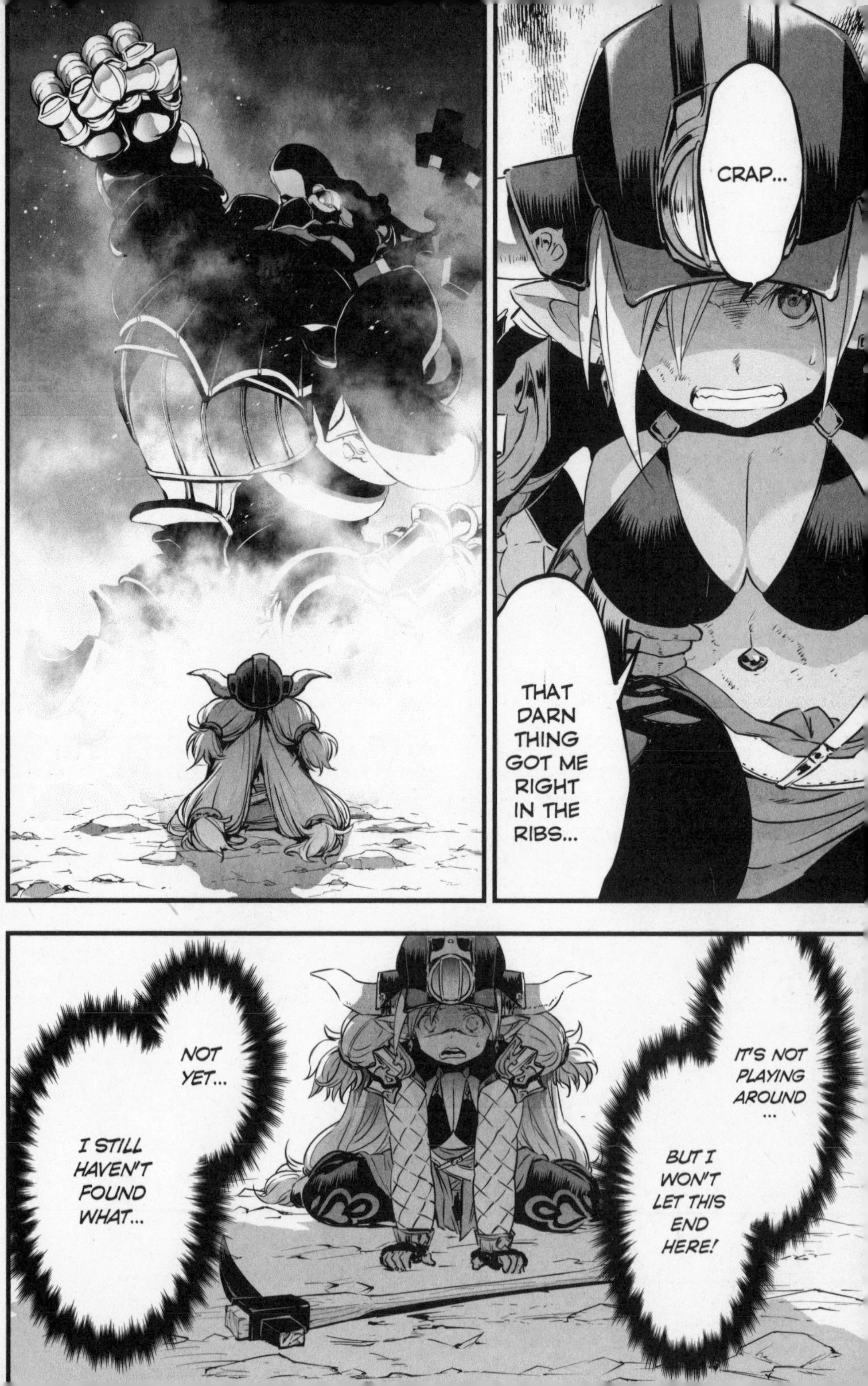
CRAP...
THAT DARN THING GOT ME RIGHT IN THE RIBS...
IT'S NOT PLAYING AROUND ...
BUT I WON'T LET THIS END HERE!
NOT YET...
I STILL HAVEN'T FOUND WHAT...

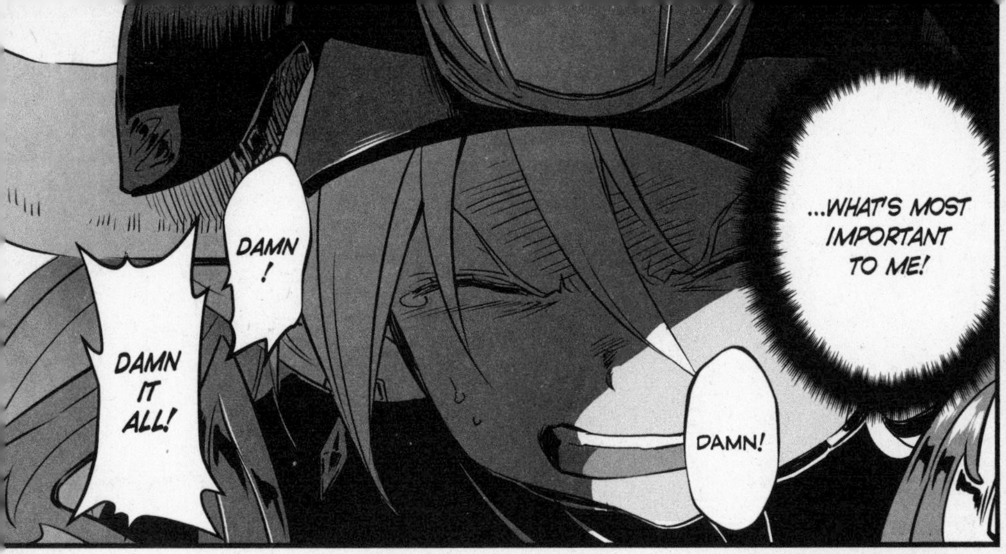
...WHAT'S MOST IMPORTANT TO ME!
DAMN!
DAMN!
DAMN IT ALL!
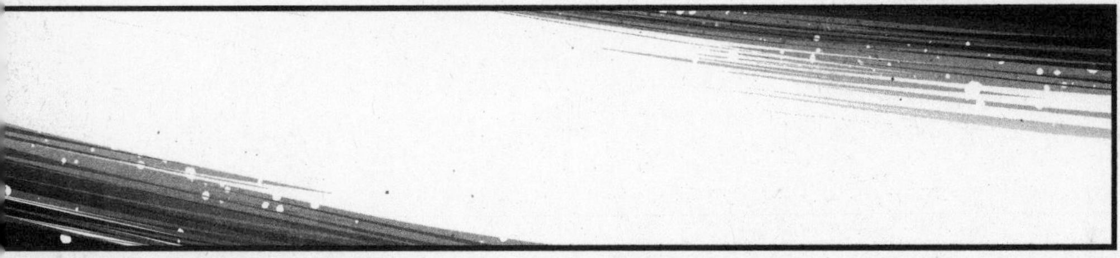
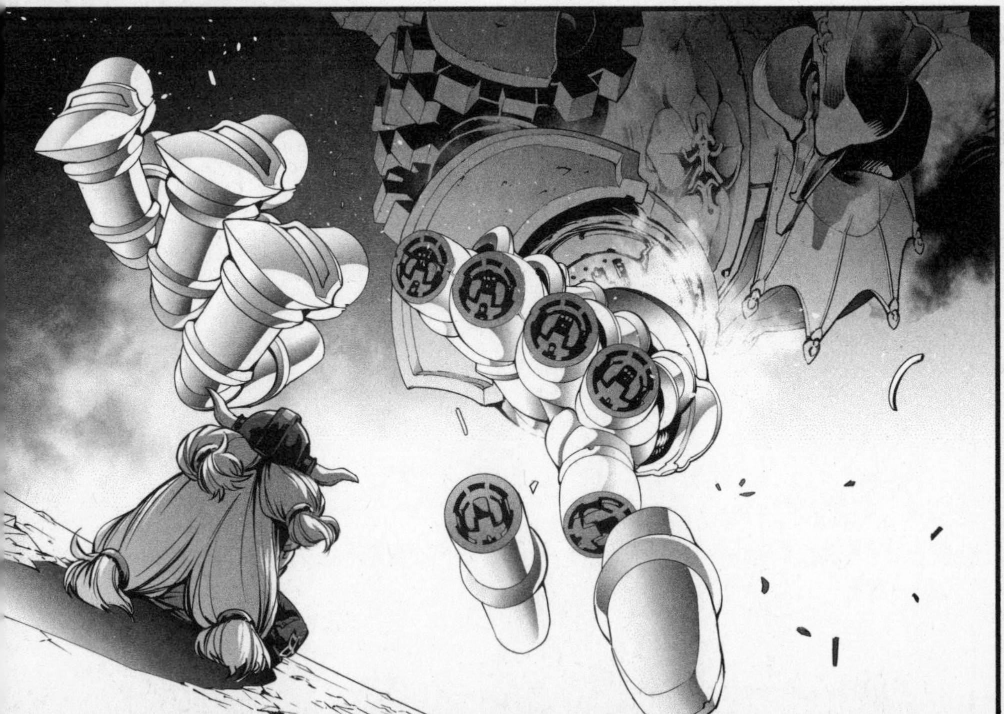

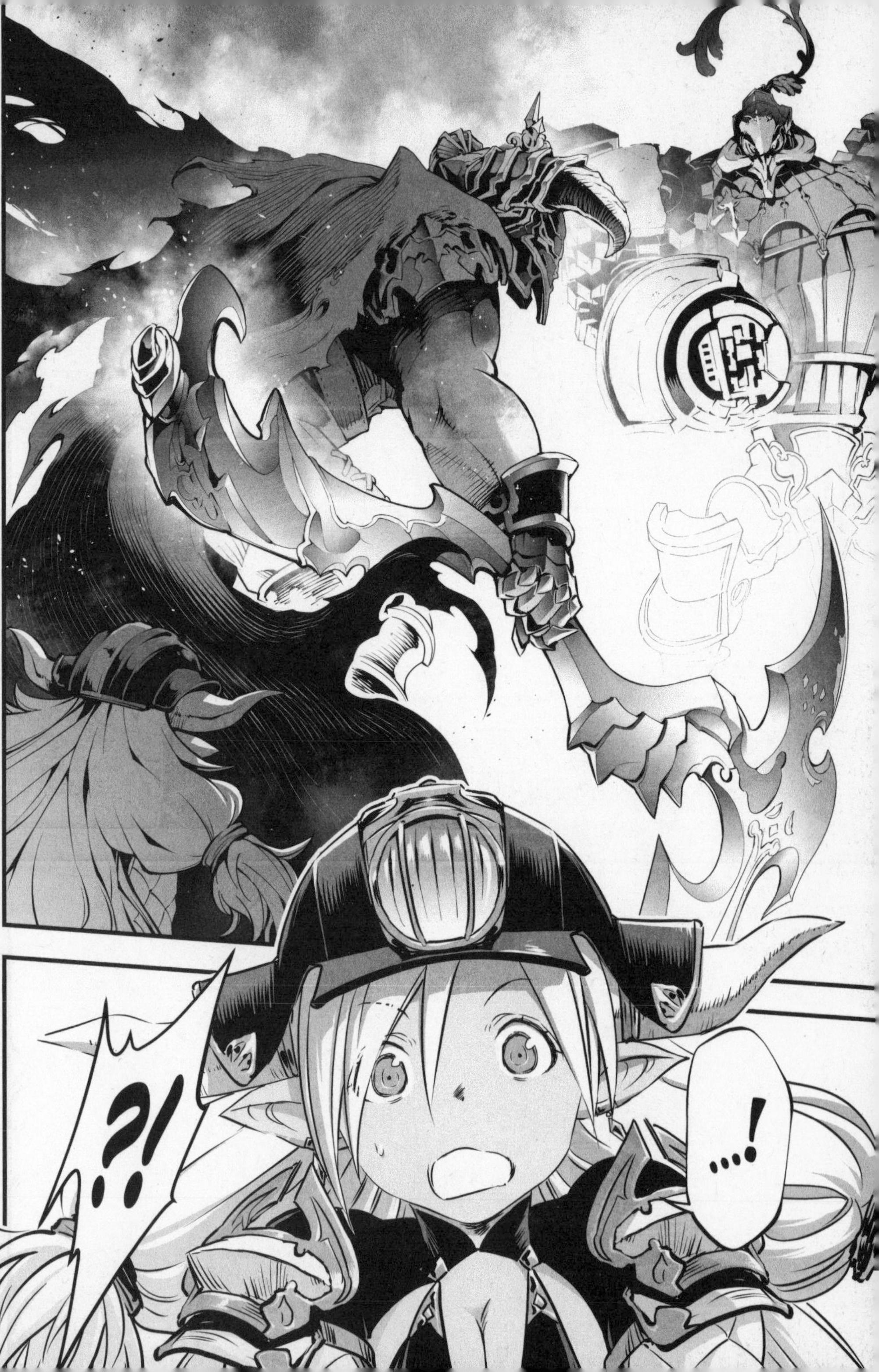
...!
?!

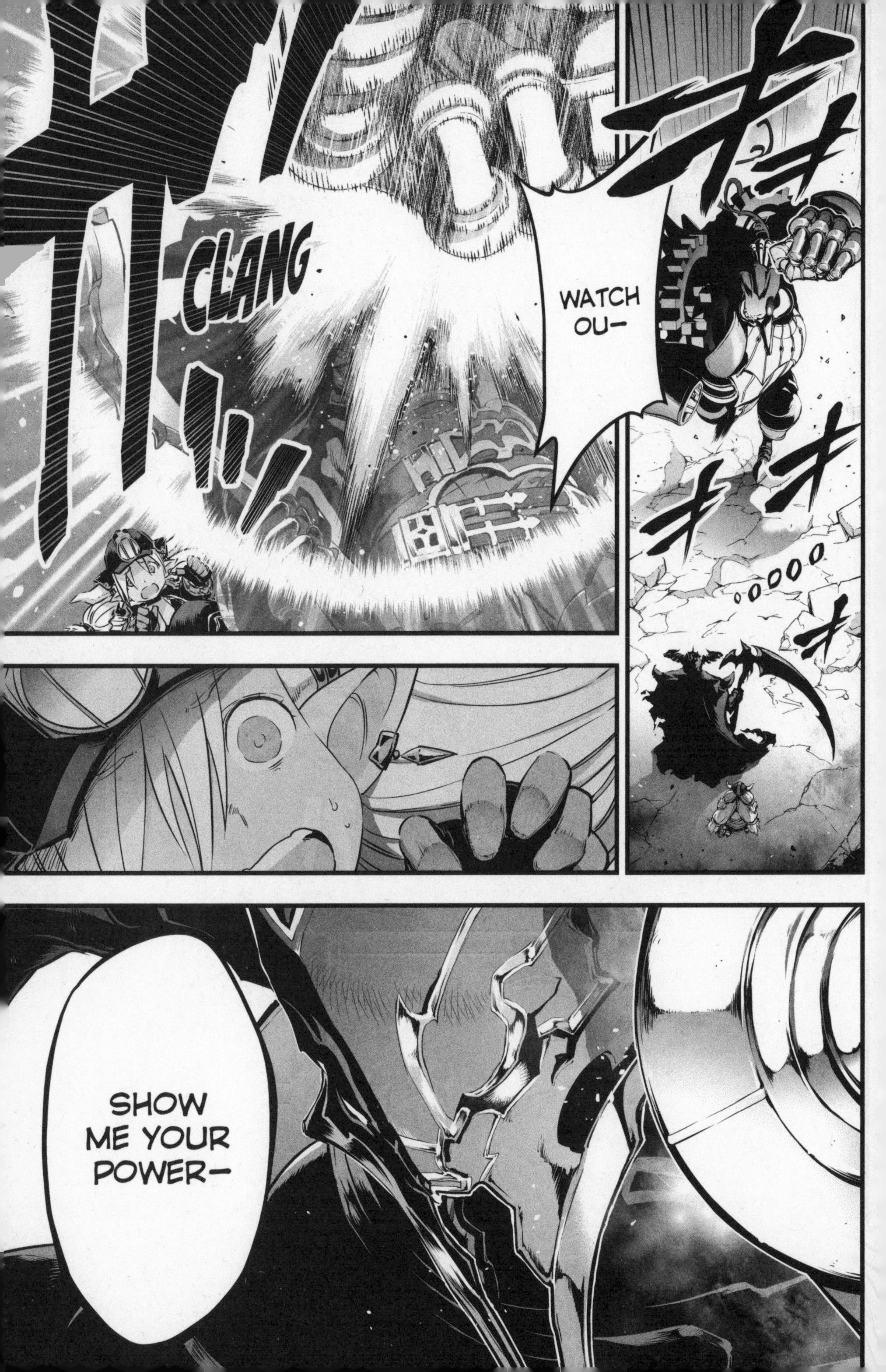
OOOOO
CLANG
WATCH OU–
SHOW ME YOUR POWER–

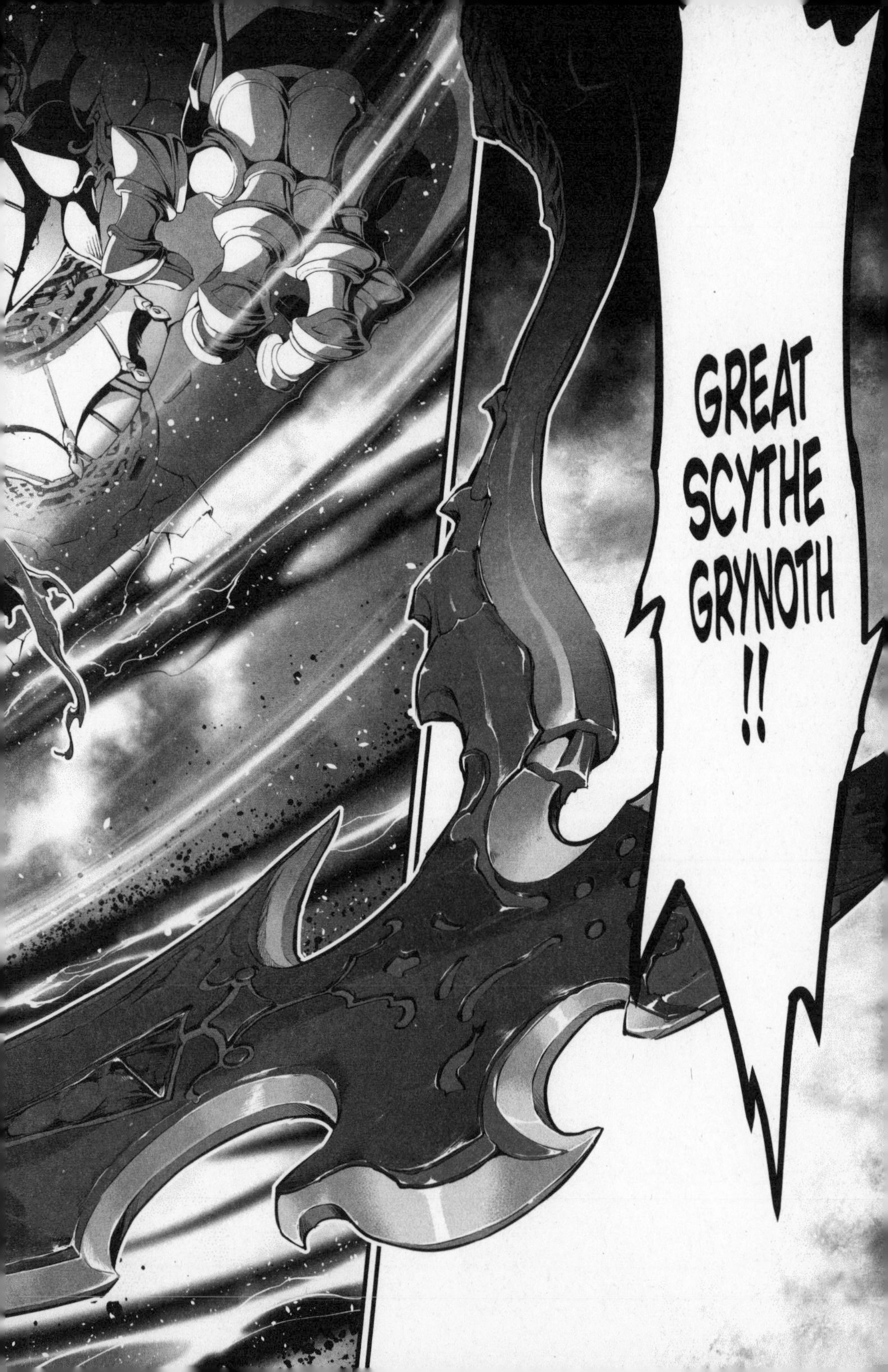
GREAT SCYTHE GRYNOTH !!

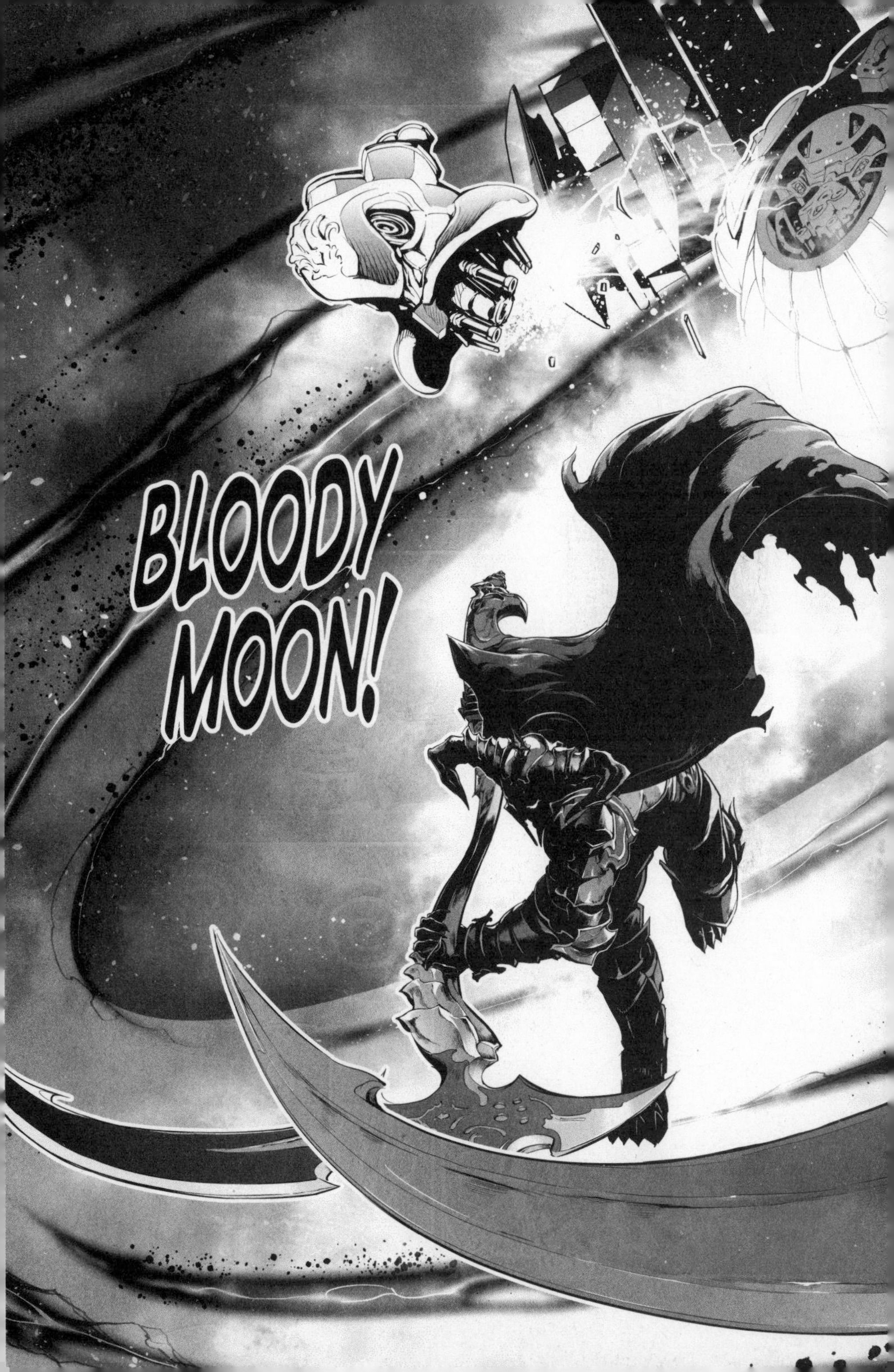
BLOODY
MOON!

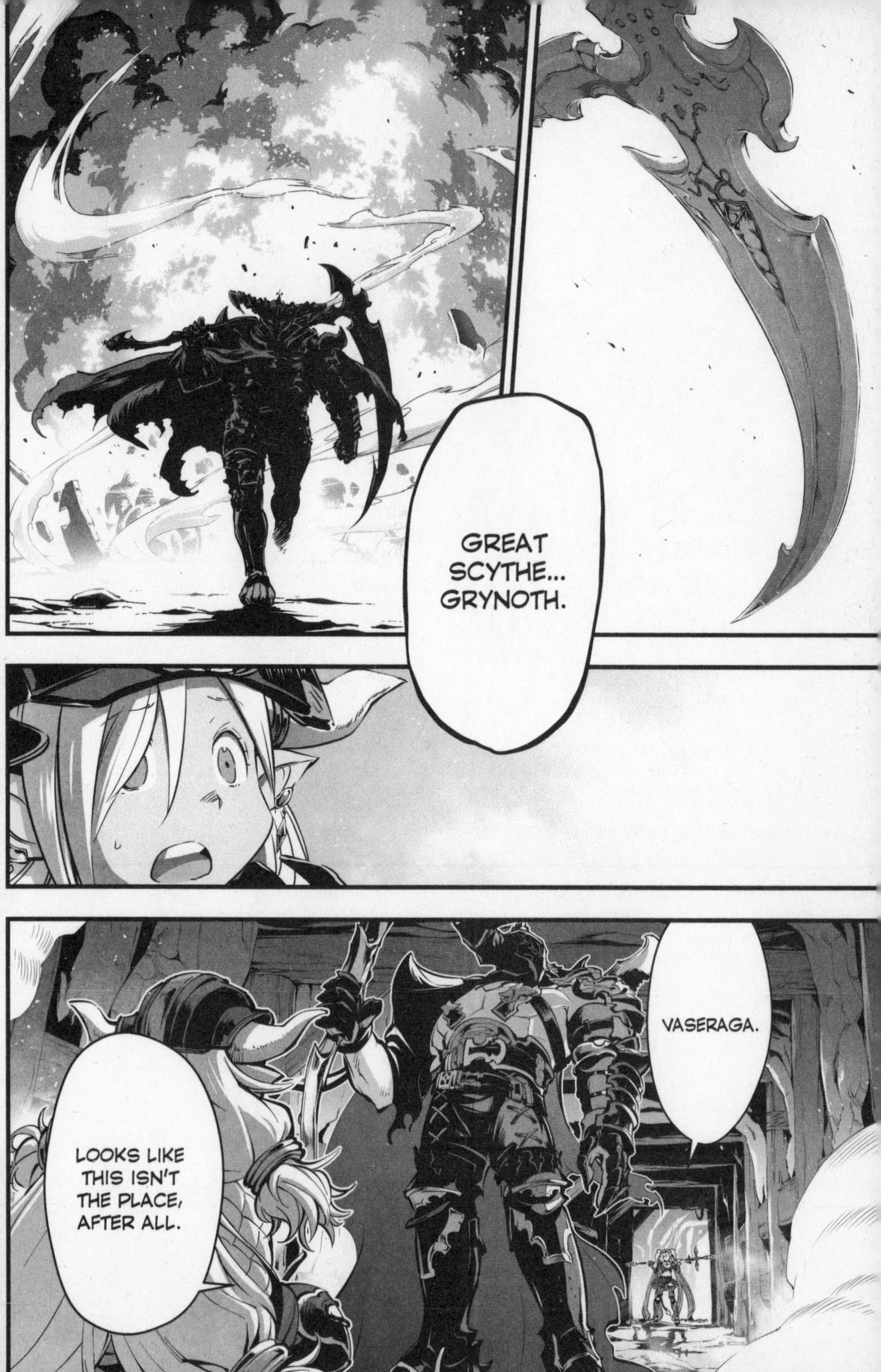
GREAT SCYTHE... GRYNOTH.
VASERAGA.
LOOKS LIKE THIS ISN'T THE PLACE, AFTER ALL.

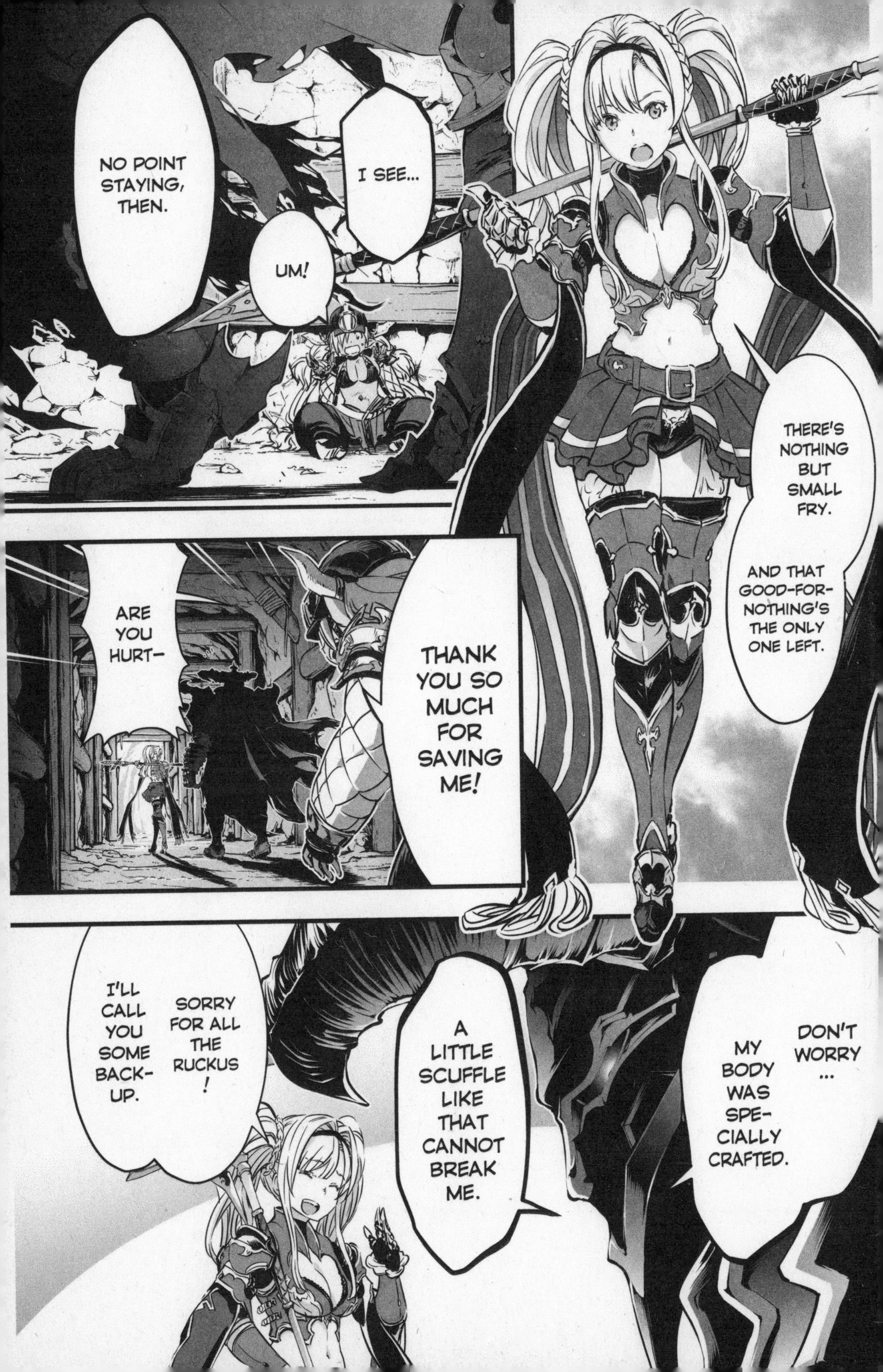
THERE'S NOTHING BUT SMALL FRY.
AND THAT GOOD-FOR-NOTHING'S THE ONLY ONE LEFT.
I SEE...
NO POINT STAYING, THEN.
UM!
THANK YOU SO MUCH FOR SAVING ME!
ARE YOU HURT-
DON'T WORRY...
MY BODY WAS SPE-CIALLY CRAFTED.
A LITTLE SCUFFLE LIKE THAT CANNOT BREAK ME.
SORRY FOR ALL THE RUCKUS!
I'LL CALL YOU SOME BACK-UP.

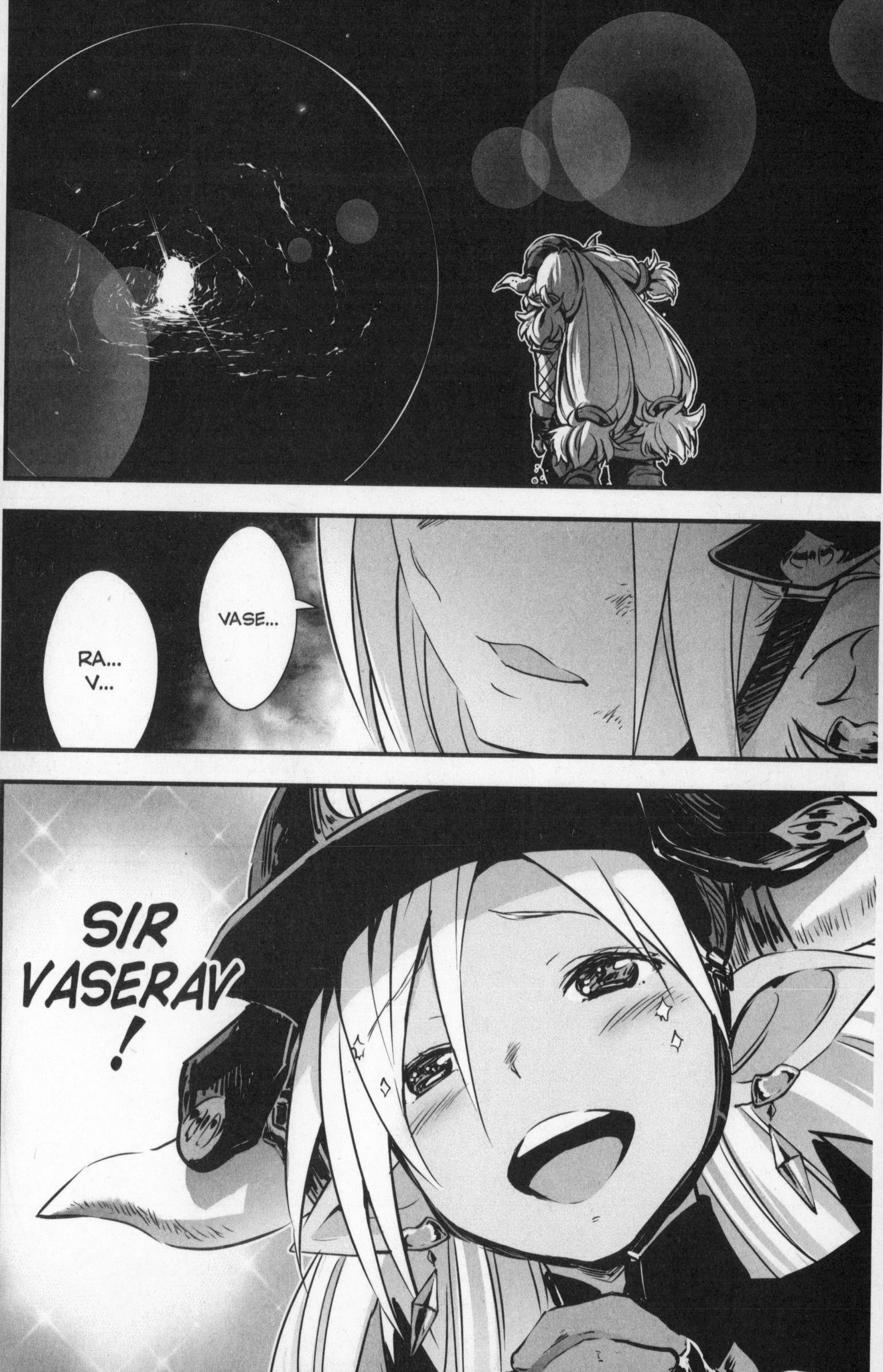
VASE...
RA... V...
SIR VASERAV!

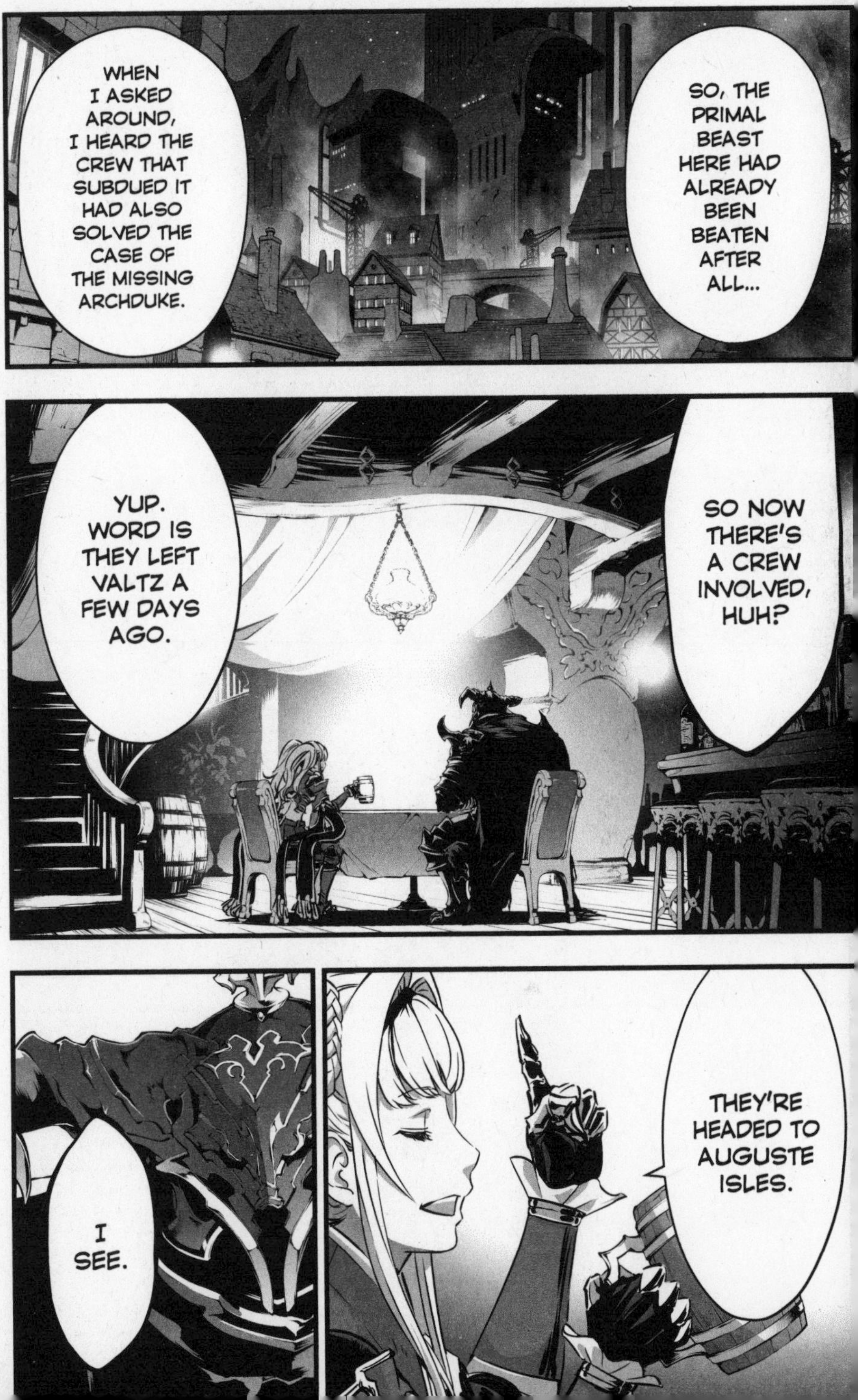
SO, THE PRIMAL BEAST HERE HAD ALREADY BEEN BEATEN AFTER ALL...
WHEN I ASKED AROUND, I HEARD THE CREW THAT SUBDUED IT HAD ALSO SOLVED THE CASE OF THE MISSING ARCHDUKE.
SO NOW THERE'S A CREW INVOLVED, HUH?
YUP. WORD IS THEY LEFT VALTZ A FEW DAYS AGO.
THEY'RE HEADED TO AUGUSTE ISLES.
I SEE.

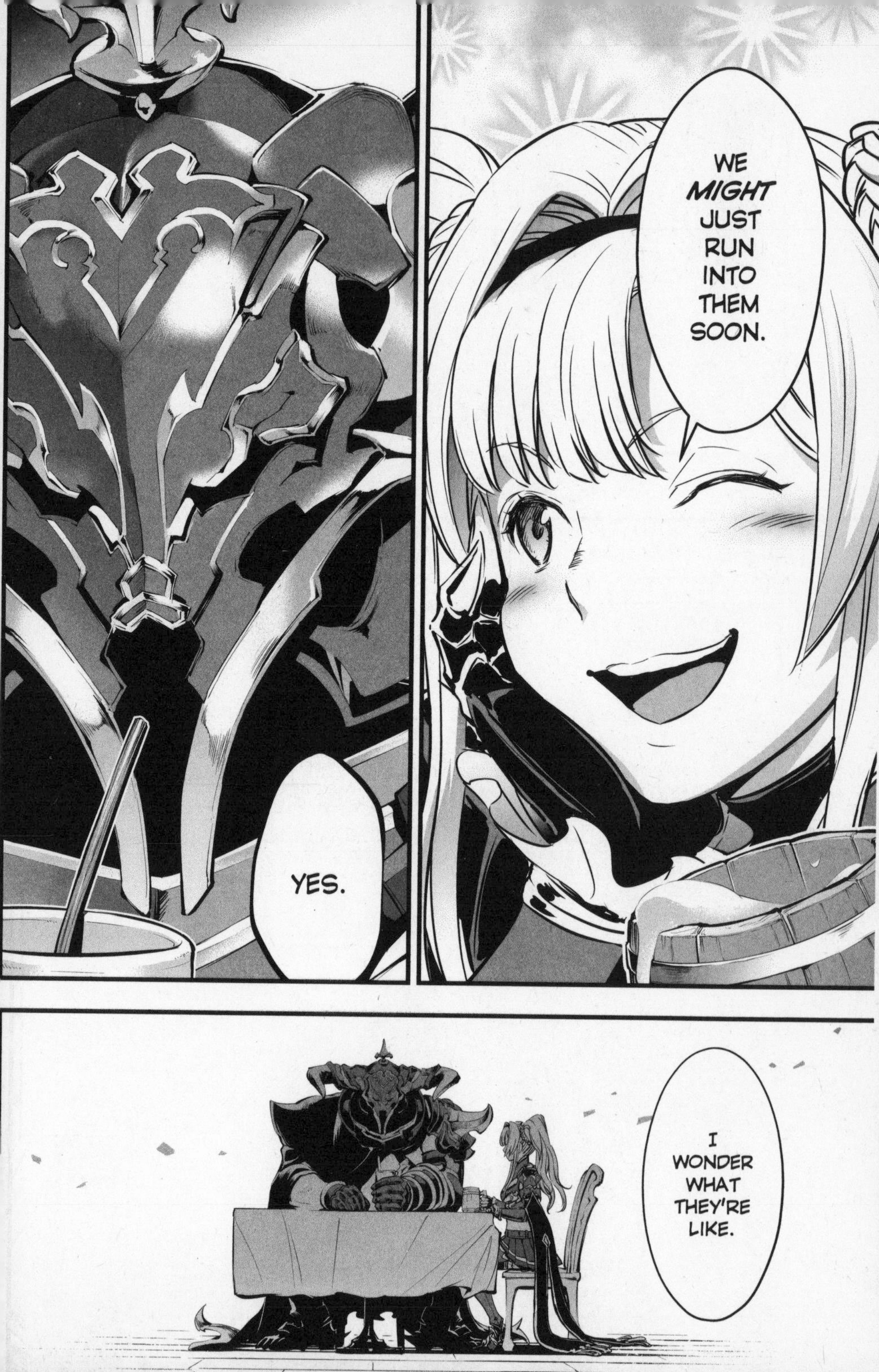
WE *MIGHT* JUST RUN INTO THEM SOON.
YES.
I WONDER WHAT THEY'RE LIKE.

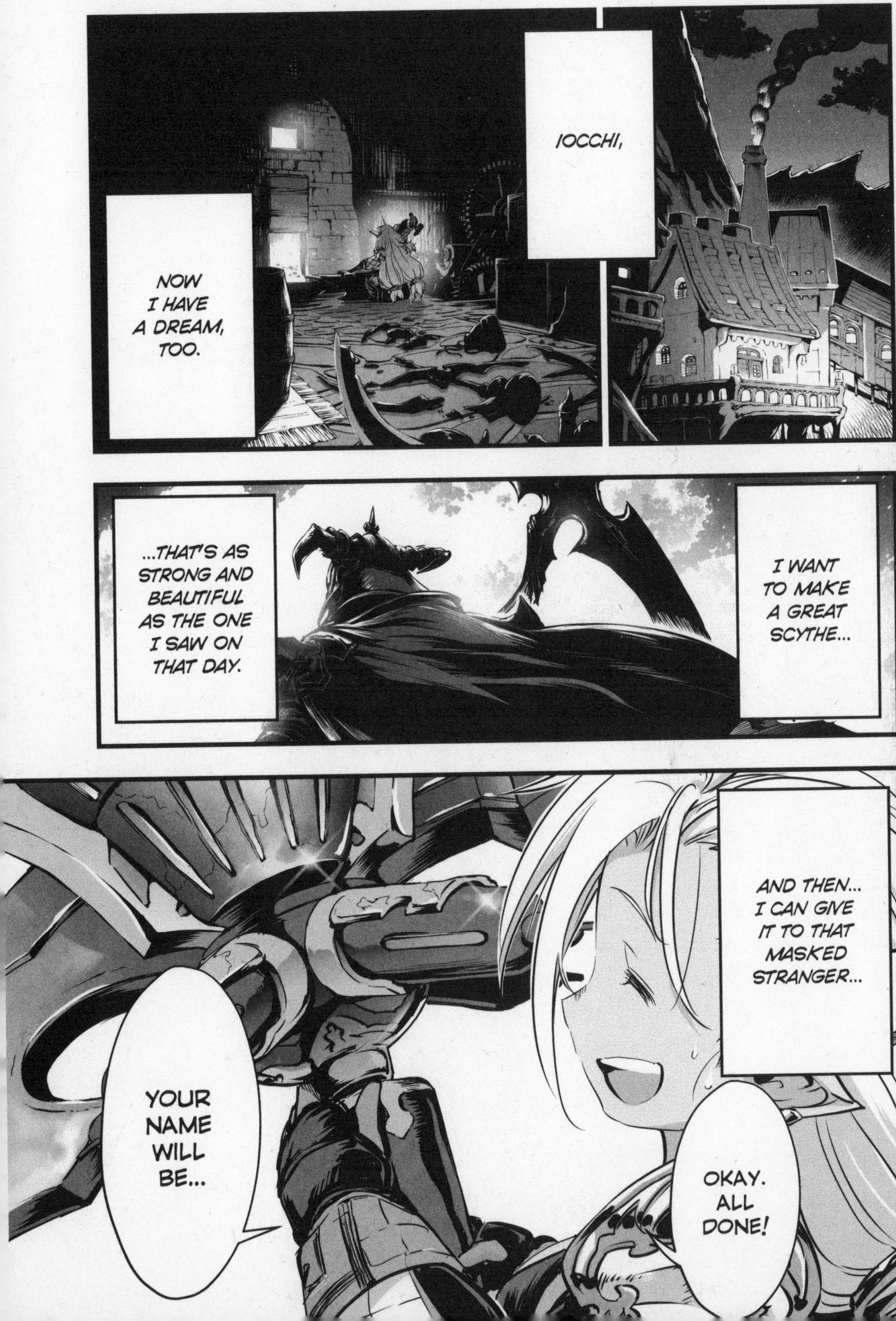
IOCCHI,
NOW I HAVE A DREAM, TOO.
I WANT TO MAKE A GREAT SCYTHE...
...THAT'S AS STRONG AND BEAUTIFUL AS THE ONE I SAW ON THAT DAY.
AND THEN... I CAN GIVE IT TO THAT MASKED STRANGER...
OKAY. ALL DONE!
YOUR NAME WILL BE...

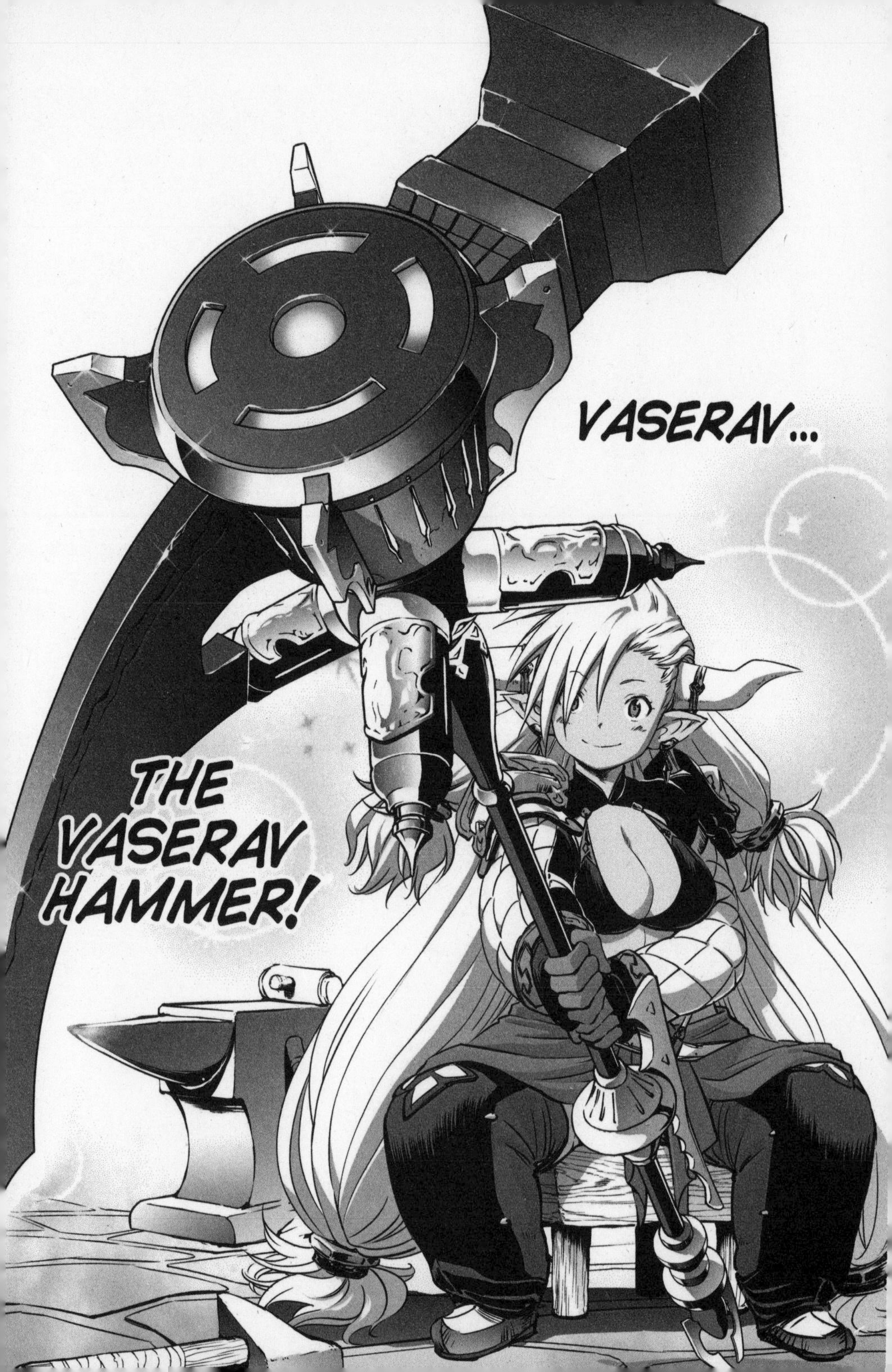
VASERAV...
THE VASERAV HAMMER!

GRANBLUE FANTASY
グランブルーファンタジー

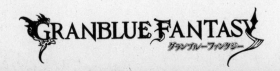

GRANBLUE FANTASY
グランブルーファンタジー

CHAPTER 23: Auguste Isles (1)

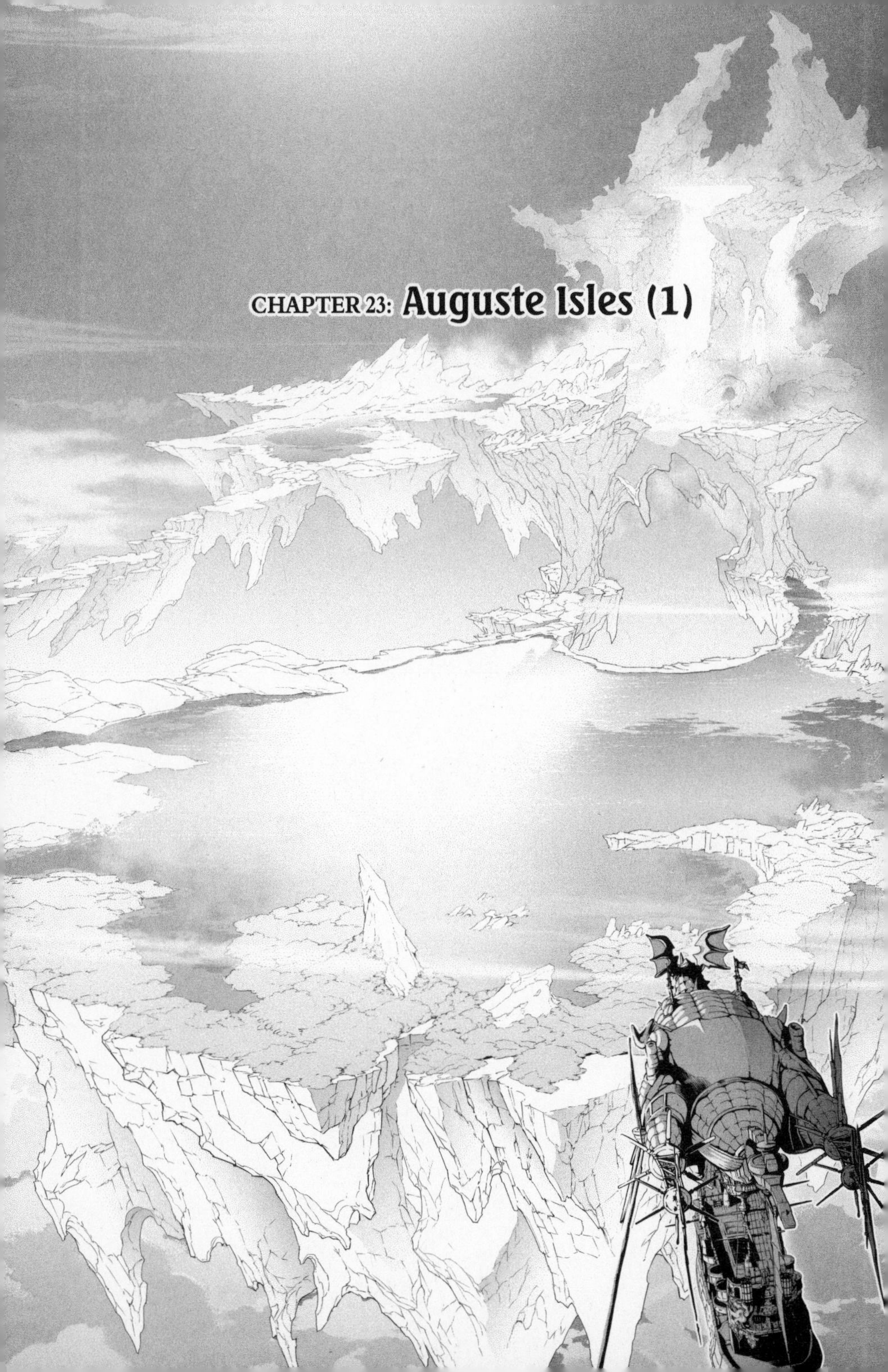

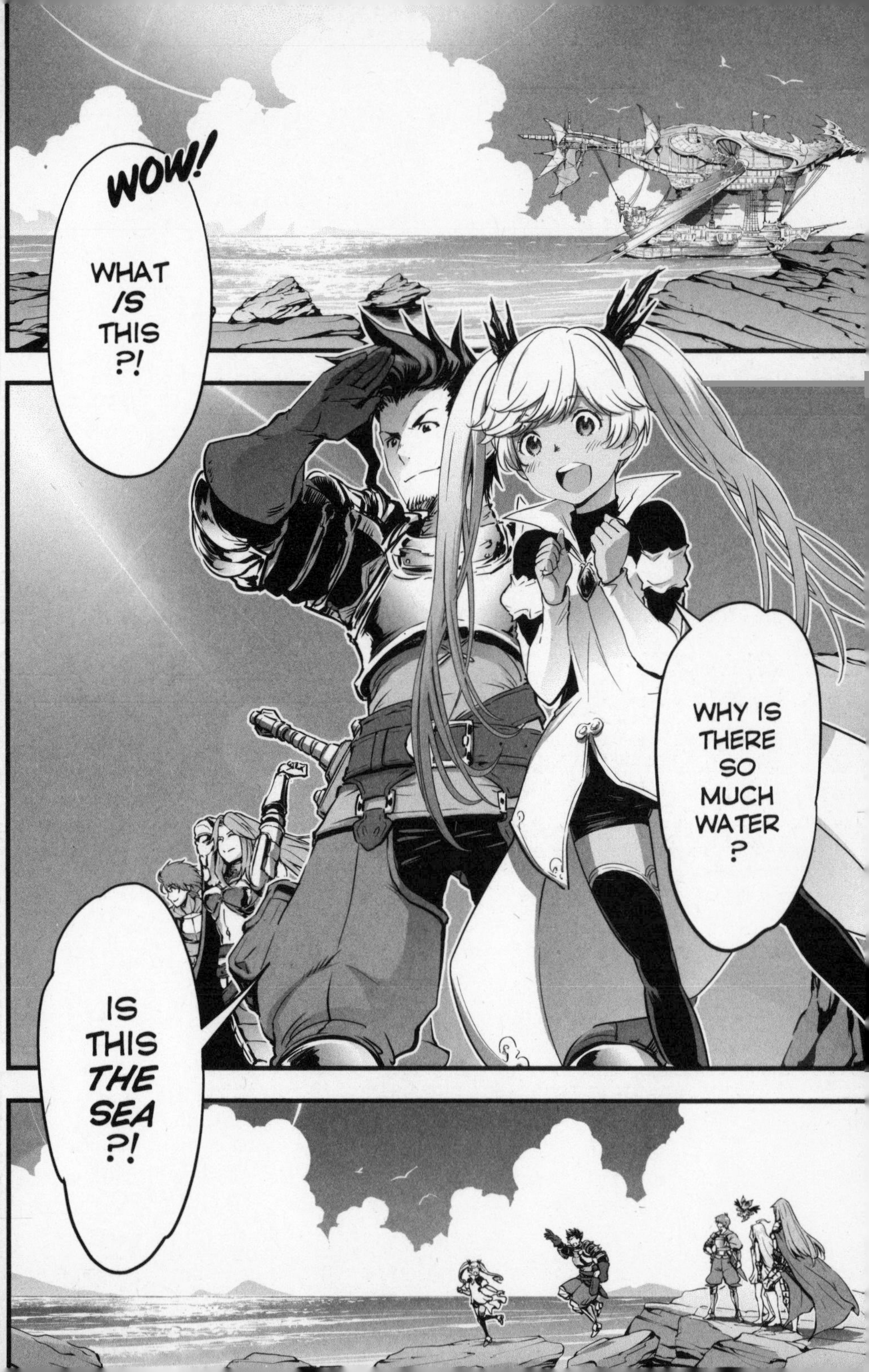

WOW! WHAT IS THIS?!
WHY IS THERE SO MUCH WATER?
IS THIS THE SEA?!

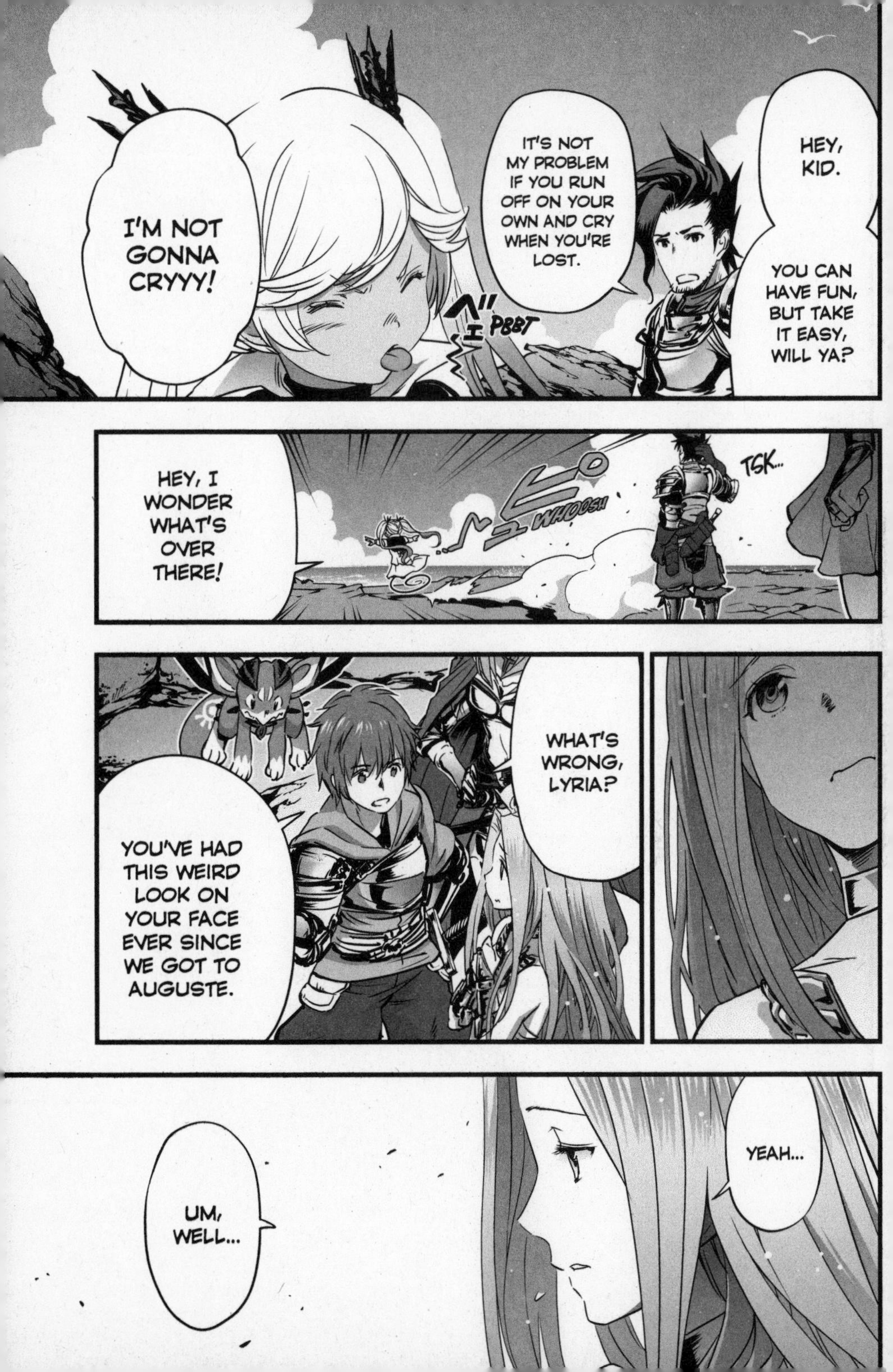
HEY, KID.
YOU CAN HAVE FUN, BUT TAKE IT EASY, WILL YA?
IT'S NOT MY PROBLEM IF YOU RUN OFF ON YOUR OWN AND CRY WHEN YOU'RE LOST.
PBBT
I'M NOT GONNA CRYYY!
TSK...
WHOOSH
HEY, I WONDER WHAT'S OVER THERE!
WHAT'S WRONG, LYRIA?
YOU'VE HAD THIS WEIRD LOOK ON YOUR FACE EVER SINCE WE GOT TO AUGUSTE.
YEAH...
UM, WELL...

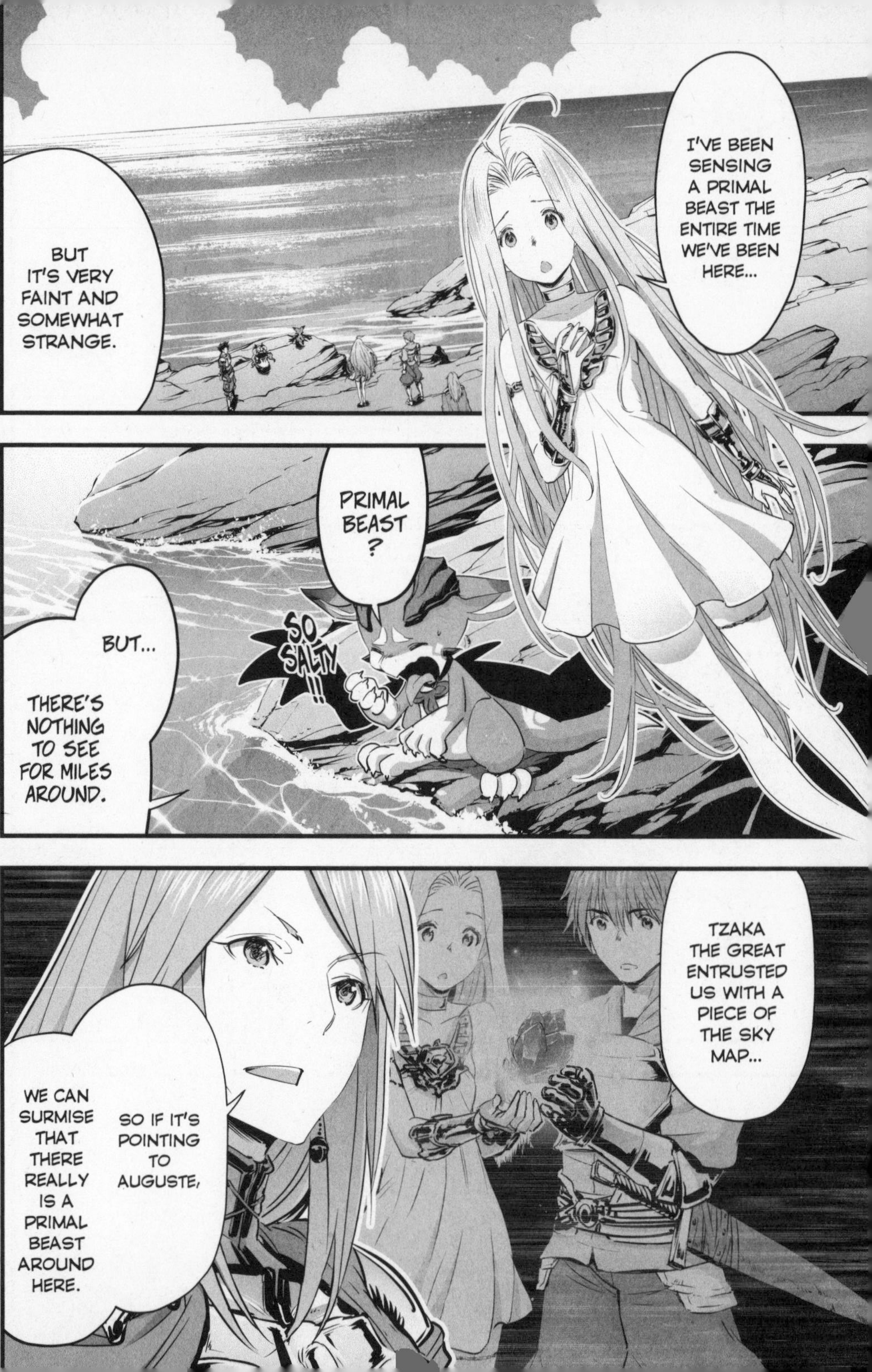
I'VE BEEN SENSING A PRIMAL BEAST THE ENTIRE TIME WE'VE BEEN HERE...
BUT IT'S VERY FAINT AND SOMEWHAT STRANGE.
PRIMAL BEAST?
SO SALTY!!
BUT...
THERE'S NOTHING TO SEE FOR MILES AROUND.
TZAKA THE GREAT ENTRUSTED US WITH A PIECE OF THE SKY MAP...
SO IF IT'S POINTING TO AUGUSTE,
WE CAN SURMISE THAT THERE REALLY IS A PRIMAL BEAST AROUND HERE.

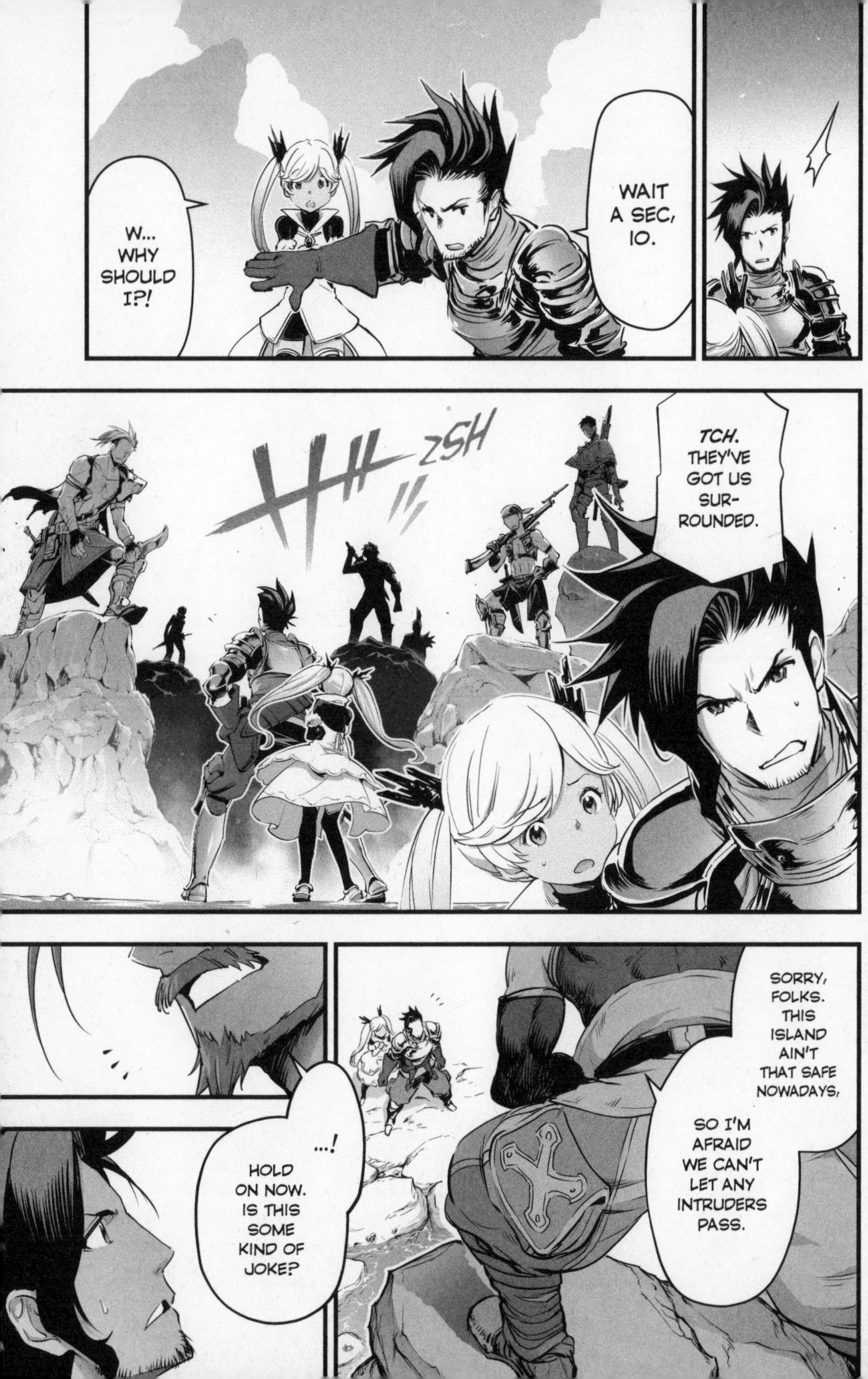
WAIT A SEC, IO.
W... WHY SHOULD I?!
TCH. THEY'VE GOT US SUR-ROUNDED.
ZSH
SORRY, FOLKS. THIS ISLAND AIN'T THAT SAFE NOWADAYS,
SO I'M AFRAID WE CAN'T LET ANY INTRUDERS PASS.
...!
HOLD ON NOW. IS THIS SOME KIND OF JOKE?

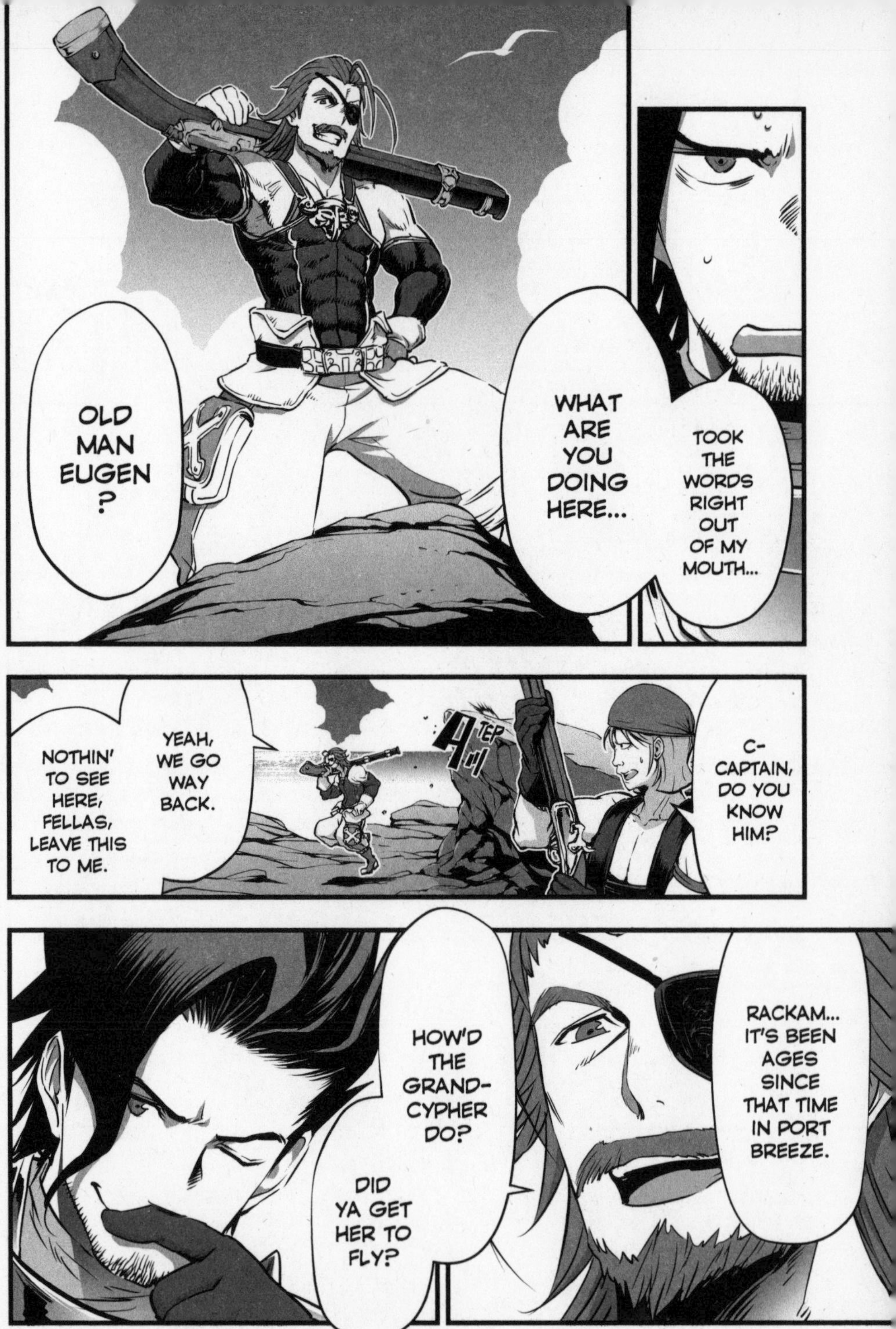
OLD MAN EUGEN?
WHAT ARE YOU DOING HERE...
TOOK THE WORDS RIGHT OUT OF MY MOUTH...
C-CAPTAIN, DO YOU KNOW HIM?
TEP
YEAH, WE GO WAY BACK.
NOTHIN' TO SEE HERE, FELLAS, LEAVE THIS TO ME.
RACKAM... IT'S BEEN AGES SINCE THAT TIME IN PORT BREEZE.
HOW'D THE GRAND-CYPHER DO?
DID YA GET HER TO FLY?

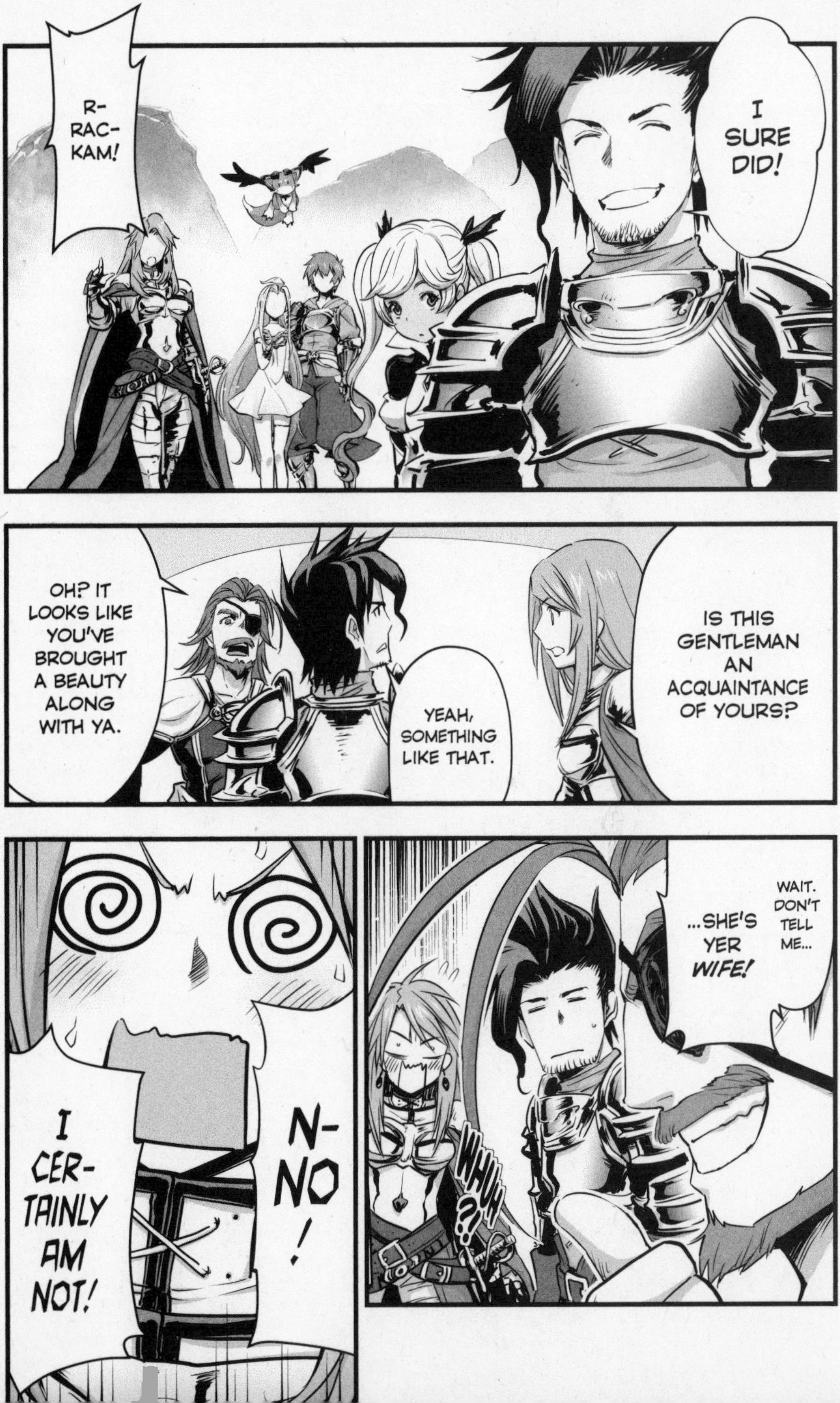
I SURE DID!
R-RAC-KAM!
IS THIS GENTLEMAN AN ACQUAINTANCE OF YOURS?
YEAH, SOMETHING LIKE THAT.
OH? IT LOOKS LIKE YOU'VE BROUGHT A BEAUTY ALONG WITH YA.
WAIT. DON'T TELL ME...
...SHE'S YER *WIFE!*
WHUH?!?
N-NO!
I CER-TAINLY AM NOT!

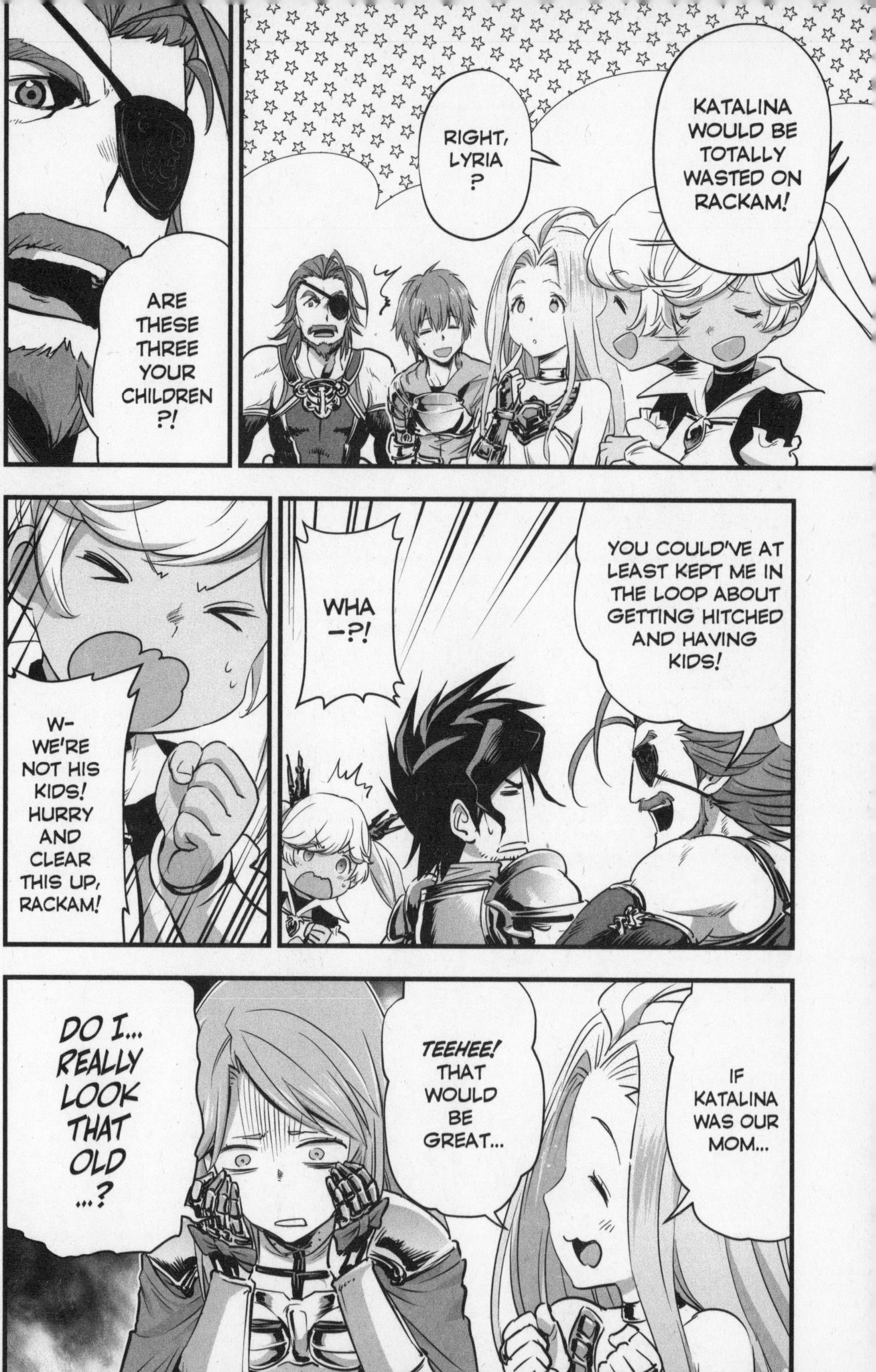
KATALINA WOULD BE TOTALLY WASTED ON RACKAM!
RIGHT, LYRIA?
ARE THESE THREE YOUR CHILDREN?!
YOU COULD'VE AT LEAST KEPT ME IN THE LOOP ABOUT GETTING HITCHED AND HAVING KIDS!
WHA-?!
W-WE'RE NOT HIS KIDS! HURRY AND CLEAR THIS UP, RACKAM!
IF KATALINA WAS OUR MOM...
TEEHEE! THAT WOULD BE GREAT...
DO I... REALLY LOOK THAT OLD...?

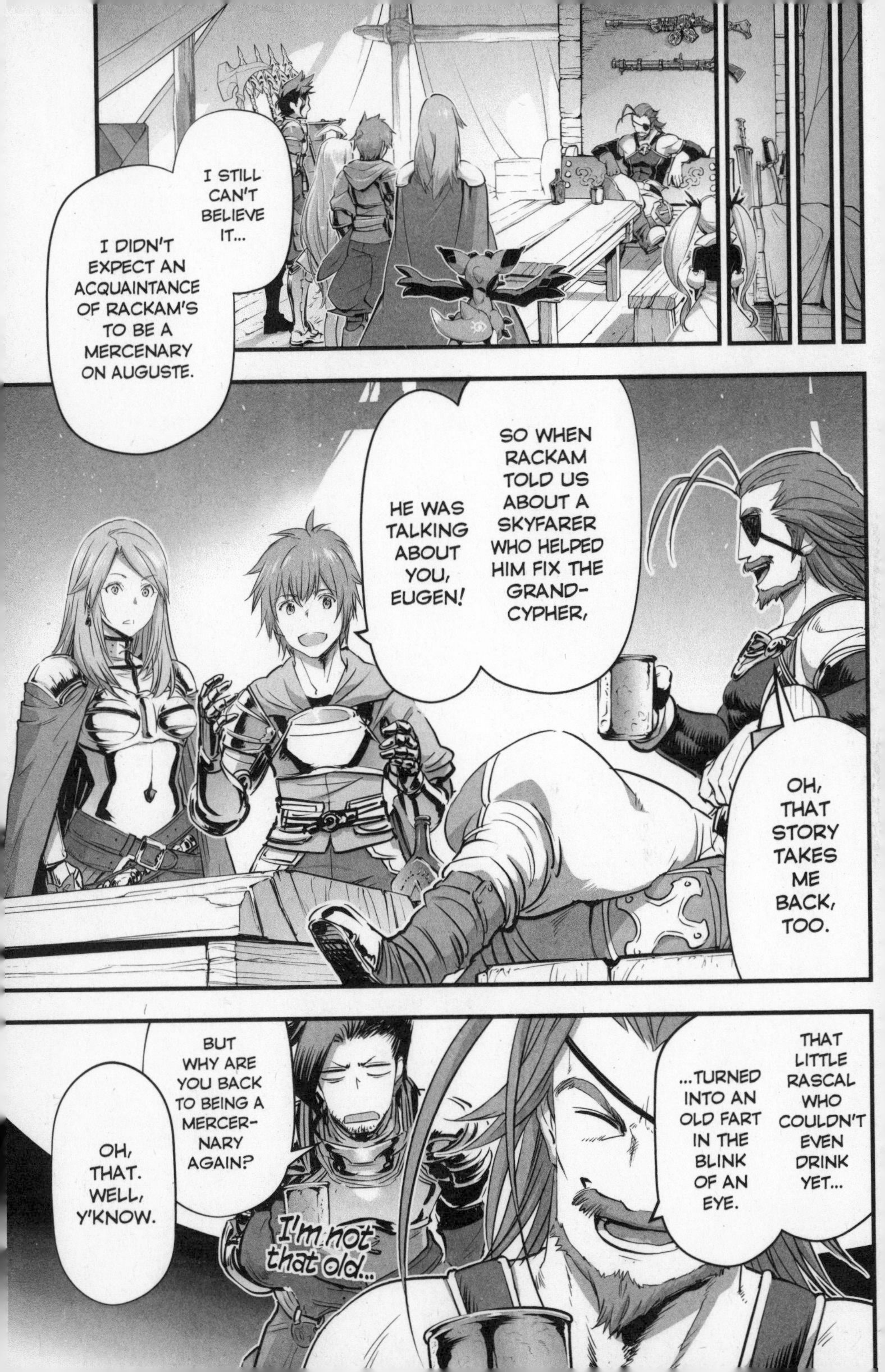
I STILL CAN'T BELIEVE IT...
I DIDN'T EXPECT AN ACQUAINTANCE OF RACKAM'S TO BE A MERCENARY ON AUGUSTE.
SO WHEN RACKAM TOLD US ABOUT A SKYFARER WHO HELPED HIM FIX THE GRAND-CYPHER,
HE WAS TALKING ABOUT YOU, EUGEN!
OH, THAT STORY TAKES ME BACK, TOO.
THAT LITTLE RASCAL WHO COULDN'T EVEN DRINK YET...
...TURNED INTO AN OLD FART IN THE BLINK OF AN EYE.
BUT WHY ARE YOU BACK TO BEING A MERCER-NARY AGAIN?
I'm not that old...
OH, THAT. WELL, Y'KNOW.

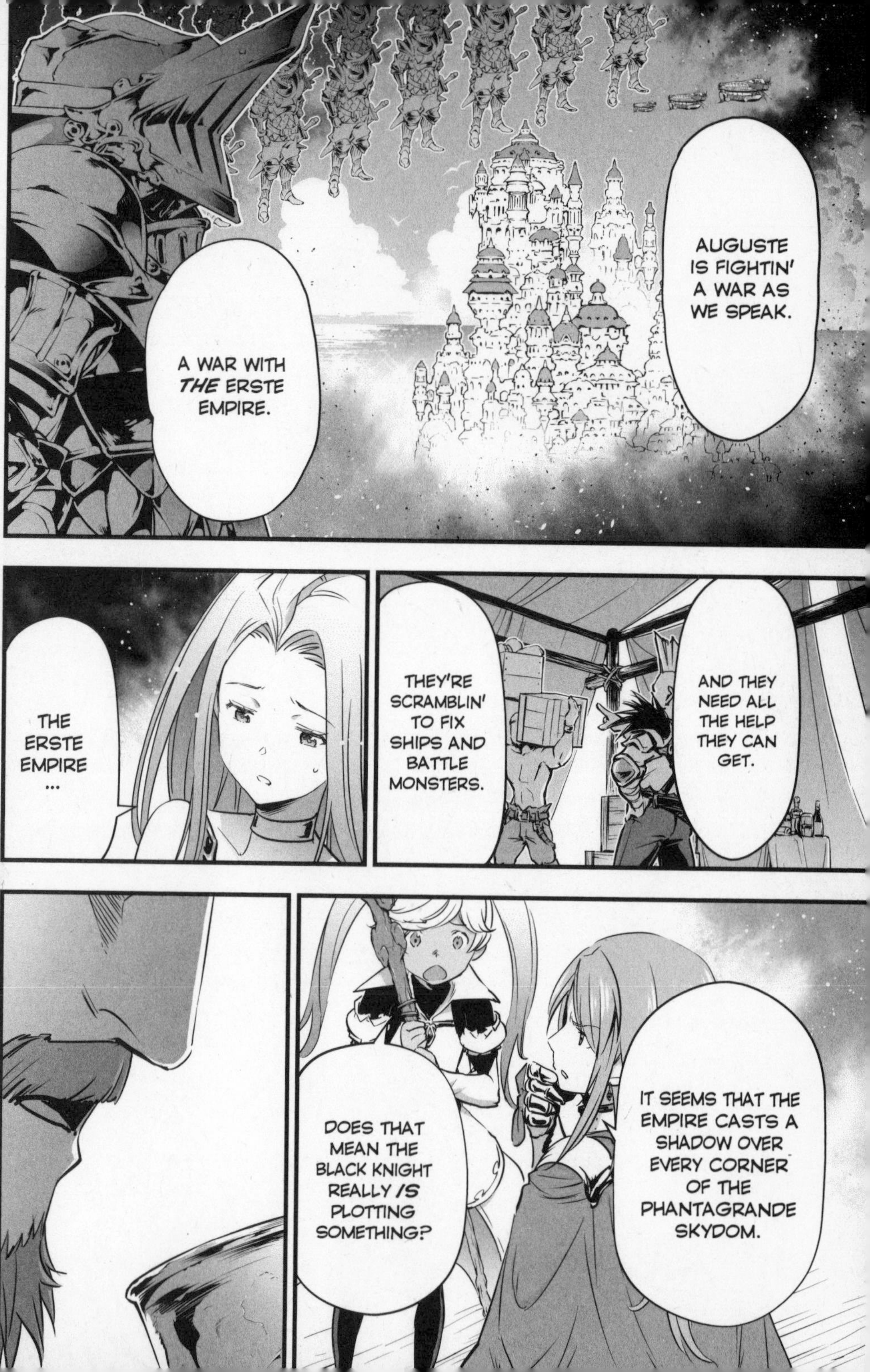
AUGUSTE IS FIGHTIN' A WAR AS WE SPEAK.
A WAR WITH *THE* ERSTE EMPIRE.
THEY'RE SCRAMBLIN' TO FIX SHIPS AND BATTLE MONSTERS.
AND THEY NEED ALL THE HELP THEY CAN GET.
THE ERSTE EMPIRE ...
IT SEEMS THAT THE EMPIRE CASTS A SHADOW OVER EVERY CORNER OF THE PHANTAGRANDE SKYDOM.
DOES THAT MEAN THE BLACK KNIGHT REALLY *IS* PLOTTING SOMETHING?

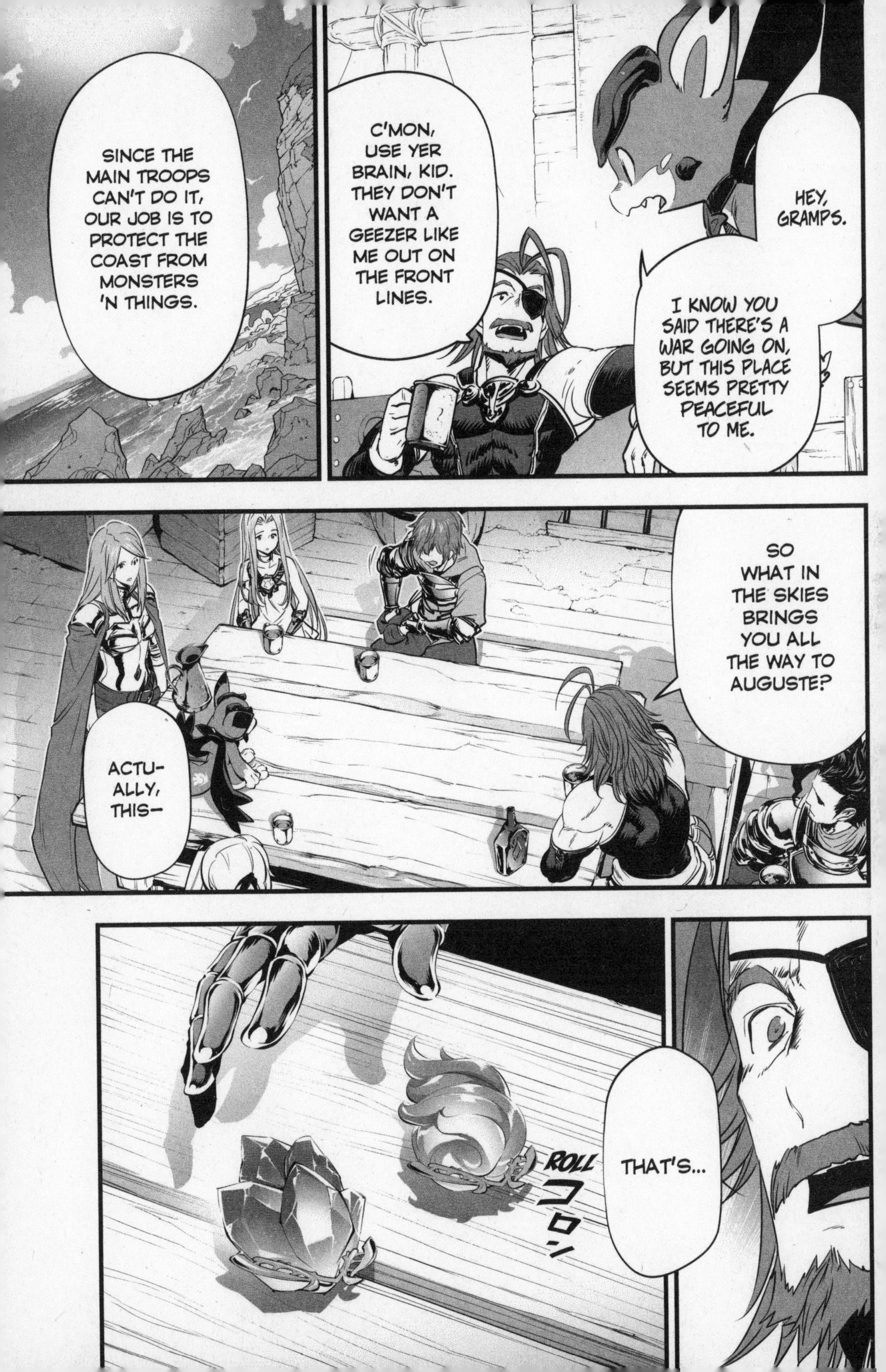
HEY, GRAMPS.
I KNOW YOU SAID THERE'S A WAR GOING ON, BUT THIS PLACE SEEMS PRETTY PEACEFUL TO ME.
C'MON, USE YER BRAIN, KID. THEY DON'T WANT A GEEZER LIKE ME OUT ON THE FRONT LINES.
SINCE THE MAIN TROOPS CAN'T DO IT, OUR JOB IS TO PROTECT THE COAST FROM MONSTERS 'N THINGS.
SO WHAT IN THE SKIES BRINGS YOU ALL THE WAY TO AUGUSTE?
ACTUALLY, THIS—
THAT'S...
ROLL
コロン

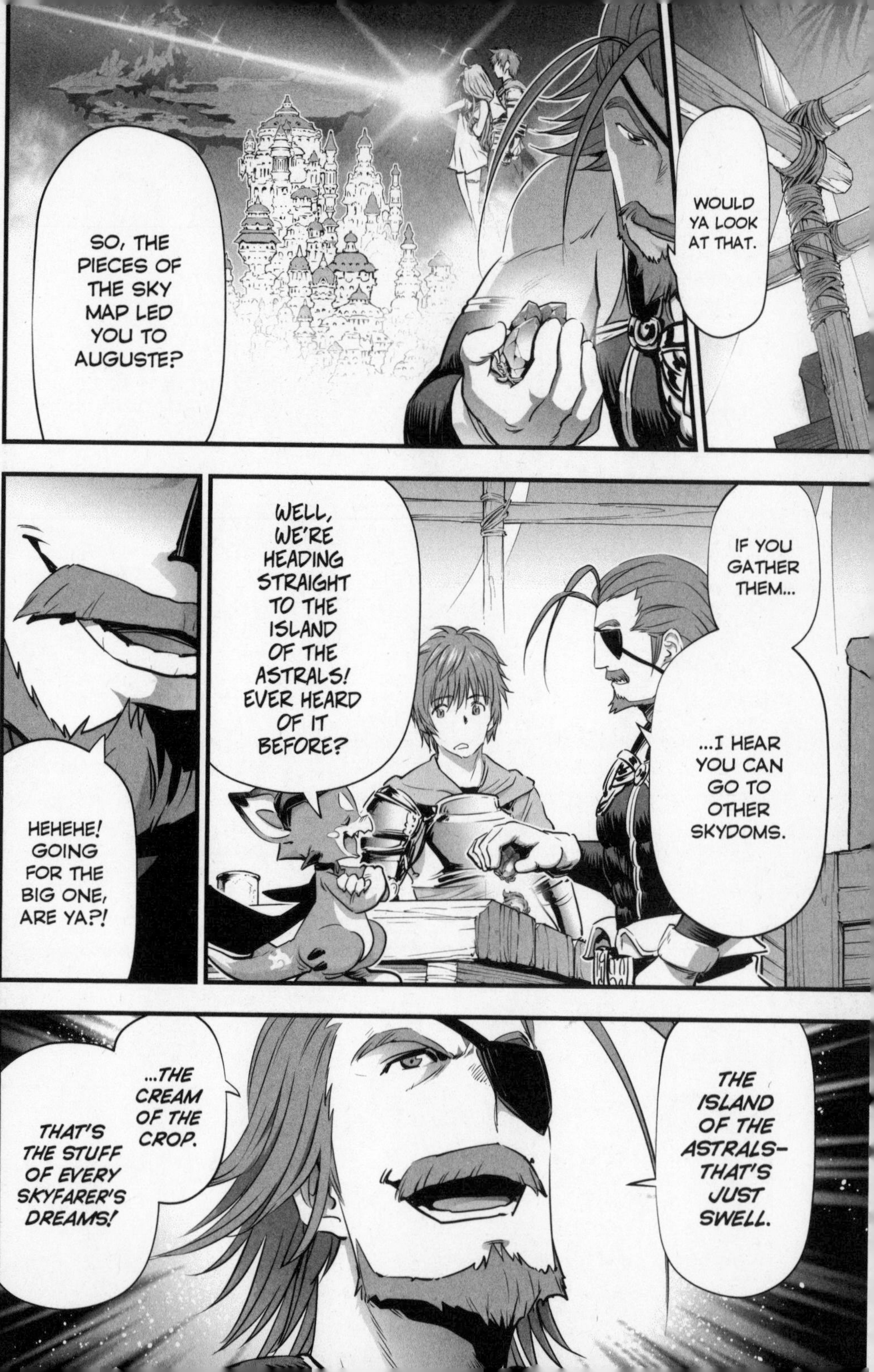

WOULD YA LOOK AT THAT.
SO, THE PIECES OF THE SKY MAP LED YOU TO AUGUSTE?
IF YOU GATHER THEM...
...I HEAR YOU CAN GO TO OTHER SKYDOMS.
WELL, WE'RE HEADING STRAIGHT TO THE ISLAND OF THE ASTRALS! EVER HEARD OF IT BEFORE?
HEHEHE! GOING FOR THE BIG ONE, ARE YA?!
THE ISLAND OF THE ASTRALS—THAT'S JUST SWELL.
...THE CREAM OF THE CROP.
THAT'S THE STUFF OF EVERY SKYFARER'S DREAMS!

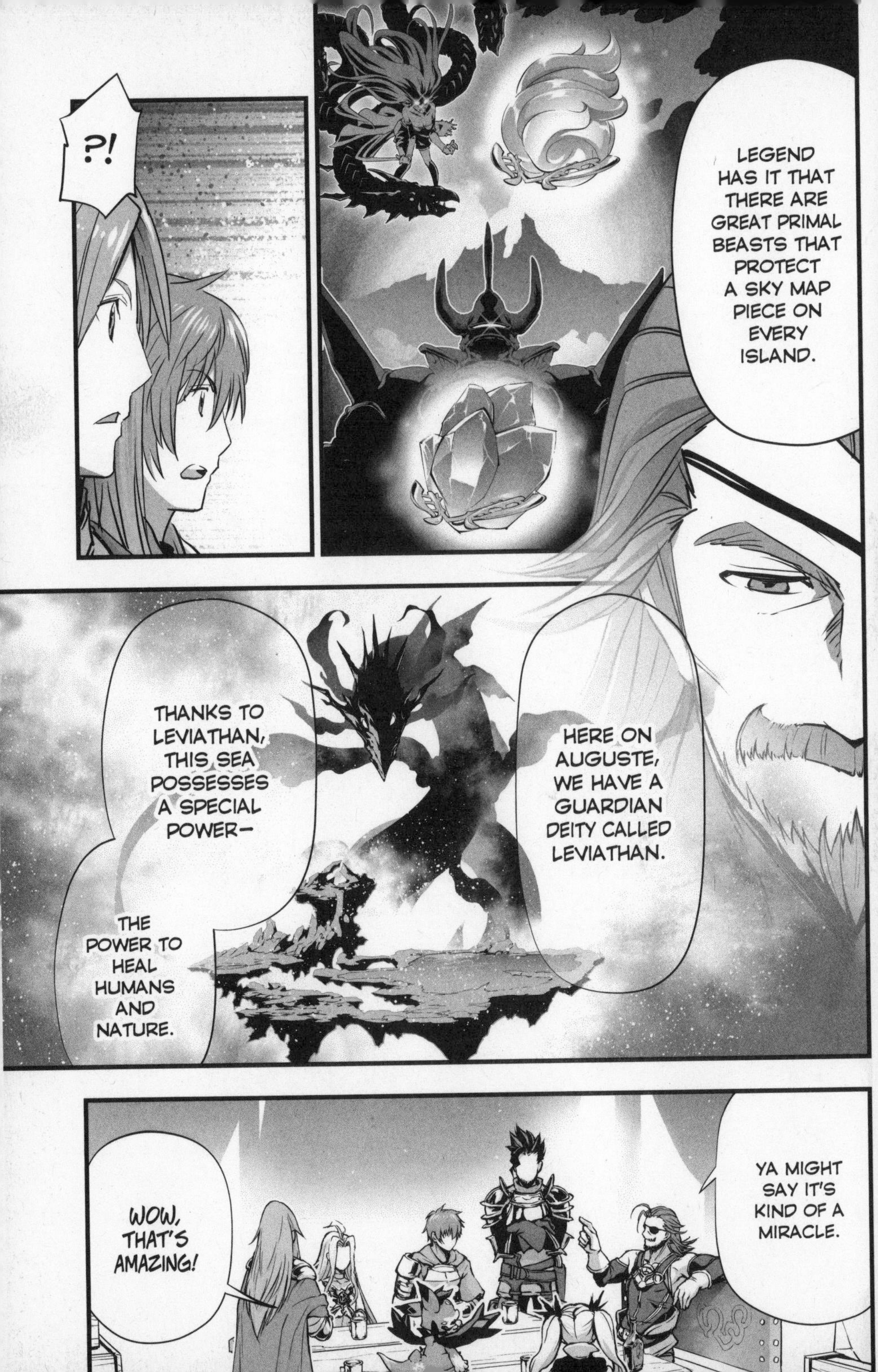
LEGEND HAS IT THAT THERE ARE GREAT PRIMAL BEASTS THAT PROTECT A SKY MAP PIECE ON EVERY ISLAND.
?!
HERE ON AUGUSTE, WE HAVE A GUARDIAN DEITY CALLED LEVIATHAN.
THANKS TO LEVIATHAN, THIS SEA POSSESSES A SPECIAL POWER—
THE POWER TO HEAL HUMANS AND NATURE.
YA MIGHT SAY IT'S KIND OF A MIRACLE.
WOW, THAT'S AMAZING!

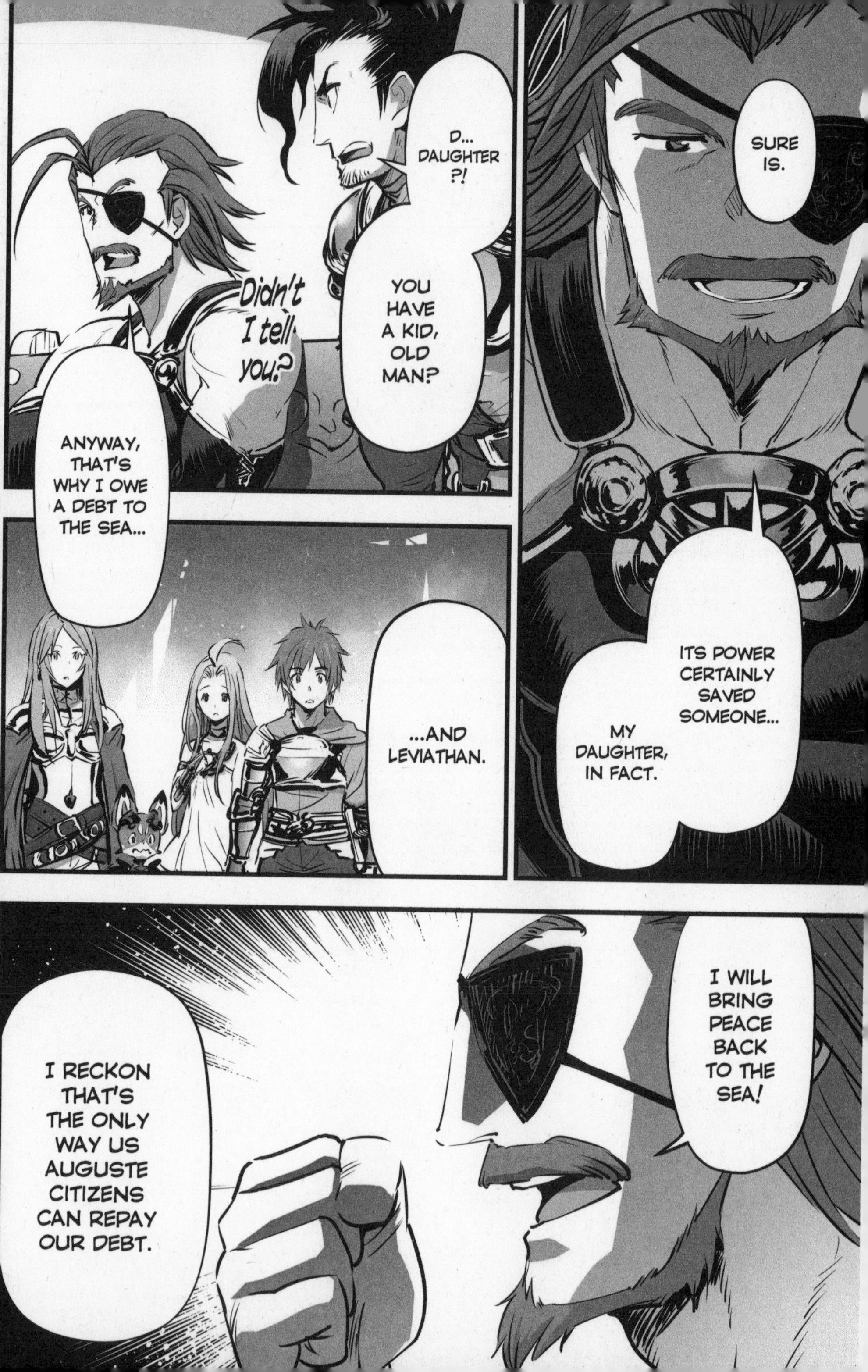
SURE IS.
ITS POWER CERTAINLY SAVED SOMEONE...
MY DAUGHTER, IN FACT.
D... DAUGHTER?!
YOU HAVE A KID, OLD MAN?
Didn't I tell you?
ANYWAY, THAT'S WHY I OWE A DEBT TO THE SEA...
...AND LEVIATHAN.
I WILL BRING PEACE BACK TO THE SEA!
I RECKON THAT'S THE ONLY WAY US AUGUSTE CITIZENS CAN REPAY OUR DEBT.

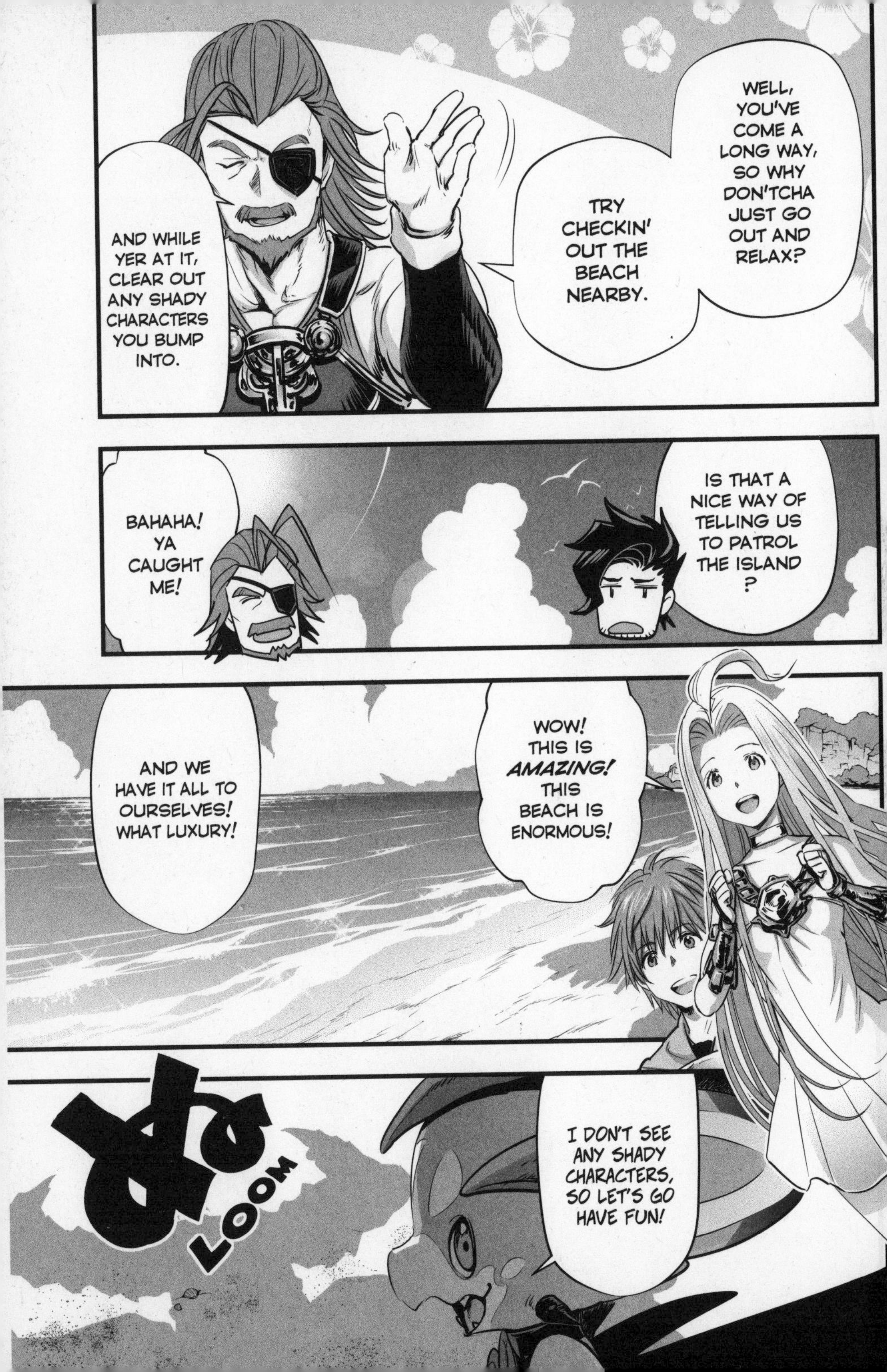
WELL, YOU'VE COME A LONG WAY, SO WHY DON'TCHA JUST GO OUT AND RELAX?
TRY CHECKIN' OUT THE BEACH NEARBY.
AND WHILE YER AT IT, CLEAR OUT ANY SHADY CHARACTERS YOU BUMP INTO.
IS THAT A NICE WAY OF TELLING US TO PATROL THE ISLAND?
BAHAHA! YA CAUGHT ME!
WOW! THIS IS *AMAZING!* THIS BEACH IS ENORMOUS!
AND WE HAVE IT ALL TO OURSELVES! WHAT LUXURY!
I DON'T SEE ANY SHADY CHARACTERS, SO LET'S GO HAVE FUN!
LOOM

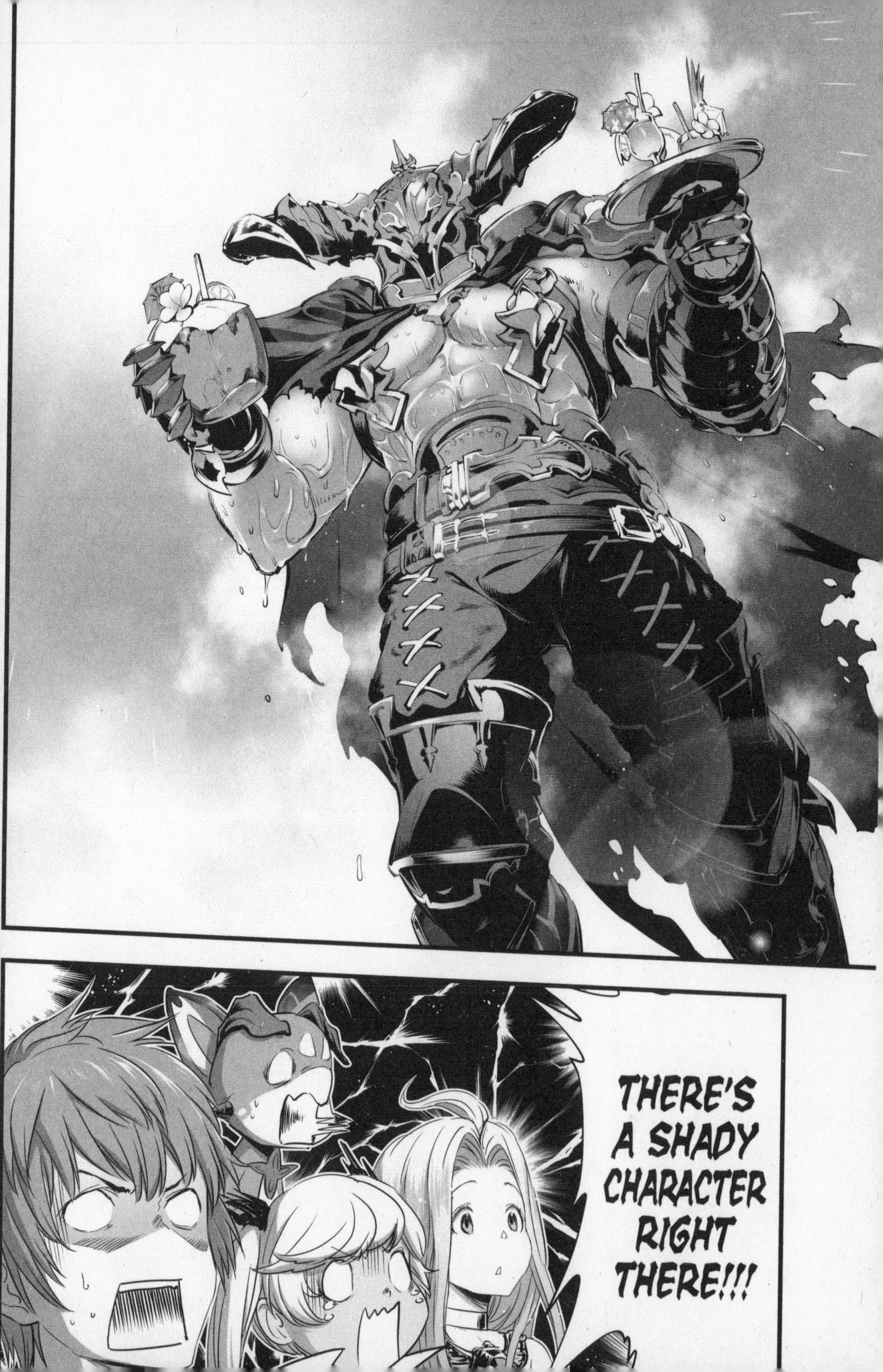
THERE'S A SHADY CHARACTER RIGHT THERE!!!

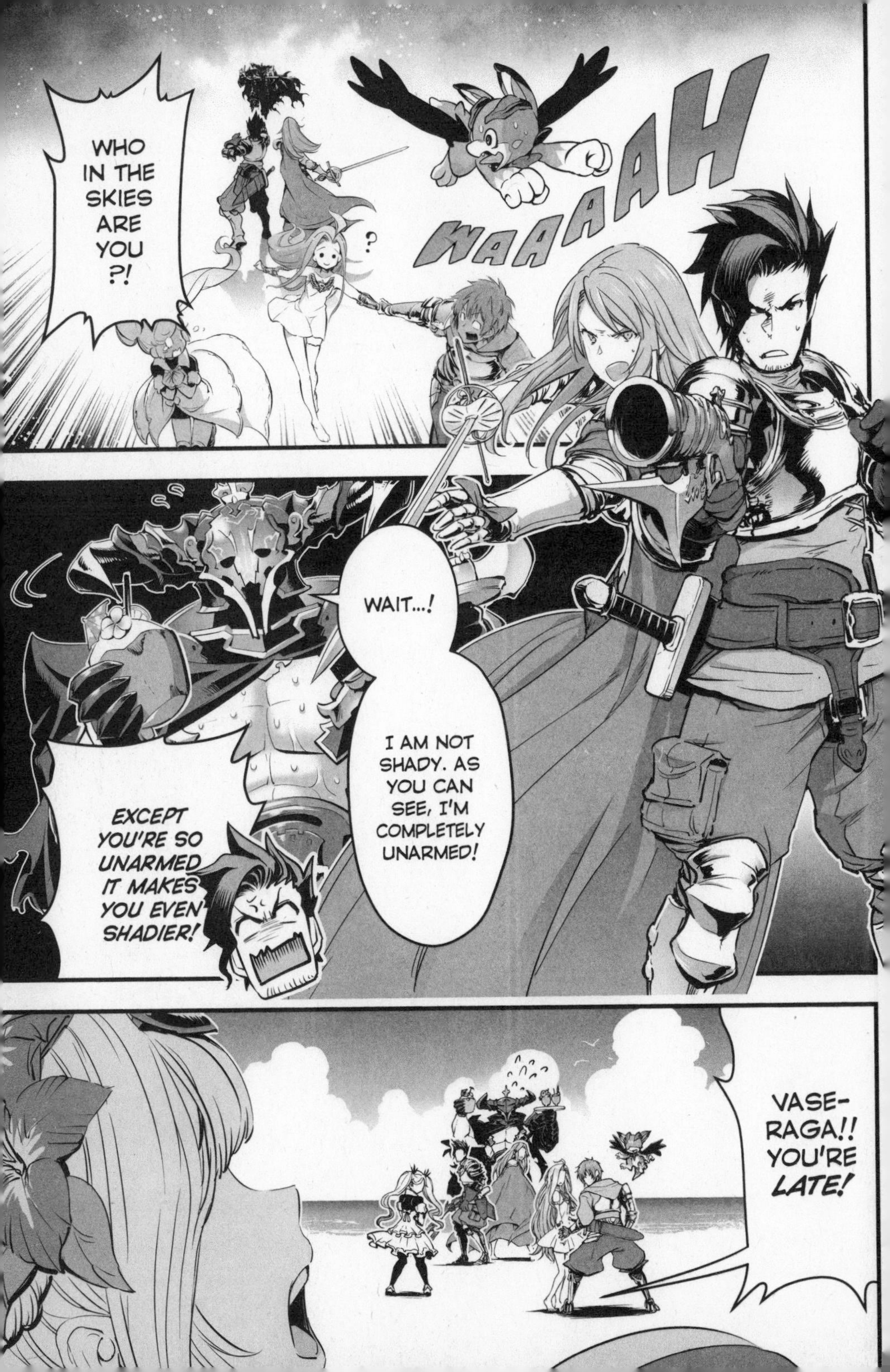
WAAAAAH
?
WHO IN THE SKIES ARE YOU ?!
WAIT...!
I AM NOT SHADY. AS YOU CAN SEE, I'M COMPLETELY UNARMED!
EXCEPT YOU'RE SO UNARMED IT MAKES YOU EVEN SHADIER!
VASE-RAGA!! YOU'RE LATE!

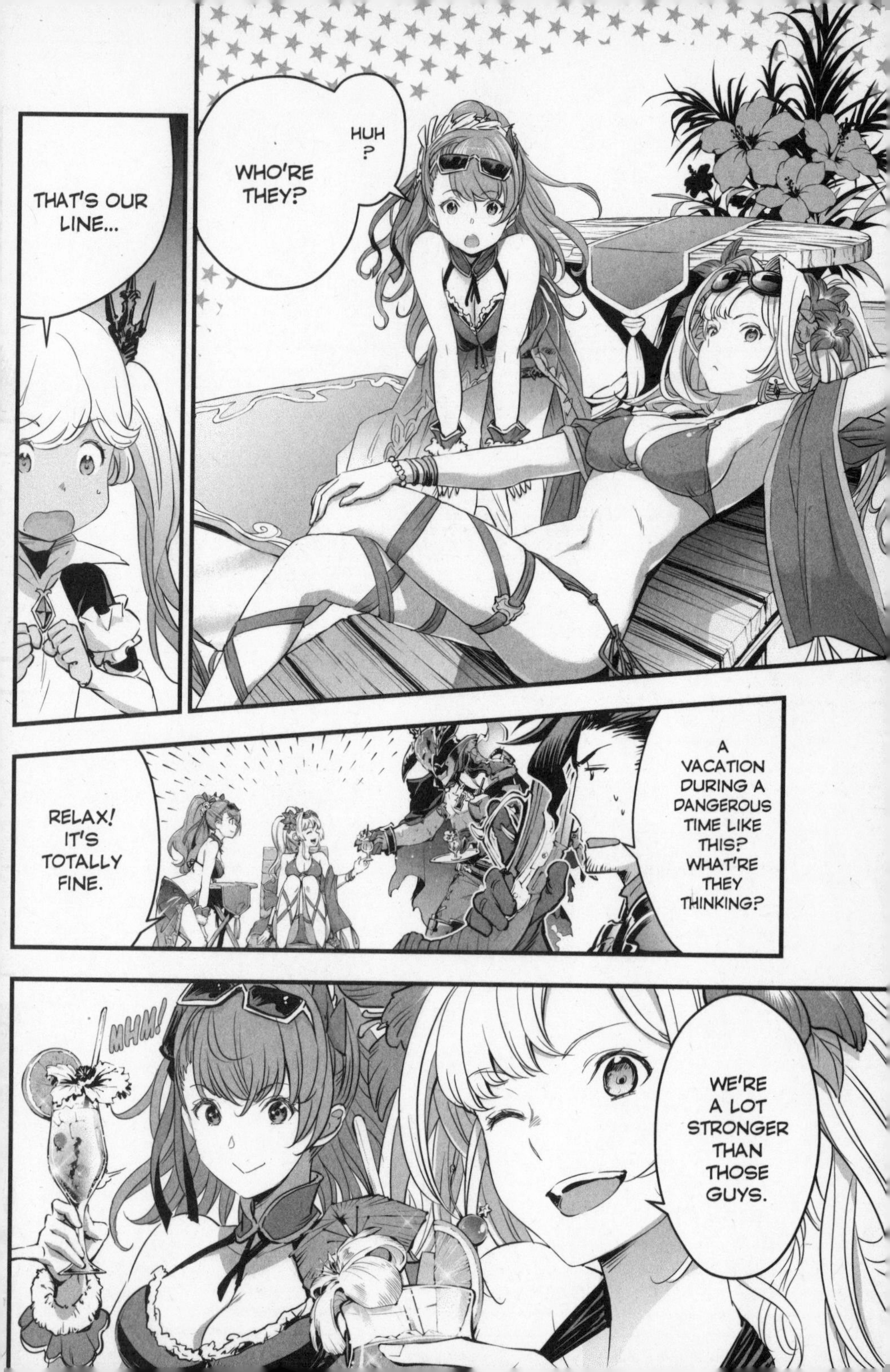
HUH?
WHO'RE THEY?
THAT'S OUR LINE...
A VACATION DURING A DANGEROUS TIME LIKE THIS? WHAT'RE THEY THINKING?
RELAX! IT'S TOTALLY FINE.
WE'RE A LOT STRONGER THAN THOSE GUYS.
MHM!

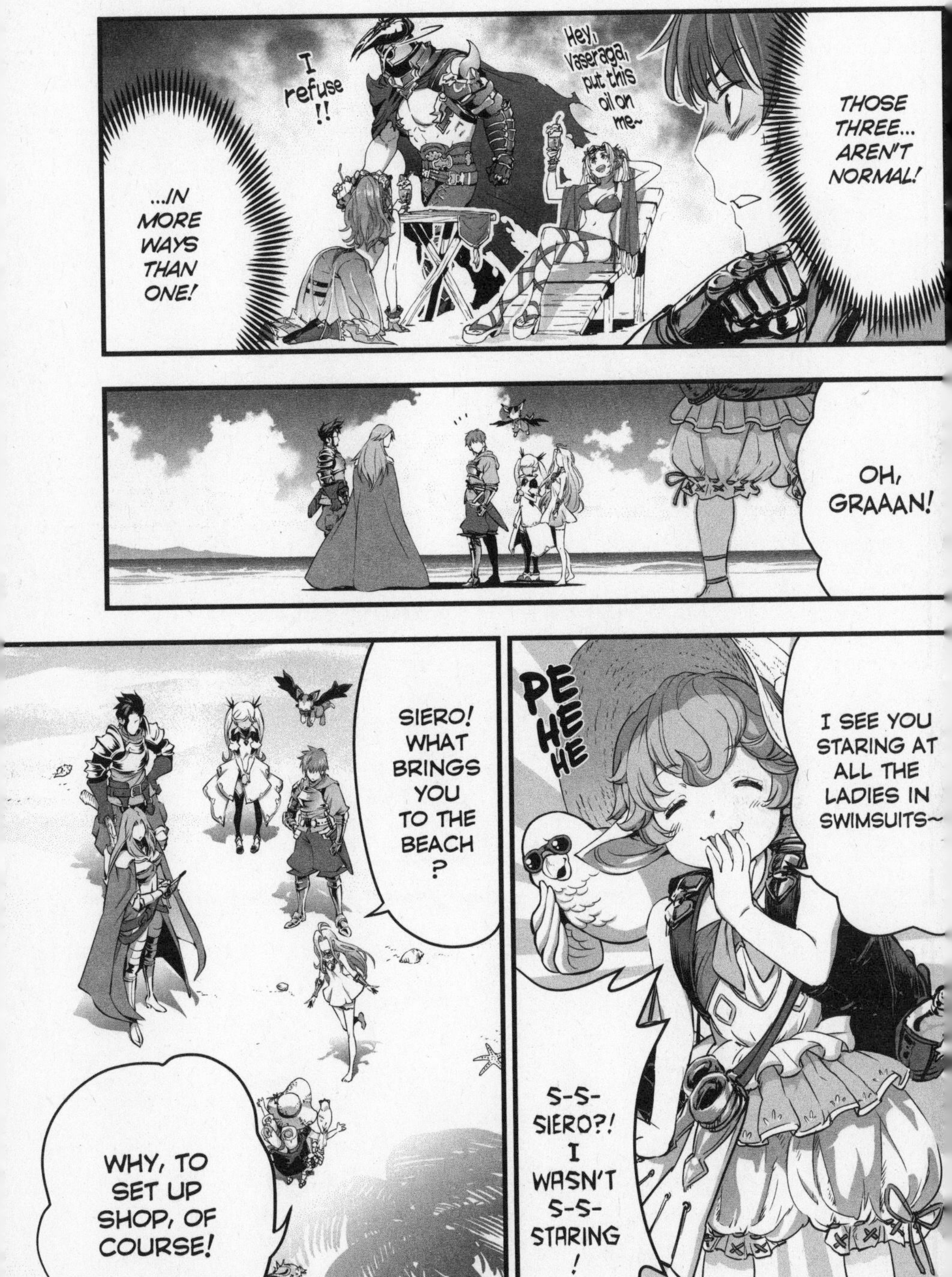
THOSE THREE... AREN'T NORMAL!
Hey, Vaseraga, put this oil on me~
I refuse!!
...IN MORE WAYS THAN ONE!
OH, GRAAAN!
I SEE YOU STARING AT ALL THE LADIES IN SWIMSUITS~
PEHEHEHE
S-S-SIERO?! I WASN'T S-S-STARING!
SIERO! WHAT BRINGS YOU TO THE BEACH?
WHY, TO SET UP SHOP, OF COURSE!

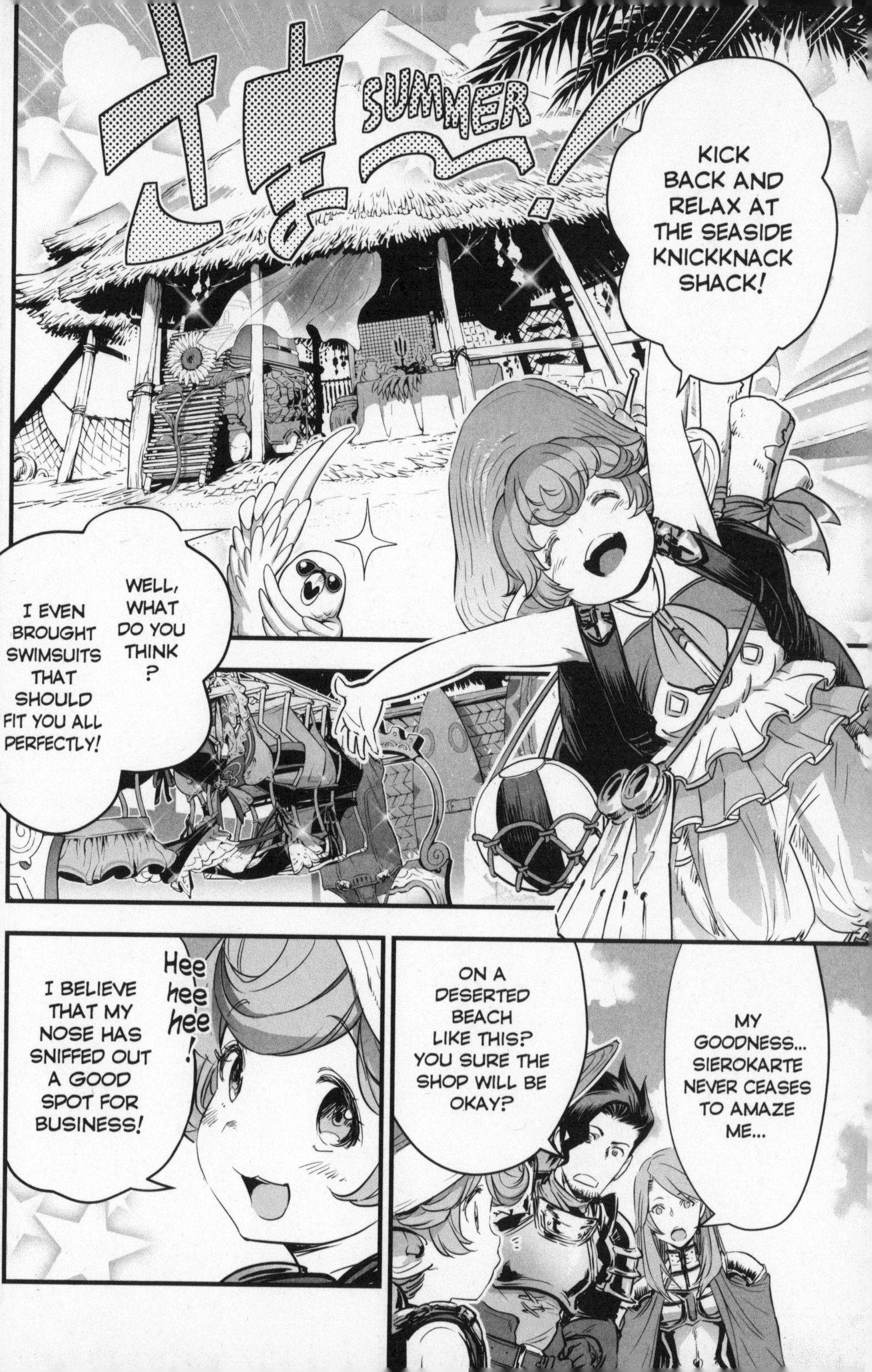
SUMMER
KICK BACK AND RELAX AT THE SEASIDE KNICKKNACK SHACK!
WELL, WHAT DO YOU THINK?
I EVEN BROUGHT SWIMSUITS THAT SHOULD FIT YOU ALL PERFECTLY!
MY GOODNESS... SIEROKARTE NEVER CEASES TO AMAZE ME...
ON A DESERTED BEACH LIKE THIS? YOU SURE THE SHOP WILL BE OKAY?
Hee hee hee!
I BELIEVE THAT MY NOSE HAS SNIFFED OUT A GOOD SPOT FOR BUSINESS!

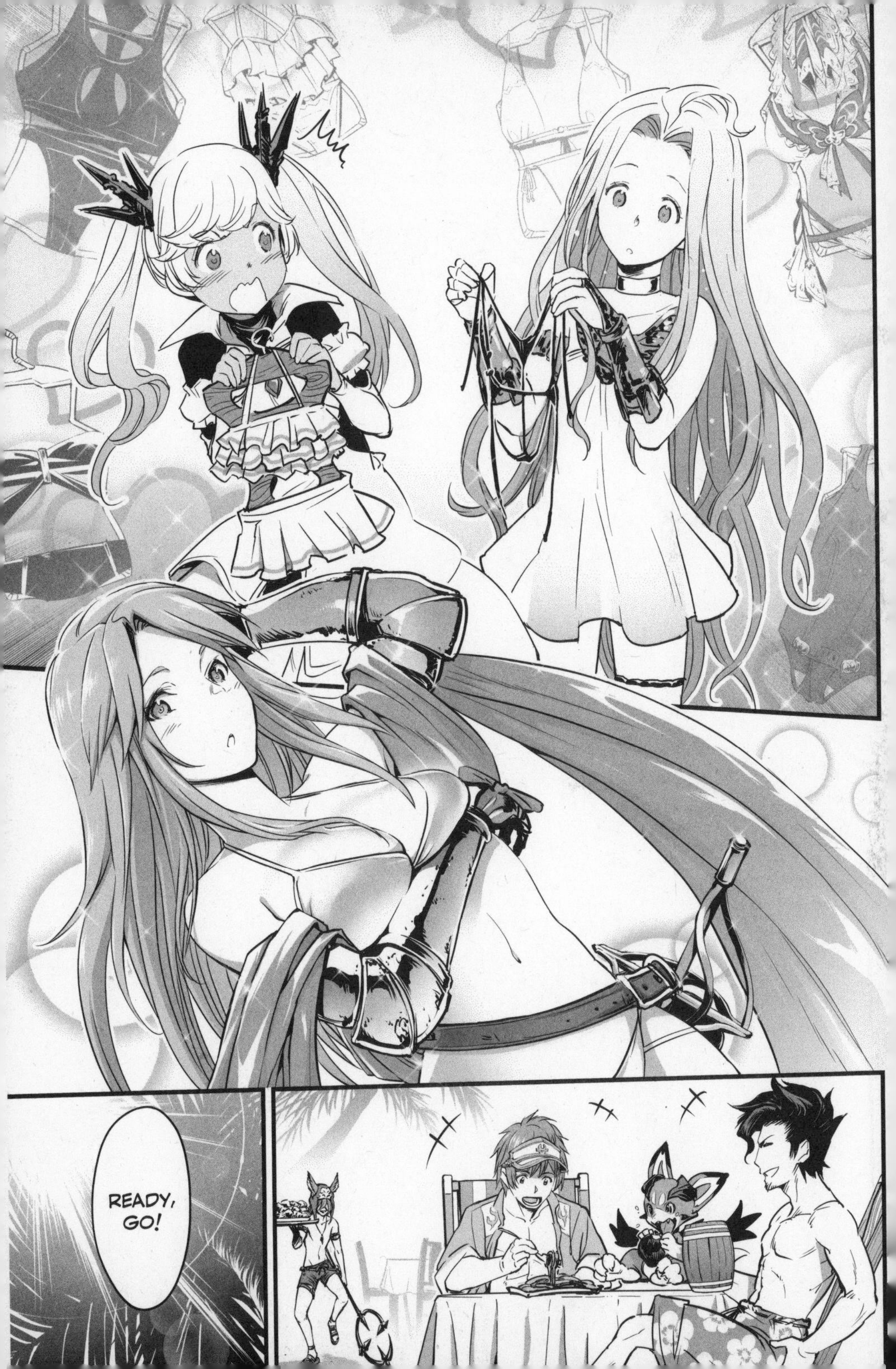
MM
READY, GO!

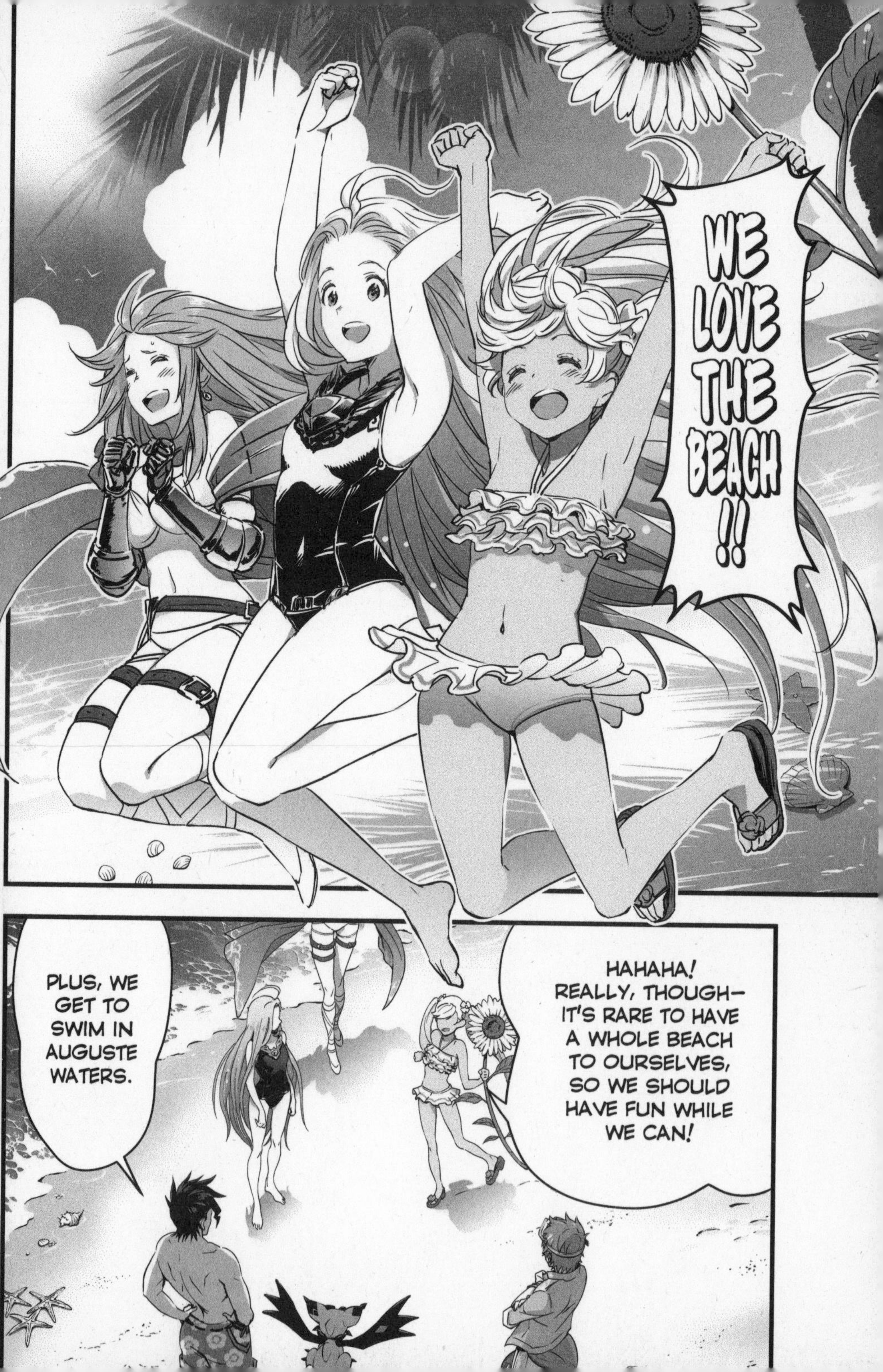
WE LOVE THE BEACH!!
HAHAHA! REALLY, THOUGH–IT'S RARE TO HAVE A WHOLE BEACH TO OURSELVES, SO WE SHOULD HAVE FUN WHILE WE CAN!
PLUS, WE GET TO SWIM IN AUGUSTE WATERS.

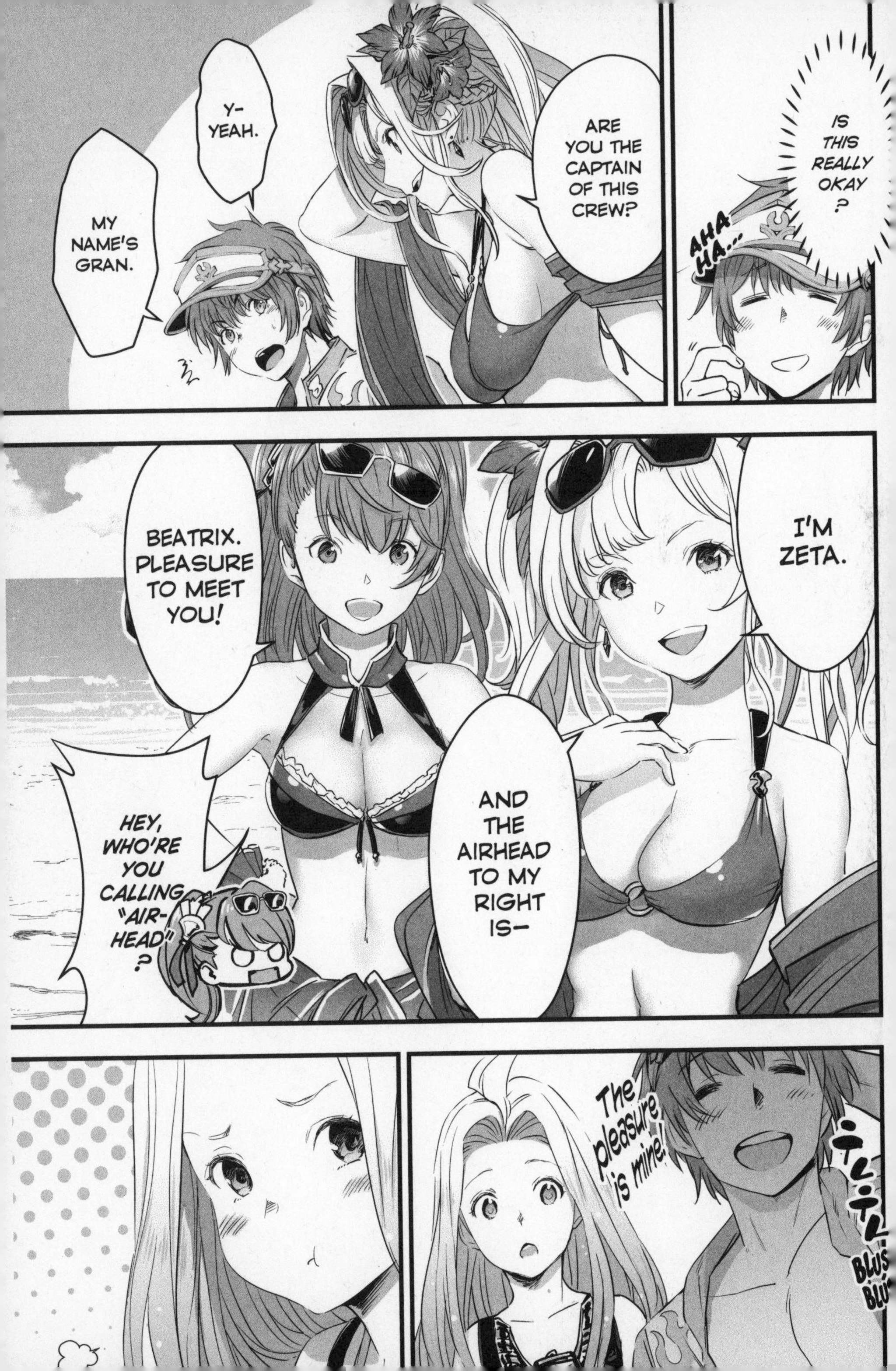
AHA HA...
IS THIS REALLY OKAY ?
ARE YOU THE CAPTAIN OF THIS CREW?
Y- YEAH.
MY NAME'S GRAN.
I'M ZETA.
AND THE AIRHEAD TO MY RIGHT IS—
BEATRIX. PLEASURE TO MEET YOU!
HEY, WHO'RE YOU CALLING "AIR-HEAD" ?
The pleasure is mine!
BLUS
BLU

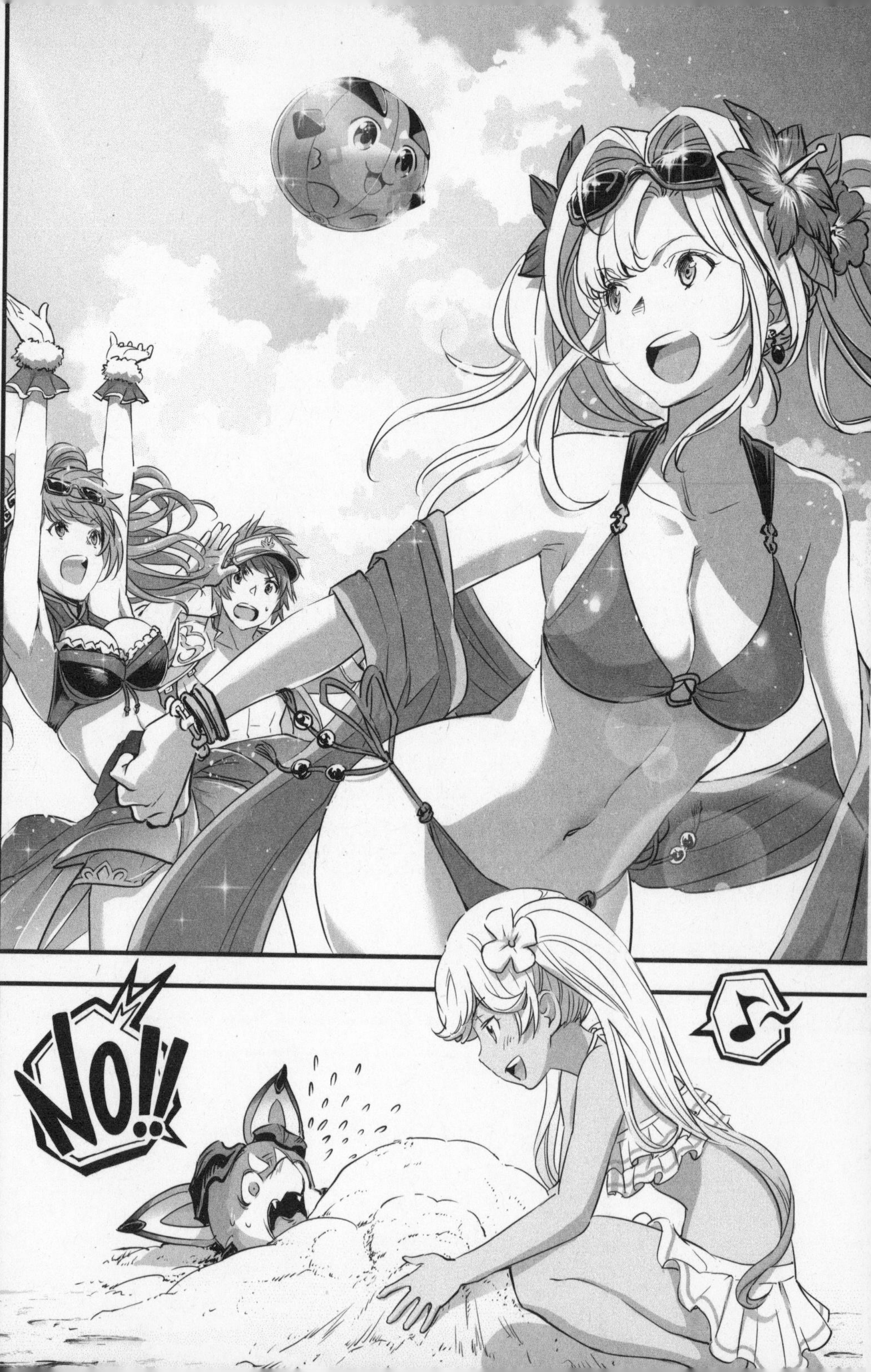
♪
NO!!

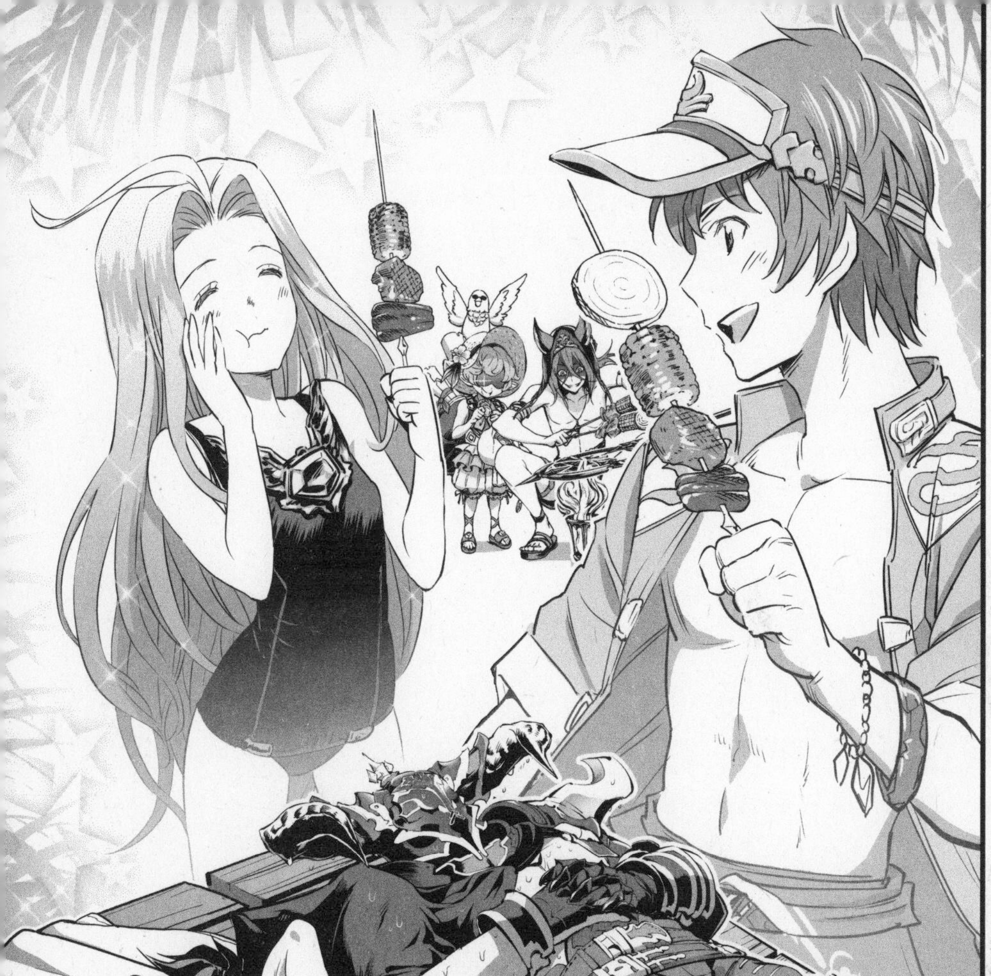

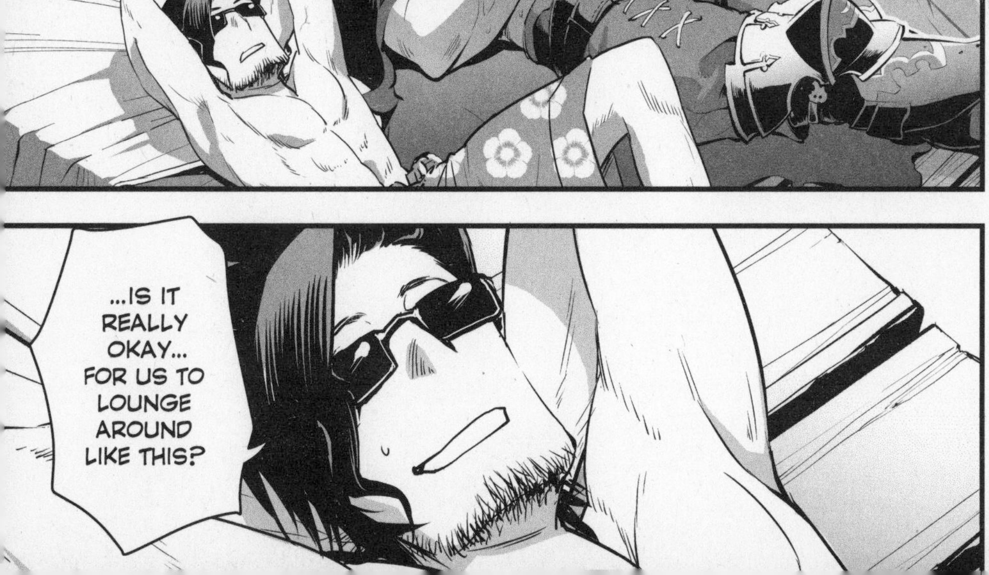
...IS IT REALLY OKAY... FOR US TO LOUNGE AROUND LIKE THIS?

GRANBLUE FANTASY
グランブルーファンタジー

CHAPTER 24: Auguste Isles (2)

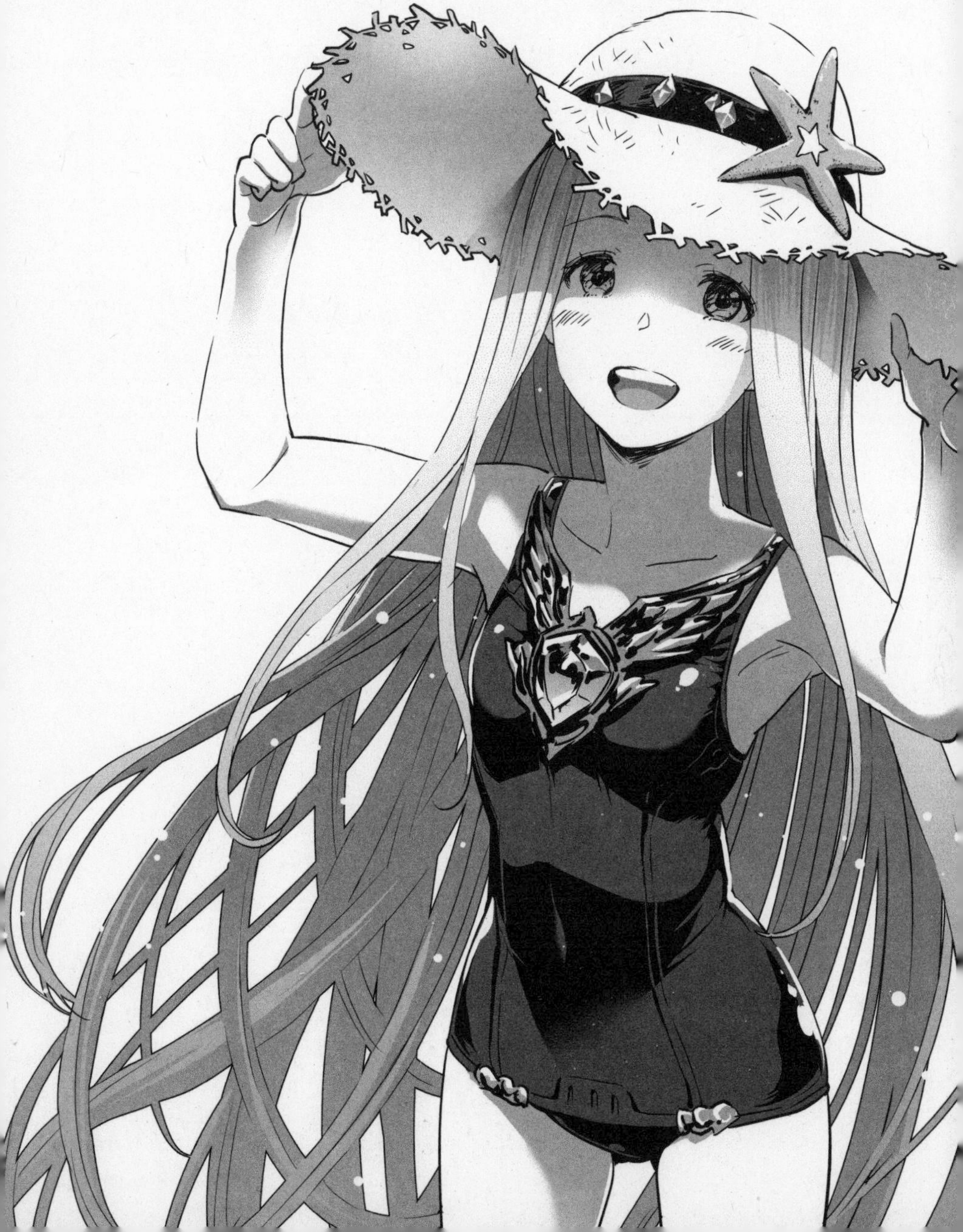

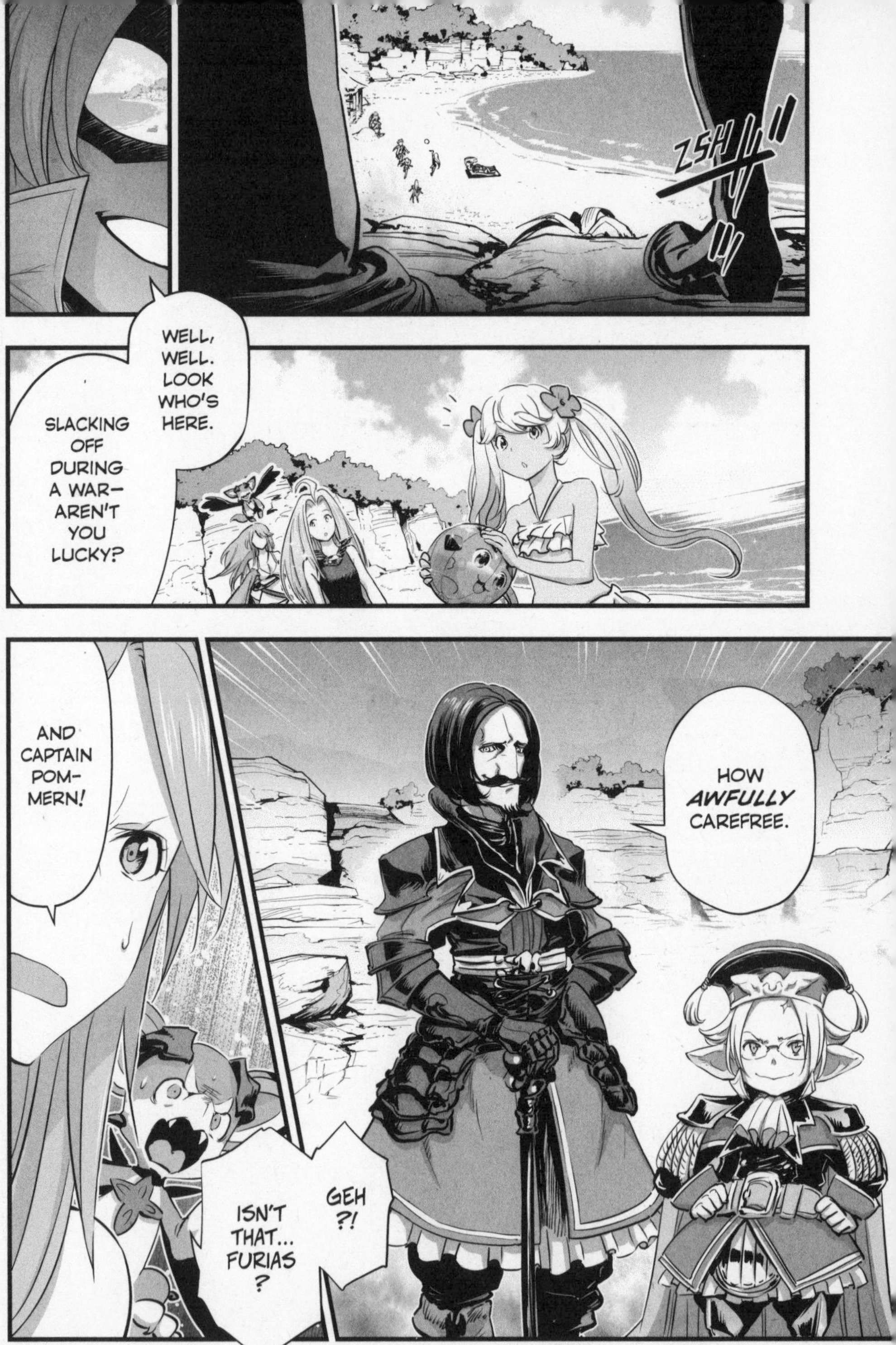
ZSH
WELL, WELL. LOOK WHO'S HERE.
SLACKING OFF DURING A WAR— AREN'T YOU LUCKY?
HOW *AWFULLY* CAREFREE.
AND CAPTAIN POM-MERN!
GEH?!
ISN'T THAT... FURIAS?

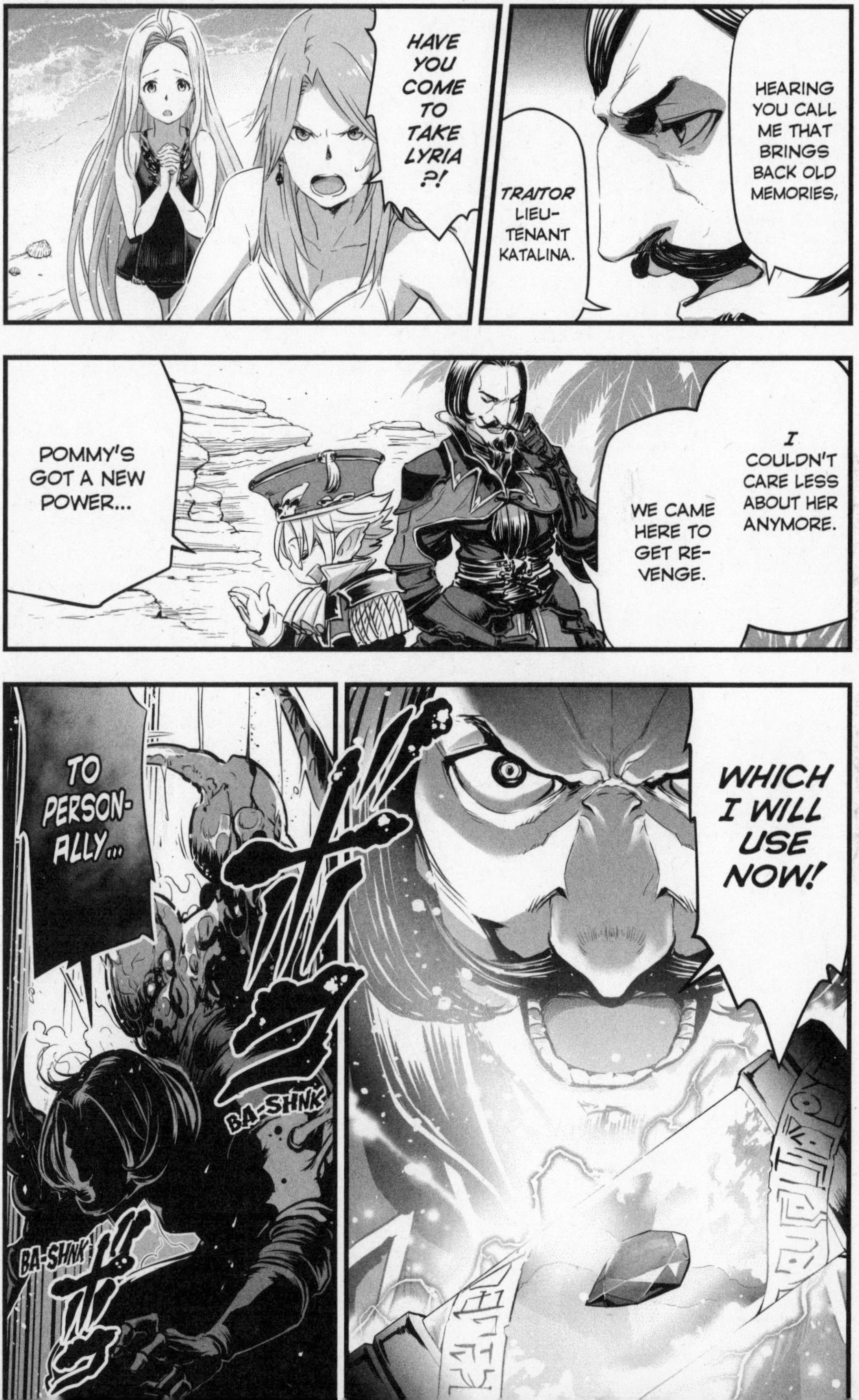
HEARING YOU CALL ME THAT BRINGS BACK OLD MEMORIES,
TRAITOR LIEUTENANT KATALINA.
HAVE YOU COME TO TAKE LYRIA ?!
I COULDN'T CARE LESS ABOUT HER ANYMORE.
WE CAME HERE TO GET REVENGE.
POMMY'S GOT A NEW POWER...
WHICH I WILL USE NOW!
TO PERSONALLY...
BA-SHNK
BA-SHNK!!

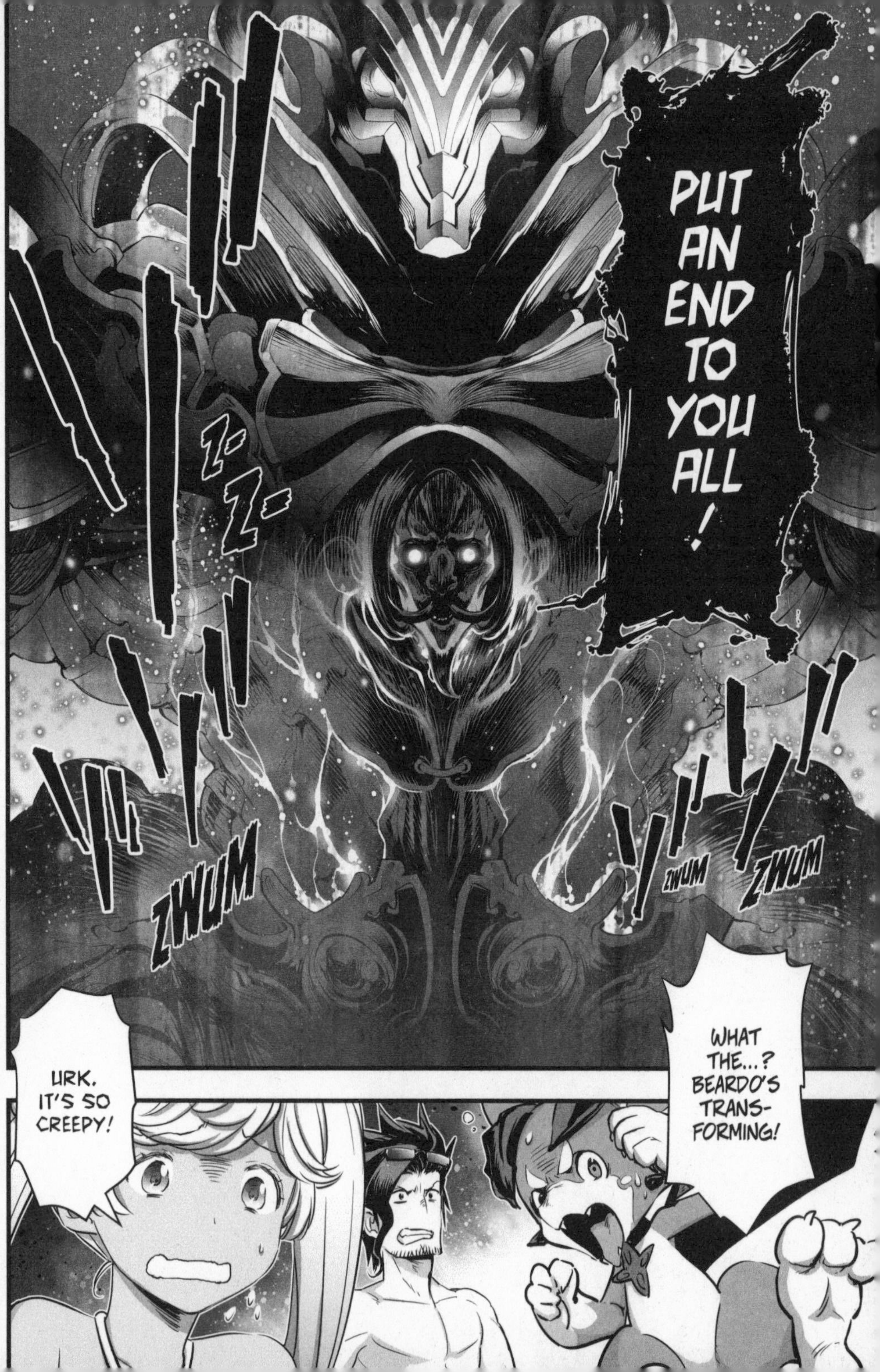
PUT AN END TO YOU ALL!
ZWUM
ZWUM
Z-Z-
ZWUM
WHAT THE...? BEARDO'S TRANS-FORMING!
URK. IT'S SO CREEPY!

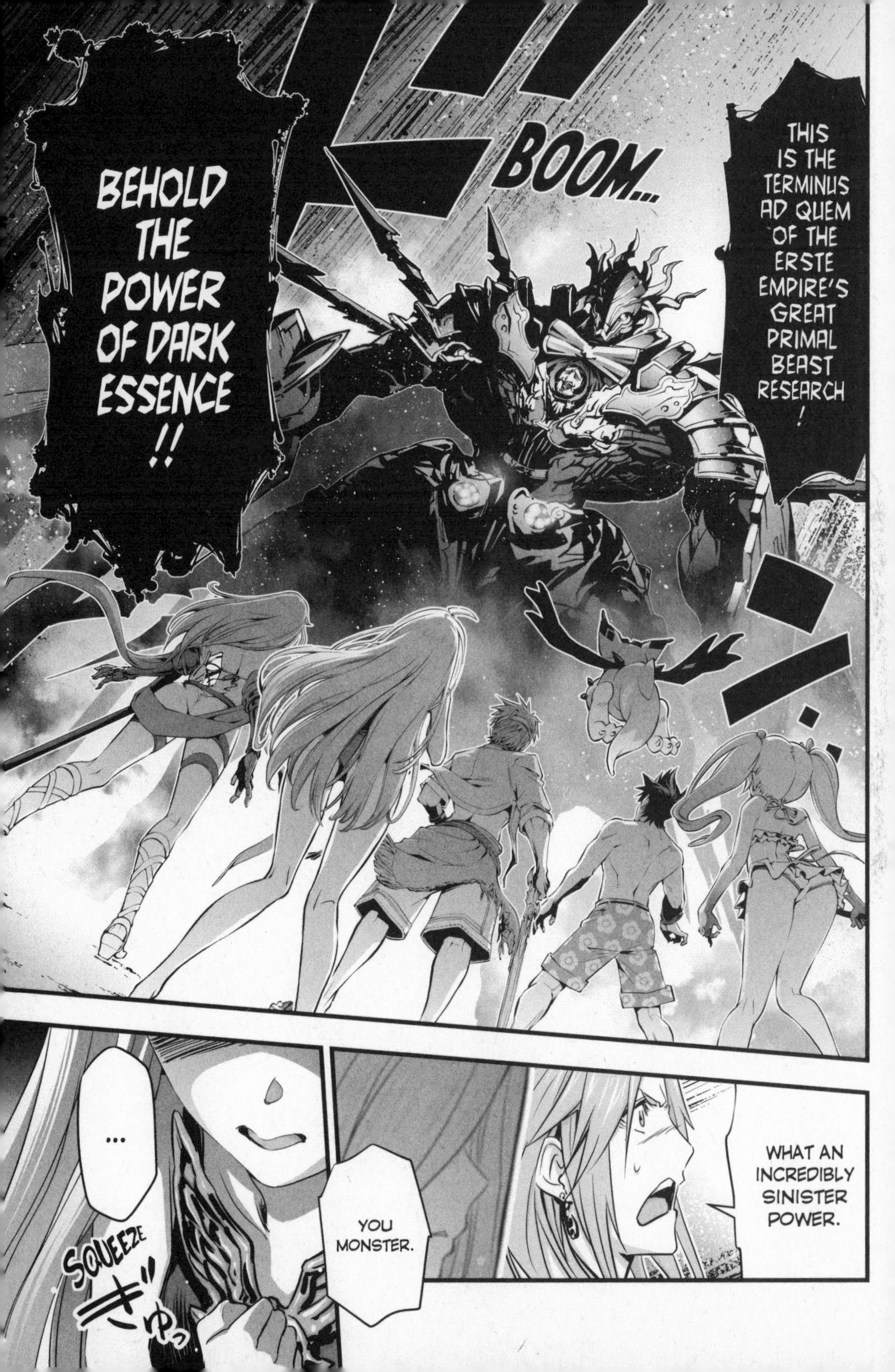

THIS IS THE TERMINUS AD QUEM OF THE ERSTE EMPIRE'S GREAT PRIMAL BEAST RESEARCH!
BOOM...
BEHOLD THE POWER OF DARK ESSENCE!!
WHAT AN INCREDIBLY SINISTER POWER.
...
YOU MONSTER.
SQUEEZE

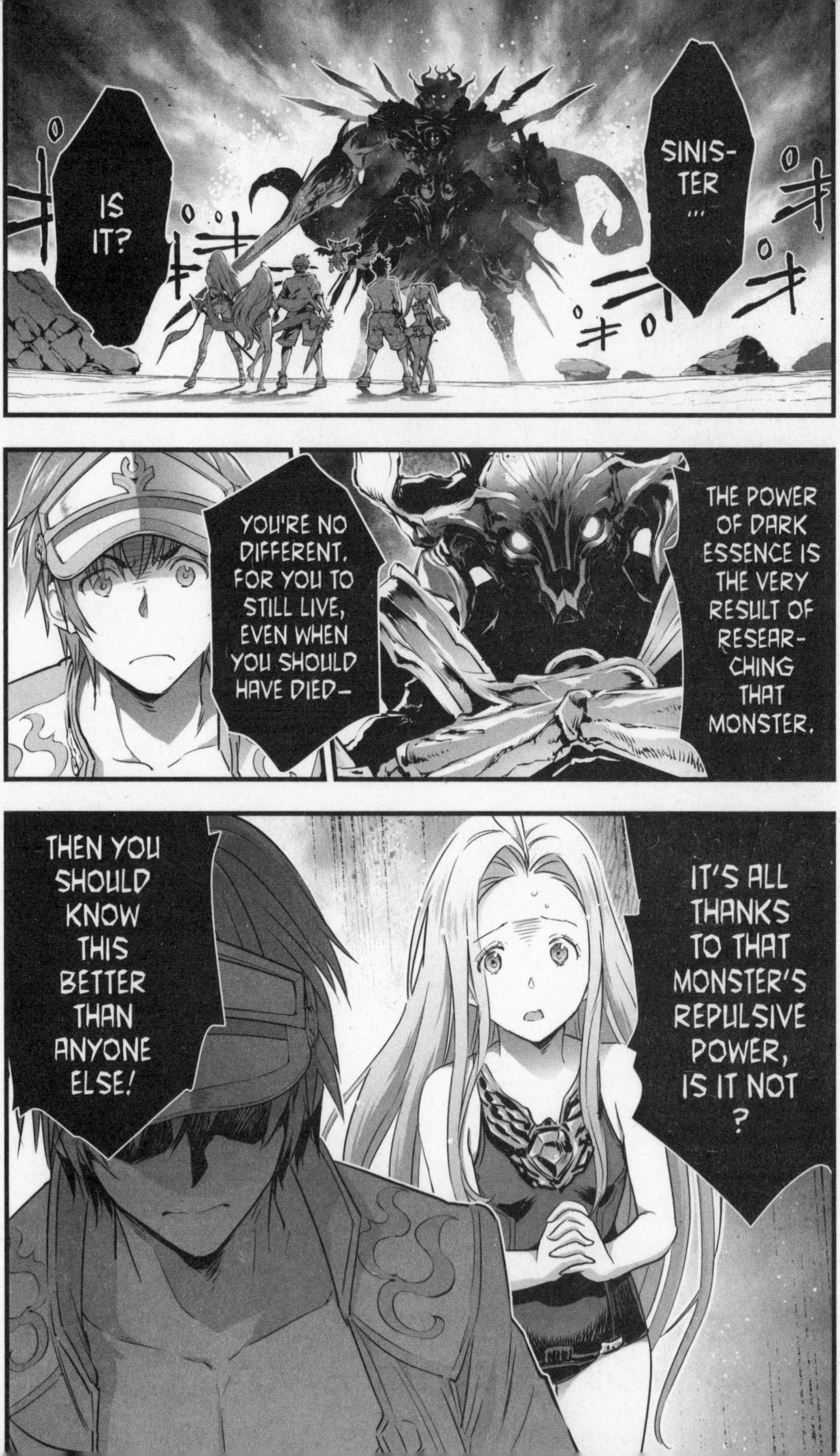
SINIS-TER...
IS IT?
THE POWER OF DARK ESSENCE IS THE VERY RESULT OF RESEAR-CHING THAT MONSTER.
YOU'RE NO DIFFERENT. FOR YOU TO STILL LIVE, EVEN WHEN YOU SHOULD HAVE DIED—
IT'S ALL THANKS TO THAT MONSTER'S REPULSIVE POWER, IS IT NOT?
—THEN YOU SHOULD KNOW THIS BETTER THAN ANYONE ELSE!

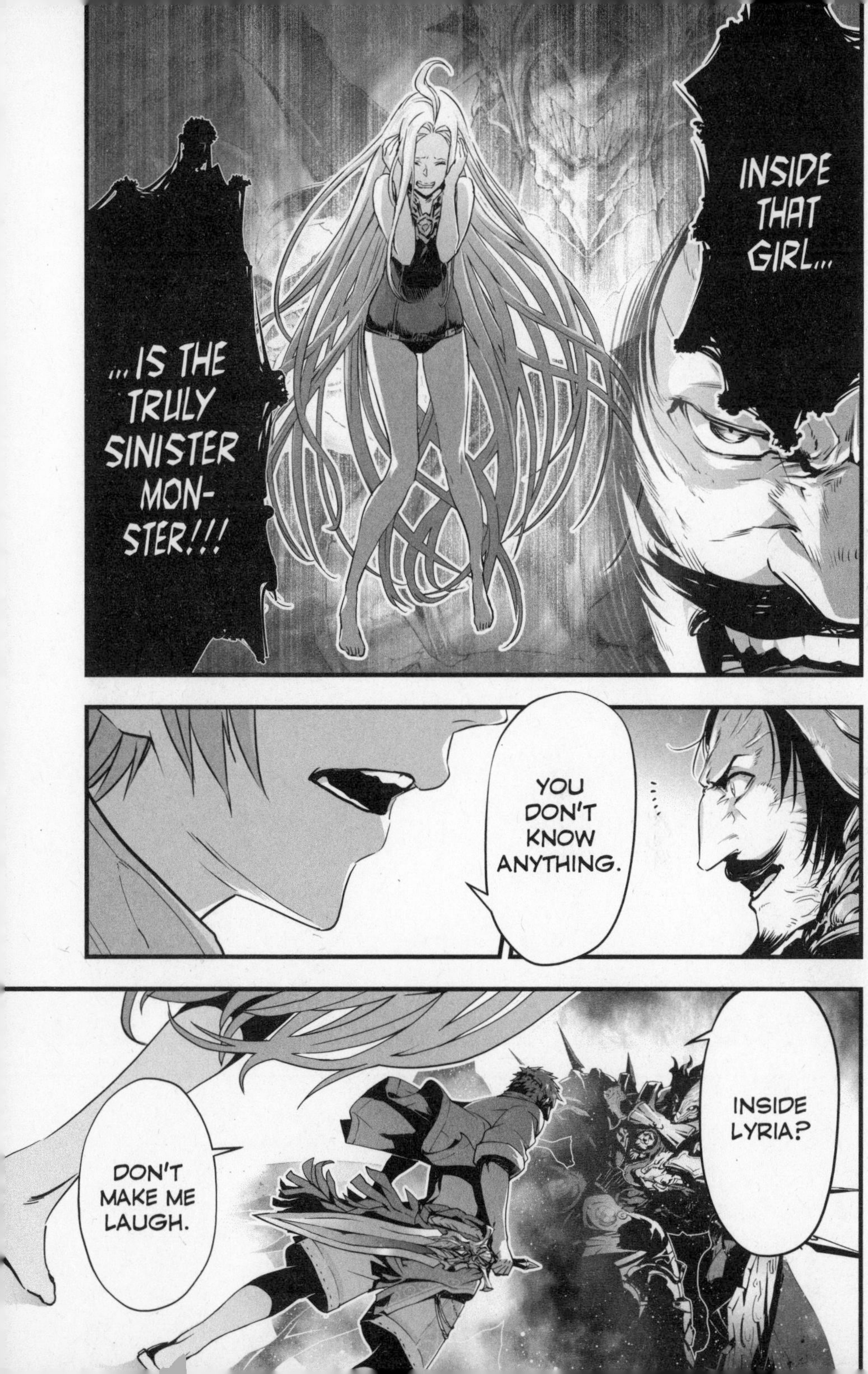
INSIDE THAT GIRL...
...IS THE TRULY SINISTER MON-STER!!!
...
YOU DON'T KNOW ANYTHING.
INSIDE LYRIA?
DON'T MAKE ME LAUGH.

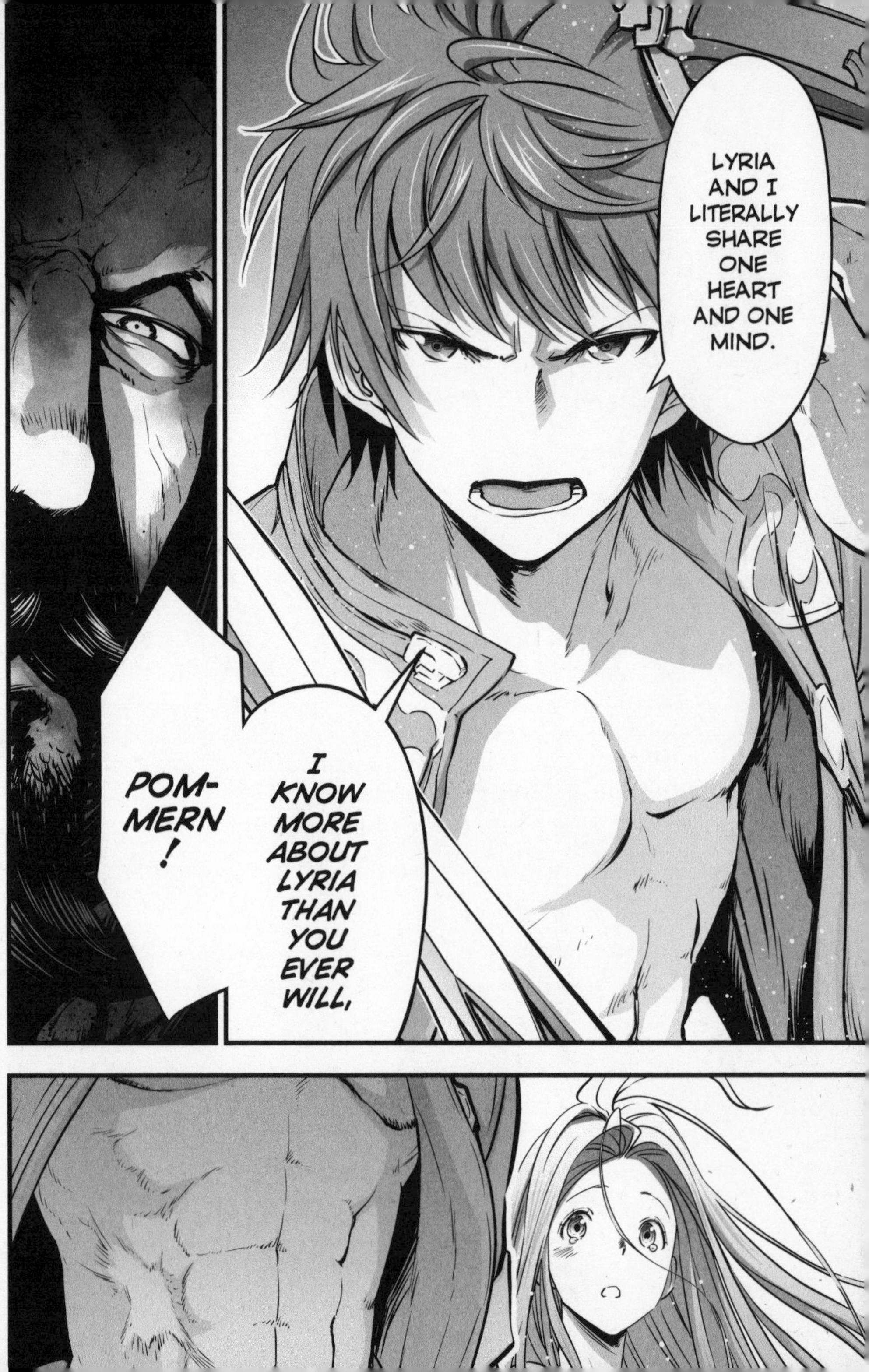
LYRIA AND I LITERALLY SHARE ONE HEART AND ONE MIND.
I KNOW MORE ABOUT LYRIA THAN YOU EVER WILL,
POM-MERN!

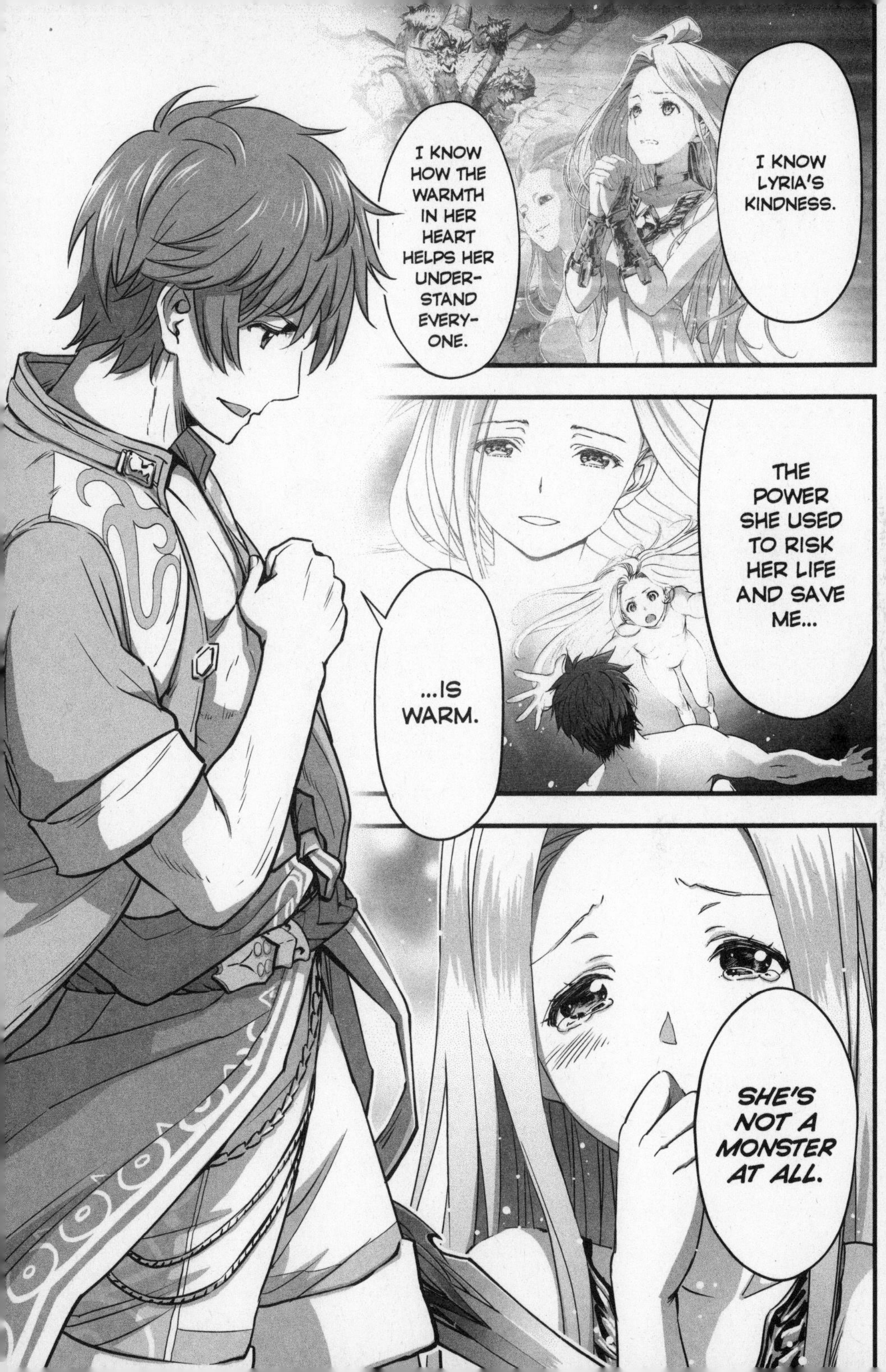
I KNOW LYRIA'S KINDNESS.
I KNOW HOW THE WARMTH IN HER HEART HELPS HER UNDER-STAND EVERY-ONE.
THE POWER SHE USED TO RISK HER LIFE AND SAVE ME...
...IS WARM.
SHE'S NOT A MONSTER AT ALL.

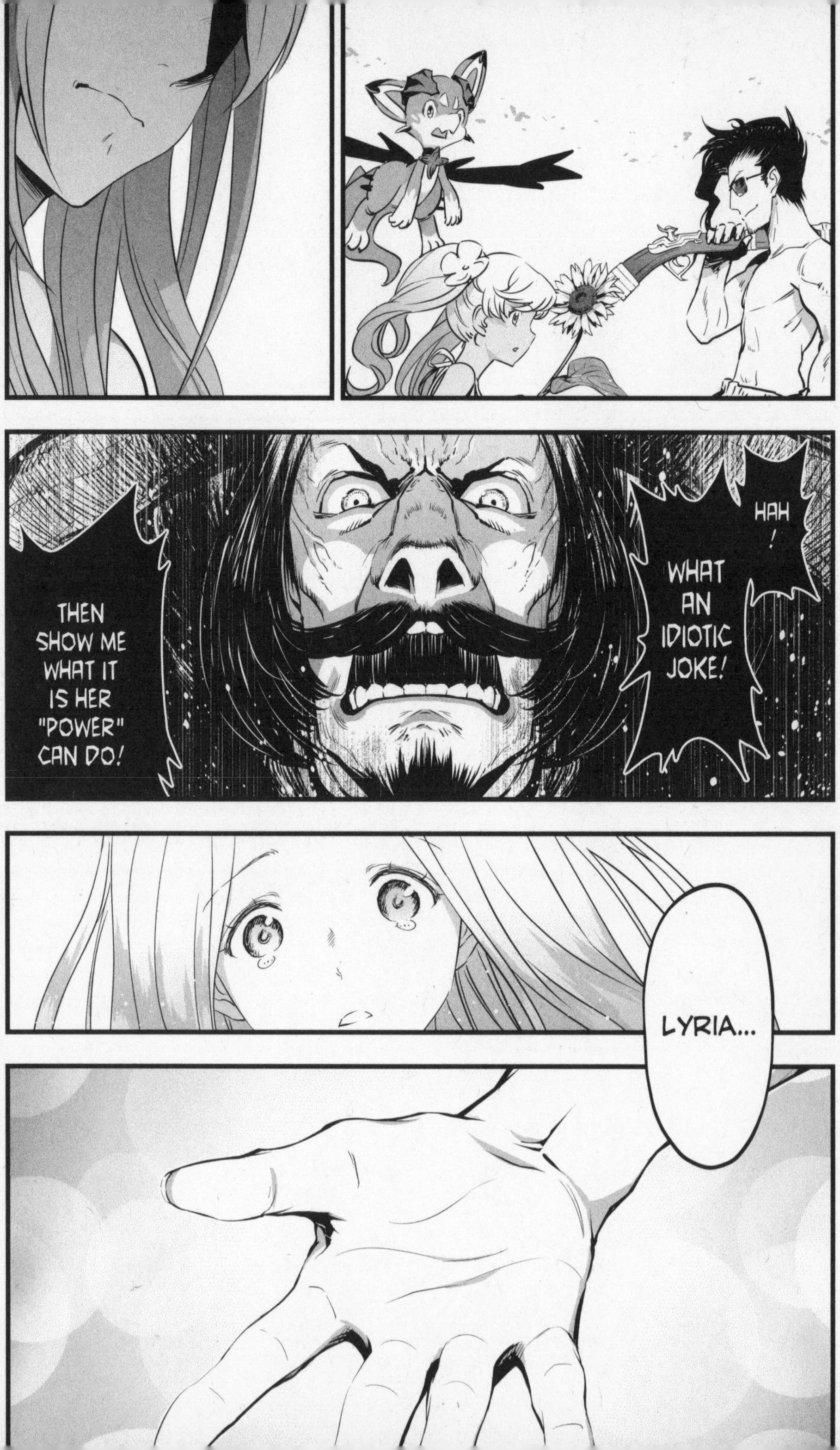
HAH!
WHAT AN IDIOTIC JOKE!
THEN SHOW ME WHAT IT IS HER "POWER" CAN DO!
LYRIA...

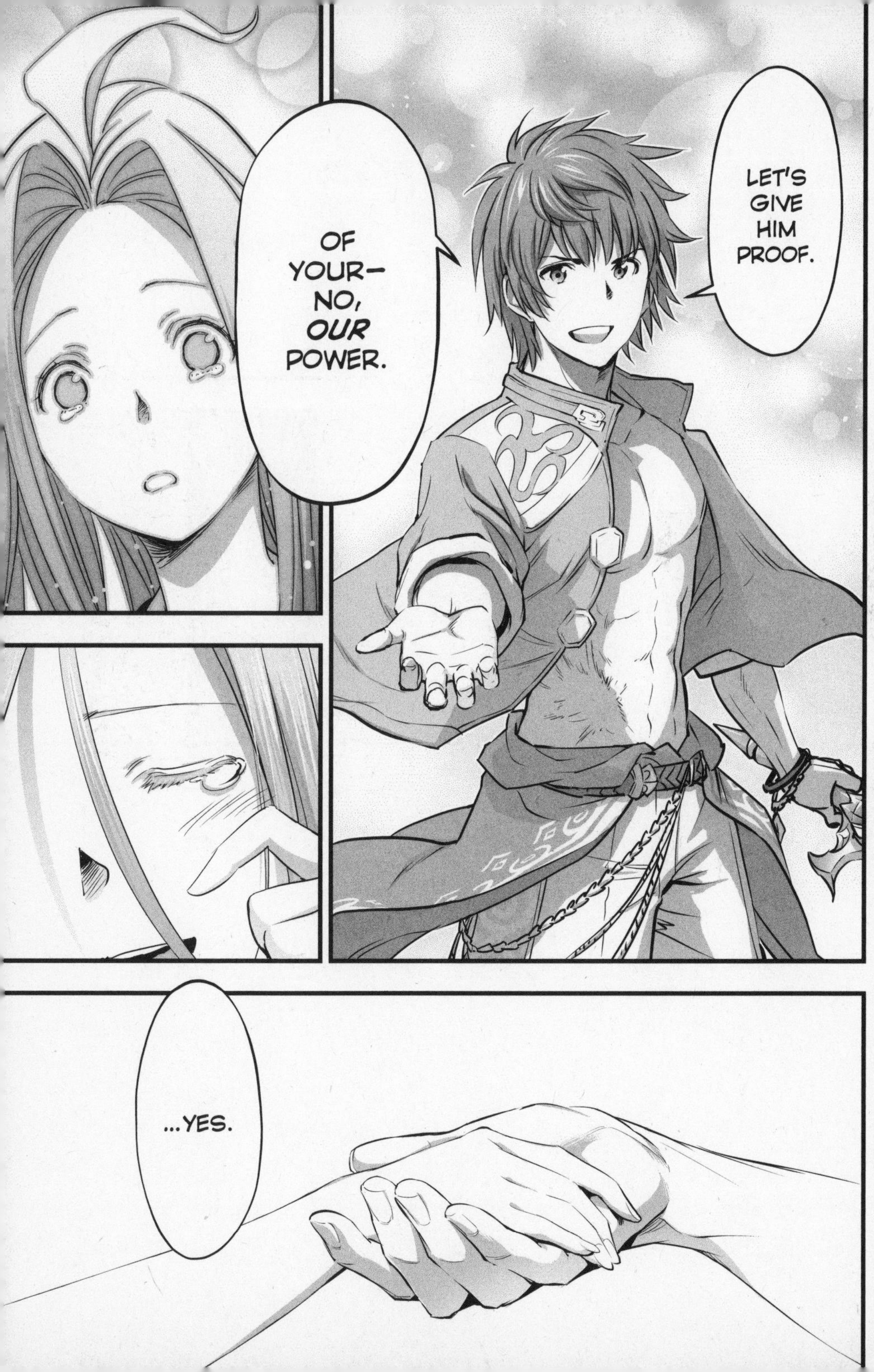
LET'S GIVE HIM PROOF.
OF YOUR— NO, ***OUR*** POWER.
...YES.

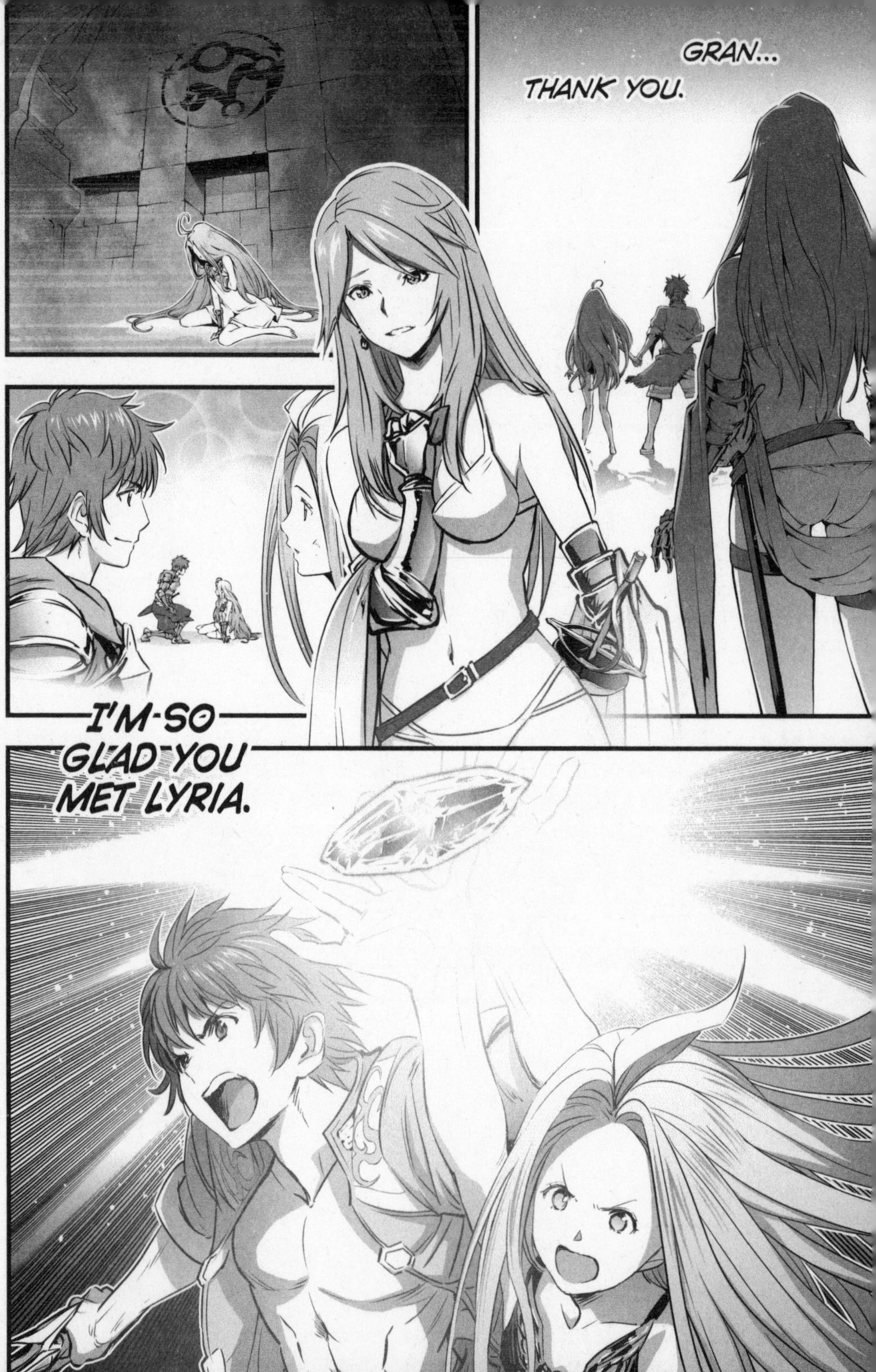
GRAN... THANK YOU.
I'M SO GLAD YOU MET LYRIA.

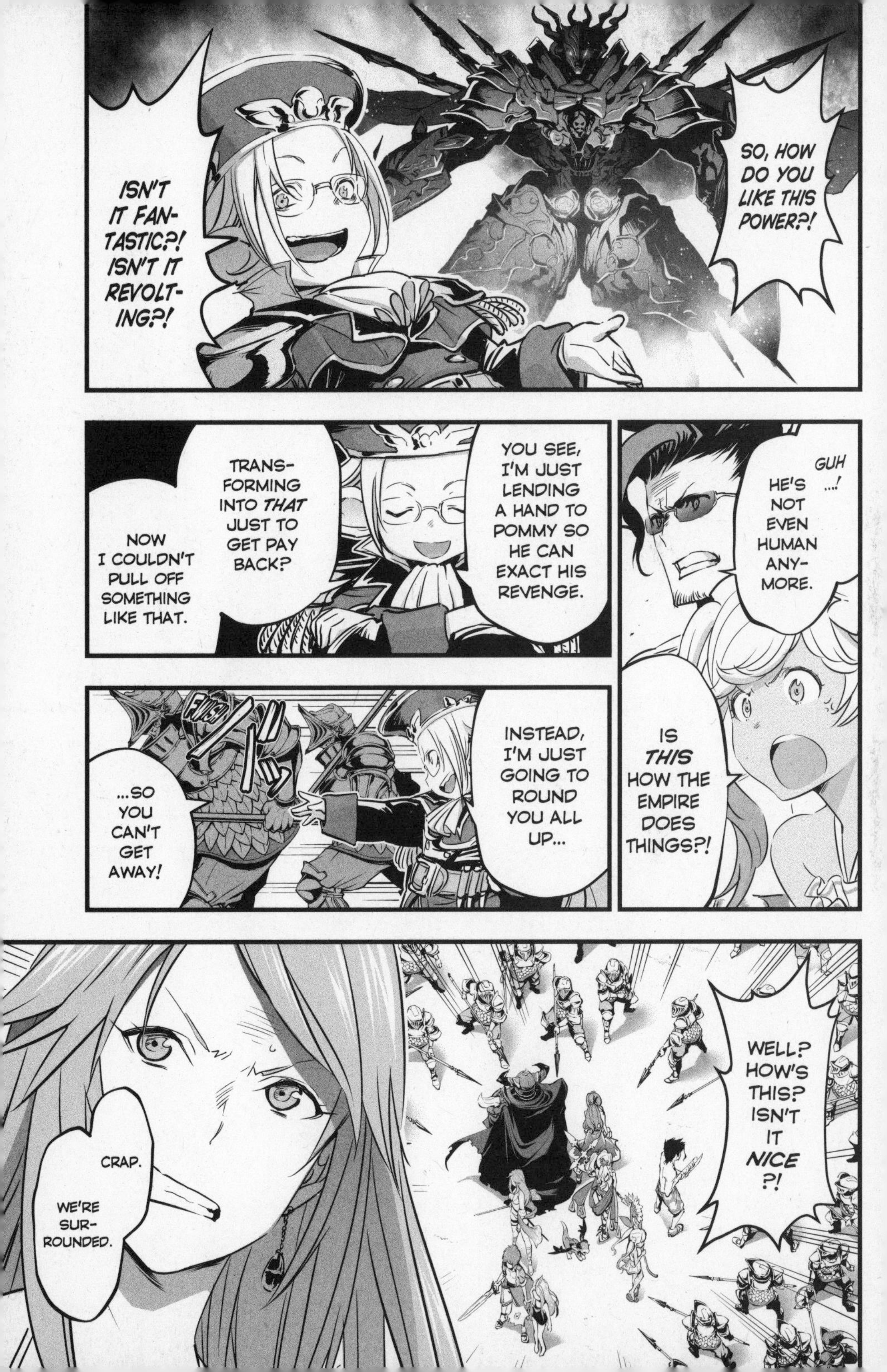
SO, HOW DO YOU LIKE THIS POWER?!
ISN'T IT FANTASTIC?! ISN'T IT REVOLTING?!
GUH ...!
HE'S NOT EVEN HUMAN ANYMORE.
IS THIS HOW THE EMPIRE DOES THINGS?!
YOU SEE, I'M JUST LENDING A HAND TO POMMY SO HE CAN EXACT HIS REVENGE.
TRANSFORMING INTO THAT JUST TO GET PAY BACK?
NOW I COULDN'T PULL OFF SOMETHING LIKE THAT.
FWISH
INSTEAD, I'M JUST GOING TO ROUND YOU ALL UP...
...SO YOU CAN'T GET AWAY!
WELL? HOW'S THIS? ISN'T IT NICE?!
CRAP.
WE'RE SURROUNDED.

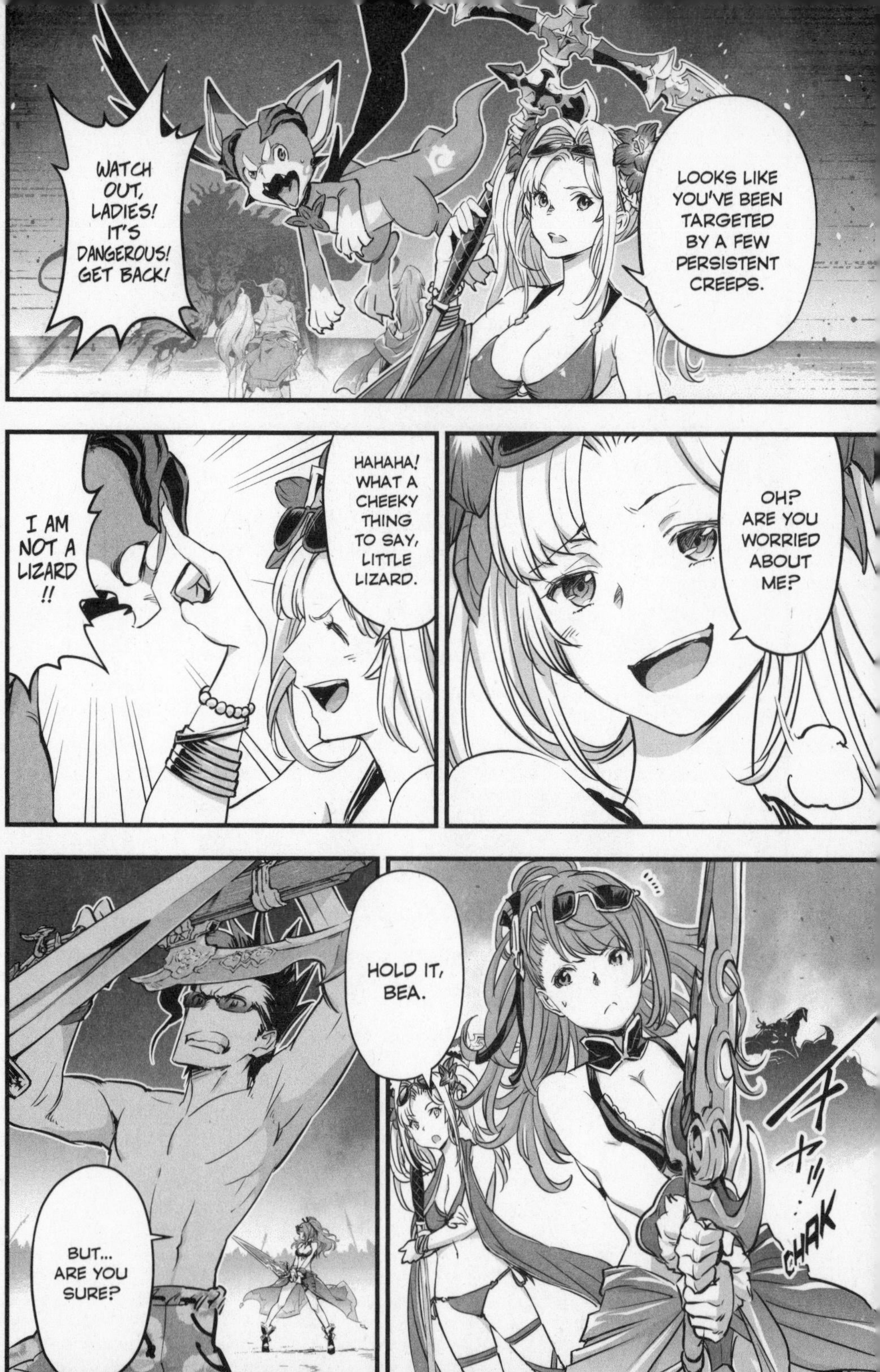
LOOKS LIKE YOU'VE BEEN TARGETED BY A FEW PERSISTENT CREEPS.
WATCH OUT, LADIES! IT'S DANGEROUS! GET BACK!
OH? ARE YOU WORRIED ABOUT ME?
HAHAHA! WHAT A CHEEKY THING TO SAY, LITTLE LIZARD.
I AM NOT A LIZARD !!
HOLD IT, BEA.
CHAK
BUT... ARE YOU SURE?

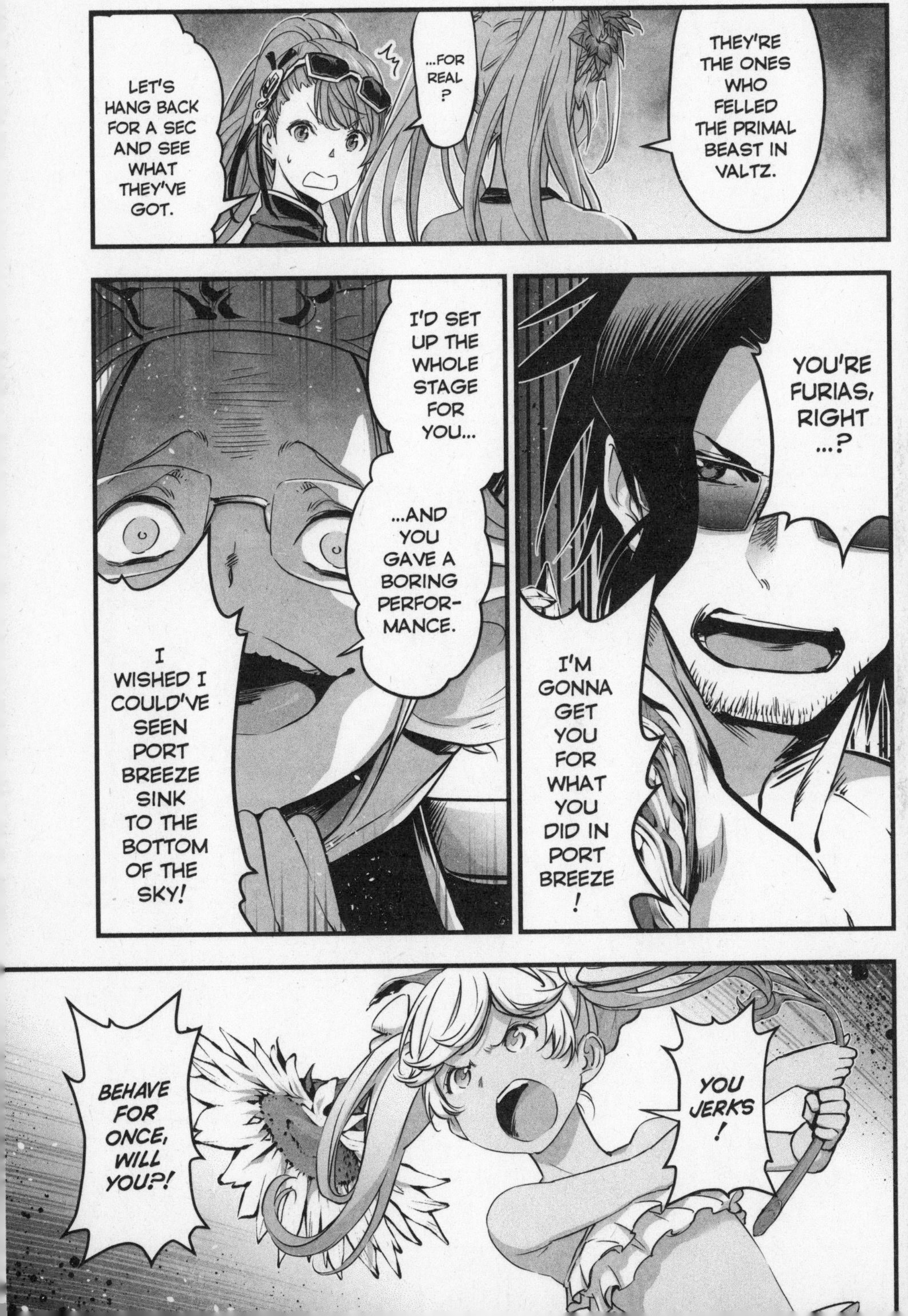
THEY'RE THE ONES WHO FELLED THE PRIMAL BEAST IN VALTZ.
...FOR REAL?
LET'S HANG BACK FOR A SEC AND SEE WHAT THEY'VE GOT.
YOU'RE FURIAS, RIGHT...?
I'M GONNA GET YOU FOR WHAT YOU DID IN PORT BREEZE!
I'D SET UP THE WHOLE STAGE FOR YOU...
...AND YOU GAVE A BORING PERFORMANCE.
I WISHED I COULD'VE SEEN PORT BREEZE SINK TO THE BOTTOM OF THE SKY!
YOU JERKS!
BEHAVE FOR ONCE, WILL YOU?!

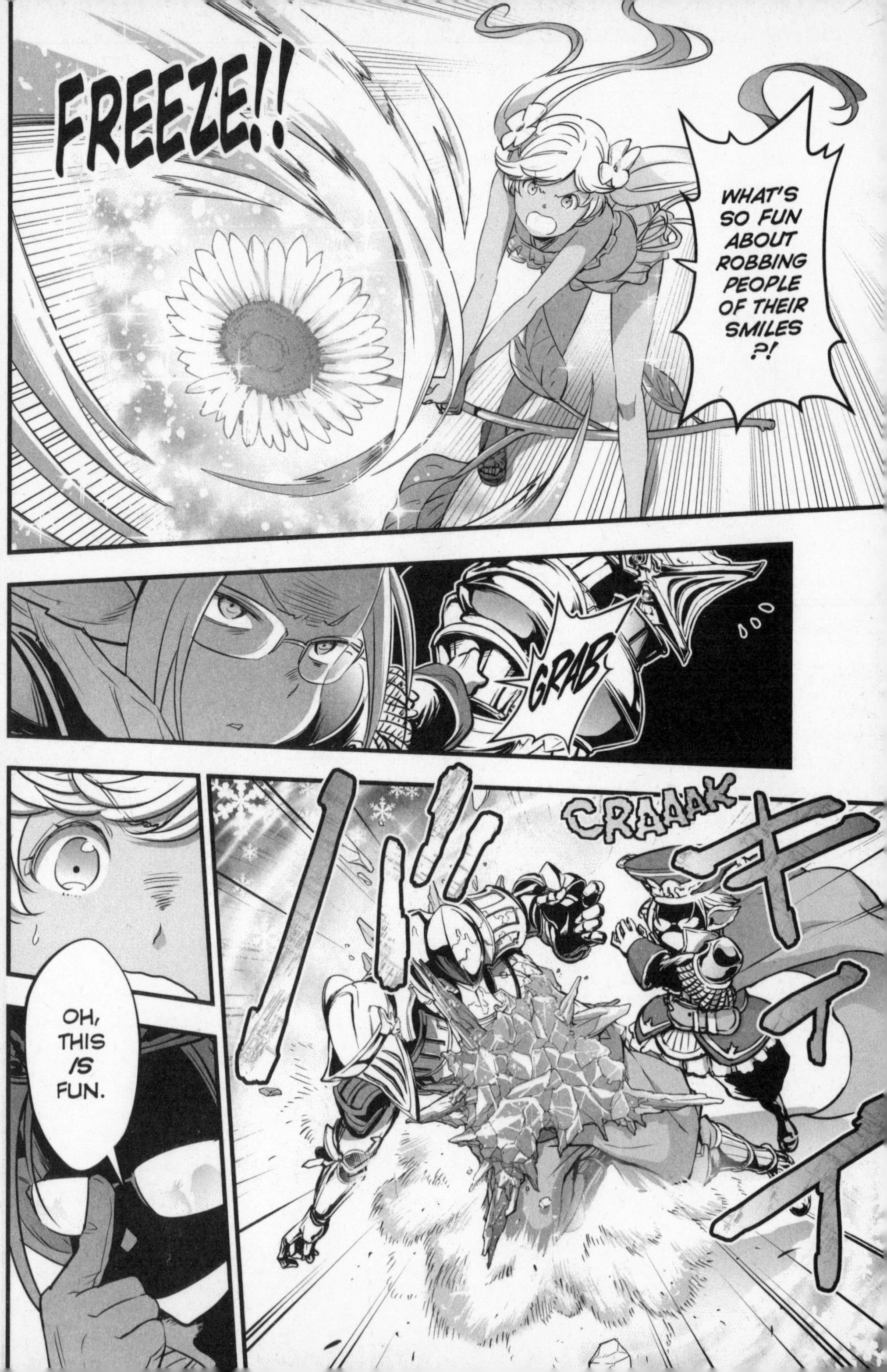
WHAT'S SO FUN ABOUT ROBBING PEOPLE OF THEIR SMILES ?!
FREEZE!!
GRAB
CRAAAK
OH, THIS IS FUN.

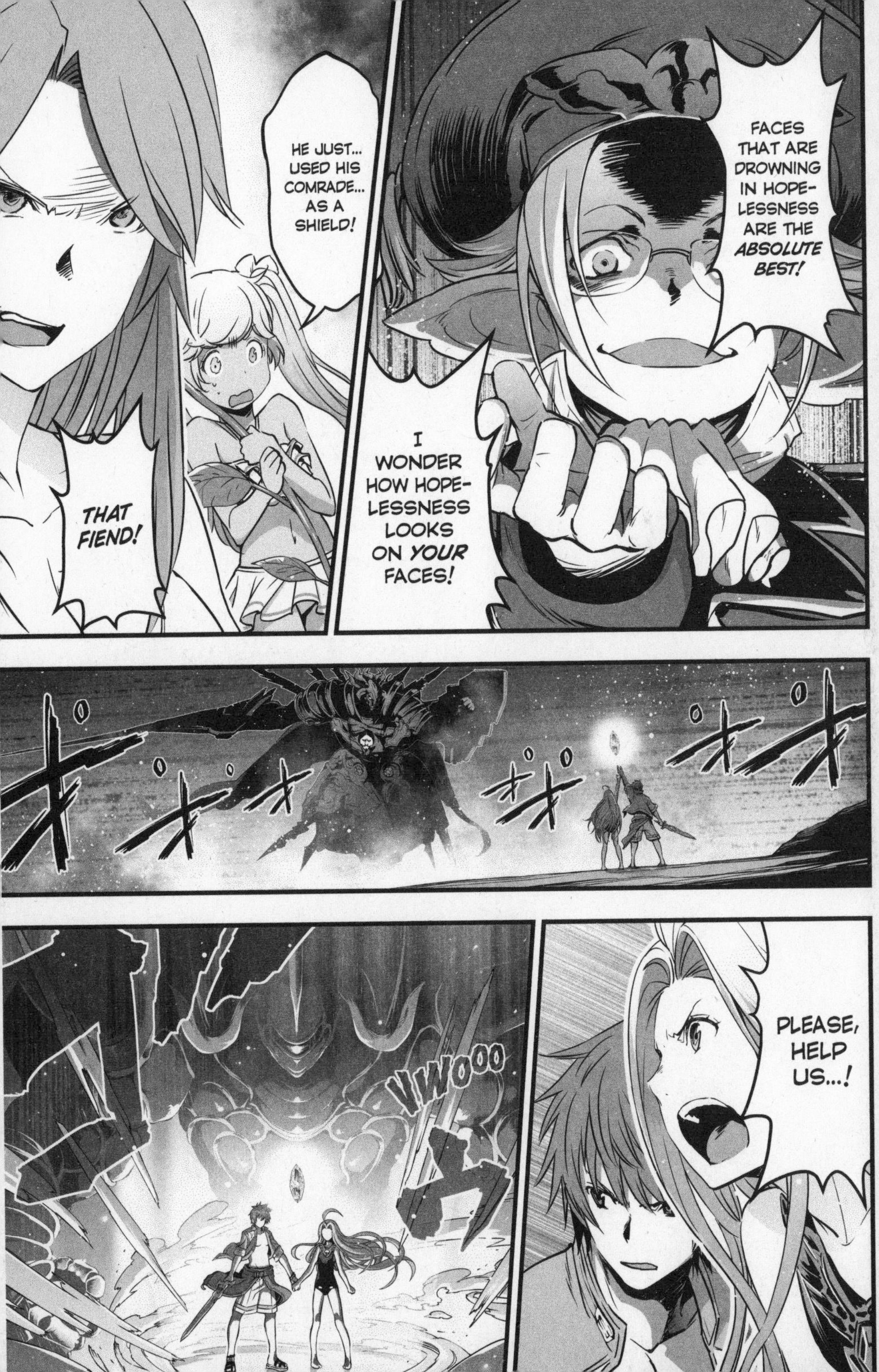
FACES THAT ARE DROWNING IN HOPE-LESSNESS ARE THE *ABSOLUTE* BEST!
I WONDER HOW HOPE-LESSNESS LOOKS ON *YOUR* FACES!
HE JUST... USED HIS COMRADE... AS A SHIELD!
THAT FIEND!
PLEASE, HELP US...!
VWOOO

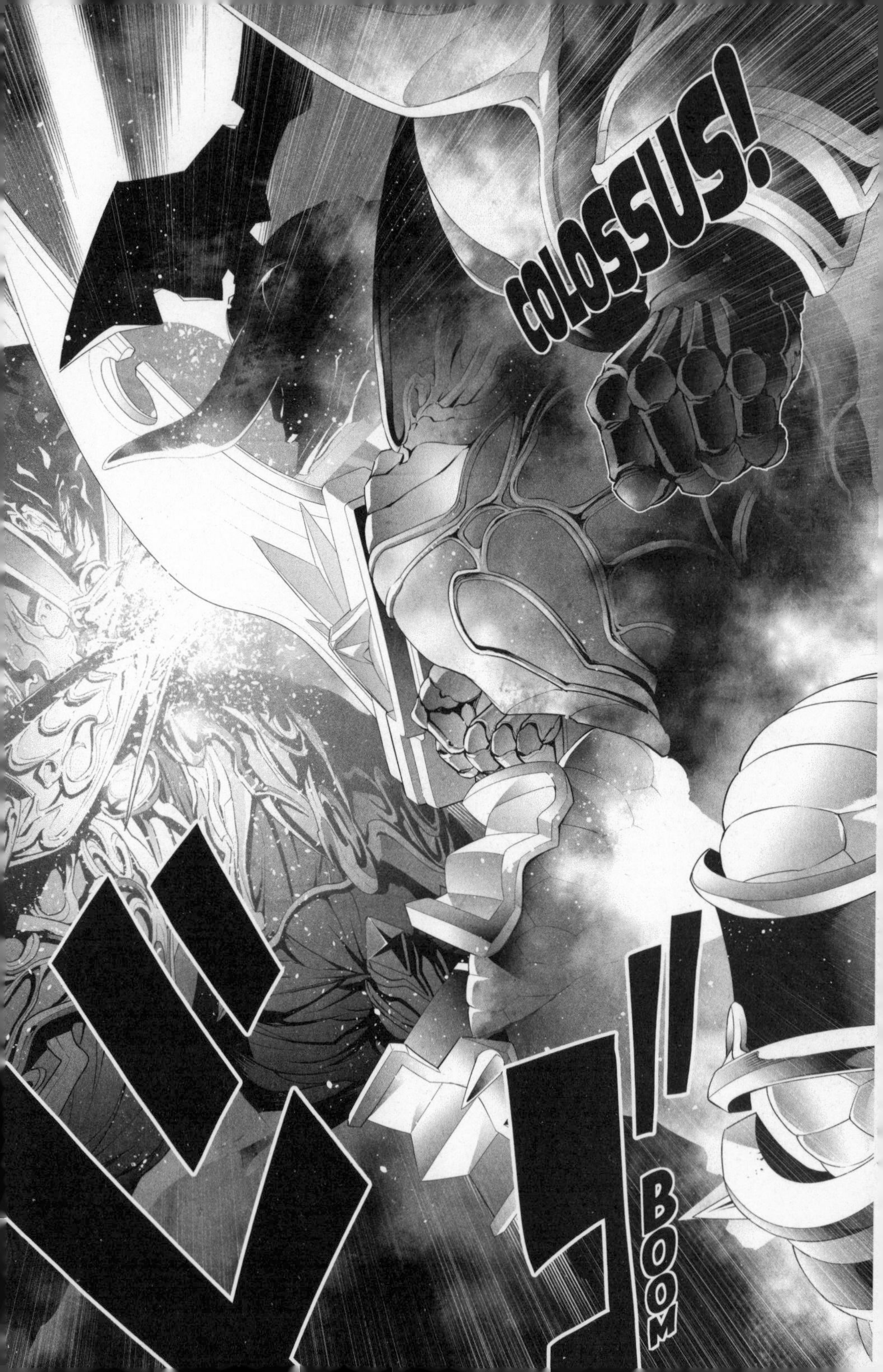
COLOSSUS!
BOOM

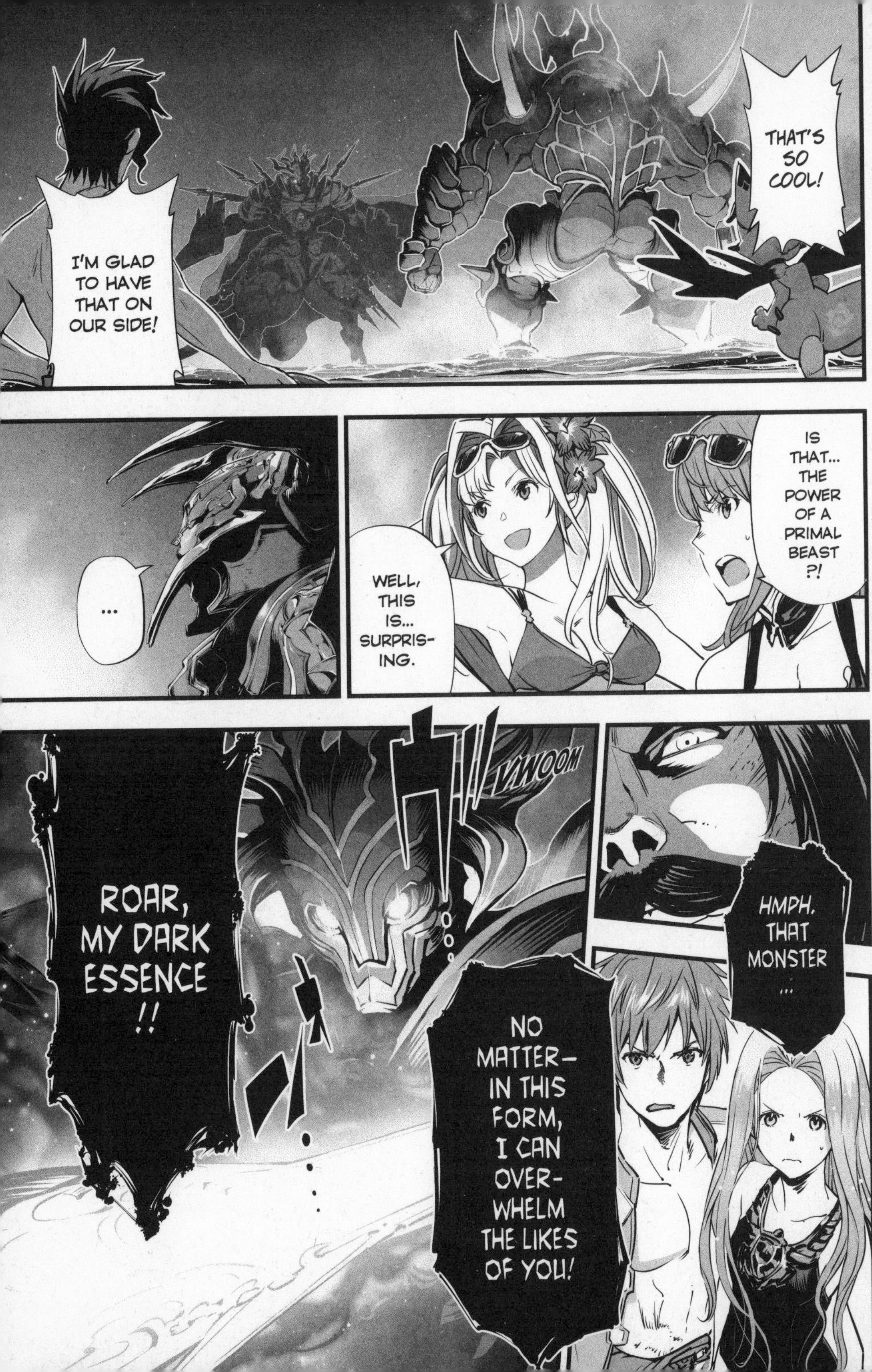
THAT'S SO COOL!
I'M GLAD TO HAVE THAT ON OUR SIDE!
IS THAT... THE POWER OF A PRIMAL BEAST?!
WELL, THIS IS... SURPRISING.
...
HMPH. THAT MONSTER...
NO MATTER— IN THIS FORM, I CAN OVERWHELM THE LIKES OF YOU!
VWOOM
ROAR, MY DARK ESSENCE!!

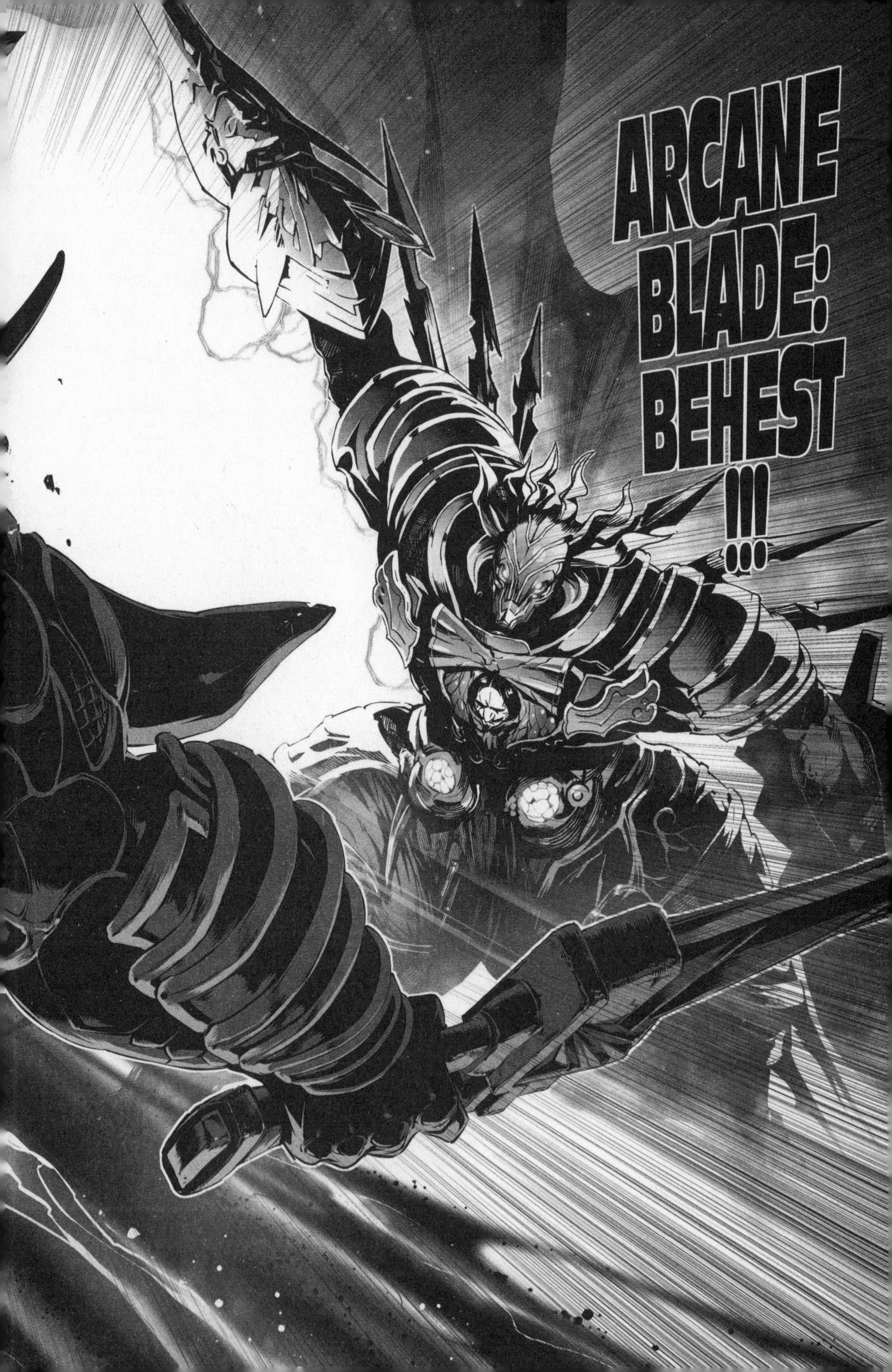
ARCANE BLADE: BEHEST!!!

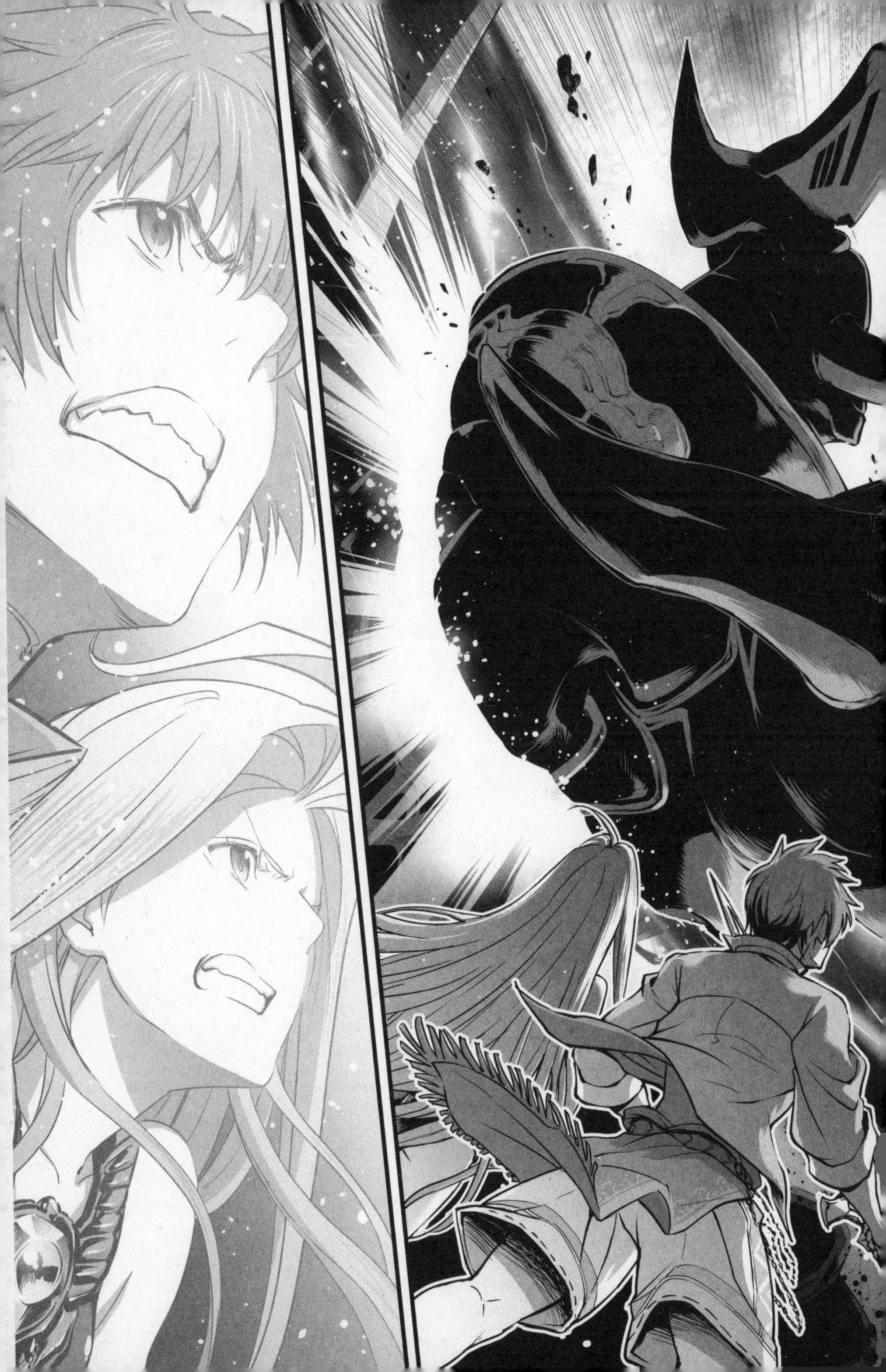

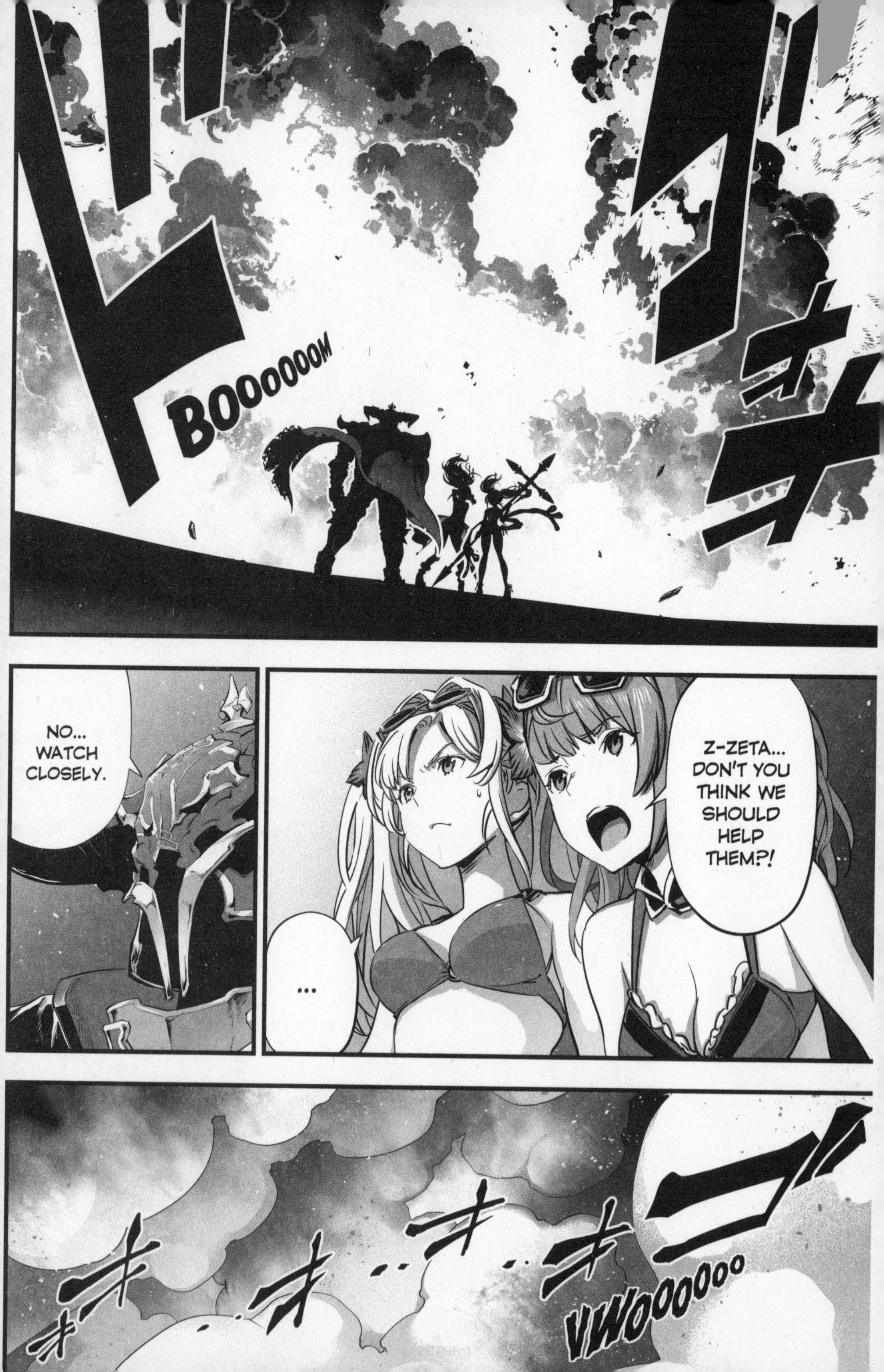
BOOOOOOM
Z-ZETA... DON'T YOU THINK WE SHOULD HELP THEM?!
...
NO... WATCH CLOSELY.
VWOOOOOO

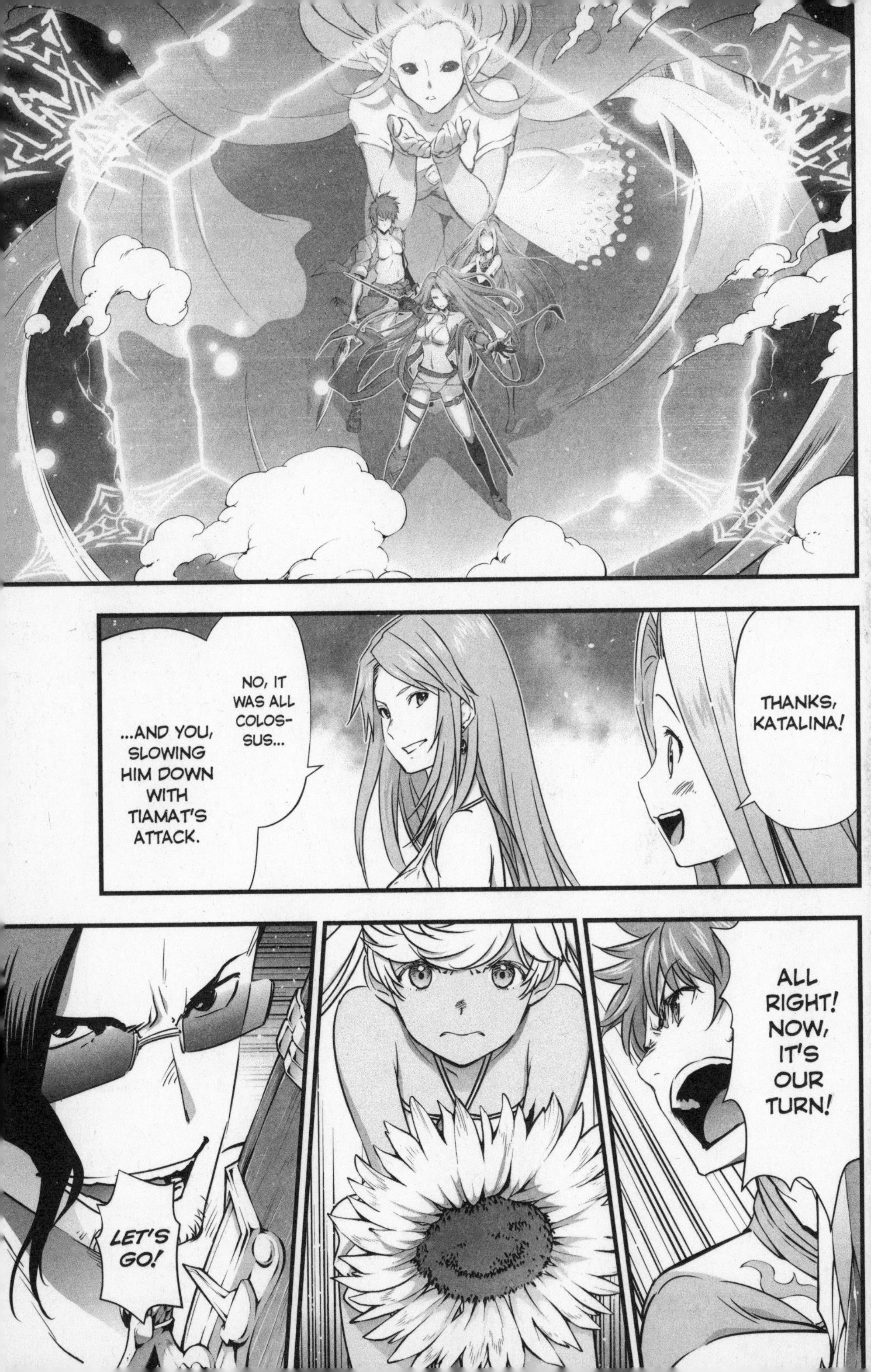
THANKS, KATALINA!
NO, IT WAS ALL COLOSSUS...
...AND YOU, SLOWING HIM DOWN WITH TIAMAT'S ATTACK.
ALL RIGHT! NOW, IT'S OUR TURN!
LET'S GO!

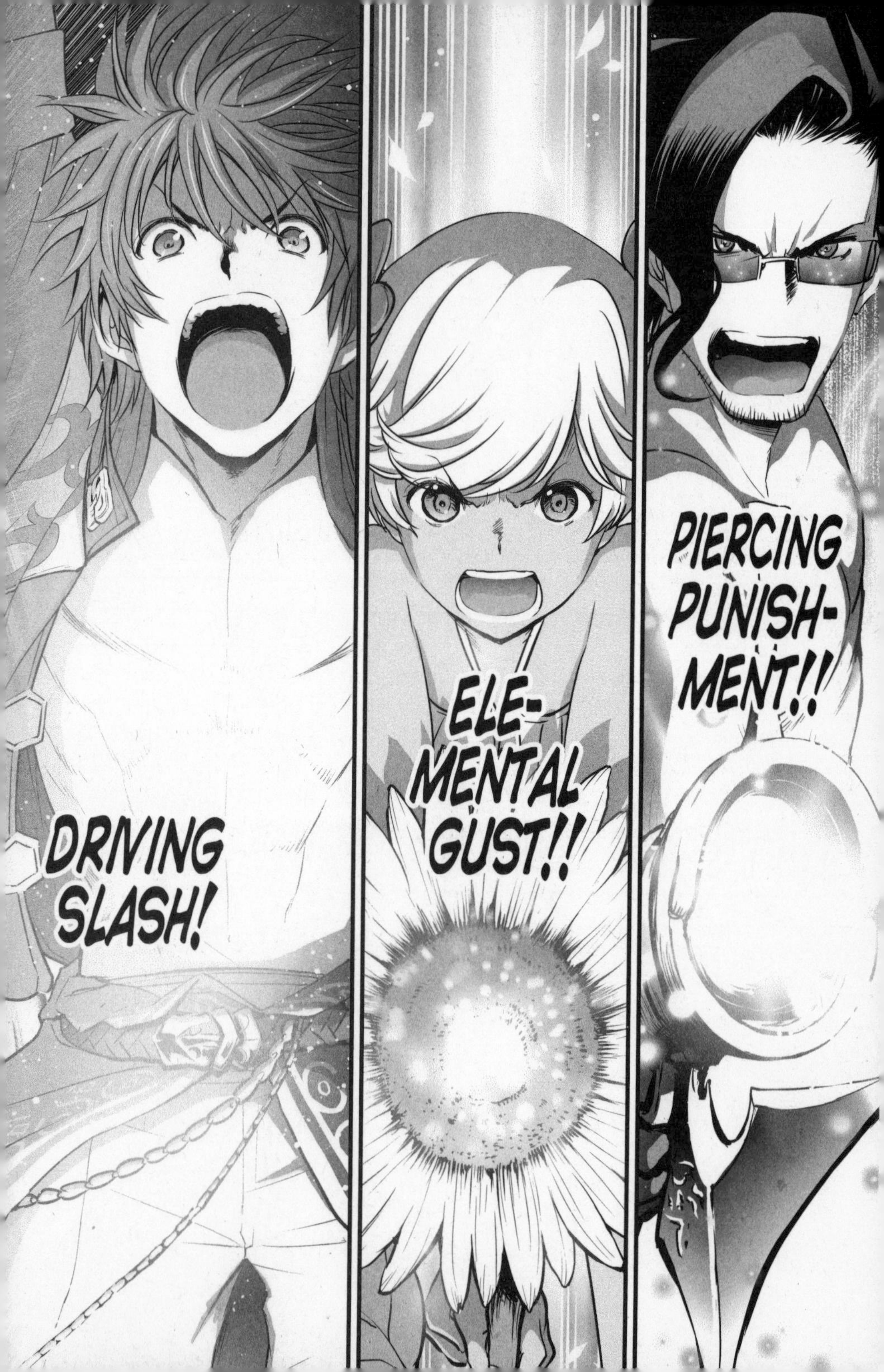
PIERCING PUNISHMENT!!
ELEMENTAL GUST!!
DRIVING SLASH!

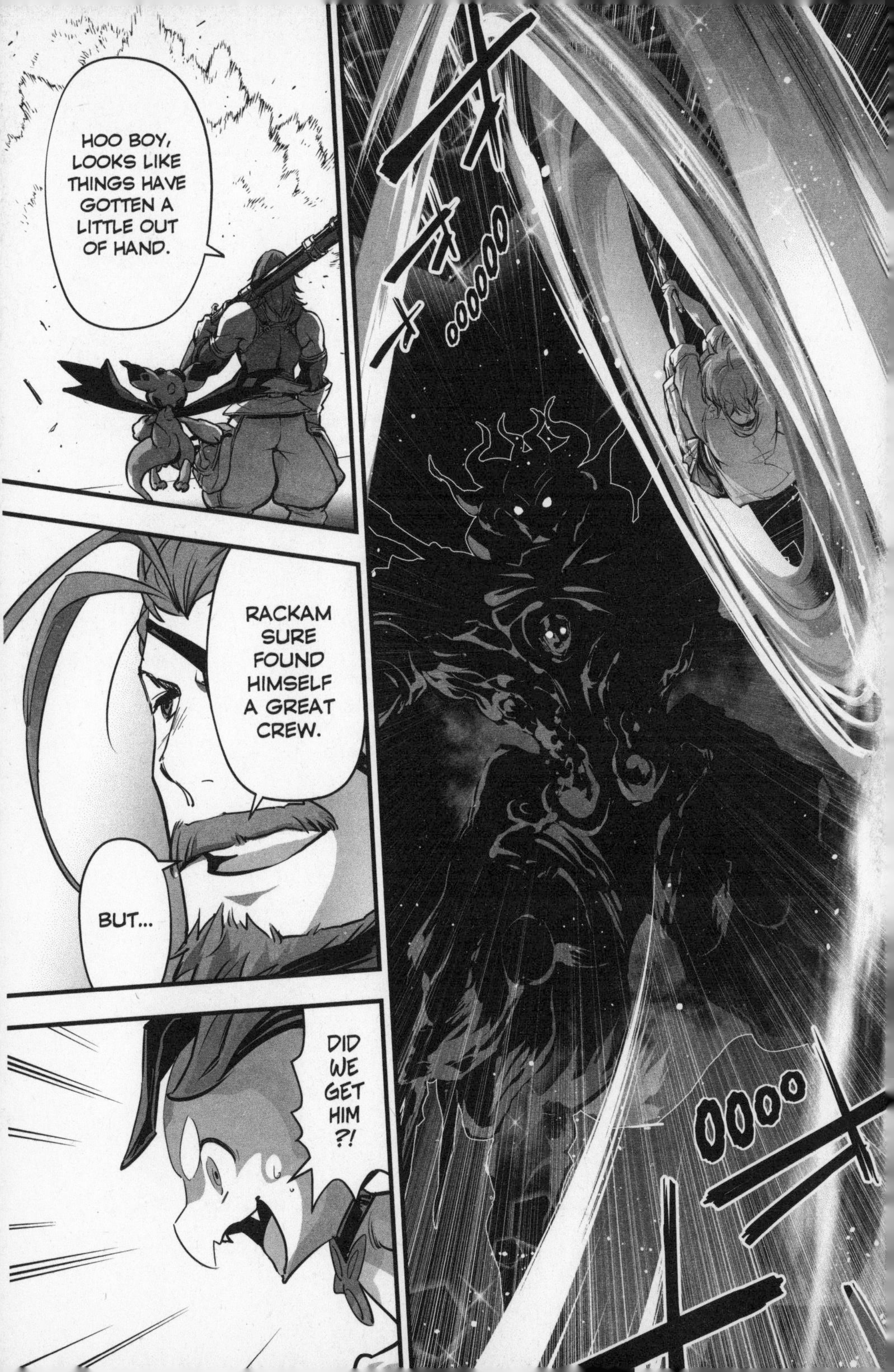
OOOOOO
OOOO
HOO BOY, LOOKS LIKE THINGS HAVE GOTTEN A LITTLE OUT OF HAND.
RACKAM SURE FOUND HIMSELF A GREAT CREW.
BUT...
DID WE GET HIM?!

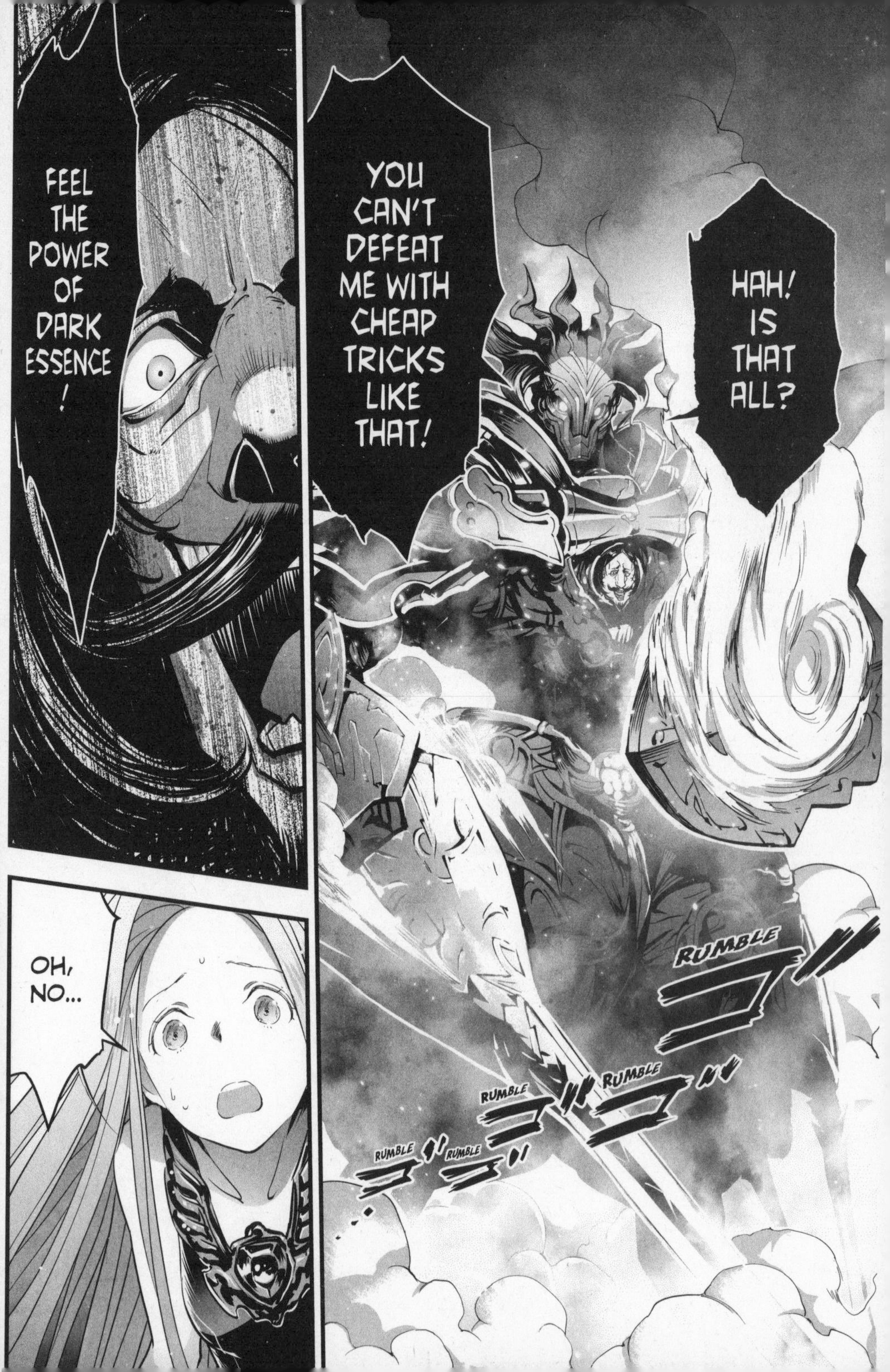
HAH! IS THAT ALL?
YOU CAN'T DEFEAT ME WITH CHEAP TRICKS LIKE THAT!
RUMBLE
RUMBLE
RUMBLE
RUMBLE
RUMBLE
FEEL THE POWER OF DARK ESSENCE!
OH, NO...

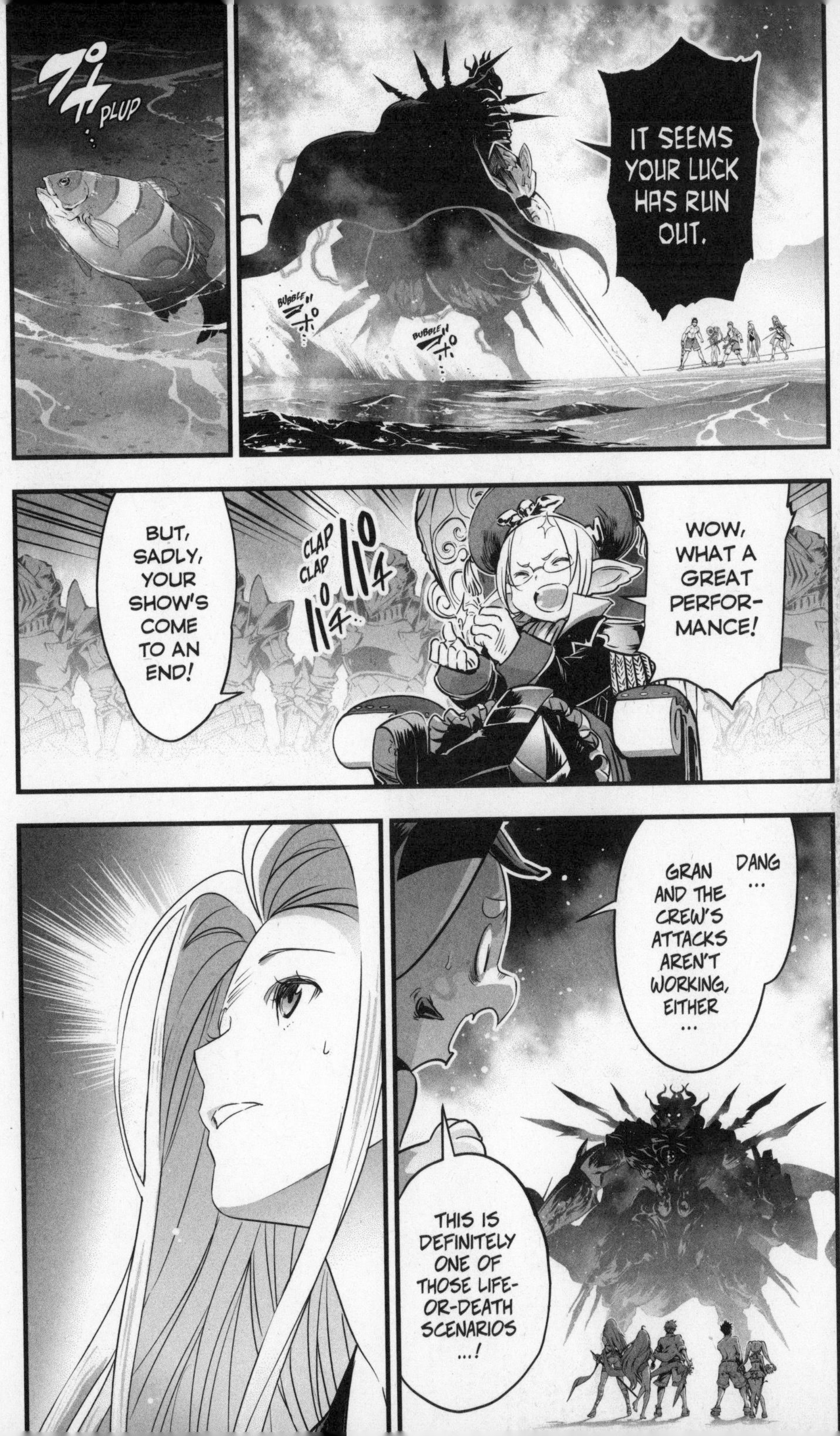
IT SEEMS YOUR LUCK HAS RUN OUT.
BUBBLE
BUBBLE
PLUP
WOW, WHAT A GREAT PERFORMANCE!
CLAP CLAP
BUT, SADLY, YOUR SHOW'S COME TO AN END!
DANG ...
GRAN AND THE CREW'S ATTACKS AREN'T WORKING, EITHER ...
THIS IS DEFINITELY ONE OF THOSE LIFE-OR-DEATH SCENARIOS ...!

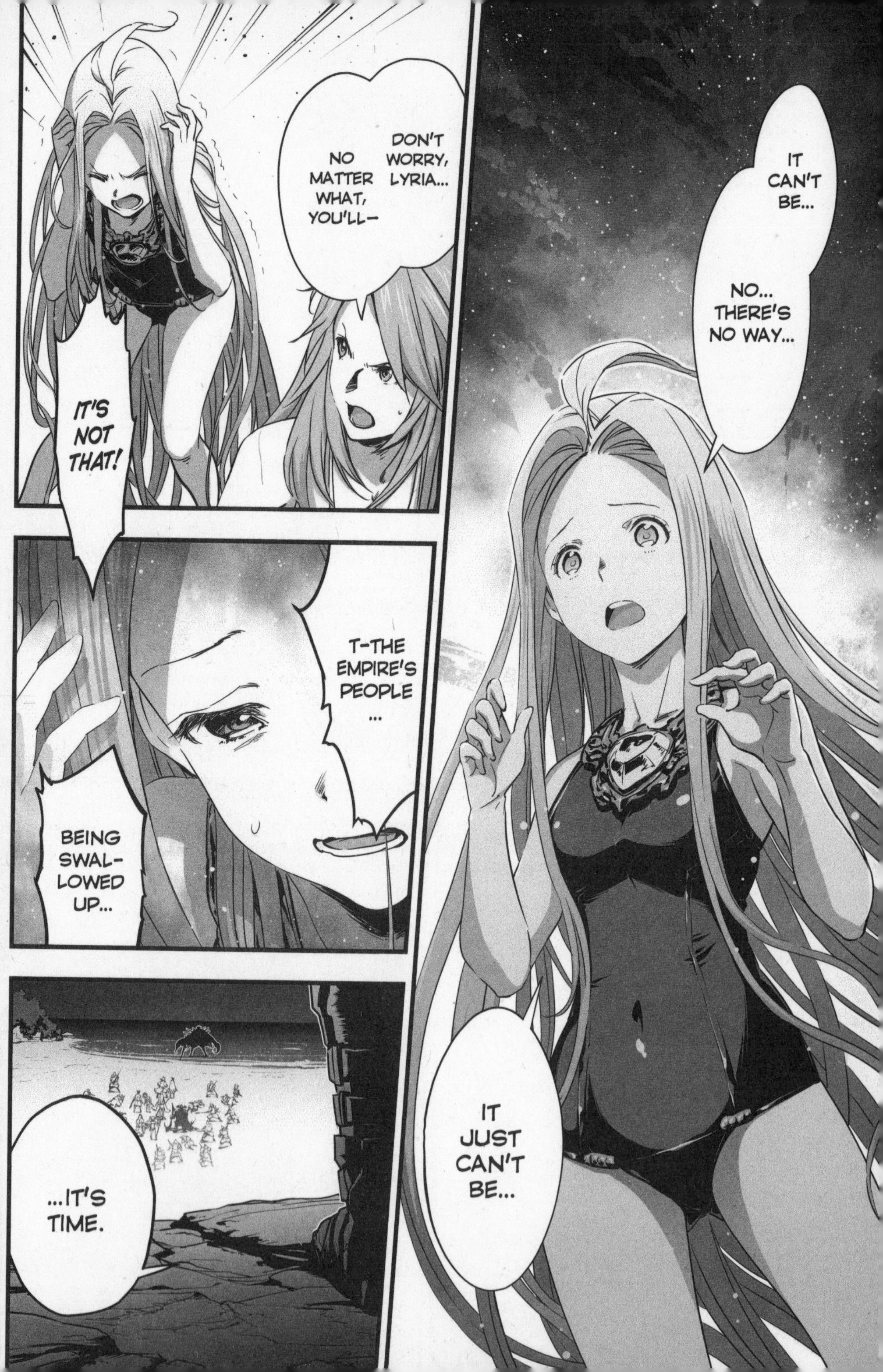
IT CAN'T BE...
NO... THERE'S NO WAY...
IT JUST CAN'T BE...
DON'T WORRY, LYRIA...
NO MATTER WHAT, YOU'LL—
IT'S NOT THAT!
T-THE EMPIRE'S PEOPLE ...
BEING SWAL-LOWED UP...
...IT'S TIME.

HUH?

WHAT IS IT?

GENERAL FURIAS! ORDERS FROM THE EMPIRE!

ARE THEY NUTS?

WHY WOULD WE RUN AWAY WHEN WE'VE GOT THEM RIGHT WHERE WE WANT THEM?!

RE-TREAT,?!

...WHAT?!

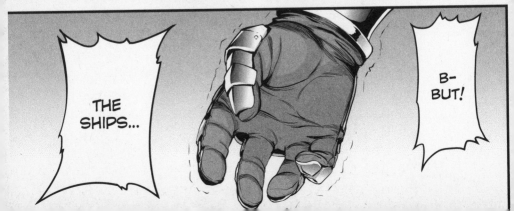

THE SHIPS...

B-BUT!

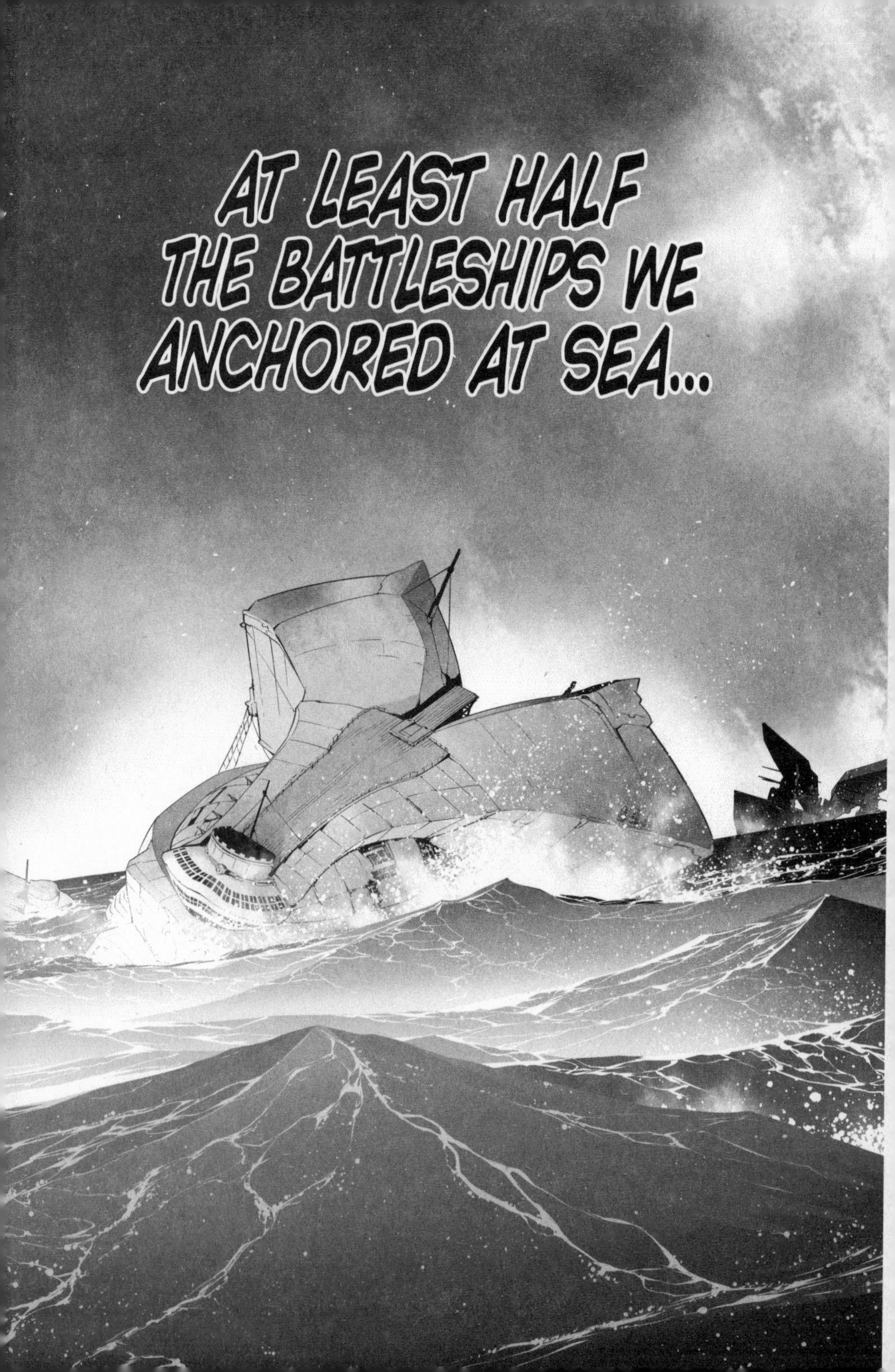
AT LEAST HALF THE BATTLESHIPS WE ANCHORED AT SEA...

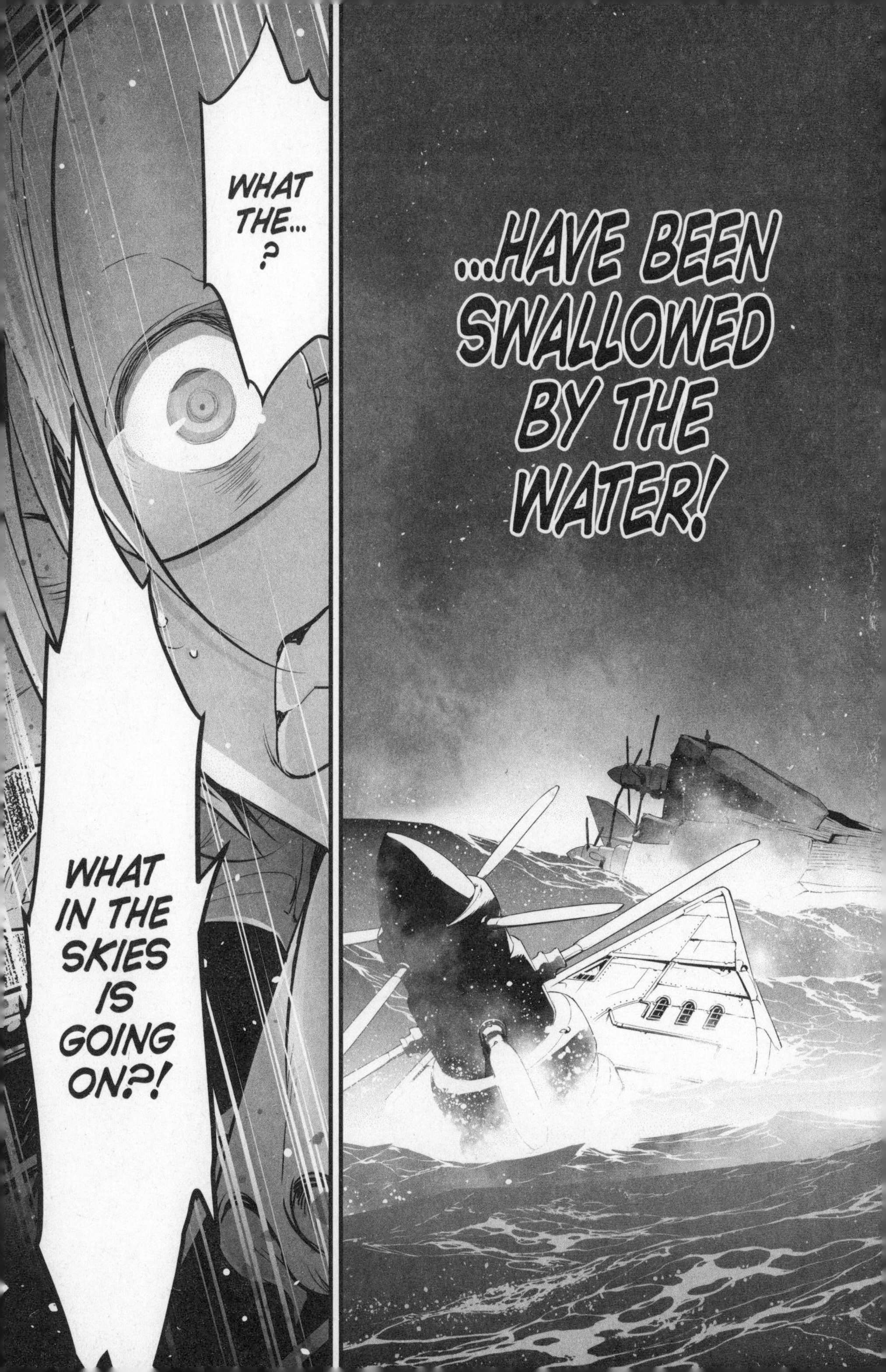
...HAVE BEEN SWALLOWED BY THE WATER!
WHAT THE... ?
WHAT IN THE SKIES IS GOING ON?!

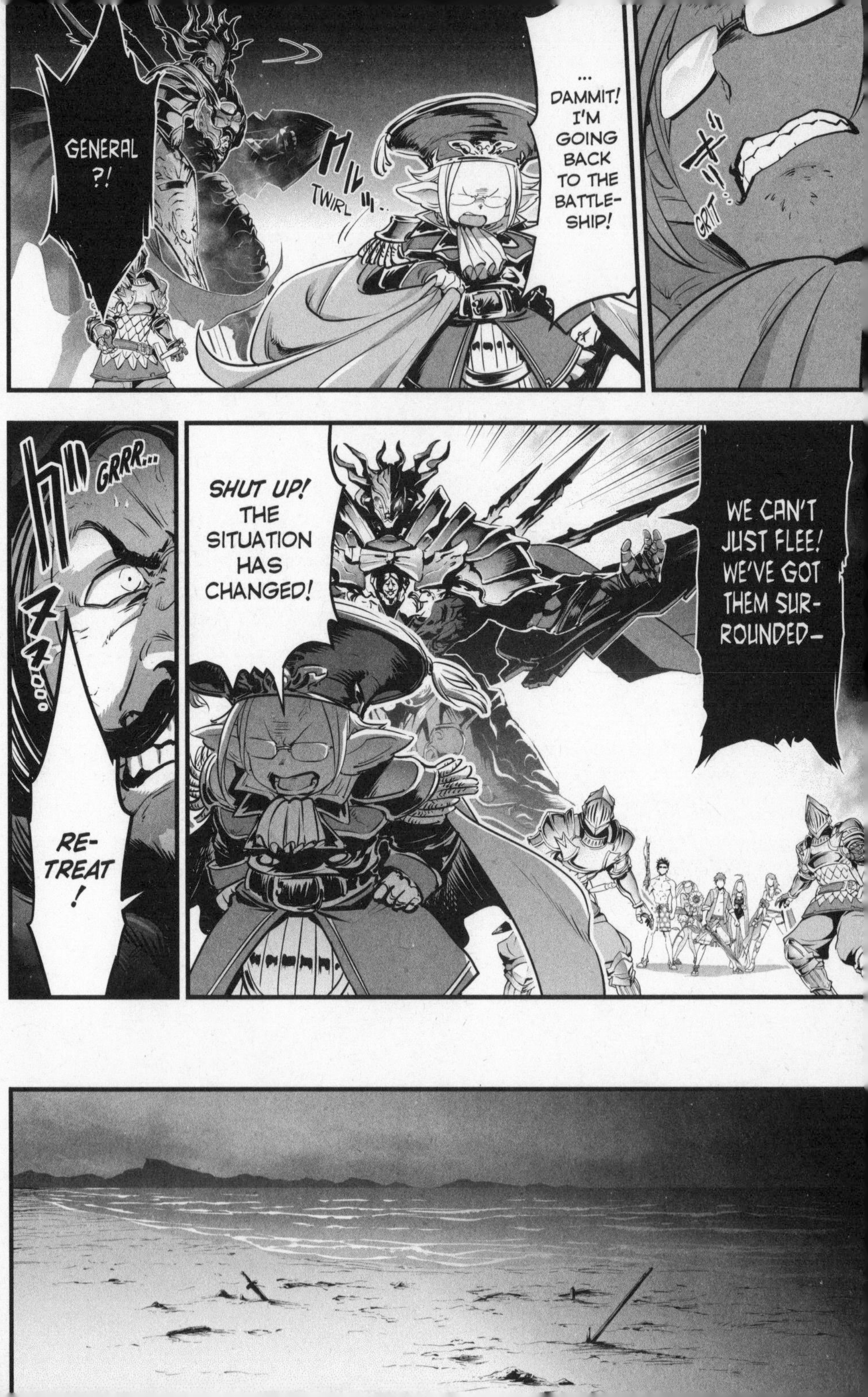

GRIT
... DAMMIT! I'M GOING BACK TO THE BATTLESHIP!
TWIRL
GENERAL?!
WE CAN'T JUST FLEE! WE'VE GOT THEM SURROUNDED—
SHUT UP! THE SITUATION HAS CHANGED!
GRRR...
RE-TREAT!

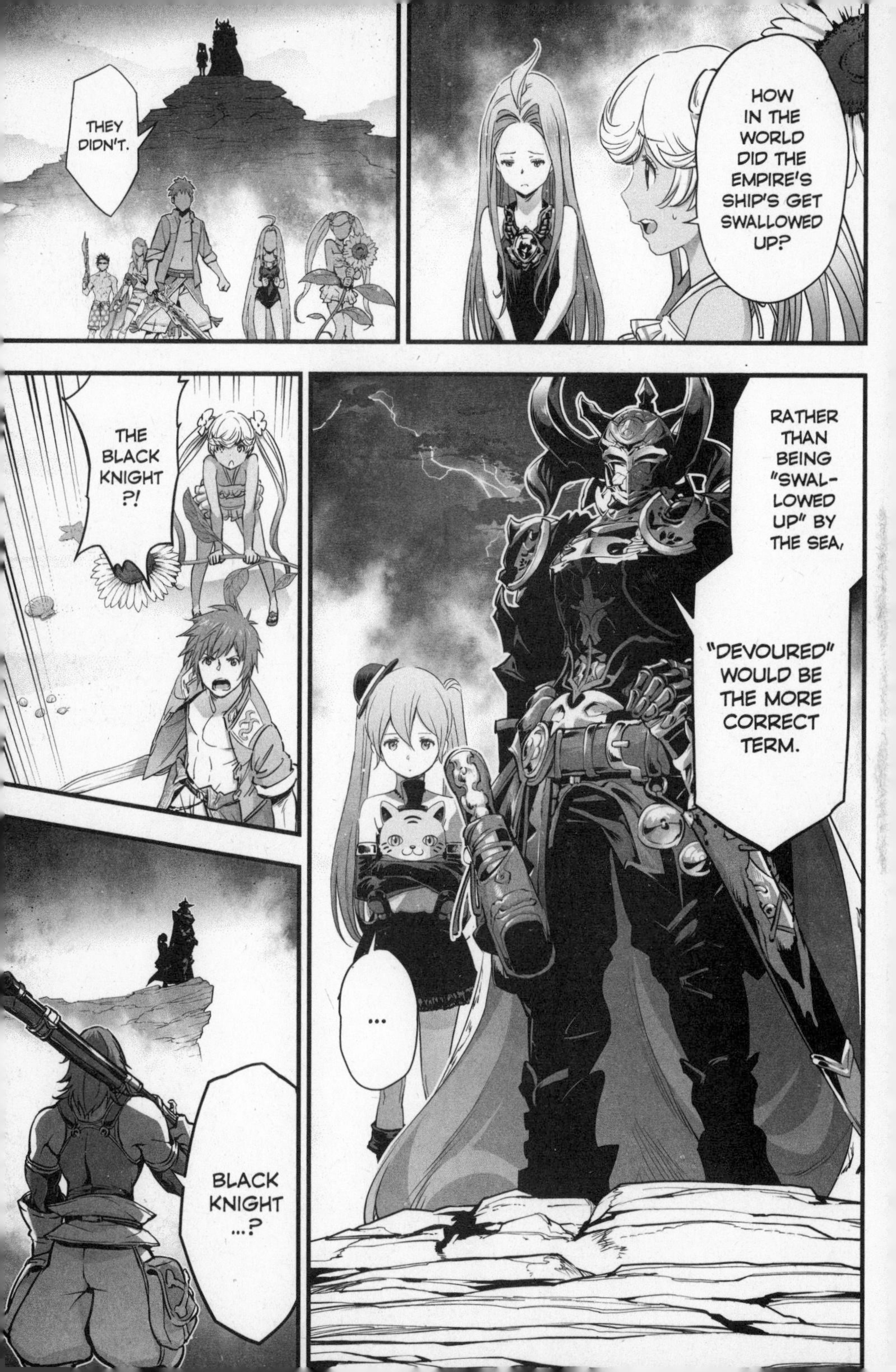
HOW IN THE WORLD DID THE EMPIRE'S SHIP'S GET SWALLOWED UP?
THEY DIDN'T.
RATHER THAN BEING "SWAL-LOWED UP" BY THE SEA,
"DEVOURED" WOULD BE THE MORE CORRECT TERM.
...
THE BLACK KNIGHT ?!
BLACK KNIGHT ...?

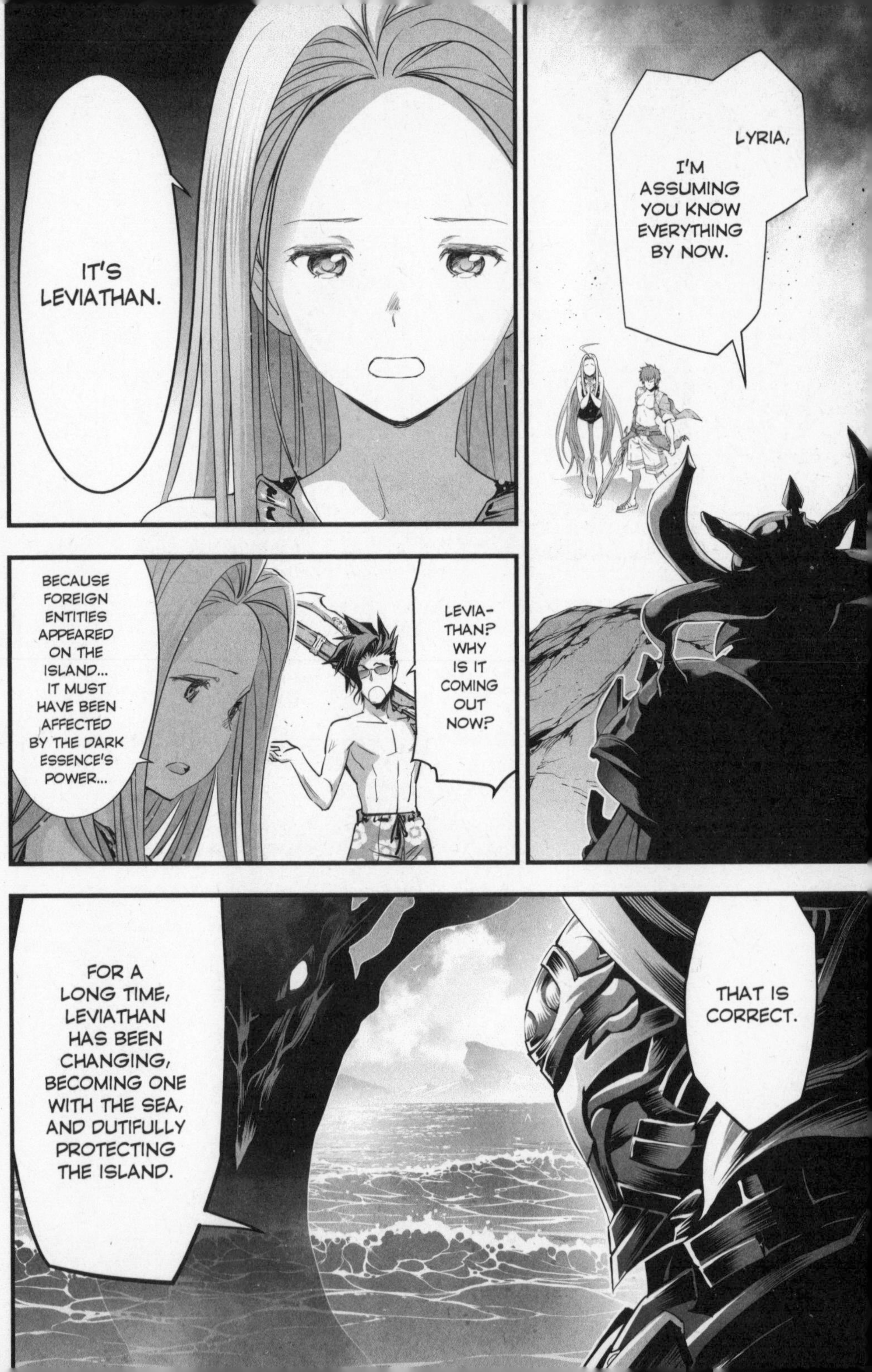
LYRIA, I'M ASSUMING YOU KNOW EVERYTHING BY NOW.
IT'S LEVIATHAN.
LEVIA-THAN? WHY IS IT COMING OUT NOW?
BECAUSE FOREIGN ENTITIES APPEARED ON THE ISLAND... IT MUST HAVE BEEN AFFECTED BY THE DARK ESSENCE'S POWER...
THAT IS CORRECT.
FOR A LONG TIME, LEVIATHAN HAS BEEN CHANGING, BECOMING ONE WITH THE SEA, AND DUTIFULLY PROTECTING THE ISLAND.

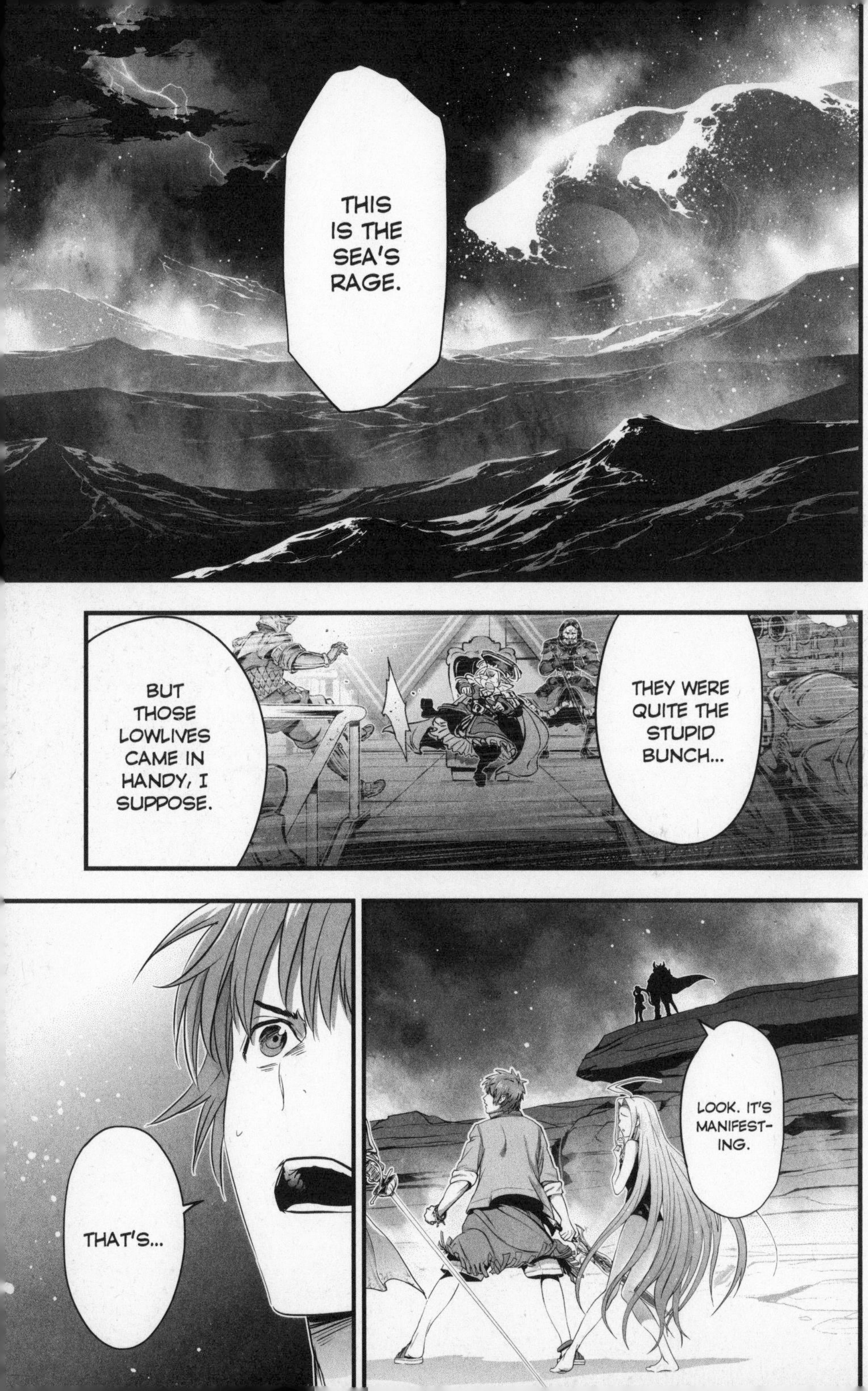
THIS IS THE SEA'S RAGE.
THEY WERE QUITE THE STUPID BUNCH...
BUT THOSE LOWLIVES CAME IN HANDY, I SUPPOSE.
LOOK. IT'S MANIFEST-ING.
THAT'S...

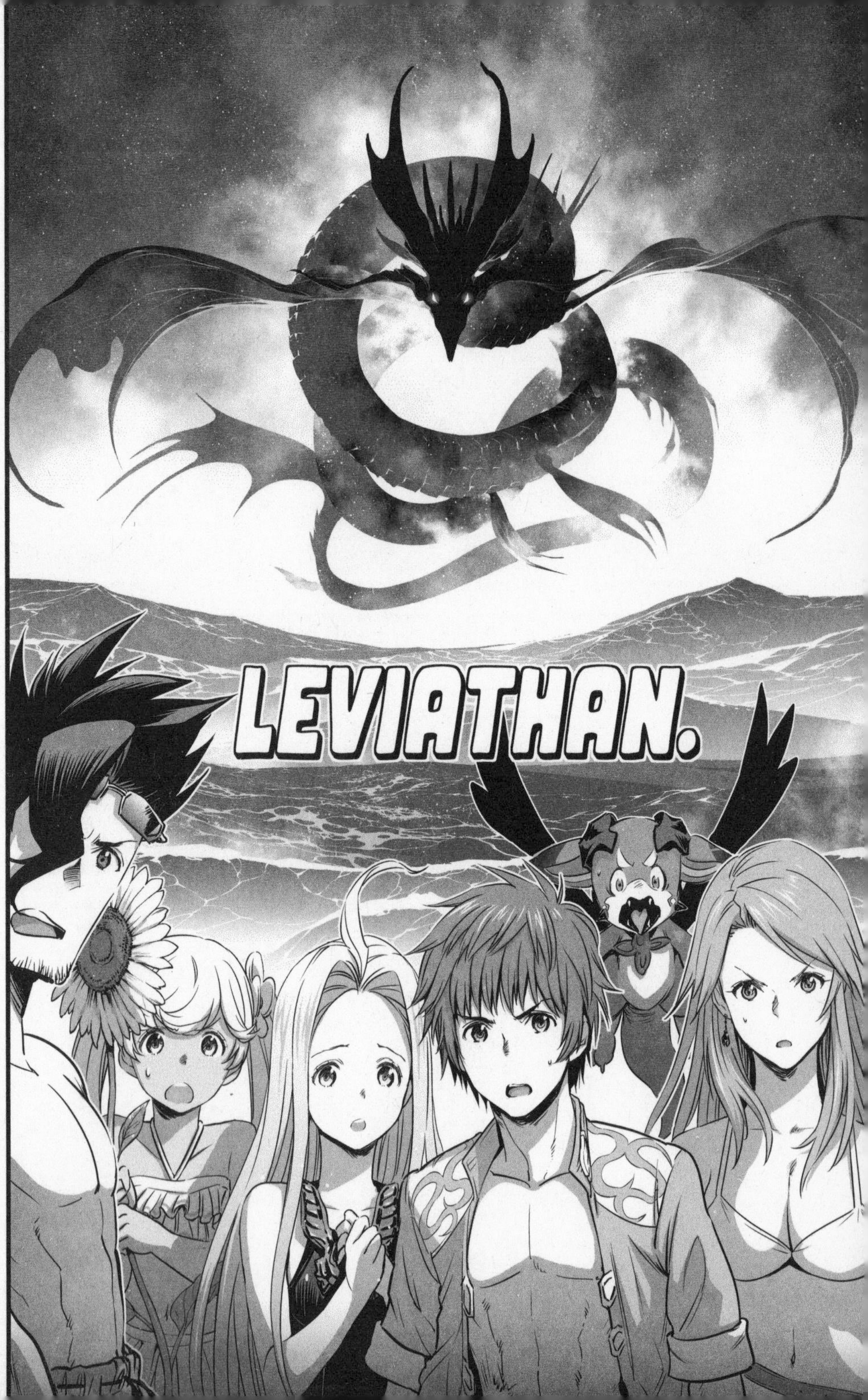
LEVIATHAN.

GRANBLUE FANTASY
グランブルーファンタジー

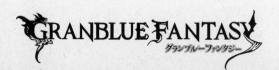

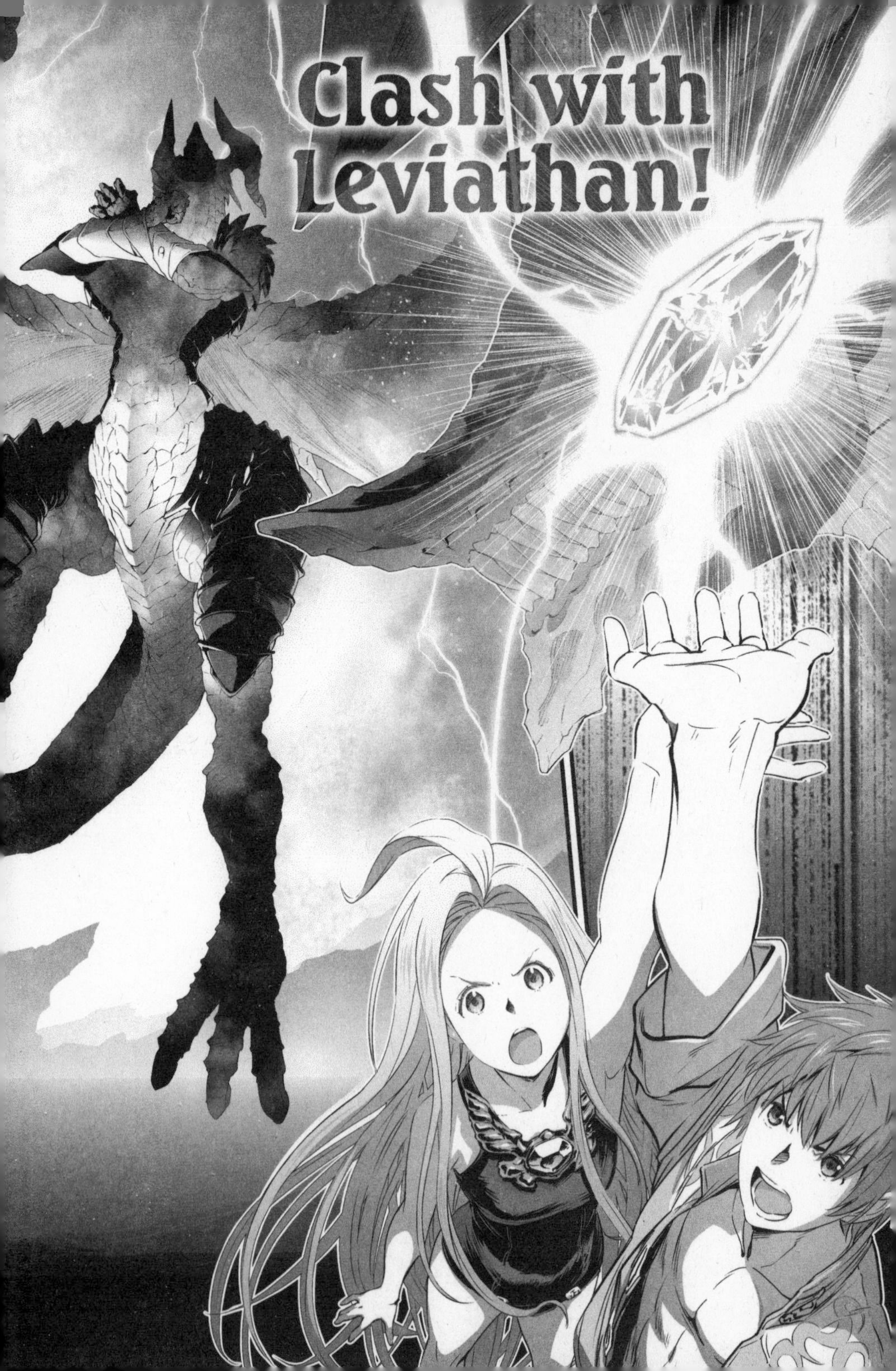
Clash with Leviathan!

NEXT
NEXT VOLUME PREVIEW
A battle for the ages...
...will come to an end!!
volume.
05
Volume Five
COMING SOON!
GRANBLUE FANTASY
グランブルーファンタジー

CAN A FARMER SAVE THE WORLD? FIND OUT IN THIS FANTASY MANGA FOR FANS OF *SWORD ART ONLINE* AND *THAT TIME I GOT REINCARNATED AS A SLIME*!

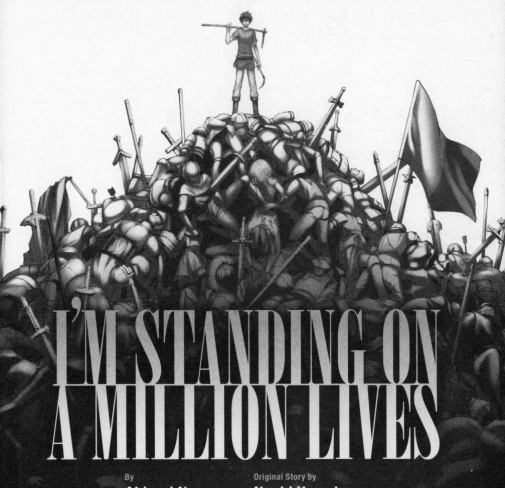

By
Akinari Nao

Original Story by
Naoki Yamakawa

Yusuke Yotsuya doesn't care about getting into high school—he just wants to get back home to his game and away from other people. But when he suddenly finds himself in a real-life fantasy game alongside his two gorgeous classmates, he discovers a new world of possibility and excitement. Despite a rough start, Yusuke and his friend fight to level up and clear the challenges set before them by a mysterious figure from the future, but before long, they find that they're not just battling for their own lives, but for the lives of millions...

KC
**KODANSHA
COMICS**

EDENS ZERO
エデンズゼロ

HIRO MASHIMA IS BACK! JOIN THE CREATOR OF *FAIRY TAIL* AS HE TAKES TO THE STARS FOR ANOTHER THRILLING SAGA!

EDENS ZERO © Hiro Mashima/Kodansha, Ltd.

A high-flying space adventure! All the steadfast friendship and wild fighting you've been waiting for...IN SPACE!

At Granbell Kingdom, an abandoned amusement park, Shiki has lived his entire life among machines. But one day, Rebecca and her cat companion Happy appear at the park's front gates. Little do these newcomers know that this is the first human contact Granbell has had in a hundred years! As Shiki stumbles his way into making new friends, his former neighbors stir at an opportunity for a robo-rebellion... And when his old homeland becomes too dangerous, Shiki must join Rebecca and Happy on their spaceship and escape into the boundless cosmos.

◄ KAMOME ►
SHIRAHAMA

Witch Hat Atelier

A magical manga
adventure for
fans of Disney
and Studio
Ghibli!

Witch Hat Atelier © Kamome Shirahama/Kodansha Ltd.

**The magical adventure that took
Japan by storm is finally here,
from acclaimed DC and Marvel
cover artist Kamome Shirahama!**

In a world where everyone takes wonders like magic spells
and dragons for granted, Coco is a girl with a simple dream:
She wants to be a witch. But everybody knows magicians
are born, not made, and Coco was not born with a gift for
magic. Resigned to her un-magical life, Coco is about to
give up on her dream to become a witch...until the day
she meets Qifrey, a mysterious, traveling magician. After
secretly seeing Qifrey perform magic in a way she's never
seen before, Coco soon learns what everybody "knows"
might not be the truth, and discovers that her magical
dream may not be as far away as it may seem...

KC
KODANSHA
COMICS

Magus of the Library

Mitsu Izumi

MITSU IZUMI'S STUNNING ARTWORK BRINGS A FANTASTICAL LITERARY ADVENTURE TO LUSH, THRILLING LIFE!

Young Theo adores books, but the prejudice and hatred of his village keeps them ever out of his reach. Then one day, he chances to meet Sedona, a traveling librarian who works for the great library of Aftzaak, City of Books, and his life changes forever...

KC
KODANSHA
COMICS

A dark and sexy body-horror action manga perfect for fans of *Prison School* and *High School of the Dead*!

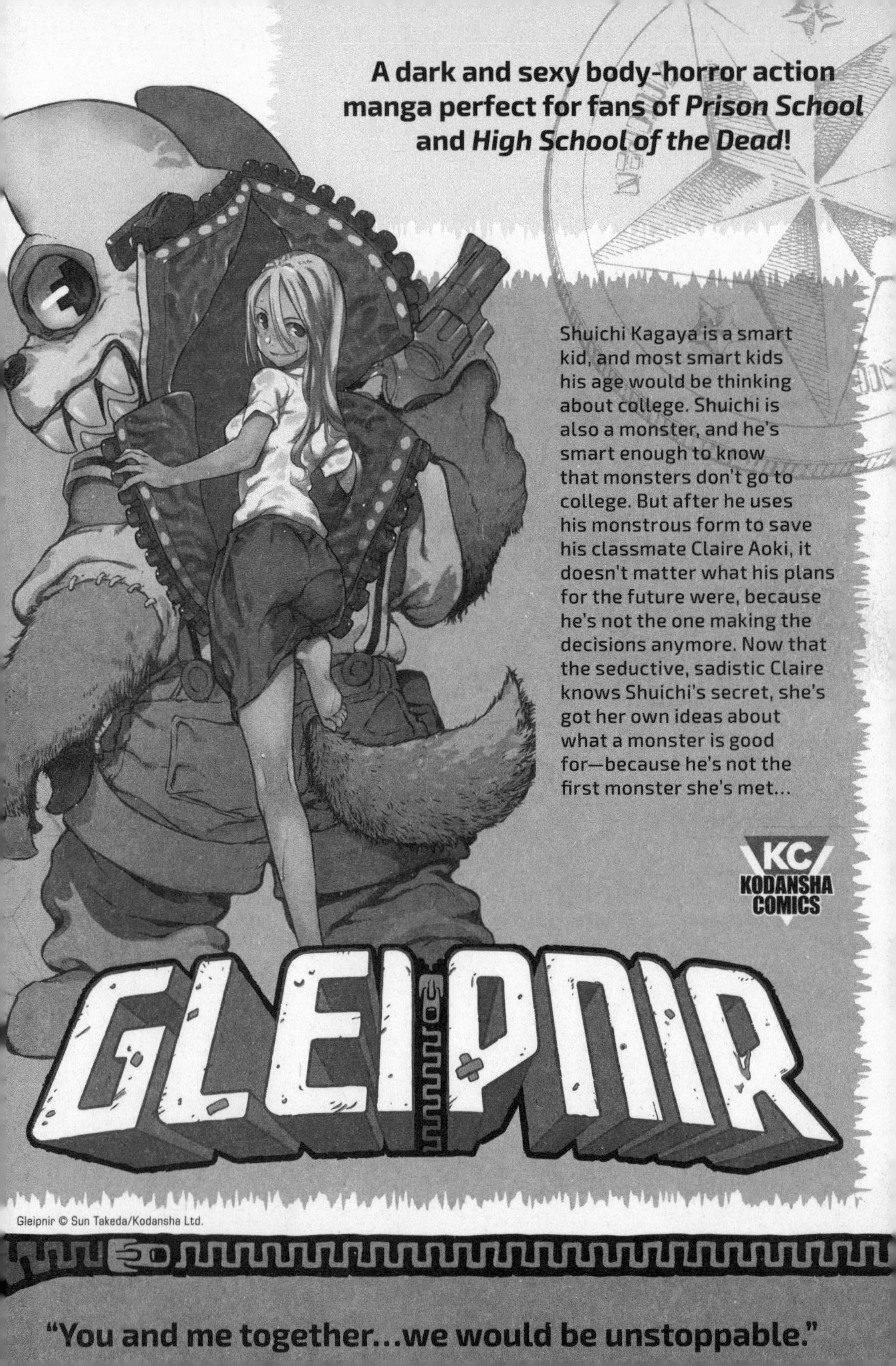

Shuichi Kagaya is a smart kid, and most smart kids his age would be thinking about college. Shuichi is also a monster, and he's smart enough to know that monsters don't go to college. But after he uses his monstrous form to save his classmate Claire Aoki, it doesn't matter what his plans for the future were, because he's not the one making the decisions anymore. Now that the seductive, sadistic Claire knows Shuichi's secret, she's got her own ideas about what a monster is good for—because he's not the first monster she's met...

KC KODANSHA COMICS

GLEIPNIR

"You and me together...we would be unstoppable."

Futaro Uesugi is a second-year in high school, scraping to get by and pay off his family's debt. The only thing he can do is study, so when Futaro receives a part-time job offer to tutor the five daughters of a wealthy businessman, he can't pass it up. Little does he know, these five beautiful sisters are quintuplets, but the only thing they have in common...is that they're all terrible at studying!

The Quintessential Quintuplets © Negi Haruba/Kodansha, Ltd.

THE QUINTESSENTIAL QUINTUPLETS

negi haruba

ANIME OUT NOW!

A Kodansha Comics Trade Paperback Original
Granblue Fantasy 4 copyright
© Cygames
© 2017 cocho
© 2017 Makoto Fugetsu

English translation copyright
© Cygames
© 2020 cocho
© 2020 Makoto Fugetsu

Published in the United States by Kodansha Comics, an imprint of Kodansha USA Publishing, LLC, New York.

Publication rights for this English edition arranged through Kodansha Ltd., Tokyo.

First published in Japan in 2017 by Kodansha Ltd., Tokyo as *Granblue Fantasy*, volume 4.

ISBN 978-1-63236-954-3

Printed in the United States of America.

www.kodanshacomics.com

9 8 7 6 5 4 3 2 1
Translation: Kristi Fernandez
Lettering: Evan Hayden
Editing: Vanessa Tenazas
Kodansha Comics edition cover design by Phil Balsman

Publisher: Kiichiro Sugawara
Managing editor: Maya Rosewood
Vice president of marketing & publicity: Naho Yamada

Director of publishing services: Ben Applegate
Associate director of operations: Stephen Pakula
Publishing services managing editor: Noelle Webster
Assistant production manager: Emi Lotto, Angela Zurlo